CULTURAL
TOURISM

The
Robert Gordon University
Heritage Library

CULTURAL
TOURISM

Edited by
J. M. FLADMARK

Papers presented at
The Robert Gordon University
Heritage Convention 1994

DONHEAD

First published in the United Kingdom
in 1994 by
Donhead Publishing Ltd
28 Southdean Gardens
Wimbledon
London SW19 6NU
Tel. 081-789 0138

ISBN 1 873394 15 2

A CIP catalogue record for this book is available
from the British Library.

Printed in Great Britain at the
Alden Press, Osney Mead, Oxford

In order to produce this book quickly for the conference
delegates, the publishers have used camera ready copy
provided by the editors and contributors

CONTENTS

REALITY OR IMAGE
The Role of Heritage Interpretation

CULTURAL SUSTENANCE
Making a Meal of Our Heritage

FOREWORD

Last year was extremely significant for Scottish tourism. For the first time, our industry generated more than £2bn in revenue, and it underwent a major review, initiated by the Secretary of State for Scotland. For too long, one of Scotland's most substantial industries has suffered, to put it plainly, from a lack of focus. No one doubted its potential, but equally, we had failed to discover the means of bringing together a fragmented business to maximise that potential.

If we have the vision to see it, a new and dynamic future for Scottish tourism is within our grasp. Over the next few years, we must concentrate all our efforts on a highly co-ordinated approach to developing the industry, and to the messages we send the outside world. Have no doubt about it, Scotland faces increasingly intense competition from several neighbouring countries, and these competitors are promoting themselves internationally with clearly defined and powerful images of what they have to offer the visitor.

To match their efforts and achieve the same degree of impact, we need to develop our tourism profile so that it bears the universally recognisable stamp of Scotland. But we can only do this effectively if we are far more co-ordinated as an industry than we have ever been before. In this respect, we could say that the Scottish Tourist Board, as the lead marketing agency, has the role of brand manager.

We need to recognise that our customer base is not homogeneous. They vary by age, sex, socio-economic grouping and aspiration. And as purchasers of a brand, they will not buy the product a second time if they are dissatisfied with it. The late 20th century tourist is an increasingly sophisticated creature, very likely to want a holiday tailored to some particular cultural, leisure or sporting interest. This requires much closer targeting of market segments, and better packaging of a wide variety of facilities.

We also must ask ourselves the basic question: what is the Scottish tourism product? A dramatic landscape; a powerful sense of history; a reputation for friendliness? Yes, all of these, but traditional virtues can only be part of what we must sell. Current tourism trends favour clean, green, unspoilt destinations. That describes Scotland very well, but we will not reap the benefits, unless we can also offer good all-weather facilities and entertainment for families with children; unless we promote ourselves to appropriate markets such as the independent European motorist; and most particularly, unless we can develop our product in such a way that it does not damage the environment.

Product development inevitably raises the question of quality, an issue which, together with value for money, features ever more prominently on the modern tourist's agenda. Scotland has to be able to offer the best quality accommodation, catering, visitor attractions and other facilities, without hitting the visitor too hard in the pocket. This will require careful, well focused investment in training, in improving and developing facilities, and also in extending the current range of grading and classification schemes.

Once we have sold the idea of Scotland to the potential visitor, we need to encourage them to come not only during the peak months; to visit not only the more obvious places; and to stay longer and spend more. We need to promote Scotland as an all-year-round destination for short breaks and second holidays. We can achieve this by understanding our markets better and by responding more specifically to what they want. Niche marketing will play an increasingly important role in the future of our industry.

The future is full of opportunity. Scotland can become one of the great international tourism destinations of the 21st century, but it will only do so if we are quick to grasp the chances and create initiatives that build on our consumer appeal. Above all, we must bring into being our vision of an industry that communicates freely and effectively, enabling everyone involved to clearly see the common goal and work towards it.

As a former graduate, I am proud to congratulate the University's Heritage Unit and its sponsors on the timely choice of theme for the 1994 Heritage Convention in Moray. The programme was designed to review existing policies and practices, with the aim of teasing out possible answers to the above issues.

The papers in this volume will stand as lasting contributions to a new agenda that will help us plan wisely for a more dynamic future. The authors have shed light on how we might go about developing a clear focus and creating a powerful brand image. They stress the need for diversity of products in response to the diversity of the market place, and they explore issues associated with sustainability and quality of services.

The thread that runs through the entire volume is a plea for better co-ordination of policy-making and action by all parties concerned. Their enduring message is that by working together we shall succeed.

Derek Reid
Chief Executive
Scottish Tourist Board

Edinburgh
June, 1994

ACKNOWLEDGEMENTS

The University is pledged to produce practitioners
who are relevantly qualified for their chosen vocations
within an educational environment that fosters
innovation, enterprise and an enthusiasm for excellence.

Our success as a university is founded on a strong commitment to partnership, our front line partners being those who come to us as students. The pledge above, from our mission statement, depends on extending this partnership approach into the community, where the relevance of our academic endeavours can be tested against the real world. Indeed, we are committed to working together with government, industry and voluntary bodies whenever possible, and we are always grateful when our initiatives meet with a positive response.

One such recent initiative is our Heritage Unit, established to enhance our capability at the interface between cultural and environmental subjects. It was launched by mounting a major heritage convention at our Kepplestone campus in 1993, and the success of this event, attended by 150 delegates from seven European countries, was in large measure due to support from government and the enthusiastic backing of the City of Aberdeen. The opening address was given by Sir Hector Monro MP, in his capacity as Minister for Agriculture and the Environment at the Scottish Office, and James Wyness, as Lord Provost, who delivered a paper on the Heritage of Aberdeen and entertained delegates at the Town House afterwards.

Our second convention is the outcome of a partnership forged at the request of Moray District Council, Moray Badenoch & Strathspey Enterprise and the Scottish Tourist Board. Many other organisations have given indispensable support, including Grampian Regional Council, Scottish Arts Council and Scottish Natural Heritage. We are particularly indebted for enthusiastic encouragement from Dick Ruane and Andy Anderson of the Local Enterprise Company, and to John Summers and Alistair Campbell of the District Council. Derek Reid and Dr Gordon Adams at the Scottish Tourist Board gave generously of their time when advice was most needed, and Anne Burgess of Moray Tourist Board let us choose a suitable picture from her collection to adorn the cover of this volume.

The content bears witness to the enormous range of talents that we were able to call upon for contributions, and we are indeed most grateful to each author for finding time to write the papers so that they could be published in time for delegates arriving in Elgin. Active encouragement by several members of the Unit's Advisory Board has been a source of strength, and we are particularly grateful to Lord Balfour of Burleigh and John Foster for their insistence on the pursuit of excellence at all times. Our special thanks go to the Unit's Director, Professor Magnus Fladmark, without whom there would not have been a convention. In his task as editor, he has been ably supported, well beyond the call of duty, by the deputy-editor and convention organiser, Brian Hill, as well as by Tom Band on whom the University has conferred an honorary appointment in recognition of his work as senior programme adviser. Other colleagues who have contributed in one way or another and deserve thanks are David Silbergh, Anne Simpson, Kirsty Fraser, Aileen Graham, Stewart Cordiner, Ernie Smith, Richard and Sheila Hill, Joan Hardie and Suzi Wood in the Faculty of Design, as well as Jim Rae, Leonard Forman, June Davis, Mitch Milmore and Martin Parker in External Affairs.

The convention tours were made possible through the generous support of many, including Robert Chalmers and Stephen Marsh of Moray College, Richard Miller of the National Trust for Scotland, Ian Shepherd of Grampian Regional Council, Ann Miller of the Chivas Glenlivet Group and Nicholas Morgan of United Distillers.

We are deeply grateful to Jill Pearce of Donhead and Robert Chaundy of Bookstyle for a high quality product, as well as for a Scottish Office presence in the person of Lord James Douglas-Hamilton MP who kindly agreed to give the opening address. The proceedings were greatly enhanced by the kenspeckle array of distinguished personalities who kindly agreed to chair or host sessions at Elgin Town Hall, ie Edward Aldridge, Lord and Lady Balfour of Burleigh, George Chesworth, Jean Cox, Iain Lawson, Gordon McDonald, Donald McPhail, Derek Reid, Gavin Ross, Dick Ruane, Oliver Russell, Robbie Shepherd and John Summers. The keen eyes of Professor Seaton Baxter, Tom Band and John Foster as members of the refereeing panel are clearly reflected in the high standard of papers to have found their way into this volume.

Professor Eric Spiller   David A Kennedy
Assistant Principal & Dean   Principal & Vice-Chancellor

The Robert Gordon University
Aberdeen

xii

INTRODUCTION

The heritage assets of land and culture are the very foundations of our civilisation, and these assets are increasingly becoming the basis for our economic prosperity as they attract tourists. Indeed, the decline of traditional industries has left many communities almost entirely dependent for their survival on income from tourists. The dilemma represented by the divergent cultures of heritage and enterprise is at the centre of this book.

What we see in museums and read in books about our cultural roots are but shadows cast by the lives of those who have vanished into the past as heroes or villains, or more mundanely, who have walked off to find a better job elsewhere. Without people, the living branches of culture are bare and tomorrow's harvest barren, and the conundrum of how to reconcile the pursuit of truth with the pursuit of profit remains.

Culture is popularly perceived as being about the true nature of our lives past and present. Yet, in truth, culture has always ridden on the back of wealth and poverty, and for many communities today tourism is the force that keeps them and their culture alive. As the economic and cultural balance shifts, it is widely feared that commercial exploitation threatens to destroy what is authentic and real. However, people must live and opportunities, like nettles, must be grasped.

As long as cultural activities were governed by their own internal philosophy and ethic, they stayed within the bounds of truth and values commonly subscribed to by society. The distinction between fact and fiction, the real and the unreal, became blurred when the commercial world entered the cultural arena with a different set of concepts and values concerned with product development, creation of brand images and marketing strategies. This has caused an unfortunate chasm to open between those who feel that they are the custodians of real culture and those whom they regard as the perpetrators of ersatz and phoney culture in theme parks and the like in a business loosely referred to as the heritage industry.

The objective set for this volume was to examine issues at the interface between these two points of view. To explore where the differences lie, and to identify common ground where both sides might gain mutual advantage from collaboration. The cultural purist has much to offer from rigour of scholarship and truthful heritage interpretation, but this must be balanced with the skills of the private operator who knows how to turn ideas into products with public appeal and how to market these effectively. The challenge is to stimulate a dialogue between the two that will set a new agenda and begin to look at guiding principles for cultural sustainability.

Individual authors were asked to explore the principles, practices and policy issues associated with achieving sustainability and to address specific themes. For example, are we loving our heritage to death by allowing it to be trivialised and worn down by the visiting hordes; who gains and who loses when the heritage industry takes over; can heritage be recreated and can it be exported from one continent to another like Euro Disney; is the competitive potential of cultural assets fully understood; is enough being done to generate a truly multidisciplinary approach to replace the blinkered vision of individual disciplines and sectors; and should we do more to learn from each other across national boundaries?

To give shape to the book, we decided to organise the papers into four thematic sections which are summarised below.

SHIFTING PERSPECTIVES

The first contains visionary contributions from authors who have sought, by choice and treatment of subject matter, to look back as well as forward and to point us in new directions. It opens with Lester Borley's paper, written from the unequalled perspective of a person who has served as Chief Executive of both the Scottish and English Tourist Boards, as well as having been Director of the National Trust for Scotland. He is now Secretary General of Europa Nostra, which has brought him close to the practical implications of there being no wall between East and West and the prospects of EU membership by former states of the Soviet Union. He gives a vivid picture of *the new map of Europe* with a multitude of cultural identities and affinities that have lain dormant behind the Iron Curtain of conformity for almost a century.

Like Lester Borley, Sean Browne and William Tramposch help us take a global view of the subject. Their papers are powerful testaments to the value of learning from each other and sharing of experience across national boundaries. From the vantage point of having been one of the leading players behind Ireland's tourism recovery, Sean Browne reveals the ideas and thinking that placed the cultural heritage centre stage in Irish tourism policy. His account also confirms the value of taking a long term approach and maintaining a consistent strategic line over an extended period of time. By implication, this is a warning not to return to the drawing board every other year, as it leads to confused policy and sends confusing signals to the customer.

We have always been puzzled by Europeans who are dismissive of North American achievements in the field of cultural tourism and heritage interpretation. The recent high profile of Disney exports may be partly to blame for this misguided attitude, and it will be to our own loss that we continue on this path of ignorance. William Tramposch focuses on Colonial Williamsburg, where he once worked. He provides valuable insights into how *heritage sites in the USA* have been recreated, funded and operated. Their role in fostering knowledge of and pride in local culture is reminiscent of their Scandinavian equivalents, and he explains how interpretive policy has been developed around themes like 'Becoming Americans'.

Tunnel vision is an affliction that spreads its infectious virus well beyond the British Isles, but its consequences are particularly evident here, whether in government policy, the organisational system or in the monocultural demarcations of the professions. Brian Evans analyses the history of *expos and garden festivals*, which are really a form of cultural tourism, and concludes that the considerable sums invested should be integrated within a broader strategy of tourism that includes folk parks, festivals and also major sporting events like the Olympic Games. There can be no doubt that much could be gained if those responsible for this multiplicity of activities talked to each other and planned their investment programmes together according to agreed objectives.

A feature of expos and garden festivals is the large sums, mainly from the public purse in recent years, which have gone into buildings and landscapes that last only for the duration of an event. Evans contrasts the 1911 Exhibition of Scottish History, Art and Industry in Kelvingrove Park, where a traditional burgh high street and Highland clachan were recreated for the benefit of visitors, with Skansen in Stockholm where traditional rural buildings have been recreated as a permanent folk museum. The Kelvingrove recreations of vernacular architecture would have made a perfect home for a Scottish folk collection, but instead it was demolished at the end of the exhibition. Why was our folk heritage thought worthy of only passing interest in 1911; was it because leading museologists of the time considered folk culture rather kitsch and not in the same league as their collections of ancient and exotic artefacts?

Professor Duncan Macmillan pursues the theme of *our cultural heroes*, stalking the statuary of Central Edinburgh for the great minds and ideas of bygone centuries, and concludes that their legacy of lateral thinking and equal concern for both high and low culture have been forgotten in our compartmentalised world of today. However, Peter Howard bravely attempts a lateral approach to present day policy making by analysing *fashions in landscape painting* as a tool for predicting which parts of the countryside might become the valued areas of the future.

The section is concluded by two provocative papers that stand as flashing red lights of warning. In a penetrating analysis of *The Highland Myth*, reflecting an academic grounding in philosophy, Phillip Hills contrasts the commonly perceived image of a nation's cultural heritage with the realities of life as lived by ordinary Scots. He finds that myths have superseded reality. Priscilla Boniface looks beyond Robert Hewison's 1987 vision in *The Heritage Industry: Britain in a Climate of Decline*. Her prognosis of who benefits and who loses in Theme Park Britain is that we might all slide further down the spiral of decline unless higher standards are set for heritage interpretation, with a premium being placed on truthful scholarship and more respect being accorded to the critical faculties of the visiting public.

POLICY AND PRACTICE

As reflected in Derek Reid's Foreword, the Scottish tourist industry stands at the crossroads after a period of having concentrated mainly on matters internal to itself. The Scottish Tourism Co-ordinating Group, chaired by a Scottish Office Minister, was formed in response to a realisation that meaningful tourism policy can be achieved only by taking it forward on a broad front in partnership with those responsible for the cultural and environmental heritage. The recent *Scottish Tourist Strategic Plan*, issued for consultation at the time of writing, is cast in this mould of multidisciplinary partnership.

The theme of Gordon Adams' paper is *the role of heritage attractions* in Scottish tourism policy. He examines their economic importance, their use in presenting Scotland as a tourist destination, the role of government in heritage presentation, the standard of services and souvenirs, and the cost per job in newly created attractions, using Glasgow's Museum of Comparative Religion as an example. Although he feels that there are already enough large attractions, he argues that the industrial heritage theme has been neglected in mainstream policy and suggests that more could be done in this field.

The paper on *theme trails* by David Silbergh et al is in part based on work which was undertaken by the authors for a presentation at the 1993 Convention in Aberdeen. Trails are of many types, and they are planned and developed by organisations ranging from national agencies to local community groups. They have become a much favoured tool in the box of tricks used by the industry. However, little research has been done on the subject and, on the basis of a review of Scottish practice, the authors define a taxonomy of trails, as well as a methodology for setting objectives, choosing a suitable theme, and for product development. The format of trails and standard of literature vary a great deal, and a strong plea is made for central guidance, together with action to establish a strategic partnership framework at regional and national levels so that a more coherent menu of trails can be presented to visitors.

The creation of a *national brand image* that will be powerful enough to raise a country to the status of a major tourist destination in international markets is the ambition that drives all players in the tourism game, the concept of major gateways being an essential element of such national strategies. This translates down to regional and district levels, where a similar game is played in a bid to outdo neighbours by capturing the attention of tourists. The secret of success at all levels is to create a clear focus, and Howard Fisher and Alistair Campbell give vivid accounts of how this challenge has been handled by two local authorities.

The section is concluded with a suite of papers addressing the question of loving our heritage to death. Access to land and buildings carries a cost penalty for the provider who has to cope with the *wear and tear of trampling feet*. Trevor Croft explains how this problem is handled at the historic houses of the National Trust for Scotland, where buildings have had to be closed because of collapsing floors, and Thomas Huxley deals with ecological impacts. Both agree that the consequences of access and the remedial work required are considerations that need to be built into site management plans. This principle is borne out, albeit at a much larger scale, by John Anfield who discusses the system developed for *planning and management in national parks* to cope with the ever increasing pressure of visitors. He also touches on the role of farm tourism in the parks, and the tailpiece of this section is a paper on the subject of *green tourism and farming*, presented at the 1993 Convention by Richard Denman.

REALITY OR IMAGE

Some authors in the first section, particularly Hills and Boniface, touch on the ethics of heritage interpretation. This section is comprised of papers dealing with the role of interpretation as practised by public agencies at their own hand, by consultants working for public agencies, and as pioneered by one industry, more precisely the whisky industry. It opens with twin contributions from Historic Scotland. Duncan Macniven provides an overview of their *interpretation policy* since becoming an Executive Agency which has given more freedom in corporate decision making. He stresses the high priority given to working in partnership with other bodies and the emphasis now given to the need for observing the principle of sustainability, but he distances himself from excessive strategic planning by government that might smack of meddling in the affairs of others.

The other contribution from Historic Scotland is by David Breeze who deals with several issues associated with *marketing and interpretation*. He stresses the need to determine *levels of tolerable impact*, the volume of visitors below which no lasting damage is done, and he warns against the danger of concentrating too much on sites with high earning power at the expense of those which are less popular. Closure of low earners might represent a loss in diversity now, and long term flexibility might be compromised if diversionary measures are called for to cope with excessive pressures at key sites in future. He also gives an interesting discourse on the ethics of *consolidation versus reconstruction* of archaeological ruins.

Presented at the 1993 Convention, the paper by William McDermott and Ross Noble is in two parts. The first is an account of the wide range of issues concerned with economic development, planning, access and land management that provide the backcloth to current work by Highland Regional Council to produce a strategy for heritage interpretation. The benefits of such a strategy are listed along with a set of five key objectives. High priority is given to community involvement and partnership, and to this end a *Highland Heritage Network* has been established. An important element of the strategy is the provision of gateway or orientation centres, one such being the proposed *Highland Folk Park* at Newtonmore, and the second part of the paper gives a full account of this ambitious initiative.

Michael Glen moves us to the Lowlands, where the first Scottish *visitor orientation and interpretation plan* for a whole town has been produced for St Andrews in Fife. He outlines the philosophy and operational style adopted by Derek Lovejoy Touchstone to discharge this pioneering initiative, then explains the methodology and procedures used for undertaking the heritage audit to select interpretive themes, and for testing the plan against market considerations. Proposals are described for a town map, orientation points, signage and interpretive panels at key locations.

The setting of Priscilla Gordon-Duff's paper is the Glenlivet Estate in hill country south of Strathspey, half way between Aviemore and Elgin. Owned and managed by the Crown Estates, it has developed a system of paths for public access in recent years. The author was engaged to carry out a study of *the oral traditions* in the area to discover how life in the earlier parts of this century was remembered by local residents. The intention is to publish an interpretive booklet based on her findings to enable visitors to gain a deeper understanding of and respect for the cultural landscape they see.

Within the private sector, the Scottish whisky industry has gained an international reputation for its sophisticated approach to utilising the heritage of the industry as a competitive asset. Evidence of their success is to be seen in a string of visitor centres which is now a vital element of tourism facilities in many areas, and Ann Miller tells the story of how the Chivas and Glenlivet Group is creating *a physical and spiritual home for Chivas Regal* at Strathisla Distillery. Writing as the acknowledged authority on the history of Scotch Whisky, Michael Moss has chosen to tell the 'alternative' story of the industry, which contrasts the reality of alcohol in the lives of ordinary people, with that of the popular myth. In Chapter 7, Phillip Hills also discusses reality and myth attached to the whisky theme.

The two papers on interpretation in museums, by Thompson and Harrison, were delivered at the 1993 Convention and have been included by popular request from those who heard them then. The section is concluded with an interesting analysis by the environmental psychologist, Christopher Andrew, that focuses on the pros and cons of the recent fashion for *cleaning stone buildings* in historic areas. He concludes that more research is required before we can answer the question: is the patina of time an essential ingredient of the true reality of our built heritage, or do tourists prefer to have the grime of ages removed so that they can see architecture as it appeared when originally built? In dealing with historic buildings, he also suggests that our actions should be alert to the fact that what is considered of little value today may become highly fashionable in the future.

CULTURAL SUSTENANCE

The concluding section starts with Charles McKean on the subject of architecture, where he puts forward a methodology for interpreting the built environment in terms of the land, climate and human condition which shaped its character. It is a significant contribution in the sense that it breaks away from the conventional preoccupation with high culture, returning to what Duncan Macmillan calls the distinctive Scottish trait of embracing 'as one both high and popular culture'

McKean refers to *two kinds of architecture*. One is popular artisan architecture, which like language and music, expresses a truly genuine Scottish character. The other is architecture infused with ideas from elsewhere created by architects and master builders whose design language has been enriched by the vocabulary of European culture. Robin Webster follows this through by allowing us into the mind of the practising architect today, where the fusion of modern technology and a sense of local culture is finely balanced.

Sheila Douglas tackles the thorny question of the roots and destiny of the Scots language. Like Billy Kay, in *Scots: The Mither Tongue*, she lays bare the linguistic roots that binds Scots to the wider family of modern European languages. For example, she lists many words that are still recognisable in a common vocabulary shared with the Danes. Considering that only about 15 per cent of Scottish children grow up in homes where standard English is the predominant language, it is truly remarkable that the rest of the population (excluding two per cent who are Gaelic speakers) is not catered for. Together with Paul Scott's excellent contribution on *Scottish literature*, their papers are eloquent statements in support of an initiative, which we believe is long overdue, to introduce a standard Scots grammar and dictionary to the school curriculum that would give Scottish children the choice of taking an examination in the language into which they were born.

John Purser's contribution to the revival of interest in the heritage of Scottish music shall remain an unmatched driving force for years to come. His book on *Scotland's Music* stands as a monument to his fertile mind and intellectual energy. One of his many achievements is to have masterminded the making of a replica based on a carnyx fragment found almost 200 years ago at Deskford in Banffshire. The carnyx was a trumpet or horn-type instrument made of beaten bronze used by the proto-Pictish tribes of Scotland at the time of the Roman conquest, and Purser's illustrated paper tells the story of how this instrument has been brought back to life after 2000 years of silence. Carnyx fragments have been found elsewhere in Europe, but no other attempt has been made to produce a playable replica and we believe that *the Deskford Carnyx* now stands as one of the most powerful symbols of Scottish culture in existence.

The last three papers, on the culture of food, gave the name to this section. Elizabeth Luard has written an amusing and provocative paper on *the role of the sausage* in the cultural and political firmament of Europe. Against this wider context, Catherine Brown focuses on *the roots of Scotland's food*. She shows that, like architecture, language, literature and music, food is of two kinds. One is served at the rural Highland table from the larder of the land, sea and river, with a distinct culture unique to its locality. The other is served at the more sophisticated tables of the capital city Edinburgh, with additional ingredients of exotic spices, vegetables and wines from Continental Europe.

Donald Carney completes the picture by applying the concept of *food ethnology* to the North East of Scotland, contrasting the diet of the workers with that of the laird. He takes us from the tradition of cooking into the realm of strategic tourism, stressing the need for quality of product and services, and arguing that the culinary expert be given a place at the high table of tourism policy making.

THE ISSUES

We opened this introduction by stating that the objective of the book was to examine how to arrive at a set of values that can be shared by exponents of authentic culture and those responsible for profit-driven enterprise. We declared our aim as being to stimulate a dialogue between the two that will set a new agenda for cultural sustainability. None of the authors set out to provide universal solutions, but their response to our original questions have highlighted three key issues worthy of special consideration by policy makers:

1. For culture to play its full part in tourism, high priority must be given to partnership and integrated policy across sectors, as well as providing a strategic framework for action at regional and local levels.
2. The culture of individual countries should be nourished, but it is vitally important not to lose sight of the wider commonwealth of shared culture, and more should be done to enable different countries to learn from each other.
3. For heritage interpretation to regain its credibility with the public, its objectives must be clearly stated and understood and there is a need to distinguish historical facts from fictional myths.

There are other issues which deserve a place on the agenda for future action. For example, the continuum between high and low culture should be kept in balance by paying more attention to the latter, and cultural assertiveness training should be encouraged to stimulate a more critical public attitude. The diversity of interpretation in Scotland could be enhanced by giving a higher profile to the industrial heritage and the heritage of popular sports. The pressures on Scotland's most valued landscapes are now so great that a more robust system of stewardship and development control is needed to safeguard their future. We also support the view that steps should be taken to elevate the Scots language in education and the media to a position where it is regarded as a cultural asset to be valued.

As contributions to knowledge, the papers in this volume confirm that culture is a fusion of divergent philosophies. It is a collective response to the conflicting forces which shape our daily lives and is as much about making sense of living as about earning a living. From many vantage points, the authors show that the path to success in tourism lies in connecting culture with the human aspirations which are the driving force of our civilisation. The process of culture is dynamic and positive, not static or negatively confrontational. Reconciling the opposites in culture means understanding them and celebrating, not denying, their differences.

Professor Magnus Fladmark   Lord Balfour of Burleigh
Director   Chairman, Advisory Board

The Robert Gordon University Heritage Unit

SHIFTING PERSPECTIVES
Visions of the Future

Tomorrow starts
with today's vision.

1

CULTURAL DIVERSITY IN A CHANGING EUROPE

Lester Borley

By way of a tribute, I have chosen to start by making reference to the recent obituaries of two men whose work I admired. The first was that for Forsyth Hardy, the former Director of Films for Scotland, whose knowledge of film-making and Scotland expressed themselves so well in his career. His obituary recounted the story of a journey with Arthur Freed, a film producer, looking for Scottish locations for shooting the film *Brigadoon*. This was an unsuccessful search because, as Freed remarked, Scotland no longer looked like Scotland. The second was that for Oliver Roskill, a well-known industrial consultant who, during his career worldwide, as his obituary said, 'became familiar with the history and terrain of the countries he visited – with their philosophies and fabric, their pictures and plants, their wine; the governance of the country, its raw materials and basic industries.' I would suggest that we keep both of these attitudes in our mind when considering the subject of the cultural diversity in a changing Europe. I think it will soon become clear that unless a tourist or a visitor has an enquiring mind, he will fail to appreciate the culture of a nation, and thus fail to value the diversity which makes Europe such a fascinating continent.

DEFINITION OF CULTURE

I suppose we should agree on what we mean by the word *culture*. I think that the title of this volume perhaps uses the word in a very narrow sense, and by linking it with art we might be misled into thinking that we should be concerned only with an artistic expression of the culture or the heritage of a nation. So what do we mean by the word culture? A dictionary describes it as 'the sum of the inherited ideas, beliefs, values and knowledge, which constitute the shared bases of social action.'

Matthew Arnold once said that 'Culture (was) the acquainting ourselves with the best that has been known and said in the world, and thus with the history of the human spirit.' Is it any wonder then that in 1936 Herman Goering was quoted as saying 'When I hear anyone talk of culture, I reach for my revolver.'

The purpose of the conference for which this paper was written, as I understood it, was to examine various aspects of our culture and to relate this to the important business of cultural tourism. That of course immediately raises the question of definition. I would like to suggest the following as a starting point:

> Cultural tourism may be defined as that activity which enables people to explore or experience the different way of life of other people, reflecting social customs, religious traditions and the intellectual ideas of a cultural heritage which may be unfamiliar.

There can be no doubt that what passes for cultural tourism in the minds of the travel industry bears very little relation to that holistic concept. During the course of this conference we shall be exploring many byways of our cultural heritage, but I think it would be useful to have some definition in mind, if only to be able to challenge it at the conclusion.

WHAT IS EUROPE?

The other important concept which requires definition is of course Europe itself. Are we talking about the Europe whose limits are imposed by the boundaries of the European Union, even taking into account the prospect of the enlargement to 16 nations? Or are we embracing that together with the six countries of Central Europe, namely Poland, Hungary, Bulgaria, Roumania and the Czech and Slovak Republics, with which the European Union engages in programmes of assistance? I am sure that it would be wrong to limit our concept of Europe to the political convenience of the European Union as we know it. Even the Council of Europe, which has been in existence far longer, recognises 32 Member States, and involves eight other 'special guest' Parliaments, which adopt its Cultural Convention. So the countries of Albania, Belarus, Croatia, Latvia, Moldova, the former Yugoslav Republic of Macedonia, Russia and the Ukraine, all consider themselves as part of a wider Europe.

Within this expanded area there are of course many traditional relationships between cultural groups. A new publication by The Times 'A Guide to the Peoples of Europe' in fact defines 100 nations occupying the geographical area which I have described.

I think we must conclude that the Europe of 1994 is certainly not the Europe of 1945, nor even the Europe of 1989, which saw the trauma of dynamic change making itself felt in many ways and causing the present

4

instability in government and uncertainty in the lives of people. As Felipe Fernandez-Armesto, who edited the *Guide to the Peoples of Europe* says, 'Nothing like today's sudden appearance of previously unfamiliar people has happened in Europe since the fall of the Roman Empire. In the familiar Europe of modern history, the arena of States and Empires, peoples are kicking up the sand, which is settling in new patterns ... the names of groups which by the last quarter of the century had become well-known only to folklorists are now key words of political discourse. The resurgence of historic identities seems to reverse a long-standing trend towards the submersion of small peoples in big states and superstates. Yet, in fascinating contrast to earlier upheavals, today's turbulence – the redrawing of frontiers, the trauma of ethnic cleansing, the development of regional associations across the frontiers of established states – happens in the undertow of European integration.'

To whom therefore do we owe this movement towards European union? We owe it I suppose to Jean Monnet who is known as 'the father of Europe'. As Jean-Baptiste Duroselle in his wide ranging book *Europe: a history of its peoples* shows, 'Jean Monnet's wholly original historic role depended upon two in particular of his extraordinary gifts: that of making friends, especially in high places, and that of finding for many problems highly original solutions, gradually worked out with his small group of colleagues and assistants, and then launched with energy and vigour.' It was his original idea to link the mining and metalworking areas of great importance in the Saar as a way of achieving Franco-German reconciliation. This idea came to fruition in what is known as the Robert Schumann Plan, but which was in fact the concept of Jean Monnet. It lies at the heart of European Union, which was of course based firmly on economic principles. In old age, Jean Monnet reflected that, if he had to do it all over again, he would have started with culture.

However, if we want to identify the earlier author of an idea for a new Europe, we must go back to the time of the Congress of Vienna in 1814, and the role played by a little-known figure, the Comte de Saint-Simon. He had served under George Washington in the American War of Independence and had travelled widely in Europe. He thought that the Congress of Vienna was the ideal opportunity to make his ideas known, and he sent every negotiator a brochure entitled: *The reorganisation of European society, or the need and the way to bring together the peoples of Europe in a single political body, while preserving the nationality of each.* His vision was of course somewhat uncomfortable for statesmen of a more traditional mind, and the eventual Congress of Vienna which was signed on 9 June 1815 did not embody his ideas.

THE MAASTRICHT TREATY

We have had to wait for the Maastricht Treaty and its tortuous route through the Parliaments of Europe to establish for the first time a clear recognition of the importance of culture. In a document of 100 pages, it only occupies half of one side, but it makes the important statement 'That the Community shall contribute to the flowering of the cultures of the Member States, while respecting their national and regional diversity, and at the same time bringing the common cultural heritage to the fore.' It goes on to say 'That the Community and the Member States shall foster co-operation with third countries and the international organisations competent in the sphere of culture, and in particular with the Council of Europe.' And, most important of all, it says 'That the Community shall take cultural aspects into account in its action under other provisions of this Treaty.'

In its reference to the Council of Europe, it has of course recognised the wider concept of Europe to which I referred above. The Council of Europe in its work has always been concerned among other things with the importance of Human Rights, and in what we might call a second Vienna Declaration, the Summit of Heads of State and Governments of the Council of Europe which met in Vienna in October 1993 charged the Committee of Ministers, 'to begin work on drafting a protocol complementing the European Convention on Human Rights in the cultural field, by provisions guaranteeing individual rights, in particular for persons belonging to national minorities.' It concluded that Europe, as a 'Community of spirit', can only be founded on common values, including in particular that which is at the foundation of all Human Rights philosophy: the equal dignity of all human beings.

Cultural identity of course is a product not of isolation but of interrelation, and therefore has to be regarded as a continuing process. It would be even more important for the countries which have recently rejoined the large family of Europe to create the framework for co-operation and integration.

EUROPEAN IDENTITY

European identity is a reflection of geography, although as a continent it suffers from being sometimes seen as 'the ragged western edge of Asia'. The eastern divide between the two continents is somewhat imprecise; some choosing the Urals and some the so-called Manych Depression. It is even more difficult to speak of a European race, having similar physical characteristics. One of the considerable problems of defining a European is caused by the diversity of nations within the name. As Felipe Fernandez-Armesto says in his Guide to the Peoples of Europe:

> At first sight the search for a common European culture seems a hopeless quest. Most of the continent is occupied by peoples long established in their heartlands, with the consequent baffling array of distinctive microcultures

which characterizes all 'Old Worlds'. Europe is scored, moreover, by long and deep cultural divides, which separate speakers of Romance, Germanic and Slavonic languages, and members of the Roman, Orthodox and Protestant communions. Historic experiences – sometimes centuries-old – have erected 'national' boundaries or barriers of hostility between neighbours of otherwise similar culture – in, for instance, Portugal and Galicia, Norway and Sweden, Serbia and Croatia, Derry and Donegal.

What we need perhaps is a new cultural paradigm, perhaps to create a new model of market integration within cultural diversity. European cultural strengths always need to be tested against comparative world cultures. The unfamiliar always fascinates, and the young must be stimulated by multicultural voices and visions. At the same time there is the danger of marginalising minority cultures, regarding them somewhat as 'folk traditions only having a value for tourism.' There is certainly a need to look beyond the superficial of tourism promotion for true cultural meaning. At the same time there is the need to be self-critical and to reassess constantly the integrity of one's affinities and one's cultural actions, not only within the wider Europe, but within the wider world.

THE COMMON MEMORY

Half the monuments of the world are to be found in Europe, which should be not only a source of wonder for those of us who are European, but also a source of awesome responsibility for those who also have to care for this *Common Memory*.

Because of the Diaspora and the migration of European peoples over the centuries, there are communities throughout the New World who share our heritage and our sense of values. Working-class poverty, nineteenth-century political strife and religious intolerance between 1815 and 1914 caused fifty million people to go overseas, establishing significant European cultural outposts. The biggest, clearly, is in the United States of America, which took in 32 million Europeans. The sources of the immigrants are interesting. Great Britain and Ireland provided 17 million, Germany 10 million, Italy almost as many, the Balkans and the Danube basin four million, and Spain, surprisingly, another four million. Only France has contributed little to the emigration of 50 million people from Europe over the past two centuries.

As we proceed through the papers in this volume to consider the strengths of our cultural heritage or our traditions, we should remember that these have values shared by millions of people who are descendants of those great waves of emigration.

The strength of the Scottish Clan system in the United States and Canada is such that many are drawn to revisit their ancestral roots. Time and distance lend a certain romance to the sad remains of West Coast black houses. Some who return to their roots from the relative comforts of North America sigh with relief that their forebears left such a bleak landscape. But many are moved by a deeper memory. The stones themselves can only suggest the hardship and despair. They cannot speak of the strength of character or the ability which could only flower and prosper when given the chance in another land. Two cousins who emigrated to Canada from this district, and who pioneered the railways, ended up as Lord Mountstephen and Lord Strathcona.

Their story is matched by similar stories of Poles and Lithuanians, Slovaks and Hungarians. Many return to invest in the future of their nations. George Soros, a Hungarian, has created a University of Europe largely based in Prague. It was Polish Americans who made it possible for Warsaw Castle, destroyed by Germans, to be restored to its previous splendour, as a symbol of a very proud people.

DEVELOPING CULTURAL TOURISM

Two years ago I spoke at a conference promoted by UNESCO in Indonesia, on the subject of *Universal tourism: enriching or degrading culture?* The subjects of that conference were markedly different from those which form the basis of this volume, and reflected a different philosophy. We considered the need to revitalise the cultural heritage of South East Asia, and talked about cultural tourism based upon such subjects as religious belief systems, the contribution of women in society and the potential of village tourism, as well as the usual discussion about how best to market cultural tourism.

One of my fellow speakers, Professor Mohammed Arkoun, Professor of Islamic Thought at the Sorbonne, concluded that 'the class of people engaged in mass tourism are culturally the less prepared to take an interest in the discovery of religious belief systems when they travel abroad. Tourists might be open and eager to discover the authentic values of a country, a religious tradition, but if the natives themselves ignore their own values, or use them in a distorted way, then one cannot expect the visitors to comprehend.' There was a need, he thought, for the teaching of the history of art and architecture as well as art activity in secondary schools and universities to educate the aesthetic taste and an historic sensitivity. It was for this reason that even the *cultivated* middle class or highly educated people did not necessarily have the emotional ability or capacity to comment upon artistic masterpieces in architecture, painting, sculpture, music, dance, furniture, costumes, etc. He stressed the need that tourist guides should be trained as high level professionals, for they must be considered what he called the 'mediators of the whole cultural identity of their countries when they present it to others from other cultures.'

I suggested that, if cultural tourism is to have any depth, then it must reflect the values which people themselves revere. It is too often true that strangers gain only a superficial impression of the significance of the cultural heritage of a people or a nation, and in my view the revitalising of a cultural heritage must commence with a clear restatement and comprehension of the values of the society who are to play host to visitors. Thus, I think it will be important for us to be clear on the real significance of those aspects of the cultural heritage which we choose to use for the purposes of cultural tourism.

Strangers are of course intimidated by a lack of knowledge. It is incumbent on the host nation to attempt to explain the roots of its own culture. This is not only to prevent the stranger unwittingly causing offence in a country whose religious principles may dictate certain patterns of behaviour, but rather for the visitor to be able to comprehend the relationship between the design of buildings, the patterns of land-use and the habits of people. Max Lerner, in his fascinating book *America as a Civilisation* captured the sense of the past in the following way:

> Like a person, a civilization is more than the sum of its parts. Describe a man's features, give his life history, tell where he lives and how, place him in his class or group, define his ethics and politics and still you will not have the man himself. What slips through is his total style, quick and dead: whatever it is that makes him himself, and different from other men. Thus St. Francis had a style, and Samuel Johnson, Martin Luther, Voltaire, and Dean Swift, Alexander and Asoka, Napoleon and Goethe, Lincoln and Carnegie and Justice Holmes.
>
> History remembers this about the great men, but the rest of us remember it also about the nameless people we have known: remember the way they moved, their tricks of speech and habit, their taut or relaxed quality, the superfluous things they did and with what grace or clumsiness, what cavalry pounded through their brain, what inner battles they fought.
>
> So it is with civilization. When you have described its people, armies, technology, economics, politics, arts, regions and cities, class and caste, mores and morals, there is something elusive left – an inner civilization style.

CULTURAL LANDSCAPES

It is not without significance that UNESCO, in attempting to list those World Heritage sites of universal value, distinguishes between the natural or cultural heritage. Within the past year, UNESCO and ICOMOS, working together, have defined the concept of a cultural landscape, which recognises that the man-made and natural heritage interact. I am sure that we would all accept that the culture of any person or nation essentially reflects an awareness of the sum of his natural and man-made environment. Although many papers of this volume deal with individual aspects of the subject, I am sure that we all recognise that they must harmonise in what we call cultural tourism.

All over the world, professionals and academics are reassessing the strengths and weaknesses of the cultural heritage in an attempt to create different forms of tourism which might seem to be more acceptable to host nations. The scope of problems and opportunities discussed in this volume are indeed similar to those facing administrators and professionals in other countries.

I have already made reference to the responsibility that those of us who are guardians of our culture have in sustaining its form and memory for those of our kith and kin who emigrated over the past two centuries. Just as Arthur Freed was disappointed in his search for Brigadoon; Gertrude Stein, when returning to her childhood home in Oakland, California, is recorded as having said 'But when I got there, there was no there there.' People today have moved rapidly from the word-of-mouth recommendation of friends to the instant imagery of electronic communication in creating anticipation of a destination. Many have preconceptions or even misconceptions about the culture of a country.

No visitor to a foreign country can remain entirely unaware or unaffected by what he sees, and the country that misrepresents its cultural heritage is therefore not going to create any substantive memory for the stranger. There are many differences between Scotland and the rest of the United Kingdom. There are many distinctive features between each of the regions of Scotland. All international tourism research indicates an interest in history and countryside, which are the principal motivators of travel. Lord Curzon wrote when he first discovered India:

> Tourism is a university in which the scholar never takes his degree. It is a temple where the supplicant adores but never catches sight of the object of his devotion. It is a journey the goal of which is always in sight but never attained. There are always learners, always worshippers, always pilgrims.

EUROPE'S PLACE IN A CHANGING WORLD

Scotland, like the United Kingdom and the rest of Europe, has to adjust to the fact that it is no longer at the centre of the world's economy. That centre first shifted to the United States of America and now has moved to the Pacific. Nevertheless, Europe continues to maintain a degree of moral leadership. The universal values that Europe has given the world, part of this moral leadership, has its roots in the fact that a major part of the cultural heritage created by man and reflected throughout the world is located in Europe.

Having lost its long-standing privileged role, it is perfectly proper for Europe to seek to gain a special place on the world scene, in part by paying more attention to its cultural heritage. We see this in the emerging democracies of Central Europe where a restatement of the cultural roots of the people helps to sustain a sense of nationhood. There is no doubt that this cultural diversity can have a strong social and economic value if properly considered, analysed and presented.

For almost half a century, Europe has been divided arbitrarily between east and west, when historically the cultural divisions of Europe have been really between north and south. Scotland's own links with the mainland of Europe have been direct and of long standing. The easy movement of scholars and adventurers since medieval times has given Scotland a clear identity. The Hanseatic League, whose influence spread widely through the trade routes of Europe, provided Scots merchants with their entree into the heartland of the continent, following the great cultural landscapes of river valleys.

The towns along the Vistula and the Baltic still retain vestiges of the *Scots Houses*, the bases for trade. When James VI went south as James I of England, the first Ambassador to seek an audience was from Poland, asking the King to stop more Scots settling in his country. For in 1604 there were 30,000 Scots living and doing business in Poland alone.

In this period of change, historic relationships are being reassessed, and in my experience, there is no doubt about the cultural identity of Scotland within Europe. The movement to recognise the importance of the flowering of cultures of Member States, which formed part of the Maastricht Treaty, is, as I have shown, matched by the Council of Europe's clear statement of the rights of the individual to his cultural identity. The framework is therefore there for Scotland to build upon its unique sense of values and traditions. To understand them and to present them as part of the cultural diversity of Europe is a challenge, not only for governments, but also for business and for society at large. So long as the culture we promote is the culture we respect, then I have no doubts about Scotland's ability to sustain its individual identity among the hundred nations of Europe.

The Author

Lester Borley CBE is Secretary General of Europa Nostra. His unmatched career has included marketing experience with the British Tourist Authority in USA, Australia and West Germany, as well as serving as Chief Executive of the Scottish Tourist Board, English Tourist Board and the National Trust for Scotland. A fellow of the Royal Scottish Geographical Society, he received a CBE for services to tourism and heritage conservation, and was awarded an Honorary Doctorate of Letters by the Robert Gordon University in 1991.

References

Arkoun, Professor M., *Cultural Tourism & Religious Belief Systems*, Indonesia, 1992
Duroselle, J.-B. and Mayne, R., *Europe: A History of its Peoples*, Viking, 1990
Fernandez-Armesto, F. (ed), *The Times Guide to the Peoples of Europe*, Harper, Collins 1994
Lerner, M., *America as a Civilisation*, Simon & Schuster, 1957

Figure 1 The Rock of Cashel is a microcosm of Ireland's heritage with an early Christian Monastery, a Norman Castle and a mediaeval cathedral, all in one landscape.

Figure 2 Grafton Street, Dublin, along with the left bank ambience of the Temple Bar, epitomises the vibrant image which has catapulted Dublin into one of Europe's prime 'city' destinations.

2

HERITAGE IN IRELAND'S
TOURISM RECOVERY

Sean Browne

In the two decades up to 1988, Irish tourism revenue was stagnant. In that year, the Irish Government set a target to double overseas tourism over a five year period. To achieve this objective, Bord Fáilte adopted a four part strategy embracing: *intensified promotion; better distribution; improved competitiveness; investment in product development.*

By 1993, overseas tourism revenue had doubled to IR£1,012 million. This represented a growth of 69% at constant prices or an average annual growth rate of 9%, well ahead of the world average. This paper focuses on the role played by product development in this success, and in particular on how the heritage component of the product was developed.

INVESTMENT IN PRODUCT DEVELOPMENT

Bord Fáilte set out to stimulate an extended range of high quality tourism projects so that we could offer more attractive holiday options to overseas visitors. This strategy was highly dependent on the creation of a more attractive investment climate. In 1989, the Government decided to make available over £160 million in EU Structural Funds over a five year period and extended tax breaks under the Business Expansion Scheme to a wide range of tourism investments. The International Fund for Ireland also contributed £14 million.

The end result was an investment programme of over IR£800 million which changed the face of the Irish tourism product. Accommodation has been upgraded and has added valuable indoor leisure and conference facilities to promote off-season business. Exciting new tourist attractions have been created and major investment has taken place in facilities for activity holidays such as angling, golf, walking, cycling, nature study and cruising.

Fifty per cent of all EU Structural Fund capital grant expenditure went into the heritage area. The range of products assisted included: *Historic Houses and Castles; Heritage Gardens; Ancient Monuments; Interpretative Centres; Genealogical Centres; National Parks; Traditional Music Centres; Cultural Centres; Industrial Archaeology; Heritage Towns; Signposted Touring Routes.*

TOWARDS A HERITAGE STRATEGY

Against a background of almost zero investment for over a decade, Bord Fáilte was inundated with grant applications from the day the grant schemes were announced. We quickly commissioned Ventures Consultancy to evaluate the current state of our heritage product, to make recommendations to us on what the market would demand and to suggest in that light how we should prioritise the applications. The consultants made some very trenchant comments:

> Your existing product is tired and unprofessional. ... Many of your new proposals are 'copy-cats' of existing attractions. ... Ireland's history is complex and many facets are being overlooked. ... Your interpretation and interpretative planning is unimaginative and lacks originality and variety. ... Projections of visitor numbers are unrealistic, marketing planning is poor and market research is almost non-existent.

They said many other things as well, but the central message was clear: 'If Ireland does not clearly decide the kind of heritage product it needs and convinces all the important players about this, then it certainly will not happen of its own accord.' We took a number of initiatives at that stage which greatly improved the eventual outcome of the process:

1. We developed a framework of themes and subsidiary storylines which, together, allowed the full range of Ireland's heritage to be explored. These themes were based, not chronologically, but on how historical events and sites touched the everyday life of the people. The main themes were: *Living Landscapes, Religion and Ritual, War and Conquest, Earning a Living,* and *The Spirit of Ireland.*
2. We tried to marry existing and proposed attractions to this overall framework.
3. We produced a very practical Directory of Consultants, which forced participants to reveal their unique expertise and we encouraged joint ventures between Irish practitioners and more experienced counterparts overseas.
4. We brought about the establishment of a heritage marketing consortium company.

5. We financed detailed research into visitor usage of tourist attractions.
6. We organised two major national conferences for developers of heritage attractions and their advisers.

THE OUTCOME

There were 85 tourist attractions charging an admission fee in 1987. By 1993, this had grown to 219. The number of admissions recorded in this period doubled from 3.4 million to 6.9 million. These visitors spent IR£24 million in 1993, a figure which has doubled in just two years. However, lest we are blinded by numbers, let us examine what our visitors said when they were researched during 1993: *80% rated culture and history as an important reason for choosing Ireland; 46% visited at least one place of cultural or historic interest; 72% rated our history and culture as 'good'.*

Overall, it seems like we should now sit back, rest on our laurels and follow the American adage 'if it ain't broke don't fix it.' I would like, however, to take a more critical look at where we now find ourselves as we look forward towards the end of the century. I will approach this task by attempting to answer a number of fundamental questions.

1. Why is it important for Ireland to continue to invest in cultural tourism? Our future strategic vision emphasises the attraction of Ireland as an island of spectacular and unspoilt scenic beauty with a unique heritage and culture and a fun-loving welcoming people. It is essential that the holiday experience of our visitors lives up to this promise. The very essence of our appeal to visitors is our distinctiveness, all those elements which set us apart from our competitors and which give us a unique identity.

Many countries can boast world renowned tourist attractions which have enormous pulling power and which are synonymous with the destination: the Grand Canyon, the Pyramids, the Tower of London, the Taj Mahal, the Eiffel Tower, Disneyland, to name but a few. In our case, we are unlikely to ever develop single attractions which we can claim will bring extra tourists to Ireland in their own right. Instead, we must mould our heritage in its broadest sense, and the way we promote and present it to visitors, so that the result is a high quality, distinctively Irish holiday experience.

2. What is the nature of the heritage we need to present to visitors? The tourist attractions of Ireland must be firmly based on the heritage of the country. This heritage can be analysed under three closely related components:

The Natural Heritage: As an island outpost on the western edge of Europe, the character of our landscape is quite distinct from the continental landmass. A small population put less pressure on this rich landscape than was the case in many congested countries so that a greater atmosphere of wilderness is still preserved.

This unspoilt landscape has created a variety of habitats, such as peat bogs and water meadows, which nurture a wealth of flora and fauna. The plants of the limestone terraces of the Burren are one of the most treasured botanical sights in Europe. The intensive farming which has bulldozed away much of the field boundaries in Europe has had less impact in Ireland.

One of the most exciting aspects of this natural heritage is that in Ireland one can still ramble freely on so much of our beaches, mountains and moorland, often hardly meeting another human being for hours.

The Man-Made Heritage: Ireland has a long history and an even longer prehistory. The landscape is dotted with the evidence of the hand of man stretching back over more than 5,000 years.

Many of the most spectacular and best preserved sites are major tourist attractions. There is also a growing appreciation of the great interest which overseas tourists have in the much-neglected smaller field monuments. Such monuments have not survived to anything like the same extent in our more industrialised neighbouring countries in Western Europe.

The Cultural Heritage: The Spirit of Ireland, heavily influenced by the landscape and man's struggle with it, is there to be discovered in our literature, traditional music, song and dance and folklore. However, tourists also want to discover the contemporary Ireland, our art and architecture, our food and drink, and our Gaelic games. They want to find out more about our daily lives, our theatres and concert halls, our art galleries, our pop music, our shopping, our pastimes. They want to learn a little about our traditional industries, our farming, our fishing, our crafts.

The Irish language is perhaps the most vivid manifestation of our distinctive cultural identity. Tourists are surprised to find so much evidence of the language in the bilingual signs, the radio and television programmes and, most important of all, in Gaeltacht areas where it is still the everyday language of the people.

These three key aspects of our heritage must be fostered and we must help tourists to explore and appreciate them. This is the fundamental goal of tourist attraction development.

3.   How will visitor demands change in the years ahead? A number of changes in society will significantly influence the future demand for tourist attractions:

Figure 3 At Ceide Fields, County Mayo, the story of the world's largest Neolithic monument and the greatest enclosed landscape in Europe is vibrantly explained against a backdrop of Atlantic cliff scenery.

Figure 4 This modern statue is a celebration of Ireland's traditional music, song and dance which is as vibrant today as it was a century ago.

Environmental Concern: More and more people are interested in the impact which industrial development, intensive agriculture and indeed tourism development will have on the social and physical environment.

Active Leisure: People will make more active use of their leisure time, not just for physical activity but for mental stimulation also.

Ageing Population: The 'baby-boomers' have moved into middle-age and will have a much greater interest in heritage and related attractions.

New Technology: Many have criticised the increasing use of simulation and animation as undermining the authenticity of heritage attractions. Few, however, would question the potential of computerisation to enhance visitor experience by better booking systems or better management of visitor flows. Even very traditional museums have demonstrated how thoughtful use of interactive multimedia systems can enhance interest and understanding.

4.   **What are the implications for how we develop cultural tourism?**
Responding to these changes means that there will have to be much more emphasis on conservation, information and participation at our tourist attractions, allied to an enhanced effort to present an interesting experience:

Conservation: The conservation objective must extend to all three elements of our heritage, the natural, the man-made and the cultural. This will require further investment in national parks, forest parks and natural heritage areas. We are working on a new initiative called *Scenic Landscapes* to extend this caring approach to all areas of outstanding natural beauty. The small field monuments which dot the countryside must be preserved and greater investment made in preserving historic buildings from decay and dereliction. Unique aspects of our culture, such as the Irish language and our traditional music, song and dance, must be kept alive and vibrant.

Information: There is a fundamental need to explain the basic nature of Ireland's heritage to visitors and help them understand the place of individual sites in the overall jigsaw. Following on that, tourists must be told clearly what there is to see and how to find it. Informative brochures and maps have a vital role to play, as do good guide books and information on 'what's on'. We plan to equip the network of Tourist Information Offices with a computerised information service. At individual heritage sites, there is a need for simple information plaques and good signposting.

Participation: Tourists want to get more and more involved in the attractions they visit. This is not just an interest in 'hands-on' attractions, it is a general quest for active-learning. This has implications for the organising of more talks and guided walks at nature attractions, farmlife attractions, living craft villages and so on. We plan a nationwide series of 'Seisiun' performances of traditional entertainment, many of them in a restored local 'Teach Cheoil'. We need to do more to entertain children at our attraction, but we must seek to entertain without trivialising. 40% of overseas visitors to our attractions now come from Mainland Europe, so we must do more to help people whose native language is not English. We also need to do more to help people encounter the Irish language and get to know those for whom it is their daily spoken language in the Gaeltacht areas.

Presentation: Commercial visitor attractions immediately spring to mind when we think of presenting heritage to visitors. There are, however, several more fundamental issues which have to be addressed in meeting the needs of increasingly sophisticated tourists. Many ancient monuments are on private property and ease of access has to be arranged. Nature trails are needed to guide people exploring the landscape and its habitats. Many heritage sites need some basic preservation. Others merit being restored as showpieces of their former glory. We must promote more major events featuring pageantry and entertainment based on unique aspects of our culture.

LESSONS FOR THE FUTURE

In answering the four questions above, I have made it clear that investment in our heritage will continue to be a major priority in the years ahead and I have looked at how changing market needs should influence this investment. I also want to integrate into this policy direction, some important issues of which Bord Fáilte is now more conscious due to the experience of the last six years.

For a small country like Ireland, 219 commercial visitor attractions may well be enough. In practice, two thirds of these attractions are very small, attracting less than 15,000 visits per annum. The reality is that it is not the number of attractions which matters so much as the nature and the quality of them. The following policy priorities are relevant to this:

1. Attraction development must be sustainable and be relevant to the local community. It should never diminish the ambience or trivialise the significance of a heritage feature.
2. Attractions should be authentic, designed to enhance a genuine feature of the heritage of the area where they are developed.
3. Attractions are still needed to enhance hitherto neglected aspects of Ireland's heritage, rather than copying other already successful attractions.
4. We need a number of major attractions of significant scale which can make a real impact on the quality of the Irish holiday experience.
5. Once the objectives and theme of an attraction are settled, the interpretation plan must be carefully worked out. Interpretation has been defined as the art of telling the story of a place and its heritage in order to enrich visitor enjoyment by stimulating interest and awareness. This can usually be done best through concentrating on a focused theme or story and doing it well. Too many so-called 'Heritage Centres' are trying to interpret every aspect of local history and end up presenting a lot of information at a common level of mediocrity.
6. Attraction planning must incorporate a total visitor management plan, which should include high quality shopping, dining and other facilities. In 1993, only 47% of visitors to our attractions spent money on items other than admission. Those who did spend on non-admission items, spent over IR£3 each on average, so there is a major commercial opportunity here.

A LOCATION POLICY FOR HERITAGE ATTRACTIONS

All things being equal, we intend to influence the locations selected for investment in heritage so that they make the optimum contribution to our overall development framework for centres of tourism. Our Tourism Development Plan proposes a four-part development framework embracing *tourism centres, rural tourism areas, touring areas and special interest centres.*

There are 41 *Tourism Centres*, each with at least 400 rooms in a 15km radius and they account for 85% of all tourist beds. There are three types of centres, graded by size, and this is a guide to the scale of attractions needed. A national programme to floodlight historic buildings is one example of the type of development we are advocating in tourism centres. Many of these centres are now being by-passed by ring roads, which is a new opportunity to breathe life back into their heritage core. Some of our larger provincial cities badly need a major weather-independent attraction. One solution would be to establish museums of total national collections in these cities, eg

Figure 5 Jameson Whiskey Centre, Midleton, located beside Europe's most modern distillery.

Figure 6 Jameson Whiskey Centre, where the original art that made Irish whiskey-making famous is brought back to life.

'The National Museum of Folk Life' for Galway or 'The National Museum of Exploration' for Cork.

By contrast, our 25 *Rural Tourism Areas* are off the beaten track, where visitors can enjoy peaceful holidays 'steeped in the living tradition of Rural Ireland.' Simple accommodation, rural attractions, visitor farms, island holidays, Gaeltacht holidays are some of the hallmarks of this experience. The most essential ingredient of all is that the visitor is taken into the heart of the local community and is helped to enjoy their normal daily lives with them.

The 25 *Touring Areas* we have identified feature the finest mountain, lakeshore, coastal, river valley and heritage landscapes in the country. Our priority will be to ensure that these areas are better managed with a view to landscape conservation and recreational amenity.

The final element of our framework is *Special Interest Activity Centres*. There are over 50 locations with the potential to be developed as centres of excellence for a wide range of special interest products. For many of these products, such as walking, cruising or cycling, the access to interesting heritage features is what can give Ireland a competitive edge over other countries as a venue for such activities.

FROM POLICY TO PRACTICALITY

In the cultural tourism field, it is all too easy to communicate coherent policy directions and then to find oneself wondering why people still come back proposing a myriad of random projects which do little to achieve the overall objectives. At times in the past six years I have found the process more akin to 'herding mice at a crossroads'. We intend to concentrate on a number of distinctive development programmes over the next few years in an attempt to improve this situation. A few of these are:

> *Heritage Towns:* These are identified as having the potential to become attractions in their own right because of the quality of their preserved heritage. Towns are selected as having a critical mass of historic and architectural potential and a community committed to the highest environmental standards. A visitor centre in each town explains its heritage features and helps visitors to explore them with the help of guides, literature and distinctive signposting. The total development initiative is a partnership between the local authority, the business interests and the local community so that the heritage features are complemented by high quality parking, planning control, pedestrianisation, amenity areas, shopping, pageantry and entertainment.

> One potential variation of the theme is Historic Cities. This would differ from the Heritage Town in that the renewal objective would

be focused in a core historic area, but this centre would be complemented by the more extensive facilities of a bustling modern city.

A second variation, at the other end of the scale, is the concept of a Traditional Village. Smaller than a Heritage Town and probably with fewer historic features, the Traditional Village would boast great charm, intimacy and character and would attend to every little detail of creating a satisfying holiday experience.

Nostalgia-Based Attractions: The lifestyle of the last century holds a great fascination for tourists. Traditional canal barge holidays can be developed for families and groups, with overnight accommodation in waterside inns. The remains of mining villages could be restored to depict the hard lifestyle of the time. We have some semi-ruined *Clachan* Villages which preserve a building tradition stretching back as far as medieval times and 17th century clustered settlement patterns. The challenge in these is to enable the present owners to continue to live their undisturbed lifestyle and enhance their comfort, while preserving, restoring and maintaining the crumbling historic buildings. Some seaside resorts have the potential to exploit their Victorian Heritage and restore their period facilities to their former glory to attract tourists seeking a nostalgic experience as an alternative to gaming parlours and waterworlds.

Coastal Attractions: Tourists who visit us are very conscious that they are coming to an island, it is one of the distinctive features of Ireland for them. Our beaches have been endorsed by the EU as having the cleanest bathing waters in the community and they are a superb facility for walking, or just lazing on a sunny day. Most of all, they are deserted by European standards. The sand dunes of our coasts are a valuable ecosystem, to be respected so that tourists can continue to enjoy the fascinating flora, plant life and wildlife.

By contrast, the fishing villages of the coastline are a hive of activity. They could be made most attractive to tourists if they were tidied up a little and cleansed of their eyesores. By encouraging direct sales of fish and investment in fish restaurants, harbour tours and intimate shopping opportunities, many busy fishing harbours could transform themselves into fascinating tourist attractions. There is major scope to develop holidays on offshore islands which are a cradle of a peaceful unspoilt lifestyle long lost on the mainland. Many of these islands boast dramatic scenery and others have a fascinating heritage of archaeology or plant life. Some are Irish-speaking.

Contemporary Ireland: This programme would help visitors capture the spirit of Ireland today in all its distinctive facets. This would range over cultural experiences such as concerts and theatre, craftwork visits. etc. In most cases, what is needed is better organisation, packaging and information rather than major capital investment. The bogs of Ireland are a unique resource and visitors would be interested in learning all about peat harvesting; the flora, fauna and archaeology of the bogs and the future of the resource.

The survival of Irish as the everyday language of the Gaeltacht is of great interest to visitors as a vital and vibrant link with our past culture. The emphasis should be on attracting people to spend their whole holiday in the Gaeltacht, immersing themselves in its distinctive lifestyle rather than on selling package tours to make, as it were, a day visit to a cultural museum. The Gaeltacht traditions of literature, folklore, crafts, music, song and dance should be made more accessible to visitors. The many decaying cottages in the Gaeltacht should be refurbished as comfortable self-catering houses and evening entertainment could be staged in a traditional 'Teach Cheoil'. Greater use of Irish names on business premises, a common distinctive signage and road maps with Irish names to integrate with the Irish road signs would all serve to create a more distinctive identity for the Gaeltacht.

CONCLUSION

In the 1994-99 period, we intend to spend IR£150 million of EU Structural Funding to promote the implementation of the vision I have outlined. Our target will be to lever a further IR£100 million in matching investment from the public, private and community sectors, to finance a total investment programme of IR£250 million.

We justify this investment on the basis that it will be one of the most crucial influences on how successful our product will be in attracting the kind of tourist numbers needed to meet the Government targets.

In the last six years, Irish tourism generated 29,000 new jobs, 70% of all nett new additions to the workforce. For the next six years, our target is 35,000 new jobs. It is comforting to realise that the heritage of our past is becoming such a potent force in creating a future for our present population.

The Author

Sean Browne is Head of Development Planning with Bord Fáilte (Irish Tourist Board). He is author of their *Tourism Development Plan 1994–99* and a leading pioneer of cultural tourism in Ireland who was formerly Chief Executive of the Mid-West Tourism Region.

References

Bord Fáilte, *Developing for Growth*, BF, Dublin, 1989

Bord Fáilte, *Developing Heritage Attractions*, BF, Dublin, 1990

Bord Fáilte, *Developing Sustainable Tourism: Tourism Development Plan 1994-1999*, BF, Dublin, 1994

Bord Fáilte, *Heritage and Tourism*, BF, Dublin, 1992

Bord Fáilte, *Heritage Attractions Development*, BF, Dublin, 1992

Bord Fáilte, *Market Growth Opportunities: The Marketing Plan Framework 1994-1999*, BF, Dublin, 1993

Bord Fáilte, *Tourism Growth: 5 Years of Achievement*, BF, Dublin, 1992

Bord Fáilte, *Tourism Opportunities: Investing in Ireland's Future*, BF, Dublin, 1991

Deane, B. and Henry, E., *The Economic Impact of Tourism*, in The Irish Banking Review, Winter 1993

Department of Tourism and Transport, *Operational Programme for Tourism*, DTT, Dublin, 1990

Foras Forbartha, *Inventory of Outstanding Landscapes in Ireland*, FF, Dublin, 1977

Irish Tourist Industry Confederation, *Doubling Irish Tourism: A Market-Led Strategy*, ITIC, Dublin, 1989

Moody, T.W. and Martin F.X., *The Course of Irish History*; Mercier Press, 1984

Office of Public Works, *Heritage Sites*, OPW, Dublin, 1990

Stevens, T., *Irish Eyes are Smiling*, in Leisure Management, May 1991

Stevens, T., *Disputed Heritage*, in Leisure Management, April 1993

Tansey, P. and Webster, S., *Tourism and the Economy*, Irish Tourist Industry Confederation, 1991

Tourism Development International, *1993 Visitor Attractions Survey*, TDI, 1994

Figure 1 The Palace Green at Colonial Williamsburg before restoration.

Figure 2 The Palace Green at Colonial Williamsburg after restoration.

3

HERITAGE RECREATED IN USA
Colonial Williamsburg and Other Sites

William J. Tramposch

In the closing moments of F. Scott Fitzgerald's novel, *The Great Gatsby*, the author resolves, 'And so we beat on boats against the current, borne back ceaselessly into the past.'[1] Of course, the message of this great American novel is that one cannot repeat what came before despite Jay Gatz's quixotic attempts to do so.

Outdoor history museums throughout the United States oftentimes claim that the past can be *relived* or *recreated*; yet obviously no one believes this, especially those who labor in the fields of the history museum profession. I am certain that even Gatsby would be amused by the fact that an institution like Colonial Williamsburg, the 18th century capital of Virginia, now requires twice the population of the town that it attempts to replicate. At its height as a colonial *metropolis* (George Washington's word), Williamsburg was home to approximately 2,000 people; while today more than 4,000 are on the Foundation's payroll. By far, it is the largest outdoor history museum in America.

Surely, these terms of *reliving* and *recreating* are used more for their marketing effect than for any other reason: and, the strategy works. Each year almost one million people visit Colonial Williamsburg, as well as Greenfield Village in Michigan, America's second largest outdoor history museum. In fact, more than half a million people visit Old Sturbridge Village in Massachusetts, our country's third largest open air site.

This paper is focused on these three prominent outdoor history museums, because from them one can learn a great deal about the movement in the United States: why and how were such museums created; how are they owned and managed; what are their various approaches to interpretation; and what have been their combined contributions to the heritage tourism trade?

Since there are more than 300 outdoor history museums in the United States, I will stress from the start that a study of these three institutions alone would hardly present a complete picture of the varied tapestry represented by our country's composite sites. Nevertheless, it is hoped that brief profiles of these three major museums will enable readers to understand better the origins and the current condition of outdoor history in America.

ORIGINS

As with their predecessors in Scandinavia, the first American outdoor history museums developed from a concern to preserve parts of a rapidly disappearing past. While Skansen served as an oasis for endangered buildings and customs in Sweden, so too did Greenfield Village and Colonial Williamsburg help to satisfy an interest to protect threatened artifactual reminders of our national heritage.

Greenfield Village and The Henry Ford Museum is oftentimes referred to as *America's Attic*. Its founder, Henry Ford, wanted to celebrate self-made American heroes who had grown from humble origins into giants of industry. Consequently, Thomas Edison, Henry Firestone, the Wright Brothers, and the educator, William McGuffey, among others, are all honored within this historic preserve. Thomas Edison was Ford's most revered hero. In fact, when Ford moved Edison's Menlo Park, New Jersey laboratories to Michigan, he also moved many train car loads of surrounding red New Jersey topsoil along with it. His intent was to save every possible shard of material that Edison left behind. More impressive (or strange, depending on how one wants to look at it) was the fact that Ford even saved Edison's last breath, now on display in The Henry Ford museum.

Scores of buildings constitute the Greenfield Village campus. McGuffey's original schoolhouse sits across the street from Noah Webster's Connecticut home, which is just down the road from a slave dwelling from the south which is but a pedal away from the Wright Brothers' cycle shop. Staff humorously recall one enthusiastic visitor exclaiming to her children, 'Isn't it remarkable, kids, that so many famous people once lived in the same town together.'

As with Williamsburg and Sturbridge, interpretive programmers at Greenfield Village and The Henry Ford Museum have had a challenging time of it during the past decade. Since the museums were originally meant to be largely tributes to American self-made men, what more modern social historical themes could be applied to the collection now? Surely, the tribute to these selected heroes of the past had lost some of its appeal in light of current historiography. The answer was an ingenious one: The theme would be *modernization*. Soon, the two Michigan sites offered a coherent interpretation of how our country had modernized itself over the past two centuries. Admittedly, there are still some rough edges to this interpretive rationale, but the theme seems to work throughout the exhibits, be they in the six acre large building that makes up the Henry Ford Museum, or within the

Figure 3 Patrick Henry addressing the Burgesses in a scene from the orientation film, 'The Story of a Patriot' at Colonial Williamsburg.

Figure 4 Costumed interpreters in front of the Royal Governor's Palace at Colonial Williamsburg.

Figure 5 The reinterpretation of the Royal Governor's Palace at Colonial Williamsburg.

expansive open grounds of Greenfield Village. To some degree, all sites that have recently readjusted themselves thematically have learned to deal with those maverick exhibits which in no way will ever relate to the more current theme.

COLONIAL WILLIAMSBURG

The idea that became Colonial Williamsburg did not first originate from the mind of a captain of industry but, rather, from that of a driven rural minister. W.A.R. Goodwin was Rector of Bruton Parish Church, a colonial structure in the heart of the town. Goodwin was keenly aware of the historical significance of the community in which he served. His pulpit stood in the midst of 88 original structures still standing from the colonial period when Williamsburg had shared the stage with other capital cities like Philadelphia, New York and Charleston, South Carolina. Goodwin considered it the town's great fortune to have been overlooked by the deleterious effects of modernization. Surprisingly, no industries had grown up around it, and comparatively few cars or railroads threatened the peaceful village in the 1920s.

His burning interest was to restore the colonial capital to its former glory, and he could see the results of these imaginings so clearly in his fertile imagination. His only problem, of course, was building the real foundations under these dreams, for as a country minister his resources were pitifully limited. Most people know the rest of the story: that he contacted John D. Rockefeller, Jr and what then followed, as they say, is history. But, few people are aware of the fact that Goodwin approached one other entrepreneur prior to the call for Rockefeller's help. Yes, it was Henry Ford. With Ford, Goodwin's tact was less than admirable as he suggested to his potential benefactor that, since the automobile was responsible for the destruction of so much of our heritage already, wouldn't Ford like to redeem a significant piece of the past by supporting the Colonial Williamsburg restoration. Not surprisingly, Ford was not impressed. Curiously, however, in the same year he began his museums.

At first, Rockefeller was enticed to purchase only one *said artifact* at Williamsburg, a brick home on The Duke of Gloucester Street. Repeated visits, however, enthused the entrepreneur so much that soon he, his wife and family, were spending extended periods of time in a colonial home on the young restoration's periphery. In the end, The Williamsburg Restoration became one of John D. Rockefeller's greatest heritage projects. He enjoyed following various aspects of the restoration, specifically the completion of some of the key structures like the Raleigh Tavern, site of so many pivotal political meetings in American colonial history.

In fact, one day while strolling down The Duke of Gloucester Street Rockefeller saw the architect responsible for the Raleigh Tavern reconstruction. He asked, 'Mr Perry, how is the Raleigh Tavern project proceeding?' Mr Perry replied to Mr Rockefeller that he felt uncomfortable responding because he was simply too close to the project and therefore not objective about its progress. He suggested that the benefactor might want to ask someone else. Rockefeller retorted, 'But, Mr Perry, I am asking you. How is the Raleigh Tavern project proceeding?' Mr Perry conceded, 'It looks like a million dollars.' Mr Rockefeller concluded by thanking Mr Perry for he was the first person to give Rockefeller 'an accurate assessment of the worth of the building.'[2]

By today's standards it is difficult to estimate the entire investment that John D. Rockefeller made in the Colonial Williamsburg Foundation, but surely nothing in the landscape of American outdoor history museums even begins to compare. Today, more than 500 buildings grace the 173 acre historic area. More than 100 gardeners tend to the myriad of historically accurate formal and informal plantings. Foundation-owned hotels and restaurants appear inside and along side the historic area, and in this regard the site resembles the extensive and service-oriented work of Disney more than the work of any other outdoor history site.

Despite his interest in the physical restoration, Rockefeller's chief interest was in the story Williamsburg could tell. He saw the restored site as a training ground for patriotism and a place where Americans could be inspired to become good and proud citizens. *The Story of a Patriot*, a very inspirational orientation film introduced millions to the historical significance of the restoration; and this film has remained so popular that (even though it was filmed before *Ben Hur*) none dare replace it with a piece that would inevitably be less stirring and more didactic.

Colonial Williamsburg's recent efforts at reinterpreting itself have focused upon the theme of *Becoming Americans,* how two immigrant cultures (one that arrived by choice, the other by force) grew together to form a distinctively new culture. With an academic thoroughness and vigor that resembles the restorative one of earlier years, the entire site has embraced this thematic effort during the past 15 years.

While the historic area of Colonial Williamsburg is impressive, equally as impressive is the restoration's influence on American taste. For better or worse, historic sites throughout the United States were soon borrowing styles and techniques employed by the restoration. Even the popular ball and chain gate pulls and winding brick paths appear in such far away and incongruous places as Wisconsin where no such historic precedent exists.

Williamsburg's influence has been felt not only by other museums but also by many less likely imitators. None other than gas stations and banks soon began to look like buildings from the colonial capital replete with grand cupolas and symmetrical baroque designs. So obvious was this influence and so clear was its source that The Smithsonian Institution launched a provocative exhibit on the Williamsburg influences upon everyday American architecture.

Within the next generation American tastes in collecting had also been stimulated by the earlier efforts made at Williamsburg. In Massachusetts, another family, the Wells, began collecting antiques on a rainy day in New Hampshire. Their original intent that day had simply been to go play golf with a friend. Rain forced them indoors and their New Hampshire host convinced them to join him *antiquing*. This was a new concept for the Wells brothers, who were the owners of The American Optical Company of Southbridge, Massachusetts, but soon they were collecting antiques on a robber baron scale.

Wells descendants tell of antique-laden trucks pulling-up to their homes in Southbridge where, from the porch, the brothers would survey the contents and buy them wholesale. Indeed, the habit quickly became a threat to domestic tranquillity, so the brothers decided to *recreate* a village in the country. In the words of one of the younger promoters of this notion, 'Only old people visit museums.' He suggested that they work to recreate an environment wherein the collection could be observed in appropriate settings and used by trained staff. Thus, began Old Sturbridge Village, the third largest outdoor history museum in the United States.

Old Sturbridge Village recreates a setting which would have been very common on the rural New England (specifically Massachusetts) landscape in the 1830s. Although the period is a younger one than Colonial Williamsburg, to many guests Old Sturbridge Village appears to be an older, simpler and a more rustic place than the colonial capital. It is a perfect setting for the study and interpretation of social history, for the story at Sturbridge is of common people and everyday events. As at Williamsburg and Greenfield Village, costumed interpreters discuss life in the past with visitors. Some interpreters are in 'role' undertaking a craft or assuming a character, while others are in 'third person'. I will discuss these concepts later.

Because Old Sturbridge Village is a recreation, the capacity for it to change shape (almost chameleon like) is great. Thus, if a researcher determines that a typical Federal period farmer in rural Massachusetts had only twelve Wiltshire-Dorset sheep rather than the fifteen currently at the Old Sturbridge Village farm, the flock would be cut back. Because it is not hallowed or original, the ground is fertile at Sturbridge for the demographic historian. Thus, since Sturbridge is a recreated village, if the meetinghouse in the Center Village was Baptist but the state religion was Congregationalist, then the departments of research and interpretation can simply change it. Sturbridge has a long-standing allegiance to *the typical*, and its campus is a barometer of what was common. Its appearance consequently changes quickly as historical research findings change.

Figure 6 The Grist Mill at Old Sturbridge Village.

Figure 7 Looking down the main lane in the recreated Separatist settlement at Plimoth Plantation, Massachusetts.

PLIMOTH PLANTATION

Nearby Plimoth Plantation in Plymouth, Massachusetts is also a recreation. The original 1620s Separatist settlement that it replicates was about one mile away. Here interpreters have not been called interpreters but, rather, *cultural informants*. Here the visitor is the *interpreter*, and the folks in costume assume a role with such fervor that none of the informants will admit to knowing a thing about life after the 1620s. Do not bother asking for a restroom in Plimoth Plantation. This is total first person interpretation, loved by some and detested by others.

Not surprisingly, Plimoth Plantation was conceived partially by a number of anthropologists from nearby Brown University. Originally the thought here was to deny the visitor access to the site itself, but rather have them peer into the walled-in settlement and observe life happening, much like one would look at a specimen through a microscope. A subsequent, more liberal idea was to have visitors don paper costumes and blend among the informants.

While most of the earlier outdoor history museums began with the help of wealthy entrepreneurs, the later ones emerged from eras during which the national preservation effort was far more grounded and thus much better supported through government and foundation grants as well as individual gifts. Plimoth Plantation is an example of such a later site. There are many others.

THE FARMERS' MUSEUM AND OTHERS

The Farmers' Museum, one of the sites I oversee, began as a result of support from the Clark family of Cooperstown, New York and New York City. In an effort to bring the clean industry of tourism to Cooperstown, Stephen C. Clark supported the founding of The National Baseball Hall of Fame in this scenic upstate New York village, for it was here that the national pastime of baseball arguably was first played. Soon the town became the *Village of Museums* with the purchasing and relocating of the New York State Historical Association and the subsequent development of the thirteen building campus of The Farmers' Museum, a museum of rural life.

The prominent interpretive themes at both the New York State Historical Association and The Farmers' Museum are rural and folk life in America, and these themes are promoted here in an outdoor museum setting as well as within an indoor art museum setting. Also on this campus is a major training ground for history museum professionals, The Cooperstown Graduate Program in History Museum Studies which offers an MA degree. The Farmers' Museum is dedicated to the promotion of rural life and agriculture, and its story resembles Williamsburg's, Greenfield's and Sturbridge's in many ways, not the least of which is that it is the result of original support from a wealthy benefactor.

As mentioned, sites emerging in more recent years tend to be the result of both more wide-based support and more current historiographic thinking. A case in point has been Plimoth. Yet, one other remarkable example is Old World Wisconsin in Eagle, Wisconsin. As one of the chief sites owned and operated by the State Historical Society of Wisconsin, Old World Wisconsin is an expansive outdoor history museum dedicated to the interpretation of the various ethnic cultures that settled the Wisconsin Territory. Hence, a typical Swedish farmstead shares part of the grounds with typical Finnish, German, and Norwegian farms. This massive project emerged from a period when state funding for such initiatives was far easier to acquire than it is today; and for many of us in the outdoor history museum field, Old World represents the last great stride in the outdoor history movement in the United States.

OWNERSHIP AND MANAGEMENT

Even the earlier sites described above have moved from a period of single benefactor support to more wide-based support over the years. The years of single-source support are mostly over in the United States, with the one notable exception of the Getty Museum in California. Relatively early in its development the founders of The Colonial Williamsburg Foundation discussed the issue of ownership following the Rockefeller years. The National Park Service was considered, but finally the concept of a holding company followed by a not-for-profit Board of Trustees was decided upon.

Most outdoor history museums in the United States are private, not-for-profit institutions: technically, 501c3s in the parlance of the Internal Revenue Service. Most are administered by a Board of Trustees elected by the membership of the institution. State supported historical organizations like Wisconsin and Minnesota have the benefit of strong state funding, so the governance tends to be aligned more with the government bureaucracy than it would be in a private, not-for-profit institution like Old Sturbridge Village or The Farmers' Museum.

Boards members are usually elected to a fixed term of between one to three years in duration. Yet, it is not uncommon for some sites to continue to cling to the older notion of life-time board appointments. Board activity is as varied as the institutions they serve. Some boards meet monthly, while others simply meet each year. There is no clear right or wrong way of undertaking governance at US outdoor history museums, and so much depends on the peculiar nature and history of the institution.

A major trend, however, is for boards to become increasingly conversant about their legal responsibilities to the institutions. Technically and legally, each board member is entrusted with the care of the institution; and with the economy pressing so harshly upon so many outdoor history museum sites of late, many boards have felt the consequent pressure of having to be more vigilant than ever. Ultimately, the board is responsible for the fiscal health of the institution, so this places an enormous strain on boards to choose their Chief Operating and Executive Officers very carefully.

Outdoor history museums throughout the United States are also embracing with a fervor the concepts of marketing and fund development. The need for larger, more diverse audiences coupled with the intense need for more support has flooded the *help wanted* pages in our trade journals with descriptions for Development Officers and Marketing Directors. Some museums, like Conner Prairie Pioneer Settlement in Indiana, have expanded their marketing efforts so vigorously that visitation has increased tremendously and earned revenues have never been more healthy.

Throughout the country, gift shops have become museum shops, historic taverns have begun to offer authentically prepared meals to paying guests. Shakertown, an original Shaker site in Kentucky, long ago turned original Shaker dormitories into hotel rooms for guests; and the Shaker's own dining room now serves splendid meals to guests three times a day. Consequently, this site has never operated at a loss. Conferences for museum professionals are replete with sessions which illustrate how we can increase our revenues while expanding our interpretive programs.

APPROACHES TO INTERPRETATION

While one dines in one of the many historic taverns of Colonial Williamsburg, one is treated to the singing of a costumed evening entertainer who sings ditties popular in the 18th century. Often, the visitors join in, especially in one of the taverns that offers ample drink. I know this because we lived directly across the street from a tavern for six of the ten years we resided in Williamsburg; and I know this because one of my daughters first sentences was, 'Dad, what do you do with a drunken sailor?'. Williamsburg is well-experienced at mixing entertainment with revenue enhancement; and why not, for this was common indeed in the 18th century. But, this is but one type of interpretation. Many others exist, and all are practiced within the realm of outdoor history sites in the United States.

There are many different ways of describing the most popular forms of interpretation, and like any emerging profession there is a rush to invent a language that eludes the comprehension of even the most clever followers. I will use the most simple terminology I know:

> **Third Person**. This form of interpretation is most common at sites throughout the country. Interpreters talk of the past and those who peopled it as *they*. There is no pretense of being a part of it

Figure 8 Interpreting change over time in upstate rural life at The Farmers' Museum, New York.

Figure 9 Agriculture over the ages at Living History Farms, Iowa.

Figure 10 Thomas Edison's Menlo Park Laboratory at Greenfield Village, Michigan.

themselves. Oftentimes such interpreters are in mufti, for costumes could simply threaten objectivity. Yet, just as often third person interpreters are in costume and, really, hardly anybody seems to mind. The important thing to remember is that while museum professionals are splitting hairs about these subtle incongruities and strategies, the public seems to accommodate any approach as long as it is explained and not threatening.

First Person. This can be threatening to the visitor if one is not careful. We employed a first person or *role playing* interpretation at the reinterpreted Governor's Palace in Williamsburg and many visitors were resentful of it. More potentially jarring, though, is the rigid first person interpretation at Plimoth Plantation.

Here is a vivid example. I was walking in the recreated village when all of a sudden a wet and warm chicken bone struck me on the shoulder. A brand new shirt had been ruined. I strolled up to the costumed Massasoit Indian who had hurled the half-eaten meal over his shoulder and asked as politely as I could, 'Just what is the point of throwing food in the direction of visitors?' I explained that I, too, worked in a museum (Old Sturbridge Village at the time) and implied that he would probably not have a more receptive audience than me on the matter. After appearing to listen he continued with his role playing which dictated, of course, that he had no knowledge of English and therefore could neither understand or respond to me. Understandably, many visitors can be alienated by such rigid methods of teaching history.

At Colonial Williamsburg, a prodigious effort was begun in the 1970s to interpret the life of African Americans, because half of the population of the colonial capital was black in the 18th century. Black actors assumed roles as slaves after doing intense research on characters. In tutorials they worked with faculty researchers to develop their roles upon firm facts. When the program went public we were not clear enough with the public about our objectives and techniques. Consequently, many people were startled to be approached by, say, a midwife hurrying to deliver a baby, or by a melancholic slave taking a break from his labors.

The rest of the Historic Area was in *third person* while several from this program were in first person roles. Soon, we became much more careful at preparing the public for these presentations and at giving them an opportunity to discuss the presentation with the role player after the delivery. This meant that character interpreters had to leave their role and come back in the third person. These changes made the entire program less threatening and more successful than before.

Crafts, or Trades Interpretation. Early in its history Colonial Williamsburg initiated a crafts program. In the early 1940s surveys were beginning to reveal that the public wanted to learn more about

Figure 11 Costumed interpretive staff at Plimoth Plantation.

Figure 12 Candlemaking, one of the 36 trades practiced in the historic area at Colonial Williamsburg.

Figure 13 African American history programming at Colonial Williamsburg.

'everyday life of ordinary people'. *Life on the Scenes* is what the resulting program was called, and soon as many as 36 colonial crafts were being interpreted throughout the historic area. The recruitment stories provide a delightful basis for another paper. Barrel makers were recruited from breweries in England; bookbinders and livestock supervisors were wooed from abroad, as well. Today, candlemakers, silversmiths, blacksmiths, harness makers, gunsmiths and housewrights all work together interpreting all-but-forgotten trades within a strict system of apprentice, journeyman, and master craftsmanship.

Crafts interpretation often gives the interpreter an opportunity to slip in and out of role, because the actual process of yesterday is taking place. There is a refreshing flexibility in interpreting the crafts not only because of the interpreter's ability to interpret in the third and first person but also because usually the actual craft process is captivating to the visitor.

Of course, many other forms of interpretation exist. I have cited only the most common living history forms which are practiced in outdoor history museums in my country. There are also plays, books, re-enactments, school tours, etc. Two very good sources of information on these are Tilden's *Interpreting Our Heritage* and Anderson's *Time Machines*, each cited in the references at the end of this paper.

CONTRIBUTION TO HERITAGE AWARENESS

Just how much of a contribution have outdoor history museums made to heritage awareness? This is one of the most fascinating questions in the field lately, because there is a great interest in visitor evaluation among museum professionals throughout the United States. This interest is driven by our desire to know and serve audiences better than ever before. A satisfied audience will visit more and lend more support to the institution.

With this in mind, Colonial Williamsburg has undertaken to survey its public on a regular basis since the forties, but the surveys become more scientific and effective each year. A recent visitor evaluation revealed that more than 50% of the visitors on any given day in Williamsburg had been there once before; and fully 19% had visited more than nine times before! This is invaluable information for programmers, marketers and development officers alike. Furthermore, the surveys revealed that as a result of a visit to Colonial Williamsburg, visitors were far more likely to participate more in civic affairs and elections. It revealed as well that visitors also tended to read more and learn a craft as a result of a visit.

These are encouraging results, especially because our country is in crisis when it comes to history education. A recent survey undertaken by the National Endowment for the Humanities revealed that more than a third of our 17 year-olds do not know which war came first, the Civil or the Revolutionary; a third were unfamiliar with the meaning of the word *Holocaust*, and equally as many were unaware of the name of the President who said, 'Ask not what your country can do for you, but what you can do for your country.' These figures are shocking, and they suggest the magnitude of the work that is ahead of us if we are to be successful at influencing heritage awareness on a large scale. Nevertheless, the repeat visitation figures cited above encourage us because they reflect well on the type of learning (and enjoyment) that takes place in outdoor history museums.

That learning is often confused with enjoyment is not surprising. At Old Sturbridge Village, we undertook surveys that asked our guests if they came for *educational* or *entertainment* reasons. Invariably (and with a sense of parental duty), if they were with their children their motivation was education; while if they were alone with one another their interest was more in the entertainment offered by the village. Clearly, the fact is that both exist within one another in the informal setting that is offered in an outdoor history museum.

This enjoyment and edification never blended so well as when Ken Burns offered his acclaimed video history of the Civil War on Public Television. And I mention this extraordinary program here because many of the successful ingredients of outdoor history interpretation were employed by Burns throughout this historical series which strove to present not only the facts but also the personalities behind the facts of the Civil War.

The Yale University historian, Edmund Morgan, once said that historians 'simplify without oversimplifying and bring to life the men and women who can speak across the ages to their human kin.' Burns did just this throughout his series by employing and blending music, diary accounts and original photographs of the all-but-nameless legions of heroes that contributed to that great war. In the end, those of us in the history museum field watched in awe as more visitors than ever before streamed into Civil War battlefields.

Attendance after the Burns video series reached an all time high for the National Park Service sites. The impact of this effective interpretation on heritage awareness was significant and very measurable. Effective sites like Colonial Williamsburg, Old Sturbridge Village, Greenfield Village, Conner Prairie and The Farmers' Museum were influenced as well, and our techniques of measuring effectiveness are refined more each year.

England has its own success stories in this regard. Heritage Industries efforts in Oxford, York and Canterbury all strive to blend historical accuracy with entertainment. Consequently, they make complex sites (like Oxford) more understandable to the casual visitor while striving not to compromise any of the facts behind the artifact. Of course these popular sites will always have their detractors who remain wedded to the idea of what I call *hairshirt history*: that is, to be effective, they feel that the learning of history must hurt somewhat. Yet, the visitor figures appear to be impressive, especially when one looks at the types of people waiting in line. Never have I seen a more democratic assemblage of visitors than at the Jorvik Viking Museum. Dons stand next to punk rockers who are just in front of families of four on holiday. This is a remarkable sight to observe.

In the years ahead, the United States will be experiencing an even more debatable form of history, and I encourage all to watch. Within cannon shot of the Civil War's most notable battlegrounds, Walt Disney will be placing a theme park devoted to an interpretation of American history. *Disney America* will interpret, for example, the Civil War and the Vietnam War, while treading gingerly on the colonial period because of nearby Colonial Williamsburg's pre-eminence in that arena. We will soon have a great deal to debate about and much of it will strike at the heart of just what it means to be an American in the 20th century.

With the zest and flair of a Gatsby, Disney may strive gallantly to repeat the past, and I predict that Disney will make the revisit so enjoyable and entertaining that the important truth (among many others) which confronted Gatsby may totally elude the millions who will cruise the rails, cotton candy in hand, through American history ... over and over again. We will see. At any rate, my intuition tells me that we will learn far more about Americans than about American history. I cannot wait to find out.

The Author

Dr William Tramposch is President of the New York State Historical Association. He was previously Executive Director of the Oregon Historical Society, Director of Interpretative Education with the Colonial Williamsburg Foundation, and Co-ordinator of Interpretation at Sturbridge Village in Massachusetts. His doctoral dissertation was on *Comparison of Mid-Career Museum Training in Great Britain and America (1986)*.

References

[1] Fitzgerald, F.S., *The Great Gatsby*, Scribners, 1925

[2] Short, J., *Oral History Project*, Williamsburg, 1982

Alegre, M.R.,. *A Guide to Museum Villages: The American Heritage Brought to Life*, Drake Publishers, 1978

Alexander, E P, *Bringing History to Life: Philadelphia and Williamsburg*, Curator, pp. 60–68, 1961

Alexander, E.P., *Museums in Motion: An Introduction to the History and Functions of Museums*, American Association for State and Local History, 1979

Association for Living Historical Farms and Agricultural Museums (ALHFAM), *Selected Living Historical Farms. Villages and Agricultural Museum in the United States and Canada*, Smithsonian Institution

Anderson, J., *Time Machines: The World of Living History*, The American Association for State and Local History, 1984

Botein, S. et al., *Experiments in History Teaching*, Harvard-Danforth Center for Teaching and Learning, 1978

Carson, C., *Living museums of everyman's history*, Harvard Magazine, pp. 22–32, July–August 1981

Cromie, A., *Restored Towns and Historic Districts of America: A Tour Guide*, E. P. Dutton, A Sunrise Book, 1979

Grinder, A.L., and McCoy, E.S.,. *The Good Guide: A Sourcebook for Interpreters*, Docents and Tour Guides, Ironwood Press, Scottsdale AZ, 1985

Hass, I., *America's Historic Villages & Restorations*, Arco Publishing Company, 1974

Hosmer, C.B. Jr, *Preservation Comes of Age: From Williamsburg to the National Trust, 1926–1949. Volume I*, Published for the Preservation Press, National Trust for Historic Preservation in the United States, University Press of Virginia, 1981

Hosmer, C.B., Jr, *Preservation Comes of Age: From Williamsburg to the National Trust, 1926–1949. Volume II*. Published for the Preservation Press, National Trust for Historic Preservation in the United States, University Press of Virginia, 1981

Huxtable, A.L., *Inventing American Reality*, The New York Review, pp. 24–29, December 3, 1992

Jones, L.C., *The Farmers' Museum*, New York State Historical Association, Cooperstown NY, The Farmers' Museum, 1948

Jones, L.C., *The Trapper's Cabin and the Ivory Tower*, Museum News, pp. 11–16, March 1962

Kopper, P., *Colonial Williamsburg. The Colonial Williamsburg Foundation*, Harry N Abrams, 1986

Loomis, R.J., AASLH Management Series 3, *Museum Visitor Evaluation: New Tool for Management*, American Association for State and Local History, 1987

Matelic, C.T., *Through the Historical Looking Glass*, Museum News, pp. 36–45, March–April 1980

McGrath, K.M., (Ed, Michael W. Robbins), *America's Museums: The Belmont Report*, The American Association of Museums, 1969

National Geographic Book Service, *America's Historylands: Landmarks of Liberty*, National Geographic Society, 1962

Schlereth, T.J., *Artifacts and the American Past. American Association for State and Local History*, 1980

Tilden, F., *Interpreting our Heritage. The University of North Carolina Press*, 1957

Ullberg, A.D., and Ullberg, P, *Museum Trusteeship. American Association of Museums*, 1981

Upward, G.C., A *Home for Our Heritage: The Building and Growth of Greenfield Village and Henry Ford Museum*, 1929–1979, The Henry Ford Museum Press, 1979

Yetter, G.H., *Williamsburg Before and After: The Rebirth of Virginia's Colonial Capital*, The Colonial Williamsburg Foundation, 1988

Figure 1 1888 Exhibition, Kelvingrove Park, showing view of the Great Hall from the river, known locally as Baghdad on the Kelvin.   *Photo: T & R Annan*

Figure 2 1901 Exhibition, Kelvingrove Park, showing the Kelvingrove Museum and Art Gallery in the middle distance, which was built with the profits of the 1888 Exhibition.   *Photo: T & R Annan*

4

A CELEBRATION OF ENTERPRISE
Expos and Garden Festivals

Brian M Evans

For nearly a century and a half the great exhibitions have amazed, delighted and informed countless millions of people. They have become icons of industrial and technological achievements and are cultural reflections of the host cities, peoples and nations. They provide a record of the hopes and fears, successes and failures in man's exploration, understanding and exploitation of industry and technology which continues not only to the present day but into the future. After the Second World War, a new and distinctive tradition emerged, that of the garden festival, representing industrial man's more mature response to his understanding of and relationship with the natural environment. European garden festivals are an investigative programme into green issues, bringing them alive and placing them before vast numbers of people.

This paper examines the evolution and development of the great exhibitions and the garden festivals, considers the Scottish tradition by examining the experience of one city, Glasgow, and concludes by looking at future themes that might enter the exposition and festival agenda in years to come.

THE GREAT EXHIBITIONS

Grand exhibitions began at Crystal Palace in London in 1851. They have origins in the holiday institution of the fair, the large industrial fairs held in France from the end of the 18th century and from a series of exhibitions of good design promoted by the Royal Society of Arts in London in 1847, 1848 and 1849. However, the *Great Exhibition of the Works of Industry of All Nations* in a magnificent 'crystal' palace of iron and glass was a wholly different and new phenomenon. Despite forecasts of disorder and disturbance, over six million people visited the extensive exhibition of 'All that is Useful and

Beautiful in Nature or in Art'. The international scope and idealistic commitment to the advancement of art and science were supported by commercial and national interests. There were no amusements, no smoking or drinking, but the exhibition was a huge success and made significant profits. The Great Exhibition began a vogue for expositions and world fairs which has continued to the present day (Kinchin and Kinchin).

Large exhibitions are the very expression of many of the key characteristics of the late 19th century. They would have been impossible without railway travel and unlike fairs they were entirely respectable, embodying the aspirations, taste and practicality of the industrial middle class and a confidence in progress, a belief that all resources, knowledge and culture could be categorised, labelled and enclosed in an orderly manner. Competition and materialism instigated and still drives the series of exhibitions. As Kinchin and Kinchin observe: exhibitions, like museums, share the celebration of the artefact, and flourish in westernised and capitalist manufacturing centres in a competitive spirit with medals awarded for the best and biggest in given classes.

The commercial benefit of exhibiting on these occasions was always apparent and, in fact, fundamental to the whole enterprise. Major exhibitions offered an international opportunity for display to the general public and industry and were effectively large trade fairs, although such a proposition is always hotly denied since exhibitions are also quite genuinely educational. The early exhibitions fuelled a curiosity and a desire for self improvement in the dissemination of ideas and information before the advent of mass media. The first Exhibitions offered a colourful and illuminated world full of strange and wonderful things, a temporary escape from the dispiriting reality of life in the Industrial Revolution.

The early success of The Great Exhibition was not easily repeated, but the 1862 London exhibition outstripped attendance of the 1851 Great Exhibition by 200,000 visitors. Paris achieved 6.8 million in 1867 and continued to become the world premiere exhibition city for the rest of the 19th century with major events in 1878 (16 million), 1989 (32.5 million) and 1900 (48 million).

Great international exhibitions have, above all, been expressions and reflections of their times. The 1851 Exhibition demonstrated the achievements of the industrial revolution and the importance of Britain. The French exhibitions in the 19th century asserted the cultural, political and economic ambition of France. The 1958 exhibition confirmed Europe's recovery from the Second World War and launched the challenge of European unity from its future capital, Brussels. Expo' 70 in Osaka announced Japan's emergence as a world technological power. Even more significantly, the 'Great Exhibitions' heralded the innovations and advances of mankind.

London's 1851 exhibition displayed industrial machinery, the Colt revolver and the lawn mower. The public was informed about oil and aluminium in Paris in 1867. Visitors to Philadelphia in 1876 were introduced to Bell's telephone, Edison's telegraph, the first sewing machines and typewriters and declared ice-cream soda a success. Electric light was shown in Barcelona in 1888 and Paris in 1889. Mass produced Ford cars were the highlight of San Francisco in 1915. Television (Chicago 1933), nylon and plastics (New York 1939), the structure of the atom (Brussels 1958), the laser beam (Montreal 1967) and moon rocks (Osaka 1970), all these developments became accessible to the public at these descendants of the 'Great Exhibitions'. The last Universal Exposition in the 20th century was held in Seville in 1992 attracting the greatest ever number of participant countries: 108 compared to 52 in Brussels in 1958, 62 in Montreal in 1967 and 77 in Osaka in 1970.

The role of promotional showcase together with their temporary nature has given an excellent opportunity to the best of architects and designers. Such patronage has been a measure of the commitment and excellence of these events. The 'Crystal Palace' of 1851 greatly influenced architectural ideas and enabled the widespread introduction of iron and glass as building materials to create lightweight and elegant buildings and structures. The Eiffel Tower of Paris (1889) created an icon of the modern world and established the strength and reliability of metal construction, further reinforced in the public's mind by the elevated railway which visitors used to reach the Chicago exhibition of 1893. The process continued with the celebrated manifestation of the Bauhaus in Mies van der Rohe's Barcelona pavilion of 1929, recently lovingly reconstructed on its original site through the efforts of Oriol Bohigas. The modernist Finnish pavilion by Alvar Aalto at New York in 1939 and Buckminster Fuller's geodesic dome at Montreal in 1967 equally captured the spirit of their times. The tradition continues today, with the contribution to the Genoa waterfront of the new Aquarium by Renzo Piano, the small but beautiful Hungarian pavilion at Expo '92 by Imre Makovecz, and Santiago Calatrava's bridges over the Guadalquivir in Seville, all opened in 1992.

In the post-war decades, expositions have begun to highlight, at first implicitly, the tensions between technology and the environment and culture. Expo '67 in Montreal was the first of two important post-war expositions held in Canada, the second being in Vancouver in 1986. Both of the Canadian events examined these tensions: fundamental issues in a huge sparsely populated country on the frontier of the natural wilderness to the north, and the developed and industrialised giant of the USA to the south. Andrew Wilson has observed that 'the political cohesion of (Canada) has always depended on the control that technology has been able to assert over a vast land and its many nations and cultures' (Wilson 1992). Expo '67 marked the centenary of the Canadian confederation against a background of a growing movement for self-determination in Quebec, the host province. The federal government built Expo '67 around a plea to Quebec to leave primitive ethnic desires and join the technological society of North America. The most poignant evocation of this tension came from Chief Dan George who spoke at the Centennial Birthday Party of 1 July 1967 (Wilson, 1992):

Oh Canada, I have known you when your forests were mine; when they gave me my meat and my clothing. I have known you in your streams and rivers where your fish flashed and danced in the sun where the waters said come, come and eat of my abundance. I have known you in the freedom of your winds. And my spirit, like the winds, once roamed your good lands.
When I fought to protect my land and my home, I was called a savage. When I neither understood nor welcomed (the European) way of life, I was called lazy. When I tried to rule my people, I was stripped of my authority.
Oh Canada, Shall I thank you for the reserves that are left to me of my beautiful forests? For the canned fish of my rivers? For the loss of my pride and authority, even among my own people? For the lack of my will to fight back? No!
Let me humbly accept this new culture and through it rise up and go on.

This evocation went largely unnoticed at the time in the kaleidoscope of technology and Utopia. Yet, it stands as one of the most eloquent and precise statement of the tensions between technology, the environment and culture which the Canadians were beginning to appreciate in the 1960s and which all developed cultures now face in the struggle to understand and implement the principle of sustainability.

Many of the new developments and techniques exhibited at Expo '67 concerned the introduction of new technologies to the land to stimulate and encourage the federal Government's programme to exploit Canada's rich natural resource base in the wake of the post-war economic boom. Many attempts were made to examine the relationship of mankind and the environment. The more memorable included Buckminster Fuller's geodesic dome at the US pavilion, but the most evocative and lasting, subsequently to make a notable contribution to planning practice, was Moshe Safdie's Habitat '67, a prefabricated concrete housing complex at Cité du Havre on the northern shore of the St Lawrence River. The design intent was modelled on the ancient paradigm of a cottage by a river which grows organically as people settle, expanding the settlement and adding stories to the buildings as necessary. It was an intriguing experiment which is recurrent in the theory of urban design notably in the contribution by Christopher Alexander (1987) and to which various noteworthy practitioners come back to from time to time, not always successfully, as with Ricardo Bofill in Barcelona.

In retrospect, the nature of Canadian culture and geography highlighted the emerging tension between technology and the environment, heralding the debate over contradictions between industrial society, economic growth and conservation of natural resources and the environment. In Germany, this facet has been taken further with the International Building Exhibitions of Berlin (Internationale Bauausstellung or IBA). The General Urban Development Exhibition of 1910 (Allgemeine Städtebauausstelling) centred on the results of an international competition for a new masterplan for the development of greater Berlin. The principal aim was to bring control to the continued expansion of Berlin and give form to the development of Germany's capital.

This was followed in 1931 by the German Building Exhibition (Deutsche Bauausstellung) which inquired into innovative low cost building techniques as a means of stimulating the construction economy after the world recession of the time. The work of this exhibition and the movement in Germany was cut short by the rise of National Socialism, but after a break of over 25 years, the work resumed in 1957 with *Interbau*. This International Building Exhibition established to achieve the reconstruction of Hansa-Viertel (largely destroyed in the Second World War) in the form of a modern, low-density city, marked West Germany's re-emergence in international architecture with the participation of many famous architects and stands in stark contrast to developments such as Karl-Marx-Allee in East Berlin.

Falling numbers of inhabitants and jobs, the possible depopulation of the inner city and a growing resistance to post-war policies of planning and urban renewal forced a radical change to town planning in Berlin in the late 1970's. The International Building Exhibitions (IBA) of 1984-87 was an ambitious programme of conservation and renewal to promote the inner city as a place to live, the most important areas being along the inner city border adjacent to the Wall. In the mid 1980's, a series of highly successful projects were carried out by renowned architects. Today this expertise is proving a substantial skill base in the unenviable task of reintegrating the city of Berlin.

The twin programmes of conservation and new building of these exhibitions have been particularly influential and used throughout Europe and North America as a extremely successful model for urban regeneration. This model of exhibition, used to research, promote and facilitate a programme of urban regeneration, has been developed further in Germany with the establishment in 1988 of 'IBA Emscher Park' an ambitious programme of reclamation and redevelopment of some 80 million square kilometres of the Rhur embracing the cities of Duisberg, Oberhausen, Essen and Dortmund in an extremely ambitious programme of ecological reclamation and industrial renewal directed to the aim of a sustainable city-region. The innovative mechanisms and exhibition nature of IBA 1984-87 Berlin and Emscher Park 1988 are highly relevant to Scotland's major urban area, the Glasgow Conurbation, a theme returned to below.

The theme of urban renewal and regeneration has proved increasingly important to recent Expositions. Expo '92 reclaimed some 400 hectares on the island of La Cartuja in Seville. A similar exercise the same year helped regenerate the old port area of Genoa and again figures as an important theme for Lisbon in 1998. In contrast with the building exhibitions of Germany, however, the urban renewal theme of these recent *expos* does not replace, merely supplement, the traditional themes of cultural exchange and city enhancement through a programme of promotion and increased visitor numbers.

Expo '86 in Vancouver, on Transportation and Communications, was constructed on a derelict industrial site called False Creek adjacent to the financial centre of Vancouver. After the Expo closed, the 90 hectare site was sold to a property developer which caused some controversy. Expo '92 in Seville was carefully planned to rehabilitate 400 hectares of the island in the River Guadalquivir and provide a serviced high technology site with direct links to the improved and expanded Seville airport and a new high speed rail link (AVE) from the site direct to Madrid. With each of these events, urban regeneration was considered a major element in the purpose, planning and after-use of the site. There is no doubt that both have been more successful in this respect than with many of the events which proceeded them. Seville left a legacy of new airport terminal and major engineering infrastructure, including a new railway station, AVE line to Madrid and major bridges over the River Guadalquivir. But the reality is somewhat different to the publicity, with organised environmental resistance to the redevelopment of the Vancouver site and long debates about the future of the Cartuja Site (see 'After Expo', Quaderns No 198).

Major expositions are regulated by the Bureau International des Expositions (BIE) which authorises events according to a system of exposition categories. It was established by diplomatic convention in 1928 in order to overcome problems caused by proliferation of events. The United Kingdom was a founder member but, apart from Liverpool 1984, no BIE events have ever been held in Britain. The 1994 International Garden Festival was provisionally registered by the Government, but abandoned in favour of purely domestic events. The problem seems to be that the Government finds it difficult to think and plan far enough ahead, eg next Universal Expo, Hanover 2000, has already been allocated and candidates for 2005 are already lined up, Canada and Japan being so far identified. Japanese policy is to use international and large-scale domestic events (including the Olympics) as a means of promoting large-scale urban developments, and hence the long sequence of projects in Japan since 1970, including no fewer than one Universal and two World Expos registered by BIE. Germany and Holland have announced international events in 2002 and 2003.

THE EXHIBITIONS OF VENICE AND MILAN

Somewhat different in conception, form and content are the international exhibitions staged regularly in Italy. The Venice Biennale and the Milan Triennale were both established by an Act of the Italian Parliament and have permanent homes within which to stage regular exhibitions under changing themes. The Venice Biennale was established in 1895 to inquire into themes in the fine arts. It is staged more or less every two years in the tranquil Biennale Gardens located to the east of the main island of Venice.

These peaceful gardens house a collection of national pavilions dominated by the massive palace of the host country behind a stern modernist facade of 1932 by Duilio Torres. The first foreign pavilion (Belgium) was constructed in 1907 to be followed in 1909 by the United Kingdom, Hungary and Germany (reworked in 1938 with fascist overtones). Several of the original pavilions have been replaced, notably the Dutch pavilion with a building by Gerrit Rietveld in 1954. Other noteworthy pavilions include the Czech Republic (Otakov Novotny), the Austrian (Josef Hoffman), the Venezuelan (Carlo Scarpa) and the remarkable Finnish pavilion by Alvar Aalto. Recently a new pavilion by the late Sir James Stirling has been built to house the bookshop and replace the earlier structure by Carlo Scarpa destroyed by fire in the 1980s.

The Milan Triennale was established in the 1920s to stage periodic exhibitions of the applied and decorative arts. The Triennale developed a reputation for exhibiting artistic and architectural culture in Italy and the most important venue for comparison with the culture and experience of other countries. Soon registered with the International Exhibitions Bureau, the Triennale played an important role in counterpoint to the Venice Biennale for introducing Italian culture to international debate which included the introduction of Italian rationalism to influences such as Mies van der Rohe, Walter Gropius, Le Corbusier and Alvar Aalto in themselves an inspiration to the neo-rationalist Aldo Rossi who launched his manifesto at the 1970 Triennale.

The Milan Triennale is housed in Palazzo dell'Arte, a fine building designed by Giovanni Muzio in 1931 and constructed in time to house the 5th exhibition in 1933. The Palazzo is located in Parco Sempione, the landscape setting of Castello Sforzesco in central Milan. These Italian exhibitions display a different rhythm and purpose to the great expositions. They personify the Italian preoccupation with culture, art and sense of place providing a highly attractive yet sustainable setting for intellectual inquiry which, in the case of the Triennale, has generated an immense, high quality yet little known documentary archive. Despite the fragile nature of their funding and organisation (especially in the case of Milan) they do provide useful pointers to a more profound and sustainable model for major expositions.

GARDEN FESTIVALS

The last major exposition in the United Kingdom was the Empire Exhibition held in Glasgow in 1938. A splendid affair opened by the King and Queen it was dogged by poor weather and overshadowed by the Second World War. The Festival of Britain of 1951 looms large in the British psyche. It was staged by the government as a celebration of post-war reconstruction, yet it was quite a small event mounted on a ten hectare site on the banks of the River Thames. In retrospect it can be seen to be a bit confused in its intent, lacking both the confidence and exuberance of pre-war events in Britain. It is necessary to go back only to the 1938 Empire exhibition in Glasgow to note the change. It was the first such event in the UK to use the term *Festival* in its title, yet it seemed to lack the celebration necessary to truly merit the term. It was altogether a diffident, subdued and, above all, austere event in the austere years of post war Britain.

In Europe, a wholly different form of reconstruction emerged. In 1951, the same year as the Festival of Britain, the fledging democracy of West Germany staged the first federal garden show (Bundesgartenschau) in the City of Hannover in 21 hectares of the Stadtpark. It attracted 1.6 million visitors. The second show was held in Hamburg in 1953 on a 35 hectare park. It was designated an international event and attracted five million people. The shows have continued in an unbroken biennial cycle ever since attracting over X million visitors and enhancing, reclaiming or redeveloping over X000 hectares of land (see table 2). Every fifth show in the third year of the decade is a full international event designated as such by the International Exhibitions Bureau. The 1963 and 1973 international shows were also held in Hamburg, but in 1983, the event moved to Munich and in 1993 to the city of Stuttgart. The early shows exhibited a particular slant to gardenesque designs and floral displays. This has been retained, but, over the years, the Germans have begun and developed a very significant inquiry into nature and the city which is now a fundamental component of each festival.

In the Netherlands, a much smaller country, a garden festival or *Floriade* is held every ten years. With full international recognition, it affords the Dutch a major opportunity to display the strength of their horticultural industry to the world. The first Floriade was held in Rotterdam in 1960. The '72 and '82 events were held in Amsterdam creating new parks, the latter at Gaasperplas creating a major new landscape feature for the people of the Bijlmelmeer, the huge peripheral housing estate at the edge of Amsterdam. The 1992 event was held on a polder landscape at the edge of the Dutch new town of Zoetermeer. The masterplan was based on the device of the goosefoot (patte d'oie) so called because the triangle of three converging axes is reminiscent of the footprint of a goose. The device has a long history in landscape design, appearing in such famous gardens as Versailles and at the Palace of Het Loo. In Floriade, the triangle was not used to define the pathways but as a framework for the landscape itself (see figure). This has created one of the best structural frameworks of any post-war Garden Festival.

The first British garden festival was staged in Liverpool in 1984. It was a flagship project for the Urban Development Corporation for Merseyside, newly established by the Secretary of State for the Environment, one of a number in English cities. Granted full recognition by the Association of International Horticultural Producers (AIHP) and BIE, it was the first full international event to be staged in Britain since the inter-war years. It took place only one year after the international event of Munich and two years after the international Floriade in Amsterdam. Both were ten years in the planning and implementation, while work on Liverpool began a mere 30 months before it was due to open on the site of a former petrochemical store and domestic refuse tip.

The second British garden festival was held in 1986 in Stoke-on-Trent on 80 hectares of derelict steelworks, exhibiting a degree of similarity with the fourth and fifth events (Gateshead 1990 and Ebbw Vale 1992) which reclaimed further gasworks and steelworks sites. Each of the British sites had a degree of topographic relief and for each the masterplan evolved in response to the site, climatic imperatives and the exhibition requirements. Liverpool and Gateshead had major riverside sites on the Mersey and the Tyne; Stoke, although landlocked, had a major canal running along the edge of the site. Only Ebbw Vale lacked any significant degree of water and in response a lake was built. The third festival in the British programme held in Glasgow in 1988 was somewhat different. A totally flat dockland site, there were no natural features to influence the masterplan and, like the flat polder landscape of Zoetermeer, the opportunity existed to create a stylised plan for the site. Heavily influenced by the event management ideas of Disney (discussed later) a masterplan was adopted with theme areas accessed from a central space (see figure).

Urban regeneration has always been the primary objective for the programme of British garden festivals. There can be no disputing the speed and efficiency with which the sites were reclaimed, nor the success of creating temporary events which promoted the host city and attracted many millions of visitors from home and abroad. But in characteristic British fashion the objectives to stimulate post-festival private sector development has been misjudged. The events themselves have been short sighted in developing any long term contribution to greening the city. In Germany, the garden festivals are enjoyed and fondly remembered and it is possible to visit the sites over the years. In Britain, the festivals were enjoyed and are fondly remembered but, as with the exhibitions before them, there is no legacy of architecture, no pavilions by distinguished architects to visit and no growing landscape to enjoy.

DISNEYLAND AND FOLK MUSEUMS

In a paper such as this it is inappropriate, however tempting, to avoid dealing with the phenomenon of the American Theme Park and the contribution to, if not the definition of, the genre by Walt Disney. His first Disneyland was opened in Anaheim California in 1956. It is organised around *Main Street USA*, a simulation of an early 20th century small American town which acts as the conduit to theme areas which stimulate the countries, cultures and environments of the world where senses are titillated in safety and comfort, secure in the knowledge that home and the hamburger are never more than 5 minutes away. It is difficult to overstate the impact of Disney theme parks on US culture and experience. In 1965, Walt Disney Productions purchased 11,000 hectares of land in Florida to create Disney World which today houses the Magic Kingdom (Disneyland, Florida style), the Experiment Prototype Community of Tomorrow (EPCOT)and MGM Theme Park together with housing, hotels, resorts and associated infrastructure. The gigantic complex is serviced by underground corridors to facilitate workers, supplies, utilities, telecommunications to service the site with storage, canteens, laundries and dressing rooms all located underground. The Disney vision of 'all the ideas and plans we can possibly imagine' is somewhat at odds with the reality of the impact of the Floridan environment. But it would be unfair to single out the Disney Enterprise for particular criticism over environmental matters, for they are merely the biggest, but by no means the only, exposition or festival to cause environmental impact. In terms of this paper, it is the culture and design of the theme parks and their impact on expositions and festivals which are important.

Disney's vision is all-embracing. From the training of staff, through management of the site to the design and enjoyment of the product. There is but one way to proceed creating a safe, prescribed and sanitised vision of the world that Alexander Wilson has described as history, environment and culture in the service of the market. In his words, Disney World 'is at once every place and no place; it is on the land, but not of it.' It is also phenomenally successful and for every detractor there are countless numbers of acolytes and Disney's techniques in respect of layout, commercial provisions, management, culture of service and quality have greatly influenced expositions and garden festivals over the last two decades.

A striking counterpoint to the nature of the Disney product is provided by outdoor museums, and two are briefly considered here. One was the product of a great exposition, that of Barcelona 1929. The other, said to be the first open-air museum in the world, is Skansen (from the Swedish, *small fort*) was founded in the Djurgården, Stockholm by Artur Hazelius in 1891 with the aim of demonstrating how people lived and worked in the past in different regions of Sweden. Hazelius taught and researched the Nordic languages and during extensive travels in Sweden was alarmed at the rapidly disappearing traditional way of life in the face of increasing industrialisation. As early as the 1870s, he began to establish an archive of the indigenous culture which formed the basis of the Nordiska Museet (Norse Museum) begun in 1888. But Hazelius' vision extended beyond interiors and artefacts to a desire to show whole houses, traditional objects, costumes and farm husbandry in an appropriate landscape setting.

His vision was implemented at Skansen and over a period of ten years (approximately the same as the gestation period of a Dutch or German international garden festival) buildings from different parts of Sweden were reconstructed and furnished, farms created and stocked with livestock and sustainable habitats for wild animals created (in an enlightened anticipation of the better quality late 20th century zoos). Over time, the exhibition of traditional farming and Lappish culture has been extended to embrace the life of the agricultural labourer, the middle classes and, with an addition in

Figure 3 1911 Exhibition, Kelvingrove Park, celebrated Scottish History, Art and Industry, and a Highland Clachan temporarily constructed in the park proved extremely popular. *Photo: T & R Annan*

Figure 4 1911 Exhibition, Kelvingrove Park, showing the 'Scottish Toonie' temporary construction which was also extremely popular. *Photo: T & R Annan*

the 1930 s and 1940 s, the form and living conditions of the tradition Swedish town.

The consolidation and extension of the park has continued until the present with the opening of a furniture factory and mechanical engineering workshop in 1991. Today Skansen attracts over one million visitors each year with a healthy mix of school children, Scandinavian and international tourists. The displays of buildings, artefacts, culture and husbandry are supplemented with a programme of festivals and events. Considerable attention has been paid to detail at Skansen with buildings and plant species such as willow and beech from the south of the country located to the south of the site and buildings and species (birch and pine) from the north in the north of the site with the obvious objective of providing a transect through the country.

The other example was built as part of the universal exhibition in Barcelona in 1929 in the park of Montjuïc, which was reused in 1992 as one of the Olympic venues. The International Exhibition of 1929 represented for Barcelona the culmination of planning and design to celebrate urban expansion and Catalan identity. Started in 1907 and interrupted by war, coup d'etat and dictatorship, the event planned for 1913, 1923 and 1926 eventually took place in 1929. In addition to the grand National Palace and avenue leading to the Placa d'Espanya and national pavilions by distinguished architects, amongst them Mies van der Rohe. On the western side of the Montjuïc Hill, Poble Espanyol (the Spanish town) was created, a reconstruction of picturesque buildings and styles form all over Spain. Unlike the great palace and avenue intended to proclaim Catalan culture and identity, Poble Espanyol is the quieter non-separatist spirit of Catatonia within Spain as a unified nation. Like Skansen, it is a well-built and thoughtful exhibit which survived civil war and was patronised during the years of Franco's dictatorship, continuing to flourish as a small and relatively profound theme park experience in Spain.

DEAR GREEN PLACE

Characteristically canny, the Scots entered into exhibitions relatively late and in the 1880s, when exhibition activity was reaching a peak, Glasgow embarked on what Kinchin and Kinchin have described as 'a highly successful career in the field'. Many characteristics of Glasgow found an outlet in its great exhibitions: its manufacturing and trading economy, its entrepreneurial spirit and its civic pride. The first international exhibition in 1888 had an attendance of almost 5.75 million; this was doubled to approximately 11.5 million in the International Exhibition of 1901, which was the largest that Britain had seen; the Scottish Exhibition of 1911 drew almost 9.5 million; and, in a decade of depression, attendance at the Empire

Figure 5 1938 Empire Exhibition, Bellahouston Park, here showing the Avenue of the Dominions, had the greatest display of modern architecture yet seen in the United Kingdom.

Photo: The Glasgow Herald

Figure 6 1988 Glasgow Garden Festival, Princes Dock where the designers adopted many of the spatial techniques of Disneyland to produce an interesting and highly structured plan, capable of absorbing large numbers of people on a relatively small flat site.

Photo: Colin Baxter

Exhibition of 1938 topped 12.5 million, two and a half time the population of Scotland.

Glasgow's first three exhibitions made substantial profits, the Kelvingrove Museum and Art Galleries were built from the profit of the 1888 Exhibition comparing favourably with the substantial losses which had to be written off in Vienna (1873), Paris (1878), and St Louis (1904). The Empire Exhibition of 1938 did not make a profit. The event suffered from appalling weather and was overshadowed by the Second World War. Despite changing emphasis, Glasgow's major exhibitions have shared the mutually reinforcing aims of all major exhibitions: to promote industry and commerce; to attract tourism; to educate; to entertain; and to project the city's identity and enhance its prestige. This last motive has been of special importance to Glasgow's exhibitions.

Throughout the 20th century, Glasgow has had problems with its image with an ever changing array of epithets used to describe it: from ' One of the Most Beautiful Small Towns in Europe' to the 'Smoking Workshop of the World', and from 'The Second City of Empire' to 'Miles Better'. For Glasgow, aggressive self promotion has always been necessary in the face of an image tarnished by tales of industrial squalor and cultural wealth procured by industrial energy. A lack of self confidence has driven Glasgow to beseech visitors to come, see and be impressed. Exhibitions have always had a role in the struggle of cities for national and international recognition and with such a rich civic pride to draw upon, Glasgow's exhibitions have been successful acts of corporate promotion.

By the early 1980s Glasgow's struggle to overcome its legacy of urban dereliction was beginning to take effect with a substantial improvement to the quality of life for its citizens. But this improvement was not yet known outside the City and, in 1985, the City embarked on a promotional campaign with the slogan 'Glasgow's Miles Better'. A play on words, the slogan was intended to appeal first to the humour and pride of Glasgow's citizens and later to the world at large. In fact, the campaign accelerated rapidly and gained a momentum of its own. It was an appropriate initiative taken at the right time, not selling a myth, but advertising a reality. And for this reason it was successful.

The attraction of more high-spending visitors to Glasgow has been seen consistently as an opportunity to boost demand for consumer services in the City and to raise Glasgow's profile. At the beginning of the 1980s Glasgow was not on the tourist map. Most visitors who came to Glasgow did so for business or family reasons.

The attraction of visitors has been one of Glasgow greatest success story in recent years. From a base level of around 700,000 per annum in 1982, generating some £68 million of expenditure, the City's visitor number rose over two million by 1988 generating £190 million and rising further to around three million with up to £350 million of expenditure in 1990. Today, Glasgow is the United Kingdom's third most popular tourist destination after London and Edinburgh. In this transformation, three milestone projects stand out. The opening of the Burrell Gallery in 1983, the Glasgow Garden Festival in 1988 and the City's reign as Cultural Capital of Europe in 1990. Once again, Glasgow used the mechanism of a great event to raise the city's profile and became the only Scottish city to stage a garden festival. The festival received over 4.3 million visitors (40% over target). The third of five UK festivals, it achieved more visitors than the preceding and successive festivals. Glasgow used its established expertise in the field to create a thoughtful but dynamic event which was effectively promoted.

Winning the title of Cultural Capital of Europe in 1990 was the result of major partnership between all the relevant public and private sector organisations in the City. To attract further visitors and enhance its international reputation, Glasgow developed a full twelve month programme (longer than any previously), which adopted a wide definition of culture. Embracing the mainstream visual and performing arts, the programme incorporated subjects ranging from history and architecture to engineering and sport. During the year, over 3,000 events were staged with nearly 10,000 performances attended by nine million people (30% above target). The total cost of the programme has been estimated at around £50 million around 40% of which came from public funds. The City and Regional Councils were the principal funding agencies and they linked expenditure into existing mainstream projects. In addition to the programme cost, £30 million was invested in the Glasgow Royal Concert Hall, and a further £2.5 million was committed to a major refurbishment of the McLellan Galleries, the City's primary space for touring exhibitions.

Glasgow has developed a deserved reputation for urban renewal and it seems a very great pity that the excellent tenemental renewal programme, the GEAR project and City Centre developments such as the Merchant City have never benefited from an integrated exhibition programme. They exhibit the twin themes of *conservation and careful renewal* so necessary to establishing the sustainable city of the 21st century and so expertly handled in IBA Berlin '84-'87 and IBA Emsher Park. It could be argued that the city should stage a further, Millennium Exhibition in 2001, the centenary of the extremely successful 1901 Exhibition on the south bank of the Clyde, to link together the series of urban initiatives currently planned for these sites in isolation.

THE LESSONS

The above review, combined with personal experience from some of the more recent initiatives, leads me to conclude with following lessons for the future:

> *Promotion*: Great exhibitions, first and foremost, are a vehicle for promotion and for celebration. They provide a mechanism for the host city and nation to celebrate its achievements. Competitiveness

and materialism instigated and to some extent still drives the series of great exhibitions and as a result they provide an iconographic journey through man's exploration, understanding and exploitation of industry, technology and the environment.

Regeneration: In the early days expositions and festivals played a major role in the dissemination of information about new developments to the general public. This role has long since been provided by the mass-media and in an effort to replace this function with an equally public-spirited role, expositions have come to be used as an ideal device for urban regeneration. The means by which reclamation and investment can be co-ordinated and focused to achieve rapid and measurable change.

Legacy: The danger of the regeneration role of expositions is that they come to represent the *quick fix*. The examples of Skansen and Poble Espanyol provides one of a number of clues for the future of exhibitions. It is becoming inexcusable within the context of sustainability for major investments, such as the celebration of Man's endeavour to leave no legacy to future generations. The legacy need not be ponderous or overly serious, it can be recreational, fun, but it must be there. Expositions and festivals, along with all other significant projects should be subject to a rigorous appraisal which considers the whole life of the contribution of the project in terms of a broadly based assessment of value as well as cost.

Patronage: In the hands of the enlightened, the opportunity of a major exposition or festival can challenge the best of architects, designers and artists to provide new and exciting innovations which in turn will both stimulate and later influence trends in design and practice.

Culture: Expositions cannot be other than a reflection of the host culture. The Italian examples of Venice Biennale and Milan Triennale illustrate how a sustainable event can be established which provides the opportunity to inquire into themes and to build an archive of depth and meaning in contrast with the shallow and transient nature of many other events.

Environment: The green themes of garden festivals and their concern for organisation of the landscape reflect a maturing awareness of Man's interaction with the land. The festivals now need to inform the exposition movement to ensure a heightened awareness of environmental matters.

For nearly 150 years, the Great Expositions and, more recently, the garden festival movement, have been used to promote and celebrate their host cities. Countless millions have passed through their doors and their design and architecture provide an iconographic record of man's interaction, understanding and exploitation of industrial processes, the environment and technology. As times have changed their role has adapted from the dissemination of information to an eager public to become an instrument of urban regeneration. Everybody loves a party and today they are as relevant and significant as ever, but expositions and garden festivals do need to face a changing agenda which makes them more relevant to society and its current needs. Foremost in this endeavour is the need to embrace the principle of sustainability, to make a lasting contribution in their layout, design and afteruse.

Another issue that deserves closer scrutiny and more explicit handling is the need for better integration with other national initiatives in the cultural sector. Indeed, their contribution to the wider community could be greatly enhanced by being better integrated into national strategies for tourism and programmes for cultural activities. The 1951 Festival of Britain Exhibition is an example on which to build. This was not just a London-based event. Many other UK cities were involved, eg the Heavy Industry Section was held for six months in the Kelvin Hall, Glasgow, and the Light Industry Section in Birmingham. The Aircraft Carrier Expo Ship Campania was a brave attempt to take the Festival to ports UK wide (Dundee, Aberdeen, Edinburgh). Add a cultural dimension and you have a working model for the future.

I welcome the ethos of convergence espoused by many papers in this volume. My concluding observation is to suggest that the phenomenon of expositions is in reality part of our productive industries which should in the future be placed within a family. It should work together in synergy with the other sectors of leisure, heritage and tourism to continue to develop and enhance the nation's productive contribution and the spirit of enterprise.

The Author

Brian Evans is a Partner of Gillespies and Visiting Lecturer in the School of Architecture, the Robert Gordon University. Deputy Design Co-ordinator for the Glasgow Garden Festival, joint author of *Tomorrow's Architectural Heritage (1991)*, Assistant UK Commissioner for the XVIII International Triennale in Milan 1992, and founding Vice-Chairman of the Geddes Awards for environmental excellence.

References

Alexander, C., et al., *A Pattern Language*, Oxford University Press, New York, 1977

Alexander, C., et al., *A New Theory of Urban Design*, Oxford University Press, New York, 1987

Bauausstellung Berlin Gmbh, *Internationale Bauausstellung Berlin 1987 – Exhibition Areas*, Berlin, 1987

Bauausstellung Berlin Gmbh, *Internationale Bauausstellung Berlin, 1987 – Prójektübersicht*, Berlin, 1987

Beaumont, R.D., 'The Role of International Garden Festivals in the Renaissance and Rehabilitation of a Debased Urban Environment', *Record of Proceedings*, IFPRA World Congress 1992, Hong Kong, pp 201-209

Beaumont, R.D., 'Garden Festivals as a Means of Urban Regeneration', *Journal of the Royal Society of Arts*, May 1985, No 5346, Vol CXXXIII, pp 405 – 421

Bimberg, I., et al, *Der Garten fur Uns Alle*, catalogue of the Bundesgartenschau Dusseldorf, 1987, Landeshauptstadt Dusseldorf & Zentralverband Gartenbau (ZVG), Dusseldorf, 1987

Edenheim, R., Larsson, L-E., and Westberg, C., *Skansen*, Informationsgruppen Hans Christiansen AB, Stockholm, 1991

Gottfriedsen, H., *Catalogue of the Bundesgartenschau Berlin 1985*, Land Berlin & Zentralverband Gartenbau, Berlin, 1985

Holden, R., 'Liverpool Garden Festival', Landscape Revisit, *Architects Journal*, 22 Jan 1986, pp 67 – 72

Holden, R., 'Garden Festivals – where are they Going?', Landscape Revisit 6, *Architects Journal*, 4 Feb 1987, pp 53 – 61

Kinchin, P. and Kinchin J., *Glasgow Great Exhibitions*, White Cockade, Oxford, 1988

Kleihues, J.P. and Klotz, H. (eds), *International Building Exhibition Berlin 1987: Examples of a new Architecture*, Academy Editions, London 1987

Kraus, M. and Wunderlich, C.(eds), *Step by Step: Careful Urban Renewal in Kreuzberg, Berlin*, S.T.E.R.N., Gesellschaft der Behutsamen, Berlin

London Docklands Development Corporation, *A Feasibility Study for an International Expo in London's Royal Docks*, LDDC, London, 1986

McNulty, R.H., Jacobson, R. and Penne, R.L., *The Economies of Amenity: Community Futures and Quality of Life*, a policy guide to urban economic development, Partners for Liveable Places, Washington, 1985

Mastropietro, M. (ed), *Colombo '92: La Città, il Porto, l'Esposizione*, Quaderni di Mostrare, Edizioni Lybra Immagine, Milan, 1992

Molas, I., 'Barcelona, a European City', *Homage to Barcelona*, Arts Council of Great Britain, London, 1985, pp 79 – 98

Mulvagh, G., Evans, B., Nelson S and Jones, S., 'The Challenge of Designing for Fun – Materplanning and Design Co-ordination of the Glasgow Garden Festival 1988', *Landscape Design*, June 1988

Mulazzani, M., *I Padiglione della Biennale: Vienezza 1887 – 1888* Electa, Milan, 1988

Myerscough, J., *Economic Importance of the Arts in Glasgow*, Policy Studies Institute, PSI Occasional Paper 44, London, 1988

Nemeskürty, I., *Guide to the Hungarian Pavilion at the Seville World Exhibition*, Ministry of International Economic Relations, Hungarian Republic, Makona, Budapest, 1992

Oakley, C.A., *The Second City*, Blackie & Son, Glasgow, 1985

Oudshoorn, W. (ed), *Floriade 1992*, Stichting Floriade '92, Zoetermeer, 1992

P.A. Cambridge Economic Consultants and Gillespies, *An Evaluation of Garden Festivals*, Dept of the Environment Inner Cities Research Programme, HMSO, London

Panten, H., *Die Bundesgartenschauen – Eine Bluhende Bilanz seit 1951*, Eugen Ulmer, Stuttgart, 1987

Roca, F., 'From Montjuïc to the World', *Homage to Barcelona*, Arts Council of Great Britain, London, 1985, pp 133 – 140

Rohrer, J., 'The Universal Exhibition of 1888', *Homage to Barcelona*, Arts Council of Great Britain, London, 1985, pp 97 – 100

Spieker, F-W. and Gupta, P.L., *Ein Erlebuis zum Aufblühen*, catalogue of the Bundesgartenschau Frankfurt, 1989, Bundesgartenschau Frankfurt, 1989

Sociedad Estatal para la Exposicion Universal Sevilla 92 S.A., *Expo'92 Official Guide*, 2nd Edition, Centro de Publicaciones Expo 92, Seville, 1992

State of North Rhine Westfalen, *Internationale Bauausstellung Emscher Park: Memorandum zu Inhalt & Organisation*, Minister für Stadtentwicklung, State of North Rhine – Westfalen

Triennale di Milano, *Le Città Imaginate: Un Viaggio in Italia – Nove Progetti per Nove Città*, catalogue of 17 Milan Triennale, Edizioni Electa, Milan, 1987

Triennale di Milano, *Beyond the City, the Metropolis*, World Cities and the Future of the Metropoles, International Exhibition of the 17 Milan Triennale, Electa, Milan, 1988

Triennale di Milano, *Life Between Artefact & Nature: Design & the Environment Challenge*, Catalogue of the 18 Milan Triennale, Electa, Milan, 1992

Vergo. P., *Vienna 1900: Vienna, Scotland & the European Avant-garde*, National Museum of Antiquities, HMSO, Edinburgh, 1983

Wilson, A., *The Culture of Nature: North American Landscape from Disney to the Exxon Valdez*, Blackwell, Massachussetts, 1992

Anon, 'After Expo', proceedings of an international workshop to examin the future of the Seville Expo Site, *Quaderns* No 198, Collegi d'Arquitectes de Catalunya, Barcelona, 1993

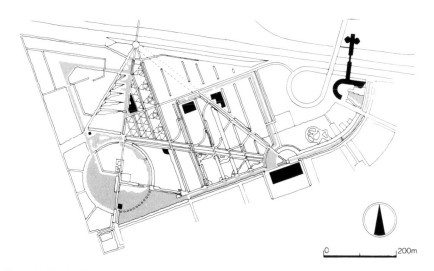

Figure 7 The highly structured 'goose foot' plan for the 1992 Floriade at Zoetermeer.

TABLE 1: SOME OF THE GREAT EXHIBITIONS

Date	Location	Type	Theme
1851	London	The Great Exhibition	Industry of All Nations
1855	Paris	Universal Exposition	The Products of Industry
1867	Paris	Universal Exposition	Work
1873	Vienna	Universal Exposition	Evolution, Culture and Economy
1876	Philadelphia	Centenary Exposition	Declaration of Independence
1878	Paris	Universal Exposition	Liberty and Understanding
1888	Barcelona	International Exposition	–
1889	Paris	Paris Exposition	Centenary of the French Revolution
1893	Chicago	Columbus Exposition	4th Centenary of Discovery of America
1900	Paris	World Exposition	The New Century
1904	St Louis	-	Louisiana Purchase
1906	Milan	International Exposition	–
1910	Brussels	Universal & International Exposition	Renewal of Mankind
1915	San Francisco	Panama-Pacific Exposition	Opening of the Panama Canal
1933	Chicago	International Exposition	A Century of Progress
1935	Brussels	Universal & International Exposition	Peace through Races
1937	Paris	Paris Exposition	Art and Technology in the Modern World
1939	New York	New York World Fair	Tomorrow's World
1958	Brussels	Universal Exposition - Expo' 58	Mankind for in a more Human World
1962	Seattle	21st Century Exposition	Man in the Space Age
1964	New York	New York World Fair	Peace through Understanding
1967	Montreal	Universal & International Exhibition - Expo' 67	Man and his World
1970	Osaka	Universal Exposition Expo '70	Progress and Harmony for Mankind
1985	Tsukuba	Expo '85	Dwellings and Surroundings – Science and Technology for Man at Home
1986	Vancouver	1986 World Exposition	World in Motion
1988	Brisbane	1988 World Exposition	Leisure in the Age of Technology
1992	Seville	Universal Exposition Expo '92	The Age of Discoveries.

TABLE 2: GARDEN SHOWS AND GARDEN FESTIVALS

Date	Location	Size (ha)	Attendance (millions)
GERMANY – Bundesgartenschau (BUGA) & Internationallegartenschau (IGA).			
1951	Hanover	21	1.6
1953	Hamburg (IGA)	35	5.0
1955	Kassel	50	2.9
1957	Cologne	48	4.3
1959	Dortmund	60	6.8
1961	Stuttgart	70	6.8
1963	Hamburg (IGA)	76	5.4
1965	Essen	80	5.3
1967	Karlsruhe	90	6.3
1969	Dortmund (Euroflor)	70	5.0
1971	Cologne	70	4.4
1973	Hamburg (IGA)	76	5.9
1975	Mannheim	68	8.1
1977	Stuttgart	44	7.0
1979	Bonn	100	7.6
1981	Kassel	235	5.5
1983	Munich (IGA)	72	11.0
1985	Berlin	90	5.2
1987	Dusseldorf	70	7.5
1989	Frankfurt	70	4.1
1991	Dortmund	60	2.1
1993	Stuttgart (IGA)	100	7.3
THE NEDERLANDS – Floriade			
1960	Rotterdam	–	< 3.0
1972	Amsterdam, Amstel Park	40	< 3.0
1982	Amsterdam, Gaasperplas	50	< 3.0
1992	Zoetermeer	90	3.4
THE UNITED KINGDOM – Garden Festivals			
1984	Liverpool (international)	49	3.4
1986	Stoke	73	2.2
1988	Glasgow	53	4.3
1990	Gateshead	73	3.1
1992	Ebbw Vale	57	2.0

TABLE 3: GLASGOW'S GREAT EXHIBITIONS

Date	Name	Location	Size (ha)	Attendance (millions)
1888	The International Exhibition	Kelvingrove Park	24	5.75
1901	Art, Industry & Science	Kelvingrove Park	30	11.50
1911	The Scottish Exhibition of History, Art & Industry	Kelvingrove Park	25	9.35
1938	The Empire Exhibition	Bellahouston Park	48	12.60
1988	Glasgow Garden Festival	Princes Dock	48	4.35

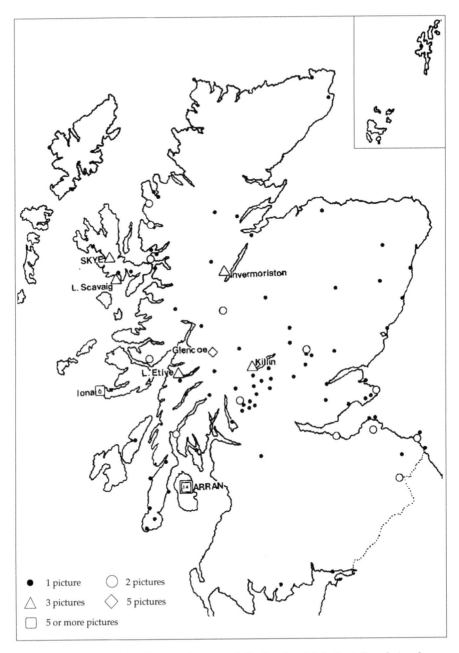

Figure 1 Location of landscape pictures of Scotland exhibited at Royal Academy, London, 1875–1899.

5

ASSET FORMATION
AND HERITAGE POLICY

Peter Howard

Formulating a heritage policy, deciding which things and places to conserve, where and how to conserve them, what story to tell about them, and to whom, must depend on knowing what is perceived as valued heritage and why it is considered important. Any effective policy must concern itself with the future, and we therefore need to know what people will consider to be heritage in ten, fifty or a hundred year's time. Our decisions now will affect people's views of heritage in the future, a heavy responsibility which museum directors have long had to bear, but we must also develop our understanding of the processes through which public perceptions assign special value to aspects of our heritage. This paper explores the concept of heritage asset formation and explores how it might aid policy formation.

Heritage asset formation does not refer, of course, to matters of scientific and historical enquiry, eg who painted this picture? when was this castle built? how was this drumlin formed? although many such questions remain unanswered, and many for which answers are available remain highly controversial, either in their factual accuracy or in their contextual interpretation. Asset formation refers to the study of how objects, or places, take unto themselves that elusive quality which we recognise as 'cultural durability', as Susan Pearce has phrased it[1]. It is this cultural durability which leads to the attempt to collect or conserve it. So the question becomes, for example, of Clovelly, a popular north Devon fishing village, when and why did who consider that such a place was of sufficient cultural value as to deserve conservation? In this case, the answer is relatively easily researched, and we can discover that it was in the early 19th century that some systematic tourists, such as William Daniell, first brought it to attention as a curiosity, and that this was greatly strengthened in the 1840s by writers and artists such as Dickens, Wilkie Collins, Hook, and most particularly Kingsley, who was regarded as having 'made the place'.[2]

Heritage is of course a cultural, not a natural, phenomenon. It is made by human beings. The Grampian mountains may have been formed in ways which have little to do with people, but its heritage value is entirely human, and doubtless there are some natural features which are scarcely heritage at all. The blue whale is much more heritage than a cockroach. The term 'natural heritage' is surely nonsense.

This paper discusses four significant causes of heritage asset formation, although there is no attempt to presume that these are exclusive, nor to deny that the causes will usually act in combination. These four are a) scholarship, b) cultural mobility, c) disinvention, and d) the arts.

SCHOLARSHIP

Probably the most easily recognised process is the discovery of interesting items by experts, which they then not only fight to protect, but through the educational process persuade others of the validity of that cause. A biologist finds a new plant, or recognises that a certain animal is nearing extinction, the archaeologists discover a complete Roman bath system under Exeter Cathedral, geographers persuade Parliament that Dartmoor should be a National Park. Most National Nature Reserves, Sites of Special Scientific Interest, and many objects in museums have their heritage origin here.

All disciplines house within themselves a variety of points of view, which dispute among themselves, and, of course, this disputation spills over into the heritage arena. Many exhibitions are the result of a particular view, as was the Richard Wilson exhibition at the Tate Gallery in 1982 that caused such a furore. Such intra-disciplinary disputes may have been at least part cause of the variety of buildings conserved, and the recent rise in significance of the vernacular heritage, the conservation of the prefab as well as the mansion. It is also worth noting the great stress laid on good research and scholarship by such bodies as the Victorian Society or the Garden History Society, which also act as pressure groups. The distinction between learned society and campaigning organisation is now dead, if it were ever alive.

Indeed, I have written elsewhere of how our country, and perhaps much of Europe, is being divided into plots of land managed by various disciplines. Just as museums, when not themselves subject specialist, are sub-divided into subject specific galleries so landscape areas represent a system of subject zoning.[3] History and geography have conspired to make this confusing; we have archaeological SSSIs within Environmentally Sensitive Areas. Architectural historians' hegemony over old churches is sometimes challenged, not only by botanists interested in the lichens, but theologists who seem to think they should have some say.

However, academics will recognise that scholarship is by no means a complete solution to asset formation, although they might wish it. For example, archaeologists surely recognise that when the purpose of a site

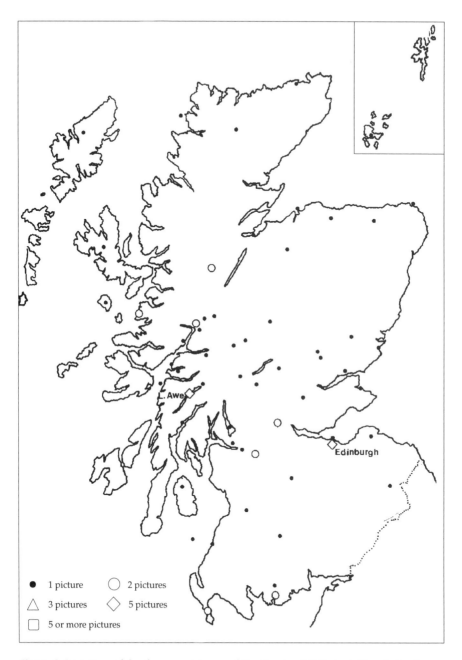

Figure 2 Location of landscape pictures of Scotland exhibited at Royal Academy, London, 1925–1949.

remains wrapped in mystery, such as Stonehenge, it always seems to have more grip on the public imagination than sites which are more or less understood.[4] I am sure that the importance of not knowing the truth is well understood by an audience so close to Loch Ness. Similarly, the scholarly fascination of a bog with superb pollen records cannot compete with Ben Nevis, uninteresting though it may be for the geomorphologist; the urge for the biggest, the unique, the Guinness Book of Records type of heritage, makes it much more conservable than say the Somerset Levels. Equally, academics and learned bureaucrats have by no means had it all their own way, or where are the Scottish National Parks?

CULTURAL MOBILITY

Christaller long ago recognised that mediaeval market towns were sited about ten miles apart because of the need to get to market; if you accelerate the mode of transport the distance increases. This question of distance, coupled with the degree of mobility now common is a matter of great concern in distinguishing the vernacular heritage. One of the important ingredients in the vernacular heritage is the way it is prized because it expresses identity and distinctiveness within an area, region, country or continent. We seem to be seeing two parallel movements; more travelling means that places tend to look similar within a very wide area, whereas it also means that the genuinely local is more and more prized.

Accessibility is not necessarily a factor in heritage. As Darvill has pointed out,[5] people are happy to save rainforests and whales which they have probably never seen, although it is also true that their heritage quality persuades many people to attempt to see them. Nevertheless, in terms of asset importance, rather than formation, access remains a factor. Dartmoor is a National Park, Bodmin Moor is not, but Bodmin is similar to Dartmoor, though smaller, lower and crucially further from London. It lies in the aesthetic shadow of Dartmoor, just as the Scottish Southern Uplands are in the shadow of the Highlands.

So travel produces new identities and reinforces those we already have. I have a whole range of identities, which I can wear all at once. First I am from Broadclyst, but a second identity is Devonian, a third is the Westcountry as a whole, and therefore someone who comes to the Highlands in summer to get away from tourists! Of course I have the slight problem of the English with national identity, English or British? The truth is both of course, English when at Twickenham or Murrayfield, but British enough when hearing a pipe band playing when abroad. I did not know I had a European identity till I went outside it. Some parts of heritage operate at one level and some at another, and this is not mere quality. Wagner for example is thoroughly German, but surely Mozart is European more than Austrian. These different identities are not hierarchical, but operate like a nest of Russian dolls.

Distinctiveness and identity (why is distinctiveness always local, and identity always national?) can only be perceived by people whose experience is wider, but is possessed in greater measure by those who have not travelled. The result of travel, sometimes even vicarious travel through television, tends both to destroy identity and reveal it. As a child I had no idea that 'spotted dick' was my heritage, I just thought it was food. Only now, when it is difficult to find and I am more cosmopolitan in my habits, does it become heritage. Only now, as many middle class English people travel widely and think of themselves primarily within a European culture, does the semi-detached house of the 1930s begin to feel like an important part of English heritage, (English rather than British I think) recognised by French tourist brochures.

DISINVENTION

The invention of the milk tanker effectively disinvented the milk stand at the farm gate which, after a decent interval in which sufficient rarity is acquired, becomes heritage now being studied by the National Trust. Do all inventions disinvent something? Can we therefore make some forecast of future heritage? If we can, that is of great practical importance. Modern farming has disinvented the small field, already recognised as heritage, whereas the disinvention of the typewriter by the word processor is not yet in that category. Once a year I visit the South West Static Diesel Engine Society's annual meet, and it seems commonplace for ordinary people to recognise the disinvented heritage long before the museum. Heritage managers should obviously welcome 'progress' since the faster the speed of innovation the more heritage is created.

There may be a reverse process as well. As Fowler has suggested[6], when something is recognised as heritage, thus commodified and rendered harmless, it may accelerate obsolescence. Certainly the commodification of heritage acts, as does design, to remove unselfconsciousness.[7] It is no longer possible nowadays, certainly not since the opening of St Mungo's museum, to practise religion in the way my parents certainly did, as an uncomplicated and unselfconscious part of their daily life. So not only does progress disinvent things which become heritage, the very act of becoming heritage accelerates the process.

ART

Artists invent new heritage sometimes just as a consequence of their style, sometimes as a deliberate fashion. The most important in heritage formation are not necessarily great artists judged by more usual criteria. On Dartmoor, for example, William and F.J. Widgery, father and son, are figures of great significance in creating the popularity of the moor, and the way in which it was usually seen, most dramatically perhaps in the Basil Rathbone film of *The Hound of the Baskervilles*. Constable's landscape taste was rather in advance of his time, and he did not become popular until taste had caught up with him.[8] Wordsworth's poetry came in the middle of a vogue for the Lake District, and did not cause it. However, the most obvious example of an artist, here a writer, causing a new vogue is that of Sir Walter Scott in the Trossachs.

A series of maps can be drawn which show the distribution of landscape paintings of Scotland hung in the Royal Academy's Summer Exhibition (see figures 1 and 2). As this is the London exhibition, these show English interest in Scotland; Scottish artists may well show a quite different pattern.[9] There are many examples of asset formation through art: in Cornwall the Newlyn School of painters was largely responsible for the discovery of the attractiveness of the fishing village and its inhabitants, giving the English (or do I mean British?) a folk hero to compare with the French peasant given them by Millet. Cezanne and van Gogh must be responsible for the English artists' passion for inland Provence, though well after their deaths. Style can be important too. Devonshire has been a county of orchards for many years, but they do not figure in the artistic output until after Impressionism. The new technique called into being a new attraction. There is also a case that the obsession with seeing landscape as geometric pattern has more to do with cubism than with the invention of the aeroplane.

Artists' ideas of what constitutes the attractive then pass through the intellectual spectrum, by way of engravings, postcards, television etc. These places and features begin to receive heritage attention, whereupon artists abandon them and move on to pastures new, western art always seeking novelty. If trade follows the flag, tourism follows art. A study of present day art can thus act as a predictor of future heritages, a glimpse into the future heritage industry. If the trickle down system is still in operation and has not been irreparably damaged by the greater alienation of art coupled with the development of other visual media, tourism managers could make use of a normal process by seeding places with art. They could stage an exhibition of painting, invite Channel Four to make a film, or, as the Council for the Protection of Rural England has done, invite major photographic figures to take pictures of the places they are trying to save.[10]

However, art is immutably elitist and, in the 20th century at least, very ego-centric. Because of its very nature, art removes a place's unselfconsciousness, and tends to transform places into the preserves of the aesthetic elite, as has happened in the Forest of Dean Sculpture Park, where the sheer incomprehensibility of most of the work persuades people that it is not there for them. It's a bit like barging into an erudite lecture on particle physics when you were expecting some lantern slides of other planets. Design has a similar effect. Brown road signs tell me that I will not find what I am looking for, which is the completely unnoticed, authentic but unselfconscious beauty spot, with an old pub for lunch. Indeed, brown road signs tell me I shall be over-charged.

CONCLUSION

The future of heritage depends on its past. If we understand the processes by which places and artefacts become valued heritage in the mind of a few individuals and then the public, we should be able to manage the heritage in a way which 'goes with the flow' and do so much more cheaply. Luckily human beings will always beat the managers. If we recognise the next great heritage demand, and we preserve it and interpret it well in advance, it will have lost both its rarity value and its unselfconsciousness, so people will ignore it, and the backers will lose a lot of money. In Exeter we now have a small but vocal movement to preserve our large Debenhams store, a 1960s glass and concrete block threatened with demolition. No doubt someone is now busy forming the Society for the Protection of Sixties Buildings.

The Author

Dr Peter Howard is Principal Lecturer and Course Leader for the BA in Heritage and Landscape, University of Plymouth. He is author of *Landscape: The Artists' Vision (1991)*, Editor of the International Journal of Heritage Studies, and Vice-Chairman of the Landscape Research Group.

References

1 Pearce, S., *Studying Museum Material and Collections*, International Journal of Heritage Studies, Vol. 1, No. 1, 1994
2 Harrison, Rev. W., *Clovelly*, Art Journal, 1896, pp. 321-325
3 Howard, P.J., *Insider versus Outsider, People versus Experts*, IALE Conference, Ceske Budejovice, October 1994
4 Darvill, T., *Value Systems and the Archaeological Resource*, International Journal of Heritage Studies, Vol.1, No.1, 1994
5 Ibid
6 Fowler, P.J., *The Times Deceas'd*, International Journal of Heritage Studies, Vol.1, No.1, 1994
7 For a discussion of self-consciousness in landscape see: Relph, E., *Place and Placelessness*, Pion, 1976
8 Daniels, S., *Fields of Vision*, Oxford: Polity Press, 1993
9 Howard, P. *Landscapes: the artists' vision*, Routledge, 1991
10 Council for the Protection of Rural England, *Legacy*, CPRE, 1992

6

HERE STAND OUR CULTURAL HEROES
But Have They Stood in Vain?

Duncan Macmillan

If you arrive in the capital of Scotland by train, you emerge in Waverley Station, probably the only railway station in the world called after a novel. As you leave the station, practically the first thing that you see is the extraordinary gothic monument to the author of *Waverley*, Walter Scott, and Scott himself in marble is seated beneath his heroic canopy. If you turn east along Prince's Street the cast of characters grows. You see the philosopher, Dugald Stewart, and his colleague at Edinburgh University and professor of natural philosophy, John Playfair, commemorated on the Calton Hill.

You turn up the Bridges and if you look back to the east, you will see that David Hume, the greatest of all Scots philosophers and the personification of the Enlightenment, is commemorated in a monument, designed by Robert Adam, which stands in the nearby Calton cemetery. Beyond Hume, on the far edge of the hill stands a monument to Robert Burns, designed in an elegant, Greek Revival style by Thomas Hamilton.

The military heroes, Nelson and Wellington, are commemorated here too, certainly, but Nelson's telescope on the Calton Hill is upstaged by the towering obelisk for the political martyrs of 1793 that stands in front of it. This is a very different kind of monument, but one with a close bearing on the significance of the others. It commemorates the confrontation between the radical politics that grew from the culture of new values formulated by the men of the Enlightenment and the conservative politics rooted in the traditional culture of feudal power that their ideas eventually helped to overthrow.

It is striking therefore how Edinburgh is a city dominated by cultural heroes. These include not just the poets, but the philosophers and in Playfair's case, even a mathematician, astronomer and geologist. If you look west from the bridges, too, this view of the importance of what we now isolate as 'culture' in early nineteenth century Scotland is endorsed, not by individuals, but by institutions. Beyond the towering Scott Monument are the two purpose-built art galleries that occupy the central site in the city (built in 1825 and 1859 respectively). High culture is thus placed visibly at the centre of society. In this context, too, in case we should suppose that this was a society dominated by the cultural heroes of the past, it is worth remembering that in these two buildings as they were designed originally, only half of one of them, the National Gallery, was used as a repository for historic art, ie heritage. Otherwise they were dedicated to the teaching and promotion of the art of the present.

Above and behind these two buildings, however, this story continues with the gothic towers of New College, not a monument to art certainly, but to the Disruption in the Scottish Kirk in 1843. Religion has a central place in any proper view of culture and the Disruption was a cultural drama of the highest importance, intimately related to the significance of the other monuments around it.

Although this makes a fine bit of townscape, does this kind of hero worship mean anything now? Can it still stand for anything useful in the late twentieth century? The effect of the particular bit of cultural hero worship expressed in Waverley station, for instance, already seems pretty ambiguous for it means that, as you enter the capital of Scotland, you do so by way of a work of fiction, quite a complex proposition, if you think about it, challenging even.

FACT OR FICTION

Does it mean that Scotland is itself a work of fiction? Some might answer, yes, it does, and for all the years that some among us have been pursuing our claim to a political expression for what we see as our legitimate identity, others of the Unionist persuasion would say that this is an irrelevant myth, a fiction indeed. But the answer to that view was given by Scott himself, and entering Scotland through a novel (or a series of novels as the first, *Waverley*, gave its name to them) is a reminder of the extent to which any national identity, although it is not a simple fiction, is nevertheless a cultural artefact. If this is so, as we honour our cultural heroes, we only pay the respect to our progenitors which our own self-respect requires.

It was Scott, through the *Waverley Novels*, who did more than any other single European to establish the legitimacy of this idea. Through him it became a major force in history, inspiring people throughout Europe to identify themselves by their culture, and to claim the right to find a political form for such an identity. He was a giant. People of all the European nations made the pilgrimage to Abbotsford and in many modern European countries you find echoes from Abbotsford at the root of the modern nation. Even where the historic nation state has a history stretching back far beyond the birth of Scott, he played a part in the birth of the modern culture as he did for instance in Denmark or in France.

The way in which it is the distinctive elements of its culture that are so widely used to market a modern nation also ultimately goes back to Scott who therefore has a place as one of the presiding deities of modern tourism, although here we see how, sadly, grand ideas can be debased. One of the things that was distinctive about the movement in Scotland, for which Scott became the principal spokesman, was the way in which it embraced as one both high and popular culture. Scott's first major publication was the *Minstrelsy of the Scottish Border*, for instance, a collection of anonymous, popular ballads, but he would be shocked at the way in which the tradition that he represented has been so often used since to concoct an ersatz popular culture.

It is certainly deeply ironic that Scotland is now virtually the only historic nation in Europe to have failed to secure for itself the right of a political manifestation of its identity. Does this mean then that Scott may be a great cultural hero, but he is of little practical use and is best left as a tourist attraction while we get on with the business of the real world?

It is not the purpose of this paper to explore these political reflections however, but to look at some of the failures in our present perceptions that have led to the debasement of the idea of culture itself which, if used in its true sense, actually embraces politics. Perhaps also, at least by suggesting the nature of these failures, it may suggest, if not how, at least why we should try to understand the original motivation of this tradition of cultural hero worship in order to return to a broader understanding of the nature of culture and perhaps a healthier and more creative way of relating it to our economic needs.

The long period through which Scotland has existed without a separate political identity, has made cultural heroes of this kind especially important and this is one reason why individuals like Scott have been raised to such heights of national acclaim, although Scott's acclaim was in his time European. His influence, not just on our own culture, but on European culture as a whole, is so vast and ramifying that it is little wonder that we are not conscious of it as a single, identifiable thing. I have already suggested how, although he was a poet and novelist, he influenced the political history of Europe, but he did so because, to a significant extent, that political history was articulated through culture. And Scott defined history as a construct, not of great events, but of the experience of individual men and women.

In this respect Scott was unique, but among his compatriots, of course, he was not alone. One thinks of Burns and Burns' Night. In a different form it is just as much a national monument and is sometimes as gothic and bizarre as the Scott Monument itself, but what Burns' Night stands for now is not perhaps what it has always stood for, and this will perhaps help us in looking at this phenomenon and its meaning.

The earliest reference that I know to a celebration for the national poet is in a letter of Wilkie's dating from 1806 which refers to a get-together for expatriate Scots in London to celebrate Burns birthday only a decade after his death. It is appropriate that it should have been Wilkie who recorded this, for he was one of those influenced by Burns and who was most sensitive to what he really stood for. Wilkie's best art is almost unthinkable without the inspiration of Burns and this is reflected in his respect for the individual, his sense of justice, his consciousness of the place of humour in any complete account of humanity and that it is never incompatible with true dignity.

But even before Burns was thought of, the members of the Cape Club in Edinburgh celebrated James Thomson's birthday, evidently regarded as the national bard before he was replaced by Burns. The idea of a cultural hero is therefore deep-rooted in the Scottish psyche. A slightly different angle is given on this by the fact that even earlier, immediately after the Act of Union in 1707 in fact, the poet Allan Ramsay was the leading figure among a group of Scots who consciously took steps to preserve parts of the distinctive heritage of Scots culture, but in a way that made it not a nostalgic refuge, but a force in the continuing development of the culture. Just think of the debt that Burns owed to Ramsay, how he proudly acknowledged it and how this has enriched our heritage. Burns' Night has fallen a long way from this and Ramsay himself was quite clear that he was not just preserving things that were quaint. For him the poetry of the makars, for instance, the 'good old bards' as he called them, was important because it enshrined values whose loss would make the world a poorer place. The poetry of Burns, or the painting of Wilkie prove that he was right.

A CULTURE OF VALUES

They were leading exponents of the expression, through art, of the idea of a culture of values. This culture was implicit in the work of the great thinkers of the Enlightenment. Central to Hume's work, was his study of human nature. He was closely allied to Adam Smith, a moral thinker who has been quite improperly hijacked by the right, and Adam Ferguson. Thomas Reid and his interpreter, Dugald Stewart, developed their thinking and transmitted it to nineteenth-century Europe. It was above all Adam Smith who drew the explicit conclusion from all this inquiry that society itself is a psychological construct. It depends on the feelings that we share with our fellow men and even our individual identities are formed by the relations we have with those around us. Hume and William Robertson extended this to approach history as the resource of memory that is an essential part of identity. It was the ideas of these men that were articulated by the artists, by the poets like Burns and Robert Fergusson, by the painters like Ramsay, Raeburn and Wilkie and by the novelists like John Galt and for the world at large above all by Scott himself.

That this, and therefore culture, also had an explicitly spiritual dimension was borne out by the events of the Disruption of the Scottish Kirk in 1843. Where most of Europe was thinking of the political revolutions which broke out in 1848, the Scots seemed strangely out of step in conducting a spiritual revolution of their own which was in effect what the Disruption was. It is given its most memorable cultural expression in Wilkie's painting, inspired by Burns, *The Cotter's Saturday Night*, and in fact looking at the warmth and humanity of such a picture, we can see how those who participated in the Disruption were prescient, even before Marx had written *Das Kapital*, in recognising as we now know too well that the crisis that would face industrial Europe would in the end be spiritual, not material. It is appropriate that the leader of the Disruption, Thomas Chalmers, should also be commemorated with a monumental statue in Edinburgh. It stands at the junction of George Street and Castle Street and it is a reflection of his status that at the other two intersections of George street stand George IV and William Pitt.

ART – NOT THE MIRROR OF WEALTH

The modern traditions of Burns' Night, or on the tourist trail, the kitsch of Burns' cottage at Alloway, suggest a much more confused vision of ourselves and our culture and that we have fallen a long way from this idealism. These Burns' traditions do at least even now do one essential thing, however. They honour a man who stood for the idea that poetry is a vital means of expressing the values by which a society lives, and by honouring him in that way, we also still honour the particular values that he stood for.

In the present, even such a rickety reflection of such beliefs as is preserved in Burns' Night is to be valued, for it is not at all clear otherwise that we know what culture is for, indeed what culture is or how our institutions should serve it. As the word is generally used to denote the leisure activity of 'the chattering classes', it would be a poor substitute for the political control of our own destiny. The whole idea expressed in that phrase (the chattering classes) is abhorrent, but it does reflect something of the way that we have debased culture from denoting comprehensively what makes a civilisation to describing the leisure activity of its wealthy minority. It suggests the twittering of H.G. Wells' Eloi in *The Time Machine*, for whom the grim reality that they were no more than cattle for the subterranean Morlocks was too harsh to acknowledge.

Seen thus, culture is no more than a refuge for frivolity and an opportunity for the display of wealth. The redecoration and rehanging of the National Gallery of Scotland a few years ago is an example of the mismanagement of one of our great cultural institutions, one of the organs of our self-respect indeed, which reflects this quite clearly. Whatever was said, and a great deal was, about the architectural authenticity of this refurbishment was a blind. The real model by which it was guided was the use of art as a means for the display of wealth in palace or country house. As such it went against a century of hanging and display which quite consciously was guided by a reaction against this tradition and in its place was shaped by the idea that it should be possible to see a work of art in a public collection without any of the connotations of wealth or movable property. Amongst those who pioneered this change a hundred years ago, Walter Crane wrote: 'The decline of art corresponds with its conversion into portable forms of property or material or commercial speculation. It is evident enough in our own time that art needs some higher inspiration than that of the cash box.'

The presentation of art that Crane and his contemporaries like Arthur Melville favoured reflected this view and the belief that whatever part it may have played in the making of art historically, the display of wealth should have no place in the approach to art of a democratic society. In its public galleries, such a society should be able to inhabit its cultural property with the comfortable unselfconsciousness with which we wear an old jacket or sit in a familiar armchair. In such a context, art turns inwards towards reflection, not outwards towards display and can fulfil unhindered the function that has been its primary objective since the Reformation, to explore our perceptions and to set them in a meaningful moral framework. It is doubly ironic that the principal new use of the revamped National Gallery is for corporate entertainment.

A GALLERY OF SCOTTISH WHAT?

Another classic example of this blindness to the real meaning of culture in Scotland has been given recently again by the National Gallery in the debate over the proposed Gallery of Scottish Art. The debate was launched with an ill-considered proposal to separate the Scottish collection from the main body of the collections of the National Galleries and ship it away to Glasgow. It was a proposal that entailed seeing the Scottish collection as superfluous in a national gallery whose real function instead of serving the nation to which it belonged was seen as one in a chain of international galleries, like a chain of international hotels all offering the same service, the same familiar masters on the walls, so that the jaded business traveller need not know what country he is in. Only the discreet tartan trews of the attendants would give a little local flavour.

This is a vision of a national institution completely divorced from the culture in which it should be an integral part. It should have been impossible for such an idea even to find public utterance. Yet, it took a huge public campaign to get the proposals rejected by the highest authority. All is not well with our culture when such a thing can happen, and we can risk being helpless, outraged witnesses to the mutilation of one of our greatest national institutions by the very body charged with its care in public trust.

If this body had had a clear idea of what the function of the National Gallery was in the first place, this would not have been possible, but they did not. How otherwise, could they contemplate alienating the Scottish collection, including the work of the cultural heroes enumerated above, from the main European collection as they originally did? The director, however, far from seeing the Scottish collections as what makes the National Gallery of Scotland unique in the perspective that it offers of European art, saw these as a provincial encumbrance, an obstacle to his claim to the international importance of the collection in his charge on which in his view his own prestige depends.

The idea also entailed closing the Scottish National Portrait Gallery, a temple indeed of cultural hero worship whose origins stretch back to the first celebration of modern cultural heroes and the starting point for this whole tradition, Theodore Beza's *Icones id est Verae Imagines, Virorum Doctrina simul et Pietate Illustrium*, a heroic iconography of the Reformers published in 1580 in Geneva and dedicated to James VI whose portrait is its frontispiece. Edinburgh University, which he founded three years later, has the remains of a similar set of portraits which have hung in the library as an inspiration to the young pretty much since that time. Like Beza's *Icones*, it celebrates the power of the individual to shape history for the better. These men were not princes or soldiers, but men driven by conscience and by a belief in freedom who by the sheer force of intellect laid the foundation of the humane system of values by which we still hope to be allowed to live. The idea of such a gallery of worthies survived in various forms to be restated by Thomas Carlyle in the nineteenth century, and it is generally Carlyle who is credited with the initiative that led to the foundation of the Portrait Gallery.

The absurd proposal to close this institution, and thus to disown this whole tradition of cultural hero worship with all it stands for, would have been impossible if this were not a society where culture and heritage, both at stake here, are too often seen merely as enterprises competing for trade. This view is confirmed by the fact that the only significant statistics produced in the argument, and they were highly dubious, were of attendance figures. We appear to be a society that evaluates its culture by the crudest head count. If that is so, we have got the government that we deserve. Our ancestors certainly did not see it this way. They did not see culture as a separate field of activity, but as the upper level of a continuous spectrum of endeavour. Among them, Patrick Geddes remarked of art, but his remark would certainly apply to the whole field of what we call culture: 'if economics is the belly of society,' he said, 'then art is its mind'.

What would he have thought of art galleries whose head-counting credentials depend on their having a good café? Jean McFadden, leader of Glasgow District Council, matched the trustees of the gallery in the narrowness of her vision of the function of the proposed Gallery of Scottish Art. From her point of view, it was simply an opportunity for jobs and economic development. As far as she was concerned it was a straight competition with Edinburgh for economic resources. It might just as well have been a car plant, and, the effect that the proposals might have on the wider cultural life of the nation, were a matter of perfect indifference to her.

Now, there is nothing whatever wrong with the exploitation of the economic energy that culture can develop, but if you look at culture first of all and only from that point of view, it will yield nothing at all. Indeed it will die on you. Jean McFadden's attitude is in fact a modern version of the goose that laid the golden eggs. The goose's ignorant owner saw no need to care for it or nurture it. He simply killed it to cut it open and find the gold inside.

To change the metaphor, culture is a difficult plant to cultivate and a difficult crop to harvest. But, like any crop, the yield is in direct proportion to the care that has gone, not just into the crop that year, but in preparing the ground over many years and cultivating the best seed stock over many generations. It cannot be reduced to so many interchangeable car plants, nor on the other hand should it be seen merely as a source of tourist attractions and the shoddy simulacra of identities that are truly fictitious. Here it overlaps with the frequent banality of the modern idea of heritage.

The National Gallery exists primarily for the people of Scotland, not for the tourist. It may attract tourists, but that is secondary to its function of provide one of the organs of identity of the Scottish nation. Underlying the fiasco, however, was a complete failure to understand this, or even to ask the simple question, what is a National Gallery for? It is a question which entails the broader question too, what is culture itself for? What purpose does it serve? Is it just another kind of industry? It is a question that is rarely asked, but it is one to which Rudolf Bing and his colleagues seem to have had an answer.

RENAISSANCE BY FESTIVAL

The Edinburgh Festival was conceived by them during the war and was launched at the lowest moment in Britain's modern history, when in 1947 after the most severe winter of the century, the country was bankrupt and on the verge of starvation. In this challenging environment, the Festival was to reassert the importance of the things for which the war was fought. It has served ever since as a motor in the development of Edinburgh as a tourist centre certainly, but it has been driven by the highest and most exacting cultural standards from the start, in other words by examples of value intrinsic to the widest idea of culture, not to the narrowest idea of its exploitation.

Often criticised by an uncomprehending city, there can be no doubt at all that, if the Festival had compromised on those standards, it would have failed long ago. As it is, it has throughout its history had an evolving impact on the development of the arts in Scotland. If culture is only a presumed good, we will not be able to defend it from the actions of those, either who regard it as superfluous, or who, like the trustees of the National Galleries and Jean McFadden or her successor, Patrick Lally, who see it as useful to pursue merely economic ends, or even personal ambition.

Before Geddes, Alexander Nasmyth expressed very clearly a holistic view of culture, very like his and very different from the one that prevails now, confirming incidentally how Geddes maintained the Enlightenment view of society and the place of culture within it. Nasmyth did this in the two pictures of Edinburgh that he painted in 1824–5. Together they give characteristically luminous expression to the idea of culture as an integral part of what makes society more than just a mindless, collective alimentary system. One picture shows the city by day with the people going about their business, including, conspicuously in the foreground, the building of the Royal Institution for the Promotion of the Fine Arts, later to become the Royal Scottish Academy and the first purpose built public art gallery in Scotland. By its site, it linked the Old Town and the New and in the picture they are seen together.

The second picture shows the citizens at rest, enjoying their well earned leisure in the summer evening sun. Leisure allows recreation and that this is an active not a passive process is shown by two details in the picture. In the centre middle ground is the Calton Jail, seen at the time, not as a symbol of power and oppression, but of reform, an even more pro-active approach to recreation, perhaps, but reflecting a belief in the ultimate sociability of all of a society's members. Beyond the Calton Jail and right on the centre line of the picture stands Hume's tomb. The philosopher directs the well-ordered society, even from his grave, but equally importantly Nasmyth thus makes visible that the high culture that Hume represents in this picture and that the Royal Scottish Academy building represents in the other is not something apart. It is integral to the well-ordered, healthy society expressed here too in the streets and squares and gardens of the New Town, Edinburgh's heroic undertaking to build a truly philosophic city.

Edinburgh's New Town is a unique expression of this vision of an integrated society. We tend to see such an architectural complex as 'heritage', and therefore governed by a particular set of values that relates to historic architecture. Heritage it certainly is, but in a much more comprehensive way, as it expresses a view of culture as part of the physiology of society. For the New Town is the tangible expression of this idea, of men and women living in harmony expressed in the style of the houses and the geometry of the streets; living in equality for the style of building renders social differences invisible; living in a kind of order which is social, but harmonious with the natural world in the ever present gardens and views to the sea and the countryside beyond.

THE FIRST CULTURAL ECOLOGIST

The person who understood and articulated these things most clearly was Patrick Geddes. For him the idea of a healthy society depended on a kind of cultural ecology that extended outward to ecology proper. It included the making of art now and the understanding and proper articulation of history. Like the builders of the New Town, Geddes saw that cities and their architecture were the anatomy of society whose health depended on the proper functioning of all the organs that the structure of that anatomy contains.

Let us now return to the tour of Prince's Street with which we began, as we do so bearing in mind some of these present cultural failures and the significance of the cultural tradition which, in spite of them, we have inherited. We left our tour looking up to the Assembly Hall. If we now look above this to the west along the hill we see the picturesque complex of Ramsay Garden. This is yet another kind of monument. As we see it, it was built by Patrick Geddes, but at its heart is the house that Allan Ramsay, the poet, built for himself in the mid-eighteenth century. Geddes consciously adopted Ramsay's house into his complex. Geddes' project was a cultural enterprise and it bears Ramsay's name, for in the history of Scottish culture, as we have seen, he is indeed a hero.

The Ramsay Garden complex was intended as a kind of colony uniting different elements in the city in a common enterprise that was designed to be educational, but at the same time would serve as a motor to regenerate the Old Town of Edinburgh. Geddes also extended this community in two directions, historically and geographically. Historically, not only by including Allan Ramsay, but by using the Scottish vernacular style and by assembling in the main meeting room a whole collection of the cultural heroes of Scotland through history in a series of paintings by John Duncan; geographically he extended the catchment of Ramsay Gardens by making it an international meeting place, pioneering the idea of the summer school.

Geddes was both an internationalist and the pioneer of the idea of the Scottish Renaissance that was taken forward by other cultural heroes in the twentieth century, men like Hugh MacDiarmid, J.D.Fergusson, William Johnstone, Neil Gunn or Sorley McLean and which continues to this day in the work of some of the great contemporary artists that Scotland has produced and who have followed in their footsteps. Ramsay Garden is, therefore, a model for an ideal of cultural tourism based on the exchange of ideas based on the strongest possible articulation of both the historic and the present culture of Scotland and set within an international framework.

Like the founders of the Edinburgh Festival after him, therefore, Geddes understood the vision of culture that is presented by the monuments that dominate Edinburgh's skyline and saw it as something living. High culture from this point of view is not just one area of leisure activity competing for resources with all the others. It is a way of enhancing the quality of life by reinforcing some of its core structure of values.

As conventional tourism is a linear activity, it is governed by a law of diminishing returns. Following only a simple view of profit, it can only increase its return by a numerical increase, either more tourists, or more areas to be exploited, but as these increases are pursued, the very resources on which they depend themselves become debased. There is certainly economic benefit in the short term for the inhabitants of the tourist area, but in the end it too may kill the goose that lays the golden eggs. Cultural tourism should not be seen simply as another market for the same kind of exploitation. Geddes suggests a model by which it is instead a renewable resource in a way in which crude tourism can never be.

Much of the machinery of cultural tourism is already in place, or is being developed. I am not proposing any radical innovation in that respect, only that as we embark on it, we should make sure that we recognise the real nature of our culture and the value of the traditions enshrined in it. We should try to make sure that that is reflected in our institutions and that they are not seen merely as part of the service industry of tourism. If they serve us well, then in the long term they will serve the tourists better than they ever would if they were geared to a crude, linear view of profitability. That is no more than an upmarket version of traditional mass tourism. The National Galleries debacle shows how close we are to going down that road and how little the meaning of the celebration of our cultural heroes is understood by some of those who are there nominally to protect and interpret our heritage in one of the primary fields of endeavour.

Instead, a vision of genuine cultural tourism in which education and tourism were allies would work at the economic level, no doubt fewer people, but spending more money. However, it would be the more valuable as it promised more lasting benefits in improvements in the quality of life: benefits of exchange and enlargement of vision coupled with a better understanding of ourselves seen through the eyes of others. This refreshment of different points of view would come from a kind of tourism that was not passive, but active. Cultural tourism could reinforce our own sense of values, not erode them. That would be true profit indeed.

On the skyline of the Old Town, just to the east of Ramsay Garden, stands the Outlook Tower. Geddes converted this into a model of his vision of the relationship of Edinburgh, the particular, to the wider world, the general. It was a model of the process of learning based on a two-way flow, knowing oneself and one's own environment and using that knowledge to lead out to an understanding of the wider world and using knowledge of the outside world to inform our understanding of ourselves. Patrick Geddes's vision is one in which this kind of cultural tourism would have a place and it would surely be appropriate to relaunch the Patrick Geddes Centre as a flagship for it. At present, Edinburgh University has a Patrick Geddes Centre, but it does not occupy the whole Outlook Tower and it needs funds to expand its activities. The ideal would be to find a way to take over the whole Outlook

Tower and to link it, through the University, with the new popular ecology centre at the foot of the Royal Mile. There would thus be a true Geddesian flow from popular tourism up to the higher level of cultural tourism. It would be a more creative kind of growth, by aspiration, not crude cash flow, and it might make us all richer.

CONCLUSION

My concluding message is that these monuments of cultural heroes from the past which adorn Edinburgh are surely far more than a fig-leaf to cover the shame of the cultural impotence inflicted on us by confused politicians, misguided bureaucrats and a consumer driven private sector. Their value as a source of inspiration for us today is that they appear self-confident in their assertion of the importance of a living culture and its heroes in a healthy society with a vision of the indivisibility of man's spiritual and material needs. It is this perception of society and of the function of art within it that is represented by these monuments. It is a vision from which we can still learn. Indeed, it represents the most important part of our heritage which we owe it to ourselves, as well as to others, to recover and articulate.

This vision of a society, as celebrated in the Edinburgh monuments, was not compartmentalised as ours is now. We divide up our world into compartments, and we sometimes seem more concerned about the lines of demarcation between them, than with the lines of communication that join them and the common ground they share. We have education, tourism, heritage, art and culture (sometimes with sport tacked on), and politics is often considered a completely separate sphere. Instead of exploiting the strength that comes from shared common ground and the structure that they form together, we weaken them all by seeing them as separate. Heritage, for instance, is useless if it is the unquestioning preservation of the past without taking from it the ideas and lessons that it contains. Likewise, culture is gravely weakened if it is cut off from the continuities with the past that are enshrined in heritage properly understood. Both are, or should be, articulated by education, and the business of politics itself, if it is without culture, is without moral values.

The Author

Professor Duncan Macmillan is an Honorary Royal Scottish Academician, Curator of the Talbot Rice Gallery, and Professor of the History of Scottish Art at Edinburgh University. He is the author of several books, including the most authoritative work ever written on *Scottish Art 1460 – 1990*. He is also chairman of University Museums in Scotland, the Scottish Society for Art History and the Edinburgh Galleries Association.

References

Boardman, P., *Patrick Geddes, Biologist, Town Planner, Re-Educator,* London, 1978

Crane, W., *The Claims of Decorative Art,* London, 1892

Davie, G. E., *The Democratic Intellect,* Edinburgh, 1961

Macdonald, M. (ed), *The Edinburgh Review,* Issue 88, Summer 1992 (devoted to Patrick Geddes, it includes a reprinting from *The Evergreen* of Patrick Geddes's seminal essays: *The Scots Renascence, Life and its Science, The Sociology of Autumn* and *The Notation of Life,* as well as *A Single Minded Polymath, Patrick Geddes and the Spatial Form of Scottish Thought,* being a review by the present author of the book by Hellen Meller listed below)

Macmillan, D., *The Bride Wore Scarlet (the redecoration of the National Gallery of Scotland)* in the 'Museums Journal', vol. 90, No. 1, January 1990

Macmillan, D., *The Canon in Scottish Art: Scottish Art in the Canon?,* forthcoming in 'Scotlands', No. 1, Edinburgh University Press

McWilliam, C., Gifford, J., Walker, D. and Wilson, C., *The Buildings of Scotland: Edinburgh,* Penguin, 1984

Markus, T. et al, *Order in Space and Society* Edinburgh, 1993

Meller, H., *Patrick Geddes, Social Evolutionist and City Planner,* London, 1990

Scott, P. (ed), *Scotland, A concise Cultural History,* Edinburgh, 1993

Youngson, A. J., *The Making of Classical Edinburgh,* Edinburgh, 1966

7

THE CULTURAL POTENCY OF SCOTLAND

Phillip Hills

When Professor Fladmark asked me if I would contribute a paper to this book, I told him roughly what I thought of the heritage industry so as to make him go away. However, he seemed to like what I said and did exactly the opposite of going away.

The theme of *Cultural Potency* came out of our ensuing discussions as we seemed to agree about how enormously powerful are people's ideas of Scotland, and how important it is for Scotland's economy that we do not depreciate those ideas by running the country as a Mickey Mouse theme park. Fladmark's suggested title may also have something to do with my job as Chairman of the Scotch Malt Whisky Society.

For those who do not know about it, the Society is a bit like a wine society, and was brought into being so that the members could get their hands on malt whiskies in perfect condition. Society malts are probably the best distilled liquors produced on this planet, and it was virtually impossible to get them until the Society came on the scene a little over ten years ago. We discovered that an important piece of Scotland was not as we had been told it was and, having discovered that, we were able to create a market for Scotch whisky at a level of quality which previously did not exist.

Indeed, when we started, it was the opinion of everyone in the whisky industry (apart from the owners of Balvenie and Glenfarclas, who for some time had been doing something similar) that nobody would drink such stuff. The Scotch Malt Whisky Society could be said to be in the heritage business, in that it has taken a piece of the national heritage hitherto obscure, brought it to public notice, and made a few bob by selling it.

Given that the whisky industry has been around a long time, it is not immediately apparent why people should have come to believe that the nation's drink in its finest form, was unfit for human consumption. But it is a fact (which is in danger of being forgotten or swamped by the weight of heritage-influenced advertising) that until the 1960s, malt whisky of any kind was virtually unobtainable in this country. This was an altogether extraordinary state of affairs, whose analysis throws some light on Scotch history and on the heritage business. How, in a free country, which has long prided itself on its knowledge of its own history, could there exist a set of beliefs which deprived the Scots of the best of Scotch drink?

THOU SHALT NOT FALSIFY

The concept of ideology has been devalued by its association with communism, which is a pity, for it is a useful term to describe a corpus of interlocking beliefs, by which societies constitute themselves and through which individuals identify and locate themselves in society. Ideologies, typically, serve mainly the interest of the dominant social class, and the interest of that class is a more important determinant of beliefs than the mere correspondence of those beliefs with reality. The cultural potency of Scotland is rooted in such a system of beliefs, and a very powerful system it is indeed. For over a hundred years, until the 1960s, the Scottish ideology incorporated the proposition that no Scotch whisky which had not been through the hands of the blenders, was remotely drinkable. What was true of whisky, was true of a lot of other things people believed about Scotland.

It is from this perspective that I propose to look at Scotland and the integrity of its heritage. If a part of the apparatus of belief about Scotland, as apparently fundamental as the nature of her national drink, is capable of being falsified by economic interest, then we must realise that the fabric of belief which is the foundation of the heritage industry, cannot be taken for granted. It is not a thing whose veracity may be assumed or its permanence guaranteed. It must be conserved as carefully as those physical relics, to which the attention of conservationists is generally directed. Conservation, however, is not about preserving everything. Value judgements must be made about what is worth preserving. Good stuff is to be kept and junk junked. The judgement as to which is which is not simple in the case of artefacts; less so in the case of ideas.

Now, still by way of prologue and, as they say, for the avoidance of doubt, I ought to tell you a little more of where I am coming from. Bob Marley's lines,[1] 'If you don't know where you bin, You don't know where you goin' apply both to this argument and to the prospects for our heritage in the long run.

I do not like travelling. I think it is tedious and disagreeable, unless on a boat, and even then it can be pretty vile. I do not enjoy holidays, which consist mostly of enforced idleness and are a violation of eudaimonia, Aristotle's principle of happiness,[2] to which I have long adhered. I regard tourism as something which may have been pleasant for its inventors, the 18th century British aristocracy, but has fallen victim to the dialectic[3] and, made popular, is shot with internal contradiction. My feelings toward tourists are similar to my feelings about oil slicks: I do not like them, but I accept them as a price we have to pay. Just as oil slicks are a cost of petrol, tourists pollute but sustain places like Ballater. The existence of Ballater and the internal combustion engine are things which we have to accept for now, however much we may deplore them in the long run.

A CAUTIONARY TALE

I have, to put it mildly, mixed feelings about heritage, in the sense the term is used against the single objective of commercial exploitation. Heritage seems to be mainly about some folk making money out of other folk's sentiment about historical events of which the latter are largely ignorant. It consists of the past presented in a form capable of being assimilated by persons unaccustomed to independent enquiry: antiquity for *couch potatoes*. The national taste for literacy and antiquarianism has resulted in more books about the history of Scotland than any country of comparable size. No-one who can read, and who desires to know about Scottish history, need go farther than the nearest library. Whatever it is they are intended to do, it does not seem that *heritage centres* are designed to supplant libraries. Over the last few months, I have visited a number of heritage centres. I do not get the impression that the imparting of knowledge is their primary purpose.

What I do see, are good things from the past being destroyed to make way for Heritage projects. Let me tell you about Oban, which, as most of you will know, is a small town in Argyll: the most important centre of population between Dumbarton and Fort William. The town has a superb setting, clinging to the hill above its bay and looking out over Kerrera to the mountains of Mull. The architecture is mainly stone, from the latter half of the last century, as is the splendid harbour, where you will find ferries to the Inner Isles, fishing boats, yachts and small coasters. There is a railway line from Glasgow which, as Victorian romanticism combined with Glaswegian sentimentality, produced a vigorous tourist trade. Facilities have always been somewhat scanty for the tourists who each year exhibit what (in a quite different context) Dr Johnson called the triumph of hope over experience,[4] by returning to traipse dolefully through the rain.

The influence of Victorian romanticism and Glaswegian sentiment are not uppermost in the minds of the wet tourists, however potent they may have been in bringing about their predicament. The complaint is always: there is nothing to do in Oban. To which one might reply: there never *was* anything to do in Oban, a fact which becomes noticeable only when it is raining, which is most of the time. Tourists by and large do not do anything, but they like not to do it out of the rain.

A few years ago, this truth became apparent to the West Highland branch of the Weltgeist,[5] and it was decided that holidaymakers should be provided with some facilities to alleviate their tedium and counter the solar attractions of the Costa Brava. Thus the Oban Experience Heritage Centre was born. Nothing wrong with that, you may say, and I guess there was not. The only problem was that to be commercially successful, the heritage centre had to be in the migratory path of the moist troopers, which meant on the Waterfront. A deal was duly cobbled together among a number of bureaucracies: the District Council, the Scottish Tourist Board, the Highlands and Islands Development Board, the development company and British Rail, who owned the fish pier.

Now the fish pier was a place where for several generations, fishermen had tied up their boats, refuelled them and repaired them; where they landed their catch; where they spread out their nets and mended them; where they parked large and unwieldy items of mysterious equipment upon which they carried out arcane operations involving arc welding. The pier belonged to the railway, but the railway, having nothing better to do with the bit of land, was tolerant, and collected its revenues for the transport of boxes of fish to Glasgow and the world beyond.

All of this was not only compatible with the tourist trade: it was picturesque and it contributed to the Oban experience, as a place in which real people did the sort of things which they required to do, to facilitate an existence which was some way removed from the urban uniformity which was the daily experience of visitors. Because the people of the Fish Pier had something to do, work, the rain did not appear to bother them overmuch. For those who, fish supper in hand, penetrated the easily-surmountable barriers, there was the fine prospect of what would now be called heritage: different-looking folk doing different-looking things and looking as though they and their forebears had been doing them for a long time.

Not now. Today there is a Heritage Centre on the site of the Fish Pier. It is called The Oban Experience. Observation suggests that the Oban Experience is about buying bits of coloured glass and woolly jumpers. There does not seem to be anything else at all, nor is there any indication of the experiential relationship of the woolly jumpers and bits of coloured glass to the history, polity or economy of Oban. The fishing boats still cling to the pier, but whatever it is the fishermen do when in port, it takes place on the boats, for there is no space for them to do it anywhere else, and it would make the place look untidy, which would not be a pleasing experience for the woolly-sweatered, glass-buying subjects of the Oban Experience.

Now I am aware that most heritage entrepreneurs will probably see nothing amiss in the Oban Experience. They will argue that the future lies in service industries and not with manufacture or with primary production such as fishing.[6] That is as it may be, although there is an important sense in which tourism is a primary producer, a point to which I will return, and to which the whole argument about heritage is relevant. For me, however, something which was real and true, has been replaced by a thing which is neither. This not to imply that the Oban Experience is a chimera,[7] however chimerical. Merely that a way of life and the customs and values of a people have been displaced to make way for an economic activity whose ostensible purpose is the promotion and display of that very way of life and those very customs. That is a contradiction in whose resolution neither truth nor reality appear to be served.[8] And, quite apart from the fact that such a proceeding is morally repellent, it is also bad business.

HERITAGE AS A COMMODITY

There is a difference between heritage as a cultural asset and heritage treated as commodity. The past may be another country, but it is one which we can package and sell as we please, and its proprietors, the dead, cannot complain. Whether the living should complain on their behalf is a thing with which I will deal below. It is an issue which, I believe, is the business of a book such as this to address.

Heritage is the business of selling potted history; of using eclectic perceptions of the past to part tourists from their cash; of marketing the past-as-product. As business, some would argue, it ought to be subject to law but not to moral considerations. I hope in what follows I will make my position reasonably clear on the moral issues, but I do not intend it to be an argument about morality. It is an argument from prudence and commercial interest. But such is the nature of the commodity, Scotland, that moral considerations are inseparable from prudential ones.

There was a time when Scotland was a mighty industrial nation. In the decade before 1914, a fifth of the world's total output of ships came from the ten miles down river of Glasgow. One was launched last year. With a very few and laudable exceptions, manufacturing industry is dead, and there are no serious prospects of its being revived. The nation's capital, the accumulated surplus of two hundred years of industry, enterprise, warfare and exploitation, has cleared off to where the margins are better. Money knows no patriotism, as any observer of the rich can tell you. Scotland has been reduced a branch economy at best; at worst, it is a Third World country, a primary producer of raw materials whose natural resources are exploited by foreign capital to fuel production which takes place elsewhere, as does the accretion of the value added by production to the raw materials.

In this context, heritage appears as a logical response to a situation. People must live, and they will make a living in any way they can: they must exploit whatever economic niches are available to them. If the only thing they have to sell is their past and their country, then that is what they must do. Our job, as I understand it, is to consider how best that may be done.

Every primary producer has two nightmares. They are resource exhaustion and product substitution. Heritage is resistant to both, but not entirely immune. The public, both at home and abroad, has maintained a surprisingly high level of interest in things Scottish. I say *surprisingly*, because of the extent to which icons of national identity, which are mostly false to begin with, have been rendered more meretricious by their employment in trivia (I mean tartan dollies and the like). One wonders whether the past is a renewable resource which can be exploited indefinitely; or whether the taste for tabloid images of Scotland is one which will pass with time.

PARTING THE PUNTERS FROM THEIR MONEY

Heritage, Scotland's past viewed as commodity, has a market value which is based solely on the belief among potential customers that Scotland is a good thing. If that belief were to disappear, so would the value. The effort which we as a nation devote to conservation must be directed not only to physical preservation, but to ideological preservation as well. For the purposes of heritage, the conservation of the remains of the past is merely a means to a present end, namely the preservation of the belief in Scotland as an object of value.

The big question is: why do people think Scotland is a good thing, what is it that they believe, and how do we sell it to them so that they come back for more? Is heritage the way to do it, or is heritage merely a passing fashion, born of national decline and destined to die of the diminution of national prestige? And if so, of which nation? If heritage or some variant of it is the way, are there things which ought to be avoided, as tending to depreciate our currency? And what is the moral angle, and does it matter?

Of the potency of what, for want of a better phrase, we will call Scottish culture, there can be little doubt. Scotland is known and valued throughout the world. Things Scottish are identifiable and are, by and large, held in high esteem. What is less than clear, is why that should be the case. What is so special about Scotland that so many people in so many places should have a high regard for it?

It is not just that, as J K Galbraith and Christopher Harvie[9] have said, the Scots have done more than any nation of similar size to create the modern world, although there can be little doubt that their having done so, is highly relevant. Rather, the actions of the Scots, and Scottish ideas, have entered the belief system of the modern world. That belief system, reflexively, holds Scotland to be of value.

The Scotland which is held to be valuable, is sometimes recognisable to those of us who live here, sometimes not. Because there are so many aspects to the Scottish identity as perceived from beyond the Scottish borders (and within them, for that matter), it is possible for any person who is well-disposed toward Scotland to be highly selective, and to adopt only those facets which are congenial. Without the discipline of evidence, constructs easily pass for reality. We all do it to some extent, but those of us who live here have to cope with recalcitrant experience. That is not the case with expatriates and foreigners, who can afford to be eclectic.

The following anecdote serves as an example. Last year I was given an excellent lunch by an eminent citizen of New York, who is the head of a charitable organisation whose declared purpose is to do good for Scotland. He described to me how his institution had raised large sums of money, which was to be used to supply a fund whose purpose was to make payments to persons of Scottish ancestry in recognition of significant achievements, I forget exactly what sort. Over lunch, my new friend explained to me that he and his colleagues were about to announce (he assumed it would be to great applause) the prospective recipient. He told me in great confidence that the lucky man was to be one Rupert Murdoch, and he watched in some perplexity as I collapsed in laughter. When I had recovered a bit, I said that any such venture would have to be without the support of the Scotch Malt Whisky Society. I do not think I succeeded in explaining why. This chap spends a lot of his time thinking about Scotland and talking to people from Scotland. Judging by his letterhead, most of them seem to have been from the aristocracy, which may explain why he has missed something which, though difficult to describe, is quite essential. It has to do with reality and truth and a sense of humour and a few other things. His view of Scotland is partial, and the part of it he sees most clearly is a part which never existed: the mythic Highlands.

THE RISE OF THE GREAT HIGHLAND MYTH

Easily the most important among the elements of perceived Scottish culture is the Great Highland Myth: the adoption of the Highland clan as a paradigm of Scottish society. Beginning in the 18th century, as soon as the '45 rebellion was out of the way and the clan system of social organisation safely on the road to destruction, Highlandism gave rise to a system of beliefs and values which had no equal until the rise of the Hollywood Western, and it is disputable which bore the less resemblance to historical reality. A myth of Scotland was erected which served the purposes of Romantics on the one hand, and the Tory party on the other; it was adapted to the industrial revolution and to the Empire; it was used to sell whisky (it still is) and today it is used to sell tourism.

The Highland identity is almost entirely fabricated, and it has been most persuasive among those who have had most to gain by it, as befits its status as an ideology. In the 19th century the emerging imperial and commercial middle classes adopted it with enthusiasm, and the Scottish aristocracy, abandoning the intellectual pursuits which had so distinguished it in the 18th century, in the 19th took to dressing up in make-believe Highland outfits and doing what Victorian sentiment imagined were the occupations of Celtic chieftains, mostly slaughtering the local fauna.

The existence of the Great Highland Myth, or rather the mythic nature of a prevailing ideology, went unremarked until relatively recently, with a few exceptions. The rise of national sentiment of the later 19th century largely failed to notice it. In 1909 Tom Johnston comprehensively (if selectively) rubbished the Scottish aristocracy,[10] and in 1922, he produced for the first time, following Engels, a comprehensive class analysis of Scottish history.[11] Neil Gunn's *Whisky and Scotland: A Practical and Spiritual Survey*, was published in 1935. It is a diatribe against the whisky distillers who, under the kilts of Highlandism, contrived, Gunn said, to deprive Scotland of her national drink by substituting the inferior, blended whisky for the real stuff, malt. Since Gunn was not only an intellectual but also an excise man, it might have been supposed that he knew what he was talking about. But the time was not ripe, and nothing much happened. The political nationalism of the 1930s and 40s was undecided, and certainly made use of a lot of tartan imagery. Chris Grieve, its most vociferous exponent, adopted a Gaelic nom de plume.

The time was ripe, however, by 1980, when Murray and Barbara Grigor[12] brought *Scotch Myths* to an astonished and delighted public. This, an exhibition of Scottish kitsch, revealed the extent to which the Highland Myth, and, by association, Scotland, had been debased for commercial purposes. What had started as a diversion for the upper classes had come to Harry Lauder and dirty postcards. Because there was no reality to the Great Highland Myth, no opposition was possible to its corruption. And anyway, the intentions of the folk who sold tartan dollies were little less elevated than those of the people who organised the junket for George IV, pink tights and all.

The phenomenon of Highlandism was given its coup de grace by Hugh Trevor Roper in 1989 in a work[13] which has been followed by several other pieces which, if more detailed, are less trenchant. One gathers from the tone of Trevor Roper's piece, that it was not intended kindly: nevertheless, it did Scotland a great service.

Throughout Scotland, authentic folk traditions had survived into the post-war period, which had nothing to do with Highlandism, but contrived to coexist with it. It was out of those traditions that came that cultural resurgence, which has been the most potent force in Scottish society in the last forty years. The main vehicle of the resurgence has been that most traditional of Scottish cultural vectors, song: what came to be called the Scottish Folk Revival. Fletcher of Saltoun was justified.[14]

The revival of an authentic Scottish culture, of which the revival of malt whisky is a part, has been at the expense of the Highland Myth. It is an assertion of the superior values of a real culture which is both popular and intellectual as against the posturings of a philistinic, aristocratic and commercial one. However, it would be foolish to deny the sheer power of some of the images, and there are signs that these are being incorporated into a new synthesis of Scottish identity, in which Highlandism survives, at least in iconic form.

This is not to suggest that Mythic Highlandism is dead and buried. It remains strong in the imaginations of expatriate Scots and Scotophile foreigners, groups for whom the authentic Scotland has no significance and to whose realities they need not accommodate. It is, moreover, capable of being resurrected in all its absurdity for specific purposes. The whisky distillers were among the leading 19th century exponents of mythic Scotland and it comes as no surprise that contemporary manifestations of Highlandism should be found advertising whisky. My favourite example, in the whisky industry, is an organisation known by the wonderful title of *The Keepers of the Quaich*. This was invented in 1989 by United Distillers PLC. It has resurrected the panoply of Harry Lauder Highlandism for the purpose, post mortem, of conveying an impression of authentic and continuing tradition to people to whom it wishes to sell (mostly blended) whisky.

REALITY AND ILLUSION

The packagers and vendors of heritage would do well to take cognisance of recent cultural movements, for they bring in their wake the two dangers mentioned earlier, exhaustion and substitution. The heritage commodity has a market value because of belief in its truth and reality. If Scotland is presented by the heritage industry in a way which diminishes those values, then the belief will fade and, with it, the market. It is with relief that one views the troubles of Euro Disney, for the Highland Myth is ripe for the Disney treatment. Belief in the reality of Scotland, having been dented by Brigadoon a generation ago, would be unlikely to survive a *Scoto Disney*.

It is probably the case that, by the power of advertising alone, the fake Scotland can be sold to enough people to maintain a heritage industry. But Scotland is not a can of beans, and it is not easy to sell by media alone. Better, surely, to go with the flow, and to sell the real thing. For the real Scotland is much more romantic and infinitely more interesting than the fake.

That is always the case: the genuine has a depth and a quality to which ersatz can never aspire. If you sell tartans on the ground of their clan associations, you are always going to be short of angles, because there is little to the idea apart from what you and your fellow-hucksters make up, and you have to avoid contact with reality for fear of exposure. It is a much better idea to admit that the idea of clan tartans was a figment of the early 19th century and to tell the astonishing story of how the notion of clan tartans came into being, and of the gang of hooligans and charlatans who invented it. We do not have to pretend that we are all good, and foreigners will like us the better for saying so.

As with tartans, so with the folk who wore them. Scots history, Highland and Lowland, is so full of extraordinary incident that it needs no faking. The exploits of Crichton or Montrose or Dalzell or Claverhouse[15] are anything but dull, and the more accurate the account, the more astonishing the story. And there is no reason why, in telling of such people, they should not be accorded the respect and the seriousness which is their due and their right. These were people who gave their lives in great causes, and they are not to be demeaned to serve the pecuniary interests of their inferiors. Nor need they be, for by according such people a due respect, we communicate our respect to those to whom we speak and, by doing so, we make evident the value of that part of our heritage.

This is one aspect of the moral dimension to which I referred earlier. There is, I believe, a happy conjunction of interest between the moral and the commercial, for only by upholding the moral, do we in the long run best serve our own interest, as individuals and as a nation.

LOWLAND DEMOCRACY

If these things are true of the Highland Myth, they apply with greater force to a different set of beliefs, which is strongly represented in the popular perception of Scotland. The demotic, democratic, sceptical tradition, of which Burns is the outstanding icon, is an important part of the Scottish identity. This is the voice of the Lowland, Scots-speaking common man. Rarely woman, for it is a profoundly mysogynistic tradition, despite Burns' liking for ladies. It has its roots in 18th century radicalism and Whiggery and it represents a strain of thinking which has persisted as a powerful element in the life of the Scottish middle and lower classes. After the 18th century, it was not found to any great extent among the upper classes, to whom its egalitarian and radical elements were unpalatable, as was its nationalism.

The democratic tradition was exported by the great Scottish diaspora of the 19th and 20th Centuries; by the economic migrants to America and by the radicals shipped to Van Diemen's Land. It pervaded the commercial dealings of the Scots overseas and it was exported, via the heroic figure of Burns and its attendant legend, to sectors of Scotophile society which otherwise would have been deeply resistant to it. Democratic beliefs are to be found among people whose political ideals are otherwise oligarchic, purely on account of their Scottish ancestry. Just as Highland myths became icons for lowland Scots, whose forebears would have regarded real Highlanders as rogues and vagabonds, there is a global constituency of people who idealise a country whose present reality would be anathema to them. Try telling a republican member of the New York St Andrews Society that an independent Scotland would be a socialist republic, and you will see what I mean.

The democratic, demotic ideal makes the Highland myth accessible, and by so doing, provides part of the ideological framework which makes it possible to sell Scottish heritage to the world. As a philosophy it may be incoherent, but it works. It provides us with some delightful prospects: of Philadelphia capitalists, who congratulate themselves on their impeccable democratic credentials because of their supposed descent from members of a rigidly-stratified clan society; of Japanese sararimen who find cultural resonances as well as golf courses in Scotland.

Such traditions do not lend themselves easily to heritage treatment. The common people and the minor gentry are not as fancy as the higher aristocracy, and the progress (if that it be) of democracy is about difficult ideas, which are not suitable for presentation as tableaux. Nor is the sheer drudgery of everyday life in times gone by. Nevertheless, these things are relevant to the heritage business.

If Scotland is not to become a theme park, the presentation of her heritage must not separate the present from the past, but must show the Scotland of today as being continuous and contiguous with the Scotland of yesterday. If in the long run, theme parks are to maintain their appeal, they must be relevant to people's lives and experience. That is, to lives which are lived in the real world, not the fantasy world of some virtual-reality, never-never land of television or heritage centres.

That requires a concern for truth and understanding: truth, in the sense of an accurate portrayal of the detail of historical events, and understanding, in the sense of an adequate conceptual framework. If the heritage business does not meet those criteria, it is likely to be short-lived. If it does meet them, there is no reason to suppose that it will be less durable than Scotland's whisky industry. It can even, in a sense, be as intoxicating.

There is a political dimension, too. Politics is a part of a national culture, and Scotland's national culture has become progressively more political in the last forty or so years. The nation has proved resistant to various sorts of encroachments in the past. The cultural potency of Scotland is not just about the visibility of tartan trash. The real, present Scotland, is a place of some cultural potency, and I suspect that it will not allow itself to be hijacked by a junk-historical fantasy, however profitable. Heritage entrepreneurs should beware.

The Author

Phillip Hills is a philosopher and former Tax Inspector who has become the 'enfant terrible' of the whisky industry. As founding Chairman of the Scotch Malt Whisky Society and contributing author to *Scots on Scotch (1991)*, he has been in the vanguard of those who have triggered the modern Renaissance in Scottish culture and enterprise

References

1 Marley, R., *Exodus*
2 Aristotle, *The Ethics*
3 Various writers about dialectic: Plato, Hegel, Marx
4 Boswell, *Life of Dr Johnson*
6 Various monetarist economists and right wing theorists 1975-94
7 Homer, *The Odyssey*
8 Various dialectical theoreticians: mainly Hegel, Marx and, more recently, T.S. Kuhn
9 Galbraith J.K.,in a BBC Television programme, 1977
   Harvie, C., *Scotland & Nationalism*
10 Johnson, T., *Our Noble Families*
11 Johnson, T., *History of the Working Classes in Scotland*
12 Grigor, M.and B., *Scotch Myths*
13 Trevor-Roper, H., *The Highland Tradition in Scotland* in Hobsbaum, E. and Ranger, T (eds), *The Invention of Tradition,* Cambridge UP, 1983 (latest edition 1993)
14 Andrew Fletcher of Saltoun: 'If a man were permitted to make all the ballads, he need not care who should make the laws of a nation.'
15 See Thomas Urquhart's fragment on Crichton
   See John Buchan's biography of Montrose
   See various biographies on Dalzell and Claverhouse

8

THEME PARK BRITAIN
Who Benefits and Who Loses?

Priscilla Boniface

In considering the concept of Theme Park Britain and assessing who benefits and who loses, I shall suggest that the concept is not, as it is popularly regarded, a new phenomenon of the 1980s. It was present in British society long before then. Stonehenge and its associated prehistoric landscape is a theme park of sorts. North Wales' skein of castles is a Plantagenet theme park, the neat culmination of which is the place of investiture of Wales' own Prince. Northern Ireland was made a country estate theme park in the eighteenth century by the English landed gentry, with consequences that are still with us today. What is Edinburgh if not a Classical and Romantic, Apollonian and Dionysian, theme park?

By Sassenachs among others, Scotland has long been thought of as the Country of Tartan and Burns, with the northern portions of that country and their Clearances being given less mention. The emergence recently of political correctness has, at its forefront, concern with the provision of greater truth and balance to national and other group stories. In the past of the imperial and colonial period, these stories were dressed up as themes for the purposes of propaganda, with a view to gaining and keeping an ascendant position.

Theme parks today represent gradations from the real to the utterly synthetic. There is such a melding of the real, the half-real, and entirely fake, that there is little to distinguish from amongst the 'olde worlde' street scenes of, for example, Chester, York, the Metro Centre's Antiques Village, and Disney World itself. With this sort of thing all about us, is it any wonder we have difficulty facing up to reality? And, as I shall suggest in considering the theme park situation, surely society loses if it cannot face facts?

Particularly through the media, books and films, and very often through promulgation in the cause of tourism, tract after tract of Britain is designated by a theme. With spotlight from the mass media, places have become sudden tourist successes and altered in character just as suddenly. To the Cookson, Herriot and Bronte stalwarts, among many others, to which is now joined the town of Stamford in theme position of *Middlemarch*.

101

In recent years, 'theming' has swept Britain to a point of saturation and staleness. And in the selection of a theme, of course, areas are choosing to ignore, suppress even, their real and natural multi-variate personalities and their features. Theming, by its very nature excludes, so that those excluded could be said to lose, if losing equates to not receiving overt recognition as being of a place or area. A brave act it was for the newspaper feeding off a territory whose majority constantly propound, and revel in, its chosen theme of 'Geordieism' to represent to readers in a special supplement their area's multi-cultural features[1].

Country life has become a theme park activity too. With diversification, old country dwellers are forced to serve as custodians of the heritage residues of their past endeavour. The newcomer or visitor, meanwhile, treats the place as a country park. Country estates, open to the public represent to their visitors country house theme parks where they may dream safely of being landlord or laird without fear of the dream's realisation. The erstwhile owner has meanwhile also benefited by escaping from being saddled anymore with the burden of the upkeep of a massive estate. The ruling classes gain subtler benefit too in that, while apparently the opening of former private domains to public scrutiny is an act of democratisation, it could be said doing so is to draw attention to the class system's existence. The country house as a theme was a strong one in the 1980s, drawing new power to its cause by recruiting new adherents and thus new potential beneficiaries through devices such as 'the country house hotel'. In the town, meanwhile, one needs look no further than the signage to attractions and services to understand that we are all inhabiting the same themed place.

Of course, towns and cities are about being places of attractions and centres of cultural life. Certain places, many among them post-industrial cities, have quite deliberately used the cultural industries as their chosen theme to encourage socio-economic regeneration. Among these cities are Bradford, Liverpool and Birmingham, in the last of which the theme of public art is so prominent as to make avoidance difficult. A comparable example is demonstrated by the outside display in the environs of the Pompidou Centre in Paris, where an art in public theme works spectacularly well.

I have referred already to Edinburgh. The fantastic visual aspect of the city, in certain style themes, is its appeal. Choosing architectural themes, with powerful associations, both from the past and often associated *with* power too, can reinforce a range of required images. Powerful images denote power. A classical theme has implications of refinement and continuity. Newcastle upon Tyne, for example, has opted to maintain the old classical appearance of well-known Grey Street, although that appearance is essentially now little more than a facade to a modern fabric. In concept, with its facadism, Grey Street is now not so different from its Metro Centre counterpart. The phenomenon is not confined to Britain: in building Palm Beach in the USA, for example, Spanish was the chosen style. Montpellier in southern France, seeking to regenerate and to emerge as a modern Heliopolis, has selected to

Figure 1 Gateshead Metro Centre.

Figure 2 Hyde Park Corner, London.

clothe its huge Antigone development, which encompasses among other features a mass of public housing, in dress of classical idiom.

In regeneration, as in other endeavours involving theming, unless an appropriate theme is chosen, it will not work. Morecambe, on the wrong side of Britain now in terms of trying to have a viable existence in the present has tried a few things. The 'Frontierland' idea for its theme park at least harks back to Morecambe's past as a stopping off place near to a point of embarkation, albeit not for the United States, as was the role of Liverpool a considerable distance further south. The brave try to re-invent Morecambe's glamorous past, through the meticulous restoration of its high quality Midland Hotel foundered in the reality of being a wet resort which now rarely attracts a clientele disposed to Morecambe's old inter-war, somewhat more up-market, heyday. Now the theme of traditional saucy postcards is being tried with blow-up depictions being placed along the roadside.

Halifax's chosen theme is of education itself, of young children. So this depressed city's main visitor attraction is in the primary colours of childhood, a Yellow Brick Road for visitors wending its way across post-industrial land, to the fount of knowledge at the Eureka! Museum for Children, the English Tourist Board's Visitor Attraction of the Year 1993. In the attempt at regeneration, a gutsy city with a proud past and of naturally monochrome hue has needed to take on the colours and aspect of a theme park. In keeping with its theme of education, it is in character for Eureka! to have a small outreach display of the Archaeological Resource Centre at York. Like its other York Archaeological Trust counterparts, among them the Jorvik Viking Centre, the Trust's product theme (although with entertainment running through it), is that of academic integrity with education as an overt function, despite occupying a city which has turned into one big heritage theme park overall.

In an attempt to achieve socio-economic regeneration, for a place not to have a recognisable theme might be regarded as a disadvantage. Against others in a competitive situation, a city or town with no obvious and distinctive heritage to provide a theme for imaging, to make the place specially memorable, might lose out. Britain *is* now a heritage theme park, exemplifying in physical form our set attitudes and ways of approach.

In the publication, *Theme Parks: UK and International Markets,* the Marriot Corporation's definition of a theme park is reported as: 'A family entertainment complex oriented towards a particular subject or historical area, combining the continuity of costuming and architecture with entertainment and merchandise to promote a fantasy provoking atmosphere.'[2] Does this sound like anywhere we in Britain know?

It is interesting that the publication observes that theme parks are 'focused on entertainment rather than education.' Theme park Britain's concern is the creation of a lucrative retail and leisure environment. From revamped old arcades to conversions of redundant buildings to shopping malls themselves, heritage theme imagery is being used to sell.

Areas requiring regeneration such as post-industrial cities *can* benefit through image enhancement achieved from their linkage with positive themes from history, in terms of what would attract outsiders or insiders to believe so well of those places that they are prepared to make investment of resources in them. If the chosen historical theme has sufficient basis in truth to have some demonstrable roots, it can be believed and have influence. However, if a fairly ludicrous myth is being perpetrated, it is unlikely to hold sway either for long or in any useful depth. Part of the problem Euro Disney had in starting out, for example, was that its storylines, loosely based on European heritage images and fairy tales, while credible at a great distance and in different territory like Florida, California or Japan, did not stand up to the scrutiny of Europeans born and bred to savouring and knowing of the authentic 'presentations'.

Of the British public, 70% are said to be among socio-economic groups C and D.[3] The cultivated connoisseur type of tourist is more likely to be found in groups A and B. Such views, of course, will have implications for the sort and style of theme chosen for mass audience presentation. In the UK, a day tripper market, generally those persons within two hour's access range of an attraction, are perceived as a theme park's constituency. Naturally, therefore, this main market's believed tastes will condition the style and form of the product with which that market is presented.

The North of England Open Air Museum is located at Beamish, between Newcastle and Durham, in the heart of the old north of England coalfield. The just lost, fading in remembrance, coal-mining community lifeway in this area, therefore, is such an obvious theme for presentation as to be almost self-selecting. An important part of that old way of life is emphasis on community and family. At Beamish, the older generation touring in family groups can use the exhibit, now overtly set in time at 1913, as a talisman for telling those who have never experienced it what the coal-mining way of life was like, or what they have now chosen to believe it was like. On the answer to the question of whether or not this helps the process of giving necessary accommodation to change within a community, can decisions be made about what and whom such presentations benefit?

While it could be seen that the coal lifeway theme in the form deployed at Beamish could have a useful purpose for its area's community, more questionable by this criterion is the use of a remaining Tyneside coal staithe, restored at considerable expense as focus to one of the ubiquitous Garden Festivals staged in post-industrial areas in recent years. Here it would appear that a token heritage item was needed to provide a focal point, to put an element of theme into a park for elucidation and amusement, which otherwise was somewhat bland, featureless and flat. It is to be gauged whether, for the regeneration agencies, let alone the community at large, the gamble of drawing such attention to the past, of using coal mining to theme the area in this way, worked and benefited the north eastern corner of England. Overall, industrial themes for an attraction can be either beneficial or non-beneficial for the groups involved, as has been the case with the coal-mining theme.

Heritage can be damaging to communities other than those that are disadvantaged. Constant pressure of tourist visits, now often extended to be year-round rather than seasonal as of old, can be wearing and intrusive on home ground and can even reduce a home's value. Bus tours enable eye-level views into first floor windows as residents of the Royal Crescent in the World Heritage City of Bath know well. In what is in effect a theme park, residents may lose, even if tourists and others are benefited.

Theming can be divisive, sometimes threateningly so. A heritage attraction, while its theme and aspect can be compelling in terms of its capacity for attracting visitors, can through its tone of superficiality or general character of affluence, strike strong vibrations of discontent in those portions of a resident community experiencing deeply present-day problems of disadvantage.

For several hundred years, Spitalfields in the East End of London has been home to rag-trade workers, often from overseas, such as Huguenots originally, and Asians most recently. It has undergone, and is continuing to undergo, a partial process of gentrification. In amongst a poor community are precious homes, among them one which is open on occasions to the public and inhabited in entirely 18th century mode by its owner. It is problematic to imagine the local community taking such themed piece as this to its heart. What a difference further east in Bow with the representation *Home* by Rachel Whiteread, the last of a working class terrace house with its implied subjects of the demise of a working class community, of homelessness and change: in winning both plaudits and brickbats from the artistic fraternity, it was an undeniable success as a visitor attraction with locals and visitors alike. The artwork, on a both intensely local and universal theme, met local community and visitor needs, while serving to develop creative links between the two and from which each could obtain benefit.

Britain's prevalence of theming can have a useful aspect in regard to the country's minority ethnic groups. If these groups are prepared to use it as such, theming, with its characteristics of using pronounced colourful aspects, can be used to serve to heighten a particular group's presence and recognition within an overall community. The Chinese-ness of Newcastle upon Tyne's Chinatown, for example, in both townscape aspect and general scene has in recent years become more and more overt. The result is that the Chinatown area is much more visually attractive than hitherto. With its basis in reality, the increased colourfulness and associated activity make the area much more entertaining and enjoyable for resident community and visitors alike. The big benefit is that the Chinese community's customs and ways are better understood locally and a strong and good inter-cultural dialogue is developed overall.

A dynamic society of the world needs the benefit of inter-cultural links with a global dimension that extend beyond a particular society's immediate scope. The Japanese Festival in 1991 provided an opportunity for a Japanese theme garden to be created within Holland Park. The resulting product, while produced by a Japanese minority, nonetheless also shows British characteristics in the stern Borough authority requirement to 'Please keep off the grass', as well as its sub-Japanese standard of maintenance in British hands. In context, as exemplar of a themed product, representing inter-cultural dialogue, its success in and benefits for Britain are undoubted.

In relation to inter-cultural mixing, it may well be that the signal attraction and theme experience of the 1990s, both as regards numbers of people visiting, and for conjuring what may transpire as the decade's defining style, is the new 'tribal-wisdom and ancient-learnings' constituency Body Shop Tour. Green theming in another manifestation, learning from the shopping malls, has gone inside from Britain's real country to the protective care and warmth of a Centerparc environment. Maybe, then, the environment can benefit from theming.

Probably the main beneficiary of our British theme park society today is the monarchy. Core to that society is a monarchy theme. On a scenario of benefit to the monarchy, of course, Windsor Castle *had* to be rebuilt, just-so, after the *annus horribilis* fire: unbroken theme and line needed to be demonstrated. In 1993, the year after the *annus horribilis*, the Queen circumspectly opened Buckingham Palace to the public for the first time. In 1994, she opened the rehoused Crown Jewels as a major 'new' attraction whose style of presentation 'took some of [the Disney] theme park ideas on board.' The Queen was reportedly 'in a very good mood from the moment she arrived and was obviously enjoying herself.'[4] It can be imagined that in 1994, the 25th anniversary year of the investiture of the Prince of Wales, in placing images of Wales before British society, the opportunity will not be lost to benefit by choosing to put before us the image of Caernarvon with its associated regal as well as Princely theme.

So, who benefits and who loses on the entertaining merry go-round that is today's Theme Park Britain? Monarchy benefits in the reinforcement of its old idiom and message. Power groups in general benefit by power of control of the type of message and political groups can benefit similarly. Entrepreneurs can benefit. Scholarship is likely to lose through a process of selection and lack of objectivity, and education can easily lose if other than an overall balance of messages is presented. Ethnic minorities can benefit or lose, depending upon the circumstances. Residents and visitors both benefit and lose. Society as a whole loses because of the lack of objectivity inherent, through selection, in the process of theming. Multi-media provide the opportunity for an informational process that is dynamic in type, but without a corresponding dynamism of mind on the part of both presenter and audience there will remain a situation of no change in the subject matter of the British theme park.

Westernised civilisations live in a 'world' of theming. In describing the meeting of the International Association of Amusement Parks and

Attractions, attended by among many others, museum representatives, the Los Angeles Times reported a 'United States... 'themed entertainment' industry' boom. The occasion was the unveiling of a virtual reality mission to rescue the Loch Ness Monster, with first-time capacity for accommodating 'large volumes of paying customers'[5].

An overall emphasis on entertainment can encourage distortion and discourage adherence to facts. In the provision of education, therefore, theming and theme parks may not always be of benefit. For example, the Cornish village of Tintagel, living off a myth, as far as the most informed present knowledge opines, that it was the seat of King Arthur and his Knights of the Round Table, literally cannot afford to take notice of this latest information. Cornwall, a post-industrial county, needs to survive: what price scholarship?

Theming, if taken seriously but without the benefit of background knowledge for providing balance, can serve as a false witness and provide opportunity for delusion and will so serve society ill. Therefore, in addressing the question posed by this paper, the answer could be that we all lose, if we do not keep a level perspective. Essentially, theming by using the material of history is about the choice of one thread from among the many, which in weft and weave form history's whole fabric.

Aspects of fantasy, diversion and colour are necessary to people's lives. If not provided for them, people will produce their own. However, in the use of the matter of history in this provision, the danger is that the demands of fantasy will obliterate and override fact. In using images with a dimension of fact to their nature, in other words history as best perceived at any one time, theme park presenters need to feel their obligation to be not to 'mix' with the facts, unless they are making separation of fact from image so strong a feature as to be entirely obvious to all their audience. If this is *not* done, society will lose by a deceit perpetrated upon it, and, in the particular instance of Britain, our true island history will not be known.

Accordingly, the fundamental question needs to be asked: is there now substance in Britain behind the many styles of history or are we merely now becoming inhabitants of a Ruritarian nation? Although we may believe that we are witnessing the 'themeparkisation' of British society now, such a prospect has been long in view, maybe ever since Britain lost its position as industrial leader, head of empire and role as major actor on a world stage.

Already, getting on for thirty years ago in 1968, in the play *Forty Years On*, Alan Bennett, an acute observer of Britain and the British, was making the prognostication:

> Country is park and shore is marina, spare time is leisure and more, year by year. We have become a battery people, a people of under-privileged hearts fed on pap in darkness, bred out of all taste and season to savour the shoddy splendours of the new civility... To let. A valuable site at the crossroads at the world... Of some historical and period interest. Some alterations and improvements necessary.[6]

It may be too late for Britain to be other than a theme park, in which case it is quite clear who loses.

The Author

Priscilla Boniface has held posts with the Royal Commission on the Historical Monuments of England and in the Department of Archaeology at Newcastle University, before becoming the Regional Director of the Royal Institute of British Architects, Northern Region. Her books include co-authorship of *Heritage and Tourism in 'the global village' (1993)*.

References

[1] *The Journal*, 15 March 1994, *'Living Together'* supplement
[2] *Theme Parks : UK and International Markets*, London, Tourism Research & Marketing, 1993, p. 51
[3] ibid., p. 10
[4] Daily Mail, 25 March 1994, p. 3
[5] *Los Angeles Times*, 22 November 1993, D2
[6] Bennett, A., *Forty Years On*, London Faber, 1969, pp. 77–78

POLICY AND PRACTICE
How to Focus Strategy and Action

The parallel lines
along which we think
will only converge in action
through partnership.

9

THE PULL OF CULTURAL ASSETS

Gordon Adams

Tourism is not a new industry, and the pull of heritage is not a new characteristic of tourism. Educated Romans went to Greece to pay homage, much as prospective American Presidents still go to Oxford:

> In the Roman period, Sparta became the world's first theme park: it became a Heritage centre living off its past, and its history and traditions were revived in a very rosy glow of romanticism and presented to the Roman tourist. The constant stream of visitors brought in wealth that enabled the inhabitants to live in quiet prosperity. It is a theme not without interest to 20th century Britain.[1]

In Scotland we have become very professional at presenting heritage. Sir Walter Scott and Queen Victoria were by far the best sales team that ever sold holidays in Scotland to the English, and tours to heritage attractions in the Trossachs were early examples of Cook's tours to the exotic destination of the world.[2]

Critics, however, often mock the British heritage industry: 'Heritage, for all its seductive delights, is bogus history. It has enclosed the late twentieth century in a bell jar into which no ideas can enter, and, just as crucially, from which no-one can escape.' So wrote Robert Hewison in his review of the heritage industry in Britain.[3] Is Hewison right? Does it matter if he is right or wrong?

THE ECONOMIC IMPORTANCE OF
TOURISM AND HERITAGE IN SCOTLAND

Heritage is part of Scottish tourism and tourism is important for the economy of Scotland. Tourism as broadly defined, supported about 171,000 people in Scotland in 1991 or about 8% of the total workforce, and growth in employment in tourism has significantly outpaced Scottish employment growth in recent years. Tourism is one of the very few industries in Scotland that offers real potential for new jobs in the next decade, and in some rural areas it seems the only industry that could compete internationally without substantial subsidies.

Scotland, in many ways the home of the Industrial Revolution, is now more famous abroad for its tourism, than for any other industry. A recent report for CBI Scotland concluded, after an international survey, that 45% of respondents associated Scotland with tourism, while only 26% associated Scotland with manufacturing.[4]

There was huge expansion of the heritage industry in the 1980s and that growth has certainly slowed down and has probably stopped. Still, in 1993 Reed Information Services produced a guide to over 1500 museums and art galleries open to the public in Great Britain and Ireland, of which 218 are in Scotland. Similarly Reed has a guide for over 1300 historic houses, castles, and gardens, of which 125 are in Scotland.

Our heritage is particularly attractive for overseas visitors and some 77% of North American visitors say they like our castles and museums (Table 1). The figure is much lower for British visitors.

Table 2 shows visitor numbers at the main built visitor attractions in Scotland in 1992 and 1993 and the role of heritage is clear. The phrase 'visitor attractions' is in many ways a misnomer for visitors of course are attracted to the scenery of Scotland probably even more than to the built heritage (see Table 1) but heritage is clearly the main attraction of Table 2. Edinburgh Castle is by far the most popular of Scotland's paid attractions and, with over one million visitors in 1993, is the second most popular historic attraction with paid admission in Britain. The Tower of London is the leading historic attraction with over two million visitors.

I do not think the Scottish heritage industry does present a bogus history of Scotland, but all history is selective and the physical artefacts of history are particularly selective. Sometimes our castles and stately homes seem to present a Scotland in which the only inhabitants were Mary Queen of Scots and Bonnie Prince Charlie, but the intelligent traveller can surely see through this façade.

THE ROLE OF HERITAGE IN THE PRESENTATION
OF SCOTLAND AS A TOURIST DESTINATION

How then should the Scottish Tourist Board present Scotland given the extraordinarily complicated history of our country? We make a basic distinction between British and overseas visitors and the heritage message is emphasised strongly for the latter. The USA provides by far our largest single overseas market worth about a quarter of all overseas expenditure which in turn is worth about £670 million to Scotland. For the USA, and the 'White Dominions' in general we try to build on associations of culture and a common heritage, while recognising that family links will diminish over time.

Colleagues who come back from tourism marketing missions to the USA talk about a dream of Scotland which is quite widespread: a kind of Brigadoon inhabited by Andrew Carnegie. We must build on this rather romanticised view of Scotland, for it would be commercially reckless, and historically misleading, simply to concentrate on the warts of Scottish history. We need to build on links with the Scottish Country Dancing societies in Alberta, and the Burns societies that still exist all over the world. Yet, I myself can remember watching a BTA presentation in Ottawa on the stately houses of Scotland, and the Canadian beside me announced, inevitably with a Dundee accent, that if he had liked that kind of stuff he would not have emigrated (expletives deleted). Some potential tourists from North America know very well what Scotland has to offer.

For continental Europeans we are tending more and more to emphasise the attractions of our natural environment, which is still relatively unspoilt, rather than our historical heritage, although for some French tourists we can still offer reminders of the Auld Alliance.

The English market is still by far our most important single market and future growth is much more likely to come from short-breaks (ie up to four days) rather than from longer or 'main' holidays. English residents, however, particularly those who have never been to Scotland, often have rather a negative view of Scotland, as a holiday destination: 'The weather, the prices and the apparent lack of facilities for lively, fun-packed holidays with plenty of entertainment for adults and children, are all reasons offered for not choosing Scotland. English holidaymakers feel they have enough heritage attractions at home, while the distance and expense of travel to Scotland are further deterrents.'[5]

For the English market, then, our current emphasis is to improve our visitor's understanding of Scotland. We need to emphasise that there is more to Scotland than memories of ancient battles. A high proportion of English visitors do return, so perhaps problems of perception are more important than problems of product quality in the English market.

According to the 9th Principle of the Charter of the Arts in Scotland: 'Scotland's cultural heritage in all its forms should be preserved, augmented and made accessible to the public.'[6] Such advice is perhaps hardly realistic. We can't preserve everything, and there are surely at least some aspects of our cultural heritage that are not all that attractive to tourists. Given the cost of a TV commercial in London we will always have to be extremely selective in our presentation of Scotland, and it is scarcely an exaggeration to say that the future of Scottish tourism does rest on the ability of Scotland to present itself to England as a country with more than history, our natural environment being the most likely attraction.

THE ROLE OF THE STATE IN THE
PRESENTATION OF SCOTLAND'S HERITAGE

Heritage attractions are seldom profitable and for this reason tend not to appeal to the private sector. The role of central and local government, and institutions like the National Trust for Scotland is, therefore, crucial in presenting our heritage to our visitors.

The role of the Scottish Office is essential in safeguarding and presenting our heritage, particularly through the work of National Museums, the National Galleries and Historic Scotland. These bodies were not set up with tourism in mind, but they are now essential for tourism, and spending by tourists is increasingly essential for the further development of the heritage institutions.

The National Museums of Scotland have their main buildings in Edinburgh at the Royal Museum of Scotland, Chambers Street, the Findlay Building, Queen Street, and the Scottish United Services Museum at Edinburgh Castle. Branch museums are the Scottish Agricultural Museums, Ingliston, the Biggar Gas Works Museums, the museum of Flight East Fortune and the Shambellie Museum of Costume (Nithsdale). The National Galleries of Scotland comprise the National Gallery at the Mound in Edinburgh, the Scottish National Portrait Gallery in Queen Street, Edinburgh, and the Scottish National Gallery of Modern Art (opened in Edinburgh in 1984). These museums and galleries are all of international significance and fame. Perhaps, however, we have not always publicised them to tourists as widely as we could, albeit over 12 million visits are made annually to all Scottish museums and galleries.

Historic Scotland is an Executive Agency of the Secretary of State which, amongst other functions, manages and presents over 300 monuments in the Secretary of State's care including our most significant castles and abbeys. Increasing emphasis has been placed in recent years on the presentation of monuments to the public with much better display boards and interpretative panels. All Historic Scotland custodians have undergone customer care training in recent years. Substantial investment has taken place at Edinburgh and Stirling Castles recently and the investment at Stirling is crucial in the programme to realise Stirling's potential for tourism.[7] The range of Historic Scotland's properties is astonishing and includes castles, abbeys, palaces, and monuments all over Scotland.

The Local Authority Districts of Scotland are all involved in presentation of heritage to tourists with collections of international significance presented, for example, by Glasgow District Council at the Kelvingrove Art Gallery and Museum, and the Burrell Collection. Many lesser known museums and galleries which are run by Local Authorities should be better known to tourists. Outstanding examples are the Kirkcaldy Art Gallery, the Robert Burns Centre in Dumfries, Tankerness House in Kirkwall, and the Shetland Museum in Lerwick. Nevertheless, many local museums still have visiting hours which are not really tourist friendly.

The National Trust for Scotland has more than 100 properties in its care, including 100,000 acres of countryside, and buildings which range from Culzean Castle in Ayrshire to Hugh Miller's Cottage in Cromarty. The National Trust, of course, is not a government institution. The National Trust castles in Grampian, for example, provide a major part of the attraction of the area for tourists.

We can present the effects of all these visitor attractions in terms of visitor numbers or in terms of visitors expenditure at sites, but for tourism the real effect is in terms of making Scotland as a whole more attractive. By and large people come to Scotland to see parts of Scotland. They stay in various types of accommodation so that they can see parts of Scotland. People stay in Edinburgh hotels so that they can see parts of Edinburgh. Yet, most of the expenditure by tourists is on travel and accommodation.

Accommodation providers, then, are often the direct beneficiaries of money spent on getting access to visitor attractions. In the jargon of the economist the accommodation providers receive *external economies* from the visitor attractions. Often investment in visitor attractions will be a more efficient method of increasing visitor expenditure in hotels than investment in the hotels themselves. And, as visitor attractions are seldom inherently profitable, government investment will be necessary so that the private sector can reap benefits.

COST PER JOB IN VISITOR ATTRACTIONS

Some economic work has been carried out recently on the employment effects of expenditure on different tourism sectors. Table 3 shows the spend required to create a Full Time Job Equivalent in attractions and in other sectors. Clearly, investment in visitor attractions has been a relatively cheap method of job creation particularly in remote rural areas. However, it should be added that these estimates would not necessarily apply to any future expenditure, and it is important that simple duplication of visitor attractions does not occur in neighbouring towns and villages.

BETTER SERVICE AND BETTER SOUVENIRS

The Association of Scottish Visitor Attractions (ASVA) is a voluntary body dedicated to maintaining and improving standards in places to visit all over the country. ASVA provides a quality assurance scheme with particular reference to safety, cleanliness, provision for disabled visits, and the welcome provided by staff. Such quality assurance programmes are becoming increasingly common in service industries where it has often proved to be much more difficult to maintain quality standards than in manufacturing industries. The ASVA quality assurance programme is typical of the kind of initiatives that are necessary if we are to improve the standards of service (and hence increase income) at our heritage attractions. STB is now working with ASVA to develop the inspection programme.

Visitor attractions in Scotland have recently become much more professional in selling related crafts and souvenirs and the standard of souvenirs has risen. Christopher Harvie has concluded: 'In the 1950s families toured the Highlands in Morris Oxfords and complained about Japanese knick-knacks. In the 1970s they could buy quality pottery and handweaves to take home in their Datsuns.'[8] However, the Scottish tourism industry is not responsible for the fortunes of the car industry. We should be thankful that at least the souvenir industry has improved. (And the Japanese, for example, at St Andrews and Turnberry have seen investment opportunities in Scottish tourism which were not observed by local people.)

GLASGOW'S MUSEUMS OF COMPARATIVE RELIGION
THE COSTS PER JOB AT A GOOD EXAMPLE OF HERITAGE

As an example of excellent heritage presentation I commend to you the Museum of Comparative Religion in Glasgow. This museum opened in 1993 after a long and complicated gestation period with the main capital funding from Glasgow District Council, Glasgow Development Agency, the Friends of Cathedral, and the Scottish Tourist Board. In the present context the long procedure of getting the funding package together need not concern us. The museum which was designed by Ian Begg is in keeping with surrounding medieval buildings, and has galleries on the art of world religions, world religions, and religions in Scotland.

Here I am mainly concerned with the economic effects of investment of over £2.3 million and the creation of about 28 jobs. Treasury guidelines for public capital investment indicate that revenue deficits as well as total public capital costs should be included in the calculation of cost per job calculations. However, it is the policy of Glasgow District Council (and of British government generally) not to charge for entry to museums. Therefore, the cost per job is inevitably higher than if a fully commercial charging policy were adopted. Moreover displacement effects have also to be included, and these are particularly difficult to estimate. We estimated cost per job figures as shown in the table below.

These are generally high figures, albeit I believe the investment was essential to realise the full benefits of the substantial public sector investment in environmental improvements to Cathedral Square. In the long run the museum should attract about 300,000 visitors a year and is unique in the UK, if not in Europe and the world, by exhibiting objects and art representing all the world's major religions. It tells the fascinating story of Scotland's important part in the history of religion, and strengthens Glasgow's appeal as a visitor destination and cultural centre to Scots and non-Scots. The Museum can hold temporary exhibitions. It is publicised by the Greater Glasgow ATB, by STB, and by BTA, and is promoted in guides in 12 languages. The Glasgow Museum of Comparative Religion makes Hewison's earlier remarks about heritage appear rather snide and banal.

	Local Level	Scottish Level
STB displacement estimate, 25% of revenue deficit, total public capital cost	£13,834	£17,590
STB displacement estimate, Treasury public sector cost calculation	£21,485	£27,548
Scottish Office displacement estimate, Treasury public sector cost calculation	£32,276	£49,092

Note: Thanks to Jon Yates and Joe Summers of STB for the cost estimates.

UNEXPLOITED POTENTIAL
THE EXAMPLE OF INDUSTRIAL HERITAGE

Scotland's industrial heritage is of international significance, but so far we have not realised its full potential in terms of attracting visitors. New Lanark has been repaired sensitively and now attracts about 350,000 visitors each year, but much of Scotland' s industrial history is still not easily available to tourists. The major omission is probably ship-building, although the Scottish Maritime Museum at Irvine does very well with limited resources. Better interpretation of the offshore oil industry is also needed.

Last year, therefore, a group of bodies with interests in the presentation of industrial heritage commissioned a review of the sector with a view to maximising visitor revenue. The chosen consultants were PIEDA, the Edinburgh economic consulting firm, and Don Aldridge who had drafted the text for STB's *Guide to Site Interpretation*.[9] The steering group for the study includes representatives from STB, Scottish Enterprise, Highlands and Islands Enterprise, The National Museums of Scotland, Historic Scotland, the Scottish Museums Council, The Association of Independent Industrial Museums and Historical Sites, Cosla, and Scottish Office.

The main aims are to identify necessary improvements in the presentation of industrial heritage for visitors to Scotland, to provide guidance for public and private bodies involved in investment in heritage sites, and to make recommendations for the future development and marketing of industrial heritage in Scotland. The report is designed to be wide-ranging and is scheduled for completion later this year.

Our reasoning is that much of Scotlands 'romantic' history is already very well presented for visitors. We are famous for our castles, abbeys and stately homes, but we have not yet presented our industrial story in a way which will interest and attract visitors.

CONCLUSION

In terms of built attractions, then, omissions in our presentation of heritage are rapidly being filled. We have built on our collection of castles and museums and galleries and added features on conventional religion (Glasgow) and on our real religion (The Golf Museum at St Andrews). We should ensure that our nineteenth century industrial heritage is well presented before direct memories recede. Then the task for the next decade is probably to ensure that our natural environment is interpreted and made available to tourists without damage to our natural resources.

It is perhaps fitting that Scotland, with its history of battles at home and abroad, should follow the Spartan example.

TABLE 1

Likes of Overseas and British Tourists about their trip to Scotland 1992

Attractive features	Western European visitors	North American visitors	All Overseas visitors	Scottish visitors	English visitors	All British visitors
The scenery	83%	90%	86%	80%	84%	82%
The friendly people	73%	76%	74%	60%	67%	64%
Castles, churches, museums and sites of historic interest	70%	77%	73%	34%	36%	35%
Peace and quiet	60%	34%	48%	62%	56%	58%
The natural wildlife	40%	26%	34%	32%	42%	38%
Range/quality of accommodation	26%	43%	34%	33%	46%	40%
Good food and drink	19%	44%	28%	36%	46%	42%

Source: STB

TABLE 2

Major visitor attractions in Scotland 1993

Attractions with free admission	1992 Visitors	1993 Visitors	% Change 1992–93
Glasgow Art Gallery & Museum, Glasgow	874,688	796,380	-9%
Royal Botanic Garden, Edinburgh	662,459	787,107	+19%
Royal Museum of Scotland (Chambers Street), Edinburgh	460,249	502,428	+9%
Museum of Transport, Glasgow	492,978	493,577	–
New Lanark Village, New Lanark	400,000 *	400,000 *	–
The Burrell Collections, Glasgow	425,380	361,980	-15%
National Gallery of Scotland, Edinburgh	358,235	332,238	-7%
Aberdeen Art Gallery, Aberdeen	349,936	321,541	-8%
People's Palace, Glasgow	313,078	312,606	–
Museum of Childhood, Edinburgh	234,808	258,038	+10%

Attractions with paid admission	1992 Visitors	1993 Visitors	% Change 1992–93
Edinburgh Castle, Edinburgh	986,305	1,049,693	+6%
Edinburgh Zoo, Edinburgh	496,084	515,823	+4%
Culzean Castle & Country Park, Maybole	353,204	332,562	-6%
Palace of Holyrood House, Edinburgh	254,782	291,220	+14%
Stirling Castle, Stirling	263,546	286,163	+9%
Blair Castle, Blair Atholl	248,679	247,157	-1%
Glenturret Distillery, Crieff	146,005	193,008	+32%
Blair Drummond Safari & Leisure Park, Stirling	169,224	181,501	+7%
Urquhart Castle, Nr. Drumnadrochit	170,551	181,489	+6%
Glencoe Visitor Centre	160,633	158,024	-2%

* Estimate   Source: STB Visitor Attractions Survey

TABLE 3

Spend required to create one Full Time Job Equivalent (£)

	Urban	Rural	Remote Rural
All Hotels	23,981	33,223	29,070
Bed and Breakfast	8,071	7,092	11,287
Self Catering	27,100	21,552	18,382
Camping & Caravans	9,569	9,217	9,524
Restaurants & Bars	25,126	17,762	24,570
Tourist Shopping	44,444	42,735	19,531
Transport	49,505	46,948	69,930
Attractions	16,667	17,301	14,881

Source: Scottish Tourism Multiplier Study 1992 Vol 1, ESU Research Paper No 31, 1993, p101–102

The Author

Dr Gordon Adams was educated at Dundee High School, the University of St. Andrews, and at Queen's and McGill Universities in Canada. Before joining the Scottish Tourist Board, where he is now Director of Planning and Development, he held posts with the Canadian Federal Government, with Highlands and Island Development Board and at Glasgow University. He has been a visiting lecturer in Poland and India, and an adviser for the United Nations in Saudi Arabia.

References

[1] Wilkes, J., and Waywell, G., *Sparta – The World's first Heritage Centre*, Current Archaeology 1992, vol X1, No10, p432

[2] Brendon, P., *Thomas Cook: 150 Years of Popular Tourism* London, Secker and Warburg, 1991, p38

[3] Hewison, R., *The Heritage Industry: Britain in a Climate of Decline* London, Methuen, 1987, p144

[4] McCann-Erickson Scotland, *Manufacturing in Scotland: a Report for CBI Scotland,* 1994

[5] Scottish Tourism Co-ordinating Group, *Draft Strategic Plan for Scottish Tourism, 1994*

[6] *The Charter for the Arts in Scotland,* 1992, HMSO, p5

[7] Scottish Tourist Board, *Stirling Old Town: Tourism Development Strategy*, STB, (unpublished report), 1991

[8] Harvie, C., *No Gods and Precious Few Heroes: Scotland 1914–1980*, Edward Arnold, 1981, p60

[9] Scottish Tourist Board, *Site Interpretation: A Practical Guide,* STB, 1993

10

A STRATEGY FOR THEME TRAILS

David Silbergh, Magnus Fladmark,
Gordon Henry and Michael Young

Theme trails have a long history, and have in recent years become a significant tool both in conservation education and national and regional tourism marketing strategies in several European countries. They feature in public and private investment programmes alike, and now command a level of resource allocation which in other fields would merit the attention of policy analysts. However, the issue of theme trails (referred to hereafter as trails), has merited little academic attention, particularly in regard to the Scottish experience. Trails as we know them in the UK today, made their debut in the 1960s (eg the nature trail at Crathes Castle) with a proliferation in the 1970s, and the small body of literature which does exist, dates mainly from this time.

Why then, should we concern ourselves with trails? If for no other reason, because such projects often attract not insignificant amounts of money from the public purse, seemingly in a policy vacuum, and with little clear evidence of the benefits which accrue from them.

The starting point for any discussion of trails, is to seek a meaningful definition. Existing attempts to define the subject range from Goodey's 1975 brief statement that a trail is 'a published guide to a specific mapped route,' to the more elaborate and somewhat 'tongue in cheek' attempt by Henry and Young (1993): 'An integrated, environmentally sensitive, sustainable, relevant interpretation of a theme, in an area, through the sympathetic development of facilities and marketing, generating economic and social benefit whilst satisfying consumer demand, local need, and environmental considerations.' Our definition for the purpose of this review is:

> A theme trail is a route for walking, cycling, riding, driving or other forms of transport that draws on the natural or cultural heritage of an area to provide an educational experience that will enhance visitor enjoyment. It is marked on the ground or on maps, and interpretive literature is normally available to guide the visitor, ie

- the theme highlights a specific feature of local, regional or national significance;
- there is a continuous right of passage;
- appropriate facilities exist to enhance visitor satisfaction, eg toilets, accommodation, refreshments, visitor centres, museums etc;
- a continuum exists from the mainly educational to the mainly enjoyment orientated experience.

A TAXONOMY

Given the above definition, a vast array of trails can be listed. As long ago as 1978, the Dartington Amenity Research Trust estimated that there were over 800 trails in existence in the UK. Yet, on the face of it many of these trails have little in common. In devising a strategy for theme trails which can be equally relevant to the 150 mile car-based *Castle Trail* and the *Aberdeen Castlegate Walk* which is just over one mile long, a taxonomy of trails is necessary for a structured analysis of the subject.

The Dartington Trust classed trails under Farm, Nature, Forest, Town, or Ancient Monument. The Scottish Tourist Board for information purposes uses the categories: Attraction, People, Town, Architectural/Archaeological, and Heritage. However, there are problems with a subject specific taxonomy. For example, *Old Perth Trail*, could easily be classified as a 'town', 'architectural/archaeological' or 'heritage' trail, which can lead to confusion rather than clarity of analysis. Furthermore, trails can often have as much in common across classes as within them, eg *Burns Heritage Trail* (people) and *The Malt Whisky Trail* (attraction) are both car-based, well signposted with specifically developed visitor facilities, and they are internationally marketed.

Our review of the literature has led us to the conclusion that the principal classification of trails should be according to the criteria of geographical *scale*. Then, there would be sub-classification according to *means of transport* which allows trails to be discussed not only in terms of their inter-relationships, but also enables trails to be planned and operated as an integrated system. For example, the regional, car-based *North East Scotland Coastal Trail,* could and should be cross-referenced to the local scale, *Aberdeen Harbour Walk,* and vice versa. This would encourage the driver to get out and walk, and it would highlight the links between the City and the rest of the North East to the Aberdeen Harbour walker. Further criteria for sub-classification would be whether trails are signposted on the ground, or are used entirely on the basis of printed literature in the form of leaflets, fold-out posters, pamphlets or guide books. Another important distinction is whether a trail is mainly used as a self-guided facility, or mainly for guided tours.

Criteria for classification and sub-classification may be listed as follows:

National	Car	Signposted
Regional	Bicycle	Printed literature
Local	Horseback	Guided
Site	Foot	Self-guided
	Public transport	

OBJECTIVES

The primary objectives of trails will differ from case to case, and we agree with Goodey (1974) who stressed that: 'those producing trails or walks should have a very clear idea as to the purpose of their proposed trail or walk before setting the process of trail-making in motion.' We suggest that, when establishing a trail, the following objectives should be borne in mind:

1. It should be designed to facilitate the discovery (education) and enjoyment (entertainment) of local heritage assets both by local residents and by visitors to an area.
2. Each route should be planned according to its strategic context, ie with due regard to and with suitable links between national, regional and local trails.
3. Planning of a route should be integrated with the presentation of local facilities such as parks, museums, visitor centres, hotels etc.
4. Trail literature should convey a cultural and/or conservation message that is appropriate for the chosen route.
5. Trails should be regarded as a means of managing visitor flows effectively, whether it is to minimise ecological impact or to maximise economic benefit.
6. Marketing potential should be considered from the outset, as part of the overall implementation strategy.
7. Projections should be made of economic, social and cultural benefits.

In regard to the last above, *Paths, Routes and Trails* by the Countryside Commission (1988) stated that: 'The tourist potential of such routes is important because of the economic benefits associated with their development in the form of spending by visitors on food, transport and accommodation. Such spending helps support the infrastructure and services in the countryside to the benefit of local people and visitors alike.' However, given the paucity of empirical data to prove or disprove whether any significant level of spending is related to theme trails, great care must be taken when assessing such statements.

Key questions are: How much money is clearly trail related, and would not have been spent without a trail? Even if trails do have a substantial effect on expenditure, is it at the expense of other areas, ie do trails succeed in changing patterns, rather than the levels of expenditure? The basic inputs for calculations are the percentage of traffic volume diverted from main trunk routes and the appropriate multiplier indices of expenditure by visitors using the proposed trail.

With regard to objective five, the ability to manage or influence visitor flows can be of great importance. As the Countryside Commission consultation paper on trails (1988) noted, 'A wide choice of well-promoted regional routes will further reduce any problems of erosion and spread both the load and the benefits.' See Thomas Huxley, Chapter 14, in this volume for further discussion of related issues.

The full implications of objective six must not be ignored. Marketing has a central role to play, as confirmed by the West Highland Way Survey (1981):

> One party in eight came from overseas, two-thirds of these from the Netherlands: from discussion with walkers it was clear that much of the Dutch interest in the Way could be ascribed to the information service provided by a single outdoor equipment retailer in Amsterdam.

For strategic planning purposes it is important to distinguish between the process of choosing and developing a specific theme for a route and the basic taxonomy proposed above. The system of classification is essentially a means of establishing a geographical hierarchy to avoid duplication and to ensure compatibility of provision at different levels of planning so that a clear and ordered picture is projected to the visitor who is deciding on what to do and where to go. A good example of confusion at present is the *Burns Heritage Trail*. This is often thought of as a national trail, because Robert Burns is a nationally important name, and is often featured prominently in national promotion campaigns, but it is essentially a regional trail.

PRODUCT DEVELOPMENT

An essential prerequisite of a successful trail initiative is a comprehensive assessment of all relevant heritage assets of an area before the process of choosing the actual theme to be used. This is done from a shortlist of theme options, and the chances of success are greatly enhanced by systematic research, defining a relevant theme that has a strong and appealing image. In the words of the Countryside Commission (1988):

> The route should not merely consist of linked rights of way but offer a theme, for example an historic route, or a geographical feature or link obvious attractive destinations. Rivers, canals and the coast have special potential.

However, Bayfield and Barrow (1976) noted that it is not unusual to find cases where:

> trails have been provided because it is fashionable to do so, little thought being given to their justification, to the writing and compilation of the booklets describing them, or to the possible undesirable side effects of increased public pressure if they are wrongly located.

To succeed, a trail must be *practicable*, ie accessible and of the appropriate length. It should also be developed with care for the environment, both in terms of its physical implementation and the interpretive information conveyed to ensure *sustainability*. For example, where used, signposting or waymarking should not only be complete, but also aesthetically acceptable. The trail user must be treated to a quality experience in all facets of the trail, from having easily read printed literature available to high standards of catering and accommodation on offer along the route. Often, the quality of a trail is judged by the quality of its poorest facility. This is why care must be exercised in ensuring that all the facilities on a trail are maintained to the same high standard.

It is essential that target groups are identified early in the process of choosing a theme (schools, local residents and/or tourists) so that their aspirations and motivations are clearly understood. The interpretive literature and promotional strategy should be designed accordingly, and once in place, the trail must be *monitored*, and changes made where appropriate in light of such monitoring. Unfortunately it is still as true today, as it was when Goodey wrote in 1975, that 'the evaluation and co-ordination of trails has run behind their production.'

Whilst the ideal trail is certainly to be aspired to, the authors recognise that it is not always easy, for example, to guarantee the quality of catering along the length of an extensive trail. However, the review of literature has revealed cases of rigorous planning and development such as, the *Cwmcarn Scenic Forest Drive Study* (1976) which analyses the development of a forest drive. The first step was a *consultation* exercise, heavily reliant on *collaboration* between the Forestry and Countryside Commissions, the RAC, and various departments of the Monmouthshire County Council and three District Councils. The *planning* phase addressed questions relating to the environmental capacity of and facilities for the drive; surfacing and construction work; pricing; interpretation; publicity; management and staffing. Very importantly, it also deals with research work to monitor the drive's implementation, assessing visitor behaviour and attitudes, and the use made of facilities. This monitoring revealed that parking and toilet provision was inadequate; there was too little interpretation; and the trail surface was deteriorating more rapidly than expected. This monitoring procedure allowed action to be taken to address these problems at an early stage.

In *Planning for Success: The Lessons of the Forest of Dean Sculpture Trail*, Orrom (1993), highlights the need to establish a trail with a concomitant *management plan* to maintain and enhance the trail on a long term basis. The plan established the following requirements:

> ... firstly to maintain the quality of experience ... and secondly to cope with the demands of the public as popularity of the trail grows. The first and overriding need will be to publish a guide and provide minimum signposting so that the public can go round the trail without getting lost ... The next considerations will be car parking, lavatories and a café. A studio, exhibition hall and classroom may have to follow.

All of which did follow, ensuring the trail enjoyed 'great success with over 100,000 visitors annually,' and it could be said that the distinguishing feature of these two forest trails lies not so much in the implementation of the trail (construction etc) but in the pre-implementation (consultation and planning) and post-implementation (monitoring) phases. Sadly, it is often all too easy for a proposed trail to be rushed into existence and subsequently suffer from lack of after care, as monitoring has not been undertaken to identify requirements for maintenance and modifications.

Following the statement of aims and the setting of objectives, the essential steps in the process of product development are:

1. Survey of heritage assets and evaluation for theme selection.
2. Profile assessment of client groups.
3. Theme selection and testing against strategic context.
4. Consultation and agreement of collaboration.
5. Planning of trail and facilities.
6. Implementation.
7. Monitoring and remedial action on feedback.

SCOTTISH TRAILS

A review of national trails in Scotland is incomplete without reference to what is fondly referred to in tourism circles as 'The Milk Run', and which has been promoted to first-time visitors to Scotland for a very long time. Taking in Edinburgh, Perthshire, Inverness and the West Coast, it has been marketed aggressively in the UK and overseas and is still regarded as the 'all-Scotland' theme trail by operators and tour planners. However, we would class this type of trail as a national 'tourist route' which has different objectives/format and is deployed for different marketing purposes to theme trails. Although such tourist routes fall outside the strict definitional framework of this paper, we would argue that they are a significant element in the family of trails and must be included in the broader framework for strategic policy formulation.

There are several formally designated car trails which in aggregate form national tourist routes that are designed to encourage motorists to slow down, get off the main roads, and to enjoy the countryside at leisure. Amongst these are the route from Tarbert, through *Argyll* to Fort William, touching the Northern end of Loch Lomond and including the Crinan Canal and Connel Bridge. Others are the *Borders*, from Carlisle to Edinburgh using the A7; the *Clyde Valley*, from Abington to Glasgow following the River Clyde; *Deeside*, from Perth to Aberdeen, through Royal Deeside; *Fife*, from the Forth Bridge through the ancient Kingdom of Fife to Dundee; the *Forth Valley*, an alternative route from Edinburgh to Stirling; *Galloway*, from Gretna to Ayr, through Burns Country; *Highland*, from Aberdeen to Inverness, through Upper Donside and the Whisky Country; *Moray Firth*, from Inverness to Loch Fleet, following the Beauly Firth; and *Perthshire*, from Dunblane to Pitlochry, through the Sma' Glen.

We have found four examples of national trails in Scotland that have been designed for use by car or coach borne visitors. One is the *Fishing Heritage Trail*, which was introduced in 1984 and covered the East Coast from Berwick-upon-Tweed to John o' Groats, with island extensions including Orkney and Shetland. This excellent initiative was unfortunately allowed to fall into decline largely due to the difficulty of retaining continuous support and commitment over an extended period of time from such a large number of organisations, including commitment and firm strategic direction at national level. Truncated into the *North East Scotland Coastal Trail*, it now only exists as a route from Perth to Inverness.

The second example is *Mary Queen of Scots* (Scottish Tourist Board, 1991). It consists of four separate tour routes, which in their entirety pass through all mainland regions. The format is a fold-out poster with a map, pictures and informative text about places to visit, as well as a concise history of Queen Mary's life and some prominent figures of her time.

Our third example of a national trail is promoted as *Explore Scotland* by the Scottish Youth Hostels Association in partnership with the relevant transport operators and Historic Scotland. It is a tour package based on mixed modes of transport, and according to the Association's literature it is designed to give visitors '. . . the freedom of Scotland. Where you go is up to you, the choice is almost as spectacular as the views. Enjoy seven days unlimited coach travel on the services of Scottish Citylink Coaches. Discover all of the Scottish mainland plus the Isle of Skye. We also include six overnight vouchers for use at any Scottish Youth Hostel, an SYHA handbook and map, an Explorer Ticket giving you free entry to many historic monuments and castles en-route.'

The Association also promotes touring the properties of the National Trust for Scotland by car or public transport while utilising hostel accommodation. The literature is in the form of a map by Bartholomew called *SYHA Hostels and NTS Places to Visit: Touring Map Scotland*, together with another map *Scotland: Travel and Budget Accommodation*. The latter is a collaborative venture between the Scottish Youth Hostels Association, Caledonian MacBrayne, Scottish Citylink Coaches and the Scottish Tourist Board. This is an approach which we recommend for future development of trails. As noted by others, the provision of walkways and cycling routes without places for people to stay, would have been of little use.

Our search turned up a fourth national car trail, *The Pictish Trail: A Traveller's Guide to the Old Pictish Kingdoms* (1989). The trail runs from Edinburgh to Golspie and is divided into eleven parts, each designed for one day's touring. Like the above, it is not generally recognised as a trail, but it is included on our list because its concept and form are of considerable interest. Most of the trails have been established by public bodies or with some support from the public purse, but this initiative seems to have been driven entirely by the enthusiasm of Anthony Jackson who wrote *The Symbol Stones of Scotland* (new edition, 1990). The trail booklet contains a summary of Jackson's speculative interpretations of the Pictish symbol system, not universally accepted but no reason for dismissal of a well presented trail initiative that is based on one of Scotland's most potent heritage themes.

Walking trails are an important element of the recreational infrastructure of Scotland. At the national scale, there are three Long Distance Routes or Ways, established by the Countryside Commission for Scotland and now funded by Scottish Natural Heritage and run by the local authorities. They are: *The Speyside Way* in Moray, from Tugnet to Tomintoul; the 212 mile *Southern Upland Way* which runs from Cockburnspath in the East to Portpatrick in the West; and *The West Highland Way*, running from Glasgow through the suburb of Milngavie, past Loch Lomond, Rannoch Moor and Glencoe to Fort William. In addition to these three, there is a short section of *The Pennine Way* which strays over the Border to Kirk Yetholm in Roxburghshire. Borders Regional Council has recently completed an alternative spur to the Way which runs north along the Roman Road of Dere Street to Melrose, so that a link now exists between the Southern Upland Way and the English route. Impressive guidebooks have been published for all these trails, except for the Speyside Way. Indeed, the popularity of walking has risen steeply in recent years and there is a strong case for a supra-national strategy. In *Access Through Hostelling*, Lawson and Fladmark (1993) set out their vision for such a strategy which they called *The European Trail*, proposing that:

> ... here would be a walkway from John o' Groats to Inverness, which would link into the Great Glen Way to Fort William, and from there we already have the West Highland Way to Glasgow. From the 'European City of Culture' goes the Clyde Walkway, which will link with the Southern Upland Way to Melrose, whence into the Pennine Way down the spine of England. This route would eventually pick up the Thames Walk into London, and from there the North Downs Way already exists to take the walker to Dover or Folkestone.

... on the French side the walker would pick up the existing network of Grandes Randonnées which runs across the country to the Mediterranean at Marseilles. Since we are already working towards the grand idea of a monetary union for the whole of Europe, it does not seem too fanciful for national routes to be linked into a grand European strategy for access. It could have spurs across the Alps and down the Appennine spine of Italy. Another spur could be across the Pyrenees and through Spain to the Rock of Gibraltar. Other options would be eastwards through Germany to the Carpathian Mountains or northwards through Belgium, the Netherlands and Scandinavia to the North Cape.

Cycle trails are less common than car and walking trails, but not less important. The Scottish Tourist Board's booklet *Cycling in Scotland* outlines a number of cycle routes of differing scale throughout Scotland, eg at a national level crossing East to West from Lossiemouth to the Point of Ardnamurchan, utilising the Great Glen Cycleway on the Inverness to Fort William stretch.

Like the national routes, the vast majority of regional trails have been designed for the car user. In the Lowlands they include the *Burns Heritage Trail* in Ayrshire, which is now more than twenty years old, and was one of the first examples of a properly planned and signposted route, designed to capitalise on the Scottish Bard's popularity both in the UK and overseas. It has been popular but is now suffering from lack of financial support and co-ordination, although there is renewed interest from the Japanese market. The *Christian Heritage Trail*, in Dumfries and Galloway was designed to divert tourist traffic from the main route into Scotland. The *Scottish Borders Woollen Trail*, a circular 100 mile long trail taking visitors from sheep-to-shop, served as a catalyst for the development of a range of visitor attractions, although original plans were subsequently affected by recession in the woollen industry. *Scotland's Mill Trail Country*, Clackmannan, is a good example of private/public partnership.

Several regional car trails exist in the Highlands and the North East. Gordon District Tourist Board established the *Castle Trail* to create an identity for itself in the marketplace. It capitalises on the area's wealth of historic properties, but its popularity has been negatively affected by an inability to provide accommodation in any of the castles, although it is a good example of signposting. The *Malt Whisky Trail* in Moray is also more than twenty years old, and is perhaps the best example of private/public sector partnership enjoying financial support from distilleries and providing high quality visitor attractions and retail outlets. There is extensive promotion in the UK and overseas, where the full-colour leaflet is in great demand and there are around 140,000 visitors per annum to the Glenfiddich distillery alone, although not all of them can be attributed to the trail. *Scotland's Quality Trail*, which had impact with both the media and the travel trade, failed because one of the main partners lost its manufacturing element and because the attractions had proved too far apart to cover in a reasonable time. It has been partly re-introduced as *Quality Around Speyside*; and finally, the *Loch Ness Monster Trail* is a 70 mile round trip circumnavigating Loch Ness, giving visitors the opportunity to enjoy the beauty of the area and explore the age-old mystery of the Loch.

In recent years regional and local cycleways have emerged as an important element of the recreational infrastructure in parts of the country. Much of recent development has been made possible through the initiative and work of the voluntary organisation SUSTRANS. Active throughout Scotland, it is dedicated to encouraging the use of sustainable transport through the provision of integrated cycle and pedestrian routes. There is now the beginning of a regional network. For example, from Glasgow the cyclist can follow SUSTRANS routes in the direction of all the cardinal points on the compass. North following the *Glasgow/Loch Lomond/Killin Cycle Way* to Killin on Loch Rannoch, or East to Edinburgh via Airdrie and Bathgate. Heading South on the *Glasgow to Irvine Pedestrian and Cycle Route*, the Lochwinnoch to Kilwinning section forms an *Art Trail* in itself, and the route literature cross-refers to other trails such as the *Paisley Town Trail*. To the West Greenock can be reached from Glasgow via Paisley and the *Johnstone and Greenock Railway Path*. Although SUSTRANS is a voluntary organisation, these routes were felt to be of the utmost importance by several public bodies, and significant resourcing was provided for their establishment by the Scottish Office, Countryside Commission for Scotland, British Rail and local authorities.

Other examples of regional and local cycleways include a *3 to 5 Day Tour of the Borders* from Peebles (including part of the Tweed Cycleway) as promoted in *Cycling in Scotland*, Lothian Regional Council's *Cycle and Walk in Lothian* and *Cycling in Ayrshire*. The authors believe that the development of cycle trails should be given higher priority than at present to reduce the reliance on the car for recreational purposes, and to minimise the impacts of mountain biking in environmentally sensitive areas through initiatives like Forest Enterprise's *Cycling in the Forest: North East Scotland*.

A great number of regional and local walking trails exist, such as the *Glen Tilt Trail* and *The Eildon Hills*. They range from the privately operated (and presumably profitable) *Audio Tour of the Royal Mile* to nature trails and forest walks. Local walking trails are often on a community scale, conceived and produced by Community Councils or other community organisations, eg *A Walking Tour of the Royal Burgh of Wick* by Wick Community Council, *Stonehaven Heritage Trail* by the Stonehaven Heritage Society. Urban and rural, architectural, forest, nature and historical, walking trails abound.

There are some excellent urban trails like the *Patrick Geddes Heritage Trail: Old Town Edinburgh* (1982) which was masterminded by David Roderick Cameron, and *Elgin Town Trail* (1983). The former was produced by a partnership comprised of the City of Edinburgh District Council, Scottish Tourist Board and the Sir Patrick Geddes Memorial Trust, and the latter by Moray District Council and the Moray Society. The scope and style of trail literature vary a great deal and there can be no preferred model. At one end of the spectrum is the straightforward fold out poster leaflet with a map and accompanying illustrated text. At the other is the handsome booklet with high quality artwork, and in this genre we found the series produced in 1977 by East Sussex County Council in a class of its own. The artistic quality of Michael Barnard's drawings is quite exquisite, and the three booklets in our collection are keepsakes in their own right *Lewes Town Walk, A Walk Round Burtons' St Leonards* and *Battle Town and Abbey Walk*.

Site trails are normally short walking trails, specifically presented as an integral part of a wider experience, for example, *New Lanark Heritage Trail, The Two Rivers Trail* at Dean Castle Country Park and *Glen Park Nature Trail* at Gleniffer Countryside Park. Site trails can be found in a vast array of locations, one unusual example from South of the Border being the nature trail at Oldbury-on-Severn nuclear power station.

A selection of literature from the Theme Trail Collection held by the Robert Gordon University Heritage Unit is listed at the end of this paper. An examination of the titles alone gives an impression of the diverse nature of trails in Scotland and elsewhere.

IDEAS IN THE MAKING

Most Area Tourist Boards and local authorities have an involvement with trails. Grampian Highlands and Aberdeen (a partnership of five local Boards, which will become one of the fourteen new tourism marketing authorities recently proposed by the Scottish Office) has developed some strong images. In response to the national *Tourism and Environment Initiative*, the Loch Lomond, Stirling and Trossachs Tourist Board has recently revamped (and much improved) *The Trossachs Trail*. The authors firmly believe that initiatives such as *Tourism and the Environment* and *Tourism and the Arts*, as well as the pending reorganisation of tourism marketing, will allow for a review of many trails. It might be said that prudent review and (where necessary) adjustments to existing trails could prove more cost-effective than a more revolutionary 'clean slate' approach to trail development.

Among new and subject specific suggestions for trail development are: *Archaeology*, Grampian Region (Gordon District in particular) has the finest examples of standing stones in the country. Plans are under way for the development of a trail, with better access to individual sites, better interpretation at each location, and a state-of-the-art visitor centre. Fraserburgh and Aberdeen have strong connections with *Thomas Blake Glover*, the 19th century Scotsman who became the 'Scottish Samurai' after founding the Japanese navy, introducing Japan to Western industrial methods and sending Japanese students to Britain. Plans include the development of the Glover family home in Aberdeen and Kinnaird Head lighthouse, where Glover's father was keeper.

Both Glasgow and Aberdeen have plans to develop around the *Environment* theme. Protection of the environment is critical in the development of any attraction or theme. The interpretation of the natural and built environment around us in an exciting, innovative and educational manner is in the long-term essential to protect the very fabric that makes Scotland the popular tourist destination it is. In respect of the *Agricultural Heritage*, there are some wonderful attractions, most notable Aden Country Park in Banff and Buchan, and there must be potential for further development of farm trails in many parts of the country to highlight the great diversity of agricultural landscapes throughout Scotland. Apart from Robert Burns and Lewis Grassic Gibbon, there must be opportunities for other *Literary Figures* like Lord Byron, Bram Stoker and Robert Louis Stevenson. *Historic Figures* like Bonnie Prince Charlie also come to mind with 1995 being the 250th Anniversary of the '45. Although there is a need for principal national and regional trails to have some permanence, we feel that a static approach might in many circumstances be counter productive, eg interpretation of a theme can and should be varied over time and components added and subtracted to encourage repeat visits.

Other interesting scenarios can emerge from new and different approaches, eg could trails be successful with more detailed maps and less signposting/waymarking? What of the potential to use theme trails as a means of bringing attention to the less attractive side of Scottish life? To quote from Goodey (1975),

> The trail should not be intended merely as a guide book and it should show the bad as well as the good . . . few trails stimulate thought on housing condition or social stress, indeed, few pass through areas where these matters may be seen as a major theme.

There are already educational trails that address such issues, eg the Aberdeen Urban Studies centre *Looking at Houses* trail encourages participants to appraise not only Georgian and Victorian structures, but dilapidated local authority flats too. Whether or not the tourist would be at all interested in such a trail is a matter of speculation, but readers should be aware that such trails have been developed to good effect in other countries, eg Harlem, USA and Soweto in South Africa.

Another important consideration is the development of public transport and walking/cycling trails that begin and end within easy reach of public transport. Fifteen per cent of British tourists on holiday in Scotland arrive by regular train/bus/air services (ie 870,000 visitors per annum). When added to the 72 per cent of overseas tourists who arrive without a vehicle (650,000 per annum), this gives a potential market of over 1.5 million people annually, excluding use by local people (*Tourism in Scotland*, 1992). In many respects the potential of public transport has failed to be recognised by trail planners, which is surprising given the potentially large market and good environmental profile which could be exploited. The Scottish Tourist Board's

Cycling in Scotland certainly gives full information on access by public transport to all listed trails.

A good example of the type of trail which the authors would like to see developed is *The Clyde Walkway*, now partially implemented by the local authorities. It was conceived by Norman Logan as a *walking and public transport trail* in two sections, the first from Glasgow Green to Garrion Bridge, and section two carrying on to New Lanark. In his 1973 series of articles, Logan noted: 'You can cover the first section to Garrion Bridge in five easy afternoon strolls, returning by train or bus.' There are public transport links available at the end of each of the sub-sections: Cambuslang, Uddingston, Blantyre/Bothwell, Motherwell/Hamilton, and Garrion Bridge. The second section from Garrion Bridge to New Lanark was described by Logan as 'paralleled by the A72 road and easily reached by car or Central SMT red bus. Hutcheson's buses cross Garrion Bridge on their way from Wishaw to Larkhall,' and he referred to this part as being possible to achieve 'in the course of three afternoon strolls.'

PROS AND CONS

When the total costs of planning, developing, co-ordinating, promoting and maintaining are considered, (signposting alone cost £26,000 for the Castle Trail in 1983) one might be forgiven for asking: Why Theme Trails? It is a difficult question to answer as there has been little, if any, detailed research on their economic benefit. However, their effectiveness as a marketing tool is generally accepted (Henry and Young, 1993) and some key benefits of theme trails are:

1. A route initiative allows several agencies to pool limited funds for both marketing and development of a joint project.
2. The whole is greater than the sum of the parts, ie castles on a promoted trail will attract more visitors than castles promoted on their own.
3. Media coverage can be gained more easily by trails than their individual attractions, eg the Press and Journal have featured articles on the Victorian Heritage and Castle trails.
4. Trails provide opportunities for enhancing an area's tourism profile, eg Kincardine and Deeside Tourist Board capitalise on their area's links with Queen Victoria for their *Victorian Heritage Trail*.
5. A successful trail can act as an inducement to improve standards at individual attractions and accommodation facilities, extending opening hours, as well as lead to expansion and new development, eg the Speyside Cooperage on the Malt Whisky Trail.

6.   Trails provide opportunities for offering special interest itineraries.

Developing and maintaining theme trails are demanding tasks and the difficulties should not be underestimated. Particular attention must be paid to the fact that even when a trail is in place it requires monitoring, maintenance and remedial development. Research by the Dartington Trust (1978) showed that 'the amount of management required was often underestimated, and many trails in the study appeared neglected in one way or another'. In respect of the West Highland Way, Aitken (1982) noted the need for a 'more active management role'. Some important considerations for trail planners are as follows:

1.   A trail theme must be relevant to the heritage assets of an area, and can be counter productive unless it has been designed according to clear aims and objectives, as well as being specifically designed for niche markets.
2.   Signposting is expensive, takes time to design, can be subject to planning restrictions and requires maintenance.
3.   Trails must have a long shelf life to be effective and, when starting an initiative, it should be borne in mind that many such initiatives are public/private collaborative ventures and such partnership between public and private sectors can prove time-consuming and frustrating, especially in relation to funding.
4.   Too many trails may bore the travelling public and the Scottish Tourist Board should monitor reaction to changing trends, care should also be taken to ensure that the overall distance and the distance between attractions is not too great.
5.   Tourism strategies should have regard to the fact that theme trails may exert a displacement effect with regard to visitor spending that is detrimental to adjacent areas and attractions.

Ultimately, achieving, maintaining and developing the essential high quality required to meet the needs of the discerning visitor of today requires continuing commitment from all partners, guaranteed funding, unflagging enthusiasm and creative thinking.

LESSONS FROM OVERSEAS

Our limited review of overseas experience has led us to the conclusion that there is an urgent need for more international exchange of information among researchers and policy-makers. There can be no doubt that there are many lessons which we in Scotland and the rest of the UK can learn from theme trail experience abroad, and The Robert Gordon University is taking action to expand its collection of trail literature from around the world.

The North Americans in particular have an impressive network of trails, many of which are in themselves historic. The best known of these, *The Appalachian Way*, was begun in 1921 and completed in 1937. Although sixteen years may appear a somewhat protracted time scale, it is remarkably short when one considers the implications of constructing a 2,100 mile route through the eastern USA from Georgia to Maine. Furthermore, that it was achieved with no support from the public sector is astounding in comparison with UK experience. Of particular interest is the *Blue Ridge Parkway*, a trail through the mountains of Virginia and North Carolina which is designated as a National Park, and in an urban setting the *Freedom Trail* in Boston, Massachusetts has achieved international renown. In Canada, a coast-to-coast-to-coast trail is planned, to be known as the *Trans Canada Trail*. When complete it will be the longest trail in the world at over 9,000 miles. As the Appalachian Way before it, this ambitious project's success is reliant on voluntary, not governmental effort. We were especially impressed by the achievements of the Province of Nova Scotia where the whole tourism product is geared to trails.

Europe, as noted above, is well placed to develop a trans-Continental network of routes. A great many routes already exist, and the French in particular have a highly successful and extensive system of trails known as Grandes Randonnées, again mainly implemented and maintained by voluntary effort. Indeed, the antecedents of walking trails are found in Europe. The Black Forest Association was formed to develop trails as long ago as 1864, *Den Norske Turistforening* was established in 1868 to promote walking trails in Norway, and Sweden's *Kungsleden* in Lapland came into being before the First World War.

Academic interest in trails has also developed to a greater extent overseas than in the UK, eg Trent University in Ontario have identified a need for expertise in the planning, development, interpretation and management of trails and has responded by establishing a Trail Studies Unit. Tried and tested methodologies for the comparative study of public policy exist, but little attention has been paid in the UK to the study of trails. This is perhaps surprising, given the tourism significance of trails and, as an attempt to address this lack of comparative study, The Robert Gordon University is now developing links with universities in North America and some European countries.

TOWARDS A STRATEGIC FRAMEWORK

Although our research for this paper can not be said to present a complete picture of all theme trails in Scotland, it has made it possible to gain a good overview of the situation and enabled us to discover some of the key issues facing the industry. Our first call is for a national strategy to facilitate more integrated planning of trails at different scales, ie better links between national, regional and local levels of action and better cross-reference between different types of trails catering for all types of transport by car, bicycle, walking and public transport.

Another key consideration is the link between theme trails and heritage interpretation strategies. A potential threat to the integrated development and presentation of trails is the dual institutional framework comprised of the national and Local Enterprise Network (responsible for tourism development) and the Area Tourist Boards (responsible for marketing). A national framework is needed to guide the process of integration and to specify the roles of the relevant actors in policy making. Indeed, the policy situation today is little altered from 1974, when Goodey wrote: 'To suggest that there is a British programme of trails and walks is, in itself, rather ambitious as there is at present, no such programme, no co-ordination of activity and little sharing of experience.'

There is now a far greater number and diversity of theme trails in existence, some with literature produced to very high standards, while many others fail to impress. Many are signposted/waymarked, many are not. The real problem lies with the lack of linkages between trails and the absence of cross-referencing from leaflet to leaflet. For example, the series of trail guides by Ayrshire Tourist Board *Car Touring in Ayrshire, Cycling in Ayrshire* and *Walks in Ayrshire* is to be welcomed as it recognises that there is more than one transport option available to those who wish to explore the area. Indeed, *Walks in Ayrshire* includes cross-references to no fewer than 38 other walks and accompanying sources of information. Whilst this is far-sighted (and has obviously been well researched) in comparison with most other trail literature, it still lacks any cross-reference to encourage multi-transport options, ie no mention is made of the companion guides for drivers and cyclists in the same series. The Ayrshire series of guides is commended as a good attempt at producing integrated literature, and by the inclusion of references to the other guides in the series the Board could achieve the fully integrated approach called for in this paper.

The importance of trails with respect to the discipline of heritage interpretation is well expressed in the words of the Dartington Trust (1978):

> Self-guided trails are the most widespread interpretive facilities in Britain. The interpretive objectives of creating self-guided trails vary according to the circumstances, but are broadly those which apply to interpretation generally – to add to the enjoyment of a visit to a place by provoking interest in and providing information about it and other aspects of the environment; and through increased awareness to promote a respect for, and hopefully better use of, the resource being interpreted.

Given this interdependence, any strategy for theme trails based on our suggested system would fit easily within the framework for heritage interpretation proposed by Fladmark (1993) in *Discovering the Personality of a Region: Strategic Interpretation in Scotland*. His proposals are for a hierarchy of interpretive plans, fitting together like Russian Dolls at the local, regional and national levels. Obvious similarities exist with our proposals for theme trails to be planned according to the Russian Doll Principle, with local, district and regional trails progressively related to a national strategy. A national strategy for interpretation should therefore provide the context for a trail strategy and vice versa, and we believe that the appropriate vehicle for introducing the necessary direction by Central Government is through the system of our National Planning Policy Guidelines. It is also our view that there is now an urgent need to establish a Scottish Register of Trails as a national reference point for those who are planning trails as well as for the industry generally.

In conclusion, it is our belief that if future theme trails are planned, implemented and monitored within a national strategic framework with appropriate reference to regional interpretation strategies, the result will be an improved product and better value-for-money, both for taxpayer and private investor alike.

The Authors and Acknowledgements

David Silbergh holds a BA (Hons) in Public Administration from the Robert Gordon University. Since joining the Faculty of Design as a research assistant in 1993, he has worked as a member of the core teams of the Centre for Environmental Studies and the Heritage Unit. He is pursuing part-time PhD studies on government policy for sustainable development in the rural environment.

Magnus Fladmark holds qualifications in horticulture, architecture and town planning. Following spells in the Scottish Office and at Edinburgh University, he was Assistant Director of the Countryside Commission for Scotland 1976–92. Appointed to establish the Robert Gordon University Heritage Unit in 1992, he was made professor in 1993.

Gordon Henry was trained at Gray's School of Art, now part of The Robert Gordon University, and at Aberdeen College of Education. Formerly Design Manager and Company Director with Aberdeen University Press, he is currently Chief Executive of Grampian, Highlands and Aberdeen. He is Chairman of the Scottish Conference Association, President of the British Association of Tourism Officers and Vice-Chairman STB UK Marketing Committee.

Michael Young trained at the Scottish Hotel School, Strathclyde University. He was Head of Tourism Marketing with Highlands & Islands Enterprise, and is now Deputy Director for UK Marketing at the Scottish Tourist Board. He is a Fellow of the Tourism Society, and a Member of the Hotel, Catering and Institutional Management Association.

The authors gratefully acknowledge the helpful advice from Dr Brian Hay, Tom Band and Martin Orrom in the preparation of this paper, as well as from Sheila and Richard Hill who kindly made available their collection of trail literature from several European countries.

References

Aitken, R., *The West Highland Way*, 3rd ed., Countryside Commission for Scotland, 1990

Aitken, R., *The West Highland Way: Report of a Survey of Walkers on the Long Distance Footpath July to September 1981*, Countryside Commission for Scotland, 1982

Bayfield, N.G. and Barrow, G.C., *The Use and Attraction of Nature Trails in Upland Britain, in Biological Conservation*, Vol. 9, 1976, pp. 267–292

Beynon, J., *Farm Trails in the Countryside*, in The Planner, Vol. 61, 1975, pp. 52–56

Countryside Commission, *Cwmcarn Scenic Forest Drive*, CCP 96, CC, 1976

Countryside Commission, *Paths, Routes and Trails: A Consultation Paper*, CCP 253, Cheltenham, CC, 1988

Dartington Amenity Research Trust, *Self Guided Trails*, CCP 110, Cheltenham, Countryside Commission, 1978

Dartmoor National Park Authority, *Guided Walks*, CCP 130, Cheltenham, Countryside Commission, 1980

Fladmark, M., *Discovering the Personality of a Region: Strategic Interpretation in Scotland in Fladmark, J.M. (ed)*, Heritage: Conservation, Interpretation and Enterprise, London, Donhead, 1993, pp. 125–140

Goodey, B., *Urban Trails: Origins and Opportunities*, in The Planner, Vol. 61, 1975, pp. 29–30

Goodey, B., *Urban Walks and Town Trails: Origins, Principles and Sources, Research Memorandum 40*, Centre for Urban and Regional Studies, University of Birmingham, 1974

Henry, G. and Young, M., *Theme Trails in Marketing Strategies*, paper delivered to 'The Robert Gordon University Heritage Convention', Aberdeen, 1993

Lawson, P. and Fladmark, M., *Access Through Hostelling: The Role and Policies of SYHA*, in Fladmark, J.M. (ed), Heritage: Conservation, Interpretation and Enterprise, London, Donhead, 1993, pp. 161–174

Logan, N., *The Clyde Walkway*, in The Scots Magazine, 1973

Long-Distance Routes Working Party, *Development of Long-Distance Routes in Scotland: The Report of a Working Party set up by CCS and COSLA*, 1986

Orrom, M., *Planning for Success: The Lessons of the Forest of Dean Sculpture Trail*, UK, paper delivered to 'Tickon International Symposium', Rudkøbing, Langeland, Denmark, 1993

Press and Journal, *By Royal Appointment: On The Victorian Heritage Trail*, in Discovering Gordon and Deeside: A Press and Journal Supplement, April 1994, pp. 4–5

Press and Journal, *History Comes Alive on the Castle Trail*, in Discovering Gordon and Deeside: A Press and Journal Supplement, April 1994, p. 3

Scottish Tourism Co-ordinating Group, *Tourism and the Arts in Scotland: A Development Strategy*, Edinburgh, Scottish Tourist Board, 1993

Scottish Tourism Co-ordinating Group, *Tourism and the Scottish Environment: A Sustainable Partnership*, Edinburgh, Scottish Tourist Board, 1991

Scottish Tourist Board, *Effectiveness of National Tourist Route and Thistle Road Signs*, RH.7, in STB, The Research Handbook

Scottish Tourist Board, *Tourism in Scotland 1992*, Edinburgh, STB, 1993

Scottish Tourist Board, *Tourist Route Signposting Research*, C.70, 1987, in STB, Research and Planning Information Handbook

Smith, R., *The Southern Upland Way Official Guide*, 2nd ed., Scottish Natural Heritage, 1994

Sutcliffe, J.D., *Nature Trails: Their Content, Information and Educational Value*, University of Wales, (unpublished MSc Thesis), 1969

Tourism and Environment Task Force, *Going Green: Guidelines for the Scottish Tourism Industry*, Edinburgh, Scottish Tourist Board, 1993

Literature held in the Trail Archive
The Robert Gordon University Heritage Unit

SCOTLAND

A Wee Bit of Victorian Aberdeen, Aberdeen Urban Studies Centre

Aberdeen: Castlegate Walk, Shearer, C. for City of Aberdeen Department of Development and Tourism

Aberdeen: City Centre Walk, Shearer, C. for Aberdeen Tourist Board

Aberdeen: Ferryhill and Bridge of Dee Walk, Shearer, C. for City of Aberdeen Department of Development and Tourism

Aberdeen Harbour Trail: Sail, Steam, Supply, Aberdeen Urban Studies Centre, 1985

Aberdeen: Harbour Walk, Shearer, C. for Aberdeen Tourist Board

Aberdeen: Old Aberdeen Walk, Shearer, C. for Aberdeen Tourist Board

Aberdeen: West End Walk, Shearer, C. for City of Aberdeen Department of Development and Tourism

Audio Tour of the Royal Mile, The Audio Tour Company

Balmacara, Kintail & The Falls of Glomach, National Trust for Scotland

Battleby Garden Guide, Countryside Commission for Scotland

The Beauty of Loch Lomond, Strathclyde Regional Council and Dumbarton District Council

Blairlogie, Stirling District Council Planning and Building Control Department

Borders Tourist Route, in British Tourist Authority and South of Scotland Area Tourist Boards, *South of Scotland*, 1993

Borders and East Lothian Tourist Route, in British Tourist Authority and South of Scotland Area Tourist Boards, *South of Scotland*, 1993

Breathing Space: Victoria Park, Aberdeen Urban Studies Centre, 1987

The Burns Heritage Trail, Scottish Tourist Board

Caithness and Sutherland: Places to Visit for Wildlife and Landscape, Nature Conservancy Council for Scotland, 1991

Car Touring in Ayrshire, Blake Graphics and Print for Ayrshire Tourist Board

The Clyde Coast and Sea Lochs Trail, Loch Lomond, Stirling & Trossachs Tourist Board

Clyde Valley Tourist Route, Clyde Valley Tourist Board

The Commemorative Plaques of Aberdeen, City of Aberdeen Arts and Recreation Division, 1992

Countryside Walks in the Scottish Borders, Borders Regional Council Physical Planning and Development Department

Cove Harbour, Borders Regional Council

Cycle and Walk in Lothian, Lothian Regional Council Highways Department

Cycling in Ayrshire, Blake Graphics & Print for Ayrshire Tourist Board

Cycling in Scotland, Scottish Tourist Board, 1993

Cycling in the Forest: North East Scotland, Forest Enterprise and Grampian Enterprise, 1994

A Day in Spey Valley, Highlands and Islands Development Board and Landmark Press

Dean Castle Country Park: The Two Rivers Trail, Kilmarnock & Loudoun District Council Countryside Ranger Service

Discover Glenlivet: A Landscape to Explore, Crown Estates and Scottish Natural Heritage, 1993

The Dovecots of East Lothian, East Lothian County Council

Dunearn Burn Walk, Moray Estates

East Lothian Coastal Trail, East Lothian District Council

East Lothian Historic Towns Trail, East Lothian District Council

East Lothian Villages and By Ways Trail, East Lothian District Council

Explore Perthshire, Perthshire Tourist Board, 1993

Explore Scotland, in SYHA, *Breakaway 93: Activity Holidays for Europe*, p. 3

The Eildon Hills, Borders Regional Council Planning and Development Department, 1986

Elgin Town Trail, Moray District Council and The Moray Society, 1983

Follow the A9 Trail, The Scottish Highlands and Islands

Follow the Highland Gateway Trail, Loch Lomond, Stirling & Trossachs Tourist Board

Forests of the Tweed Valley: Forest Walks, Forest Enterprise, 1994

Formartine and Buchan Way: Section from Dyce to Ellon, Grampian Regional Council, 1993

Forth Valley Tourist Route, in British Tourist Authority and South of Scotland Area Tourist Boards, *South of Scotland*, 1993

Galloway Tourist Route, in British Tourist Authority and South of Scotland Area Tourist Boards, *South of Scotland*, 1993

Glasgow to Irvine Pedestrian and Cycle Route: Paisley to Lochwinnoch & Kilmacolm Section, Cunninghame District Council, Irvine Development Corporation and Renfrew District Council, 1992

Glasgow to Irvine Pedestrian and Cycle Route: Kilwinning to Lochwinnoch Section, Cunninghame District Council, Irvine Development Corporation and Renfrew District Council, 1992

Glasgow to Irvine Pedestrian and Cycle Route: Irvine to Kilwinning & Ardrossan Section, Cunninghame District Council, Irvine Development Corporation and Renfrew District Council, 1992

Glasgow/Loch Lomond/Killin Cycle Way, Loch Lomond, Stirling & Trossachs Tourist Board, Stirling District Council and Forth Valley Enterprise

The Glen Ogle Trail, Stirling District Council Planning and Building Control Department

Glen Park Nature Trail, Renfrew District Council Leisure and Recreation Department, 1978

Glen Tilt Trail, Dundee College of Commerce

Johnstone & Greenock Railway Path, SUSTRANS Scotland, 1991

Looking at Houses, Aberdeen Urban Studies Centre, 1993

Looking for Clues, Aberdeen Urban Studies Centre, 1989

The Malt Whisky Trail: Scotland's North East, North East of Scotland Co-ordinating Committee for Tourism and Scottish Tourist Board

The Malt Whisky Trail: Speyside Scotland, Benison Design for British Tourist Authority, 1993

Mary Queen of Scots, Scottish Tourist Board and British Tourist Authority

New Lanark Heritage Trail, New Lanark Conservation Trust

North East Scotland Coastal Trail, NESCOT

Old Aberdeen: The Medieval High Street and King's College, Aberdeen Urban Studies Centre, 1992

Old Perth Trail: A Walk Into History, Perth Partnership

The Old Town of Edinburgh, Edinburgh Old Town Renewal Trust, 1993

Patrick Geddes Heritage Trail: Old Town Edinburgh, Patrick Geddes Group, 1982

The Pentlands Pocket Book: A New Guide to the Hills of Home, Morris, A. and Bowman, J. for Pentland Hills Regional Park, 1991

The Pictish Trail: A Traveller's Guide to the Old Pictish Kingdoms, Jackson, A., The Orkney Press, 1989

Quality Around Speyside, Moray Badenoch & Strathspey Enterprise

Ross and Cromarty Museums, Ross and Cromarty Museums Service

Scotland Travel and Budget Accommodation, SYHA, CalMac, Citylink and STB

Scotland's Castle Trail, Gordon District Tourist Board and British Tourist Authority, 1993

Scotland's Fishing Heritage Trail, Scottish Tourist Board, 1984

Scotland's Fishing Heritage Trail: Tourist Map of St. Andrews, The East Neuk and North-East Fife, St. Andrews & North-East Fife Tourist Board

Scotland's Mill Trail Country, Loch Lomond, Stirling & Trossachs Tourist Board and Clackmannan District Council

Scotland's Quality Trail, NESCOT, 1991

The Scottish Borders Woollen Trail, British Tourist Authority and Scottish Borders Tourist Board, 1992

Short Walks Through the Long History of Leith, Leith Enterprise Trust

Sluie Walk, Moray Estates

Solway Coast Heritage Trail, in British Tourist Authority and South of Scotland Area Tourist Boards, *South of Scotland*, 1993

Southern Upland Way Official Guide & Official Route Map: Eastern Section, Andrew, K., for Countryside Commission for Scotland, 1984

Southern Upland Way Long Distance Route, Scottish Natural Heritage, 1992

Southern Upland Way Long Distance Route, Scottish Natural Heritage, 1993

The Southern Upland Way: Scotland's Coast to Coast Footpath, Scottish Natural Heritage

Stonehaven Heritage Trail, Ritchie, G.J.N. for Stonehaven Heritage Society, 1991

Street Explorer, Aberdeen Urban Studies Centre, 1989

Street Search: A Georgian Trail, Aberdeen Urban Studies Centre, 1988

Strontian Car Tours: Ardnamurchan, HMSO, 1972

Strontian Car Tours: Lochaline, HMSO, 1972

Strontian Car Tours: Polloch, HMSO, 1972

Strontian Car Tours: Kinlochmoidart and Glenfinnan, HMSO, 1972

SYHA Hostels and NTS Places to Visit: Touring Map Scotland, Bartholomew for SYHA and NTS

Torridon: A Guide to the Hills, National Trust for Scotland

Traffic Trail, Aberdeen Urban Studies Centre, 1989

The Trossachs Trail, Ideas Design for Loch Lomond, Stirling and Trossachs Tourist Board

The Trossachs Trail, Visible Means Ltd for The Trossachs Tourism Management Programme

By Tummel and Rannoch Forest Walks, Forestry Commission

Unravel the Mysteries of the Stone Circle: Discover Gordon's Early History, Gordon District Council, Gordon District Tourist Board, Grampian Regional Council and Grampian Enterprise

Victorian Heritage Trail, Kincardine and Deeside Tourist Board

A Walk Around Haddington, East Lothian District Council

A Walking Tour of The Royal Burgh of Wick, Wick Community Council, 1990

Walks in Ayrshire, Blake Graphics & Print for Ayrshire Tourist Board

Walks: Stirling District, Stirling District Council Planning and Building Control Department

West Highland Way Long Distance Route, Countryside Commission for Scotland

West Highland Way Long Distance Route, Scottish Natural Heritage, 1992

West Lothian Walks: Beecraigs & Almondell, West Lothian District Council Leisure and Recreation Department, 1984

Wester Ross Coastal Route, Ross and Cromarty Tourist Board

Yellowcraig Nature Trail, East Lothian District Council Physical Planning Department

ENGLAND and WALES

Barn Trails, East Sussex County Council Planning Department

Battle Town and Abbey Walk, Barnard, M. for East Sussex County Council

Canoe Trail, British Waterways

The Cleveland Way, 2nd ed., Countryside Commission and Central Office of Information, 1978

The Cofton Circulars: Public Footpath Walks in the Cofton Area, Urban Fringe Countryside Action

Cornwall Coast Path, 2nd ed., Countryside Commission and Central Office of Information, 1977

Cumbria Coastal Way, Cumbria County Council Planning Department

Cwmcarn Scenic Forest Drive, Forestry Commission

Cycle Route Guide Around North Worcestershire: Across Four Waters, Hill, S. and Cadence Cycling for Urban Fringe Countryside Action Project, 1992

Cycle Route Guide Around North Worcestershire: Over Two Hills, Hill, S. and Cadence Cycling for Urban Fringe Countryside Action Project, 1992

Cycle Route Guide Around North Worcestershire: Past Ten Churches, Hill, S. and Cadence Cycling for Urban Fringe Countryside Action Project, 1992

Dorset Coast Path, 2nd ed., Countryside Commission and Central Office of Information, 1978

Hay-on-Wye: A Guide and Brief History, Hay-on-Wye Tourist Information Bureau

The Icknield Way Walk No. 1: Public Footpath Walks from Forhill Picnic Site, Urban Fringe Countryside Action

The Icknield Way Walk No. 2: Public Footpath Walks from Forhill Picnic Site and the North Worcestershire Path, Urban Fringe Countryside Action

The Icknield Ways Walk No. 1: Public Footpath Walks from Forhill Picnic Site, Wythall Parish Council for Urban Fringe Countryside Action

The Illey Way, Urban Fringe Countryside Action and Dudley Countryside Management Project

Lewes Town Walk, East Sussex County Council

Milton Keynes Heritage, Milton Keynes Development Corporation, 1983

North Downs Way, Countryside Commission and Central Office of Information, 1978

Offa's Dyke Path, Countryside Commission and Central Office of Information, 1978

The Offa's Dyke Path National Trail, Countryside Commission and Countryside Council for Wales

On the Trail at Oldbury Power Station, Earl & Thompson Marketing Ltd for Nuclear Electric

Pembrokeshire Coast Path, 2nd ed., Countryside Commission and Central Office of Information, 1978

The Pennine Way, Countryside Commission and Central Office of Information, 1977

The Ridgeway Path, 2nd ed., Countryside Commission and Central Office of Information, 1978

Sculpture Trail: Forest of Dean, Forest Enterprise, 1993

Severn & Wye Valley Holiday Trail, Dowland Press

South Devon Coast Path, Countryside Commission and Central Office of Information, 1976

South Downs Way, 2nd ed., Countryside Commission and Central Office of Information, 1978

Ten Good Walks, Consumers' Association, 1993

The Upland Management Trail: Great Langdale, Countryside Commission

A Walk Round Burtons' St. Leonards, Barnard, M. for East Sussex County Council

OTHER EUROPEAN COUNTRIES

Circuits Pour Visiter: Perigueux Ville d'Art, 1992

Come and Discover the Lot, Comité Départemental du Tourisme du Lot

Experience Amberg: A Walk Around the Town, Town of Amberg Tourist Information Office

Five Major Walking Tracks in Corrèze, in Corrèze Comité Départemental du Tourisme, *Corrèze Pays Nature*

Historical Roads Through the Quercy: from Brive to Figeac

Itinéraires Touristiques dans le Lot, Comité Départemental du Tourisme du Lot

Nancy Itinéraire 1900, Nancy Office de Tourisme

Promenades et Randonnées: La Vallée de la Dordogne et le Causse de Martel: Circuits de Une Heure à Une Journée, Comité Départemental du Tourisme du Lot, 1993

Randonnons: Autour de Bealieu-sur-Dordogne

The Royal Road: Praha

Stadtführung Amberg mit dem Kassettenrecorder, Town of Amberg Tourist Information Office

Tour of the Old Figeac

Velotours 1993, Aktiv-Reisen, 1992

Walks and Cycling: Trebon, in Trebon Information and Cultural Centre, *Information Guide Trebon*

Along the River, Through the Woods: A self-guided trip through the Francis Marion National Forest, Berkeley County Chamber of Commerce

Blue Ridge Parkway, National Park Concessions

Edisto Memorial Gardens Nature Trail, City of Orangeburg, 1993

Fort Monroe Virginia: Guide to Historic Points

Freedom Trail, in Morris J., (ed.) *Best Read Guide: Boston including Cambridge*, Vol. 1, No. 4, Community Publishing Company, Fall 1993

Salem Heritage Trail, Creative Concepts, 1993

The Sea Oats Nature Trail, in South Carolina Department of Parks, Recreation and Tourism *The Natural Areas of Huntington Beach State Park*

Skyline Drive, in Front Royal-Warren County Chamber of Commerce *Front Royal, Virginia*, 1993 and *Virginia's Mountain Playground: Schenandoah National Park*, 1993

South Shore Heritage Trail: Quincy to Plymouth, Massachusetts, Plymouth County Development Council

Trans Canada Trail: A Natural Way to Love Our Land Forever, Trans Canada Trail Foundation

11

THE IMAGE OF A REGION
The Need for a Clear Focus

Howard Fisher

This is the East coast with winter
Written into its constitution
And so is very productive of men
Who do not wait for good
In case there is none.

George Bruce of Fraserburgh[1]

The image of a region, an area or even a city, is a complex amalgam of its people, the ethnic mix that is contributing or has contributed to its character, its architecture, its overall aesthetic appeal, climate and industry. It is also governed by geography and the setting of an area amongst its neighbours and the images they in turn emanate. Reflected glory can be important in human relationships and so in relationships between neighbouring areas.

Defining the image of an area is important to those who have to promote and sell the area for reasons of tourism business, but it is also important in terms of attracting business investment across the board. Much has been written about inward investment in Scotland and the reasons why new industries are attracted to an area and, perhaps mistakenly, it is still seen in terms of the capability of the area to offer attractive financial incentives in the form of grants, rate and rent free holidays amongst a sheath of similar goodies which decorate any advertisement or economic development brochure. Perhaps these cash linked inducements are important when bidding internationally for large scale plants, such as vehicle assembly or manufacture of bits of electronic gadgetry on a large scale. However, most of those in the inward investment attractor business[2] now agree that the number of internationally foot-loose factories, employing hundreds of people are few and far between. In retrospect one might question the long term return to Scotland of such captures and maybe the concept of sustainable development seems to have been overlooked.

There is much in common in any analysis of an area's potential between its attractiveness to business investment and its attractiveness as a tourism venue.[3] Essentially much the same sort of package is being marketed, a complex mix of attributes. Much of what the purchaser or 'visitor' is buying is ready made and off the peg, and rarely is a made to measure package credible or viable. The first try on or fit has to be comfortable and one that inspires a sense of well being and confidence. The choice of accessories, such as cash incentives, be that a factory rent holiday or a special offer hotel break is almost subsidiary and certainly more straightforward if the cultural package overgarment fits.

Even in tourism terms the aesthetic attractiveness of an area is not a prerequisite. In all fairness most of Grampian for example could be, and has been, described as 'nice but not spectacular'.[4] Aesthetic beauty is subject to fashion and is very much in the eye of the beholder. Perhaps a revealing, if somewhat racist, anecdote is the occasion where representatives from a number of European holiday consumer guide publishers were trying to devise a point scoring system for aesthetic appeal of a resort. The French and the British seemed to be reaching some accord on this nearly impossible task, but the Germans seemed miles away. They returned constantly to a fundamentally important question, for them anyway, and that was, 'Yes, but how many times a day are the towels changed?'

Seemingly unlikely places are now being successfully promoted as tourism destinations. Places such as Bradford, Wigan and even that 'dear green place' Glasgow are now serious players and indeed competitors to Grampian for tourists from both England and overseas. There is no room for any elitist view by this part of the world. Indeed, a look at our success in Grampian in attracting tourists should dispel any sense of smugness that we may have a superior product. We have a good product, that suits some, but not others, and is unknown to most.

A starting point for selling a region or city to business, to visitors, to advertisers in our newspapers and on local radio and television is to try and objectively perceive the area as others might. That is difficult for those born and bred in the area and perhaps even more difficult for the convert incomer (converts are always more loyal than the king). Most native and convert Grampians perceive the region as exceptionally beautiful, rich in culture, well known and the envy of many. Individually, many of these claims are true or nearly true, but does the overall package scream 'come on over' and 'you'll all be real welcome and feel at home here', again be that addressed to a new business or a tourist. Plainly it does not, at least as measured by a number of indicators. It is perhaps best illustrated by the following questions:

1. Why are the big institutional investors reluctant to invest in large property deals in Grampian?
2. Why do Locate in Scotland rate us low for inward investment interest?

3. Why is Aberdeen the butt of so many jokes, eg the Furryboots City of the (Glasgow) Herald?
4. Was the *Radio Buckie* cameo an accident of choice in the much acclaimed *Tutti Frutti* TV series, or was it saying something about external perceptions (and a lot about the great East/West Scottish divide)?
5. Why is so little known about Aberdeen and the North East in say Woking, Milton Keynes, or Northampton?

A *vox pop* in the High Street of any of the above chosen towns and cities would likely return the following words and phrases: oil, cold, expensive, a long way away, somewhere in far north and perhaps 'Dons' by a connoisseur of Scottish football results. The package does not add up to one which is choc-a-bloc with warm, comfortable and inviting words, if personal experience is correct.

In a survey[5] by Grampian TV some five years ago, the questions of Grampian that London based advertising account managers asked give a clue to perceptions: is there corporate life, and is there cocktail society? The questions are perhaps not important as regards fact, more important is their insight to the perspective of outsiders or those representing firms that might invest in one way or another in Grampian.

Social class is not irrelevant, although it is easy to be derisive about the cocktail society question. It is certainly very relevant in either tourism or inward investment if you wish to target a certain sector of the market, be that in terms of business decisions or holiday destination decisions. Indeed, one might lead to the other. Although some find it repugnant or even ephemeral, geographical areas can be rated in terms of perceived smartness. In a recent newspaper article, Aberdeen ranked very low, but Moray in terms of field sports and *country pursuits* rated fairly high.

The problem for the North East at present is that we do not have a co-ordinated view as to what is our market, or even if we really want to be players in this competitive market at all.[4 & 6] How far is this a reflection of our culture, that amalgam of attributes including history, geography and economy, that provide the raw material to set out our market stall? At present some might say the blinds are down and with an ageing sign 'Back in five minutes'.

There is no doubt geography and climate play a large part in the cultural mix and the transmitted message. The concept of remoteness is closely linked to culture and perception and has little to do with miles. All areas suffer or enjoy degrees of parochialism. Buckie and Keith in Grampian are ten miles apart, but the distance was perceived far too far to travel for a training course. A further example was personally observed during a workers breakfast break on a farm four miles north of Southend-on-Sea in Essex, when one individual was recounting how a former work mate had just gone to be a contract worker on the Falkland Islands. Some one asked: 'Which way did he go then?' Back came the reply: 'He went off up Ashingdon way.'

Ashingdon is two miles north of the shed in which that conversation took place. South East Essex is hardly a remote backwoods area in anybody's estimation.

Geography is more than distance and topography, it is about access and distance from the main arteries of travel, be that business or tourism. It is difficult to find a large town or city in South East England that can be said to have a distinct culture that has not been swamped by that of London, in spite of the worthy commitment of locally based radio and TV stations. It is not necessarily size related. The Southampton-Portsmouth conurbation is probably the largest concentration of population in South East England outside the London metro area, but as for a distinct culture, then one is hard pressed to distinguish it. Perhaps Norwich alone has achieved a perceptible, identifiable and separate culture by virtue of its isolation from the main travel arteries. It is one of the few remaining cities in England without a motorway connection, and only relatively recently achieved a high speed rail link. Also relevant is that one does not pass through Norwich on the way to anywhere, you have to set out to go to it.

If ever there were two self-contained city regions in the UK, surely they must be Aberdeen and Norwich. Both regions are off the main travel routes, have no competition in terms of domination of their areas and have a strong and distinct local character and culture. However, in reality Norwich is still only a little over 100 miles from London. Both cities have a tendency to revel in their *isolation*, and when development comes it is perhaps more thrust upon them rather than actively sought: oil for Aberdeen and the electrified railway and the boom of the Thatcher years for Norwich. There are in fact some close and more direct links between Norfolk and Grampian. The legacy of the catching and processing of herring brought many families from both areas together in Great Yarmouth and many other ports between Grampian and East Anglia.

Many discerning tourists will actively seek out peace and tranquillity, but for most this is either consciously or subconsciously distinct from perceived isolation. Furthermore, that isolation is rarely measurable in terms of miles, particularly in the confines of these isles, but is a combination of vibrations emanating from an area that adds up to a *cold* message. It may be simply an aversion to putting all one's eggs in one basket by giving up at least two days to make a detour to say Grampian from the A9 road and buying into the relatively unknown. The option is to play safe and keep to what you know and perceptions that are warm and inviting. Sometimes the cold messages from an area may be ascribed to no information, no projected image, and an impermeable information membrane which retains all cultural messages.

Stereotypes may accurately reflect an area's culture, or they may crudely distort it. However, stereotypes, like it or not, play a part in our choice of business or pleasure destination. Many regional stereotypes in the UK may seem unkind, but have become accepted as *endearing* over the years and have been used positively in promotions. In the same bracket as stereotypes, media personalities can often have the same beneficial or deleterious effect and similarly TV series and soap operas. The latter seem to have been wholly beneficial in recent years: Herriot Country,[7] Emmerdale Country, Last of the Summer Wine Country, Coronation Street/Salford City, Take the High Road and Loch Lomond and Taggart for Glasgow. Indeed, Scottish local authorities now corporately promote[8] themselves as film and TV locations realising that the filming process itself is good for local business, but also tourism and business investment that follows.

Prominent individuals can sell a whole culture package by themselves, and here again the list is a long one, ie Freddie Truman, Fred Dibnah of steeplejack fame, Billy Connolly (always controversial and especially in Glasgow), Max Boyce, Arthur Daley/George Cole and even George Melly. But when we come to Grampian and Aberdeen, where are the potted culture projectors on our behalf that escape our borders and more importantly are recognisable in England, our main opportunity market in many respects. Robbie Shepherd and Scotland the What? Few fit the bill and few will associate James Naughtie with a distinctly Grampian culture and similarly Evelyn Glennie.

I suppose we have one characteristic that is associated with Aberdeen, but is now somewhat tired and unhelpful at any stretch of the imagination and that is Aberdonians and meanness. Even here, in fact probably tighter with their brass, Yorkshiremen, have managed to turn this into a perceived endearing characteristic. Herriot et al helped and the better known Yorkshire dialect adds to a warmer received message. The reality is that Aberdeen has a good record of charitable giving, but perhaps the myth is often a more marketable commodity than the reality?

How have we in North East Scotland lost out in the alchemy of projecting an image that is well known, clear, defined (even if mangled in common perception) and that substitutes warm descriptions in place of cold words and concepts like North, wind, North Sea, granite, northern lights, wilderness and oil and rigs in inhospitable environments?

Even our festivals, all of them absolute gems, we manage to keep a secret to all but a local audience. Our Woking Man will of course have heard of Notting Hill, Edinburgh, Bath and likely Pitlochry, but the person who will have heard of the Aberdeen Youth Festival will take on the status of a collectors' item. A pity, because the Youth Festival is a superb occasion and probably unique in feel and coverage. Here is something that radiates 'warmth' all over and is the equal of Glasgow's Mayfest, although refreshingly different.

There is no doubt a challenge in promoting Grampian, that tests all the theories, both by experts and public bar pundits. Just over four years ago Dr Michael Kelly of Glasgow's Miles Better Campaign visited Grampian in his consultancy capacity. Over lunch he compared the challenges of promoting Glasgow and Edinburgh. The key to both was the culture of the people and not bricks and mortar assets, number of orchestras and business parks.

Dr Kelly saw Glasgow's great strength as the single perception of the City and its destiny shared by Glaswegians right across the social and educational spectrum. Jimmy in the Maryhill Road and the lawyer in Kelvinside only had to be told once that Glasgow is the greatest and to a man and woman this was shared and repeated by all. In Edinburgh Dr Kelly saw a society totally divided into two by school, class, money and little or no shared belief in their city's destiny. And Aberdeen? Dr Kelly admitted defeat, or we could not afford the fee it would take to crack the nut. What he did say is that we had a problem.

In a series of brain storming sessions that led eventually to the Grampian Tourism Development Strategy,[6] a recurring theme was that maybe an obstacle to the region's success in attracting more tourists is a local *attitude problem*. Although all economic development agencies in Grampian put tourism high on their list of industries ready for growth, we have an uncanny knack of finding every excuse why we should not build a new tourism facility here and expect more tourists there, even by those in the business. A recent project to provide a very attractive and imaginative facility to promote our rich legacy of pre-history, to be known as Archaeolink, has brought some local objections to an area that provides little local employment except for farming. The Irish have already done something similar.

One thing all experts agree on is that there is no shortage of raw material on which to base a better promotion of Grampian. The Grampian Initiative,[9] a public-private sector partnership established by the Regional Council, has consistently highlighted these attributes over the last six years. It represents a small pocket of true visionaries in the Region, and the Regional Council has not received the recognition it deserves here in maintaining its commitment to a clear vision for Grampian. Working in the Grampian Initiative can be a lonely experience.

Marc Ellington of Towie Barclay, a local businessman and an expert in the heritage business, considers that, whereas places like Glasgow need formal museums and collections like the Burrell Collection, we in Grampian are blessed with a collection that is in its natural and original setting and Grampian could be packaged as a living Burrell type collection.

Whatever the interpretation of the extract from George Bruce's poem (above), be that clear sighted strength or cold pessimism, we can point to its legacy. It takes the form of a unique type of 5000 year old stone circle (recumbent), vitrified forts, a plethora of Pictish stones, but also a rich sequence of castles and palaces running from thirteenth century castles like Kildrummy to one of the greatest Renaissance chateaux in Scotland at Huntly. The Improving Movement of the 18th and 19th Centuries found a vigorous response in the industrious, unflinching characters described by Bruce, to the extent that we can claim that the landscape was completely recreated at that stage.

Some would, and do, argue that like oil reserves under the North Sea, we should exercise restraint in the use of other resources and husband them for future generations. Is this what sustainability is really about? In practice it is difficult to simply stop the clock, either in terms of physical development or in terms of the growth and change of the culture, and indeed in terms of maintaining or growing local prosperity. At least we have to adapt our culture to accommodate badly needed incoming investment, ideas, entrepreneurs and workers. If we get it right the culture and the economy is the richer.

As we move to the millennium, societies and their representative bodies across Europe and beyond are considering their role and placement in a society that is likely to be very different, where national borders will be less important or less reassuringly protective. It will be a more competitive world and a more demanding world in terms of quality of goods and services demanded by customers. There will be little room for those that come second, and winning in your chosen area or areas of expertise will be crucial.

There is likely to be a number of cities, or city regions, in Europe that will dominate fashion, information and entertainment provision, scientific research and development, learning (including distance learning), broadcasting, music and the arts generally. Already a number of these cities are making their pitch and are visible, eg Barcelona, Amsterdam, Lyons, Milan and maybe Glasgow in some sectors? If you clearly are not able to be a member of that select group, also mirrored outside Europe, smaller communities will seek appropriate alliances now with partners that will give a group strength or associate status to one of the lead cities.

Grampian Regional Council has again demonstrated some remarkable foresight and has established one of the first civic strategic alliance links, ie with Calgary[10] in Canada's Alberta Province, and with Murmansk and Tyumen in Russia. Grampian Region is also negotiating similar strategic alliances with San Antonio in Texas and providing links to Mexico, and Nova Scotia on Canada's maritime east coast. In parallel, and with the blessing of the European Commission, we have worked hard at linking with local authority regional groupings in the European Union, including the Conference of Peripheral Maritime Regions, and the North Sea Commission. Oddly national governments, or at least HMG, seem less keen on this *subsidiarity* development and as to reasons why, these are best left to your own conclusions reflecting your particular political bias.

None of this is political tourism, or trips for the Council boys (and girls), but is securing a place at the political table of future Europe. Long term relationships, in business and in civic relations will become increasingly important where partners share challenges and look for complementarity in business and soft edge business projects including culture, which is very much a business. One has to be realistic in seeking partners. Over-pitch and one risks either ridicule and an early divorce, but under-pitch and one could lose out altogether.

Grampian Regional Council's documented vision is currently to be *a Region the envy of the UK*,[3] and the Grampian Initiative logos of *Grampian*

Going Places, and *Grampian, Scots for Quality*, as well as the quality keystone of the *Together to the Future*[3] economic development strategy, are all geared to realising this vision. Due perhaps more to the recession and the bad luck of others, we have realised that vision set in 1989. In economic terms and in terms of individual disposable income, we are the envy of the UK. However, a bigger role and destiny beckons.

Grampian and its premier city Aberdeen could join that select group of cities that will lead Europe in the next century. Aberdeen could be that focus of northern culture, of learning and of trade, in an arc stretching from Reykjavik to St. Petersburg. Ambitious? Certainly. Realistic? Yes, if history and culture of the North East of Scotland is any guide, then the vision is realisable.

The Author

After a distinguished career in the civil service, Dr Howard Fisher came to Aberdeen in 1989 as Director of Economic Development and Planning with Grampian Regional Council. He has taken an active interest in the formulation of a strategic approach to tourism development in the North East of Scotland.

References

[1] Bruce, G., from poem 'Praising Aberdeenshire Farmers', in *Poetry of Northeast Scotland*, Alison, J. (ed), 1976

[2] Locate in Scotland, *Marketing and Operational Plan* 1991–92 to 1993–94

[3] Grampian Regional Council, *Together to the Future*, Chapter 3, 1990

[4] Arthur Young Ltd, *Grampian Tourism Strategy*, Grampian Initiative Tourism Task Force, 1989

[5] Grampian Television PLC, *Market Research*

[6] Grampian Tourism Strategy, *Working for Success*, Grampian Tourism Focus Group, December 1992

[7] Herriot, J., series of books on veterinary practice in the Yorkshire Dales, PAN

[8] *Scottish Screen Locations*, Film House, 88 Lothian Road, Edinburgh, EH3 9BZ

[9] Grampian Regional Council, *Grampian Initiative, Annual Review 1992–93*

[10] Grampian Regional Council, Economic Development and Planning Committee, August 1990

12

A HERITAGE STRATEGY FOR MORAY

Alistair Campbell

Moray District offers a microcosm of the best of Scotland. Rich lowland farming, a necklace of quiet beaches, cliffs, crags and fishing villages, rolling hills and powerful salmon rivers, and the Cairngorm Mountains. Some 30 miles to the west is Highland Inverness, some 50 to the south east is Aberdeen. Its economy is based on the indigenous industries of farming, fishing, forestry, food processing, agricultural engineering and whisky distilling. The very names of Glenlivet, Glenfiddich, Glenfarclas, Cardhu and Macallan sing their own songs for the knowledgeable. Two RAF bases inject a large spending power into the community while tourism plays an increasingly important role.

The main town in Moray is historic Elgin with a population of 20,000. The ancient burgh of Forres lies on the Moray Firth near the mouth of the Findhorn River. Further east, flanked by fishing villages, are Lossiemouth and our prime fishing port, Buckie. Inland there is Keith, once a thriving textile town now having to claw its way back to economic survival, and Dufftown, on Speyside, at the heart of the whisky industry. The landscape, scenery and heritage of Moray have much to offer the visitor. Yet, in terms of major tourism impact, the area is in danger of remaining a holidaymakers' no man's land, trapped between Aberdeen and Royal Deeside to the east and south, and the immensely popular Highlands to the west. This is despite many excellent initiatives and developments by both the public and private sectors.

During the last fifteen years, we have seen the development of the malt whisky trail, attracting a staggering number of visitors, many from overseas, as they taste this part of Moray's heritage. Glenfiddich Distillery alone attracts some 150,000 visitors each year, underlying the importance of Dufftown as a potential major gateway to the remainder of Moray. The recent development of the Cooperage Visitor Centre at Craigellachie reflects a welcome diversification of the whisky theme. Baxters of Speyside Centre at Fochabers with some 180,000 visitors combines interpretation of the Baxter family heritage with that of the local area and offers factory tours, retail outlets, restaurant facilities and riverside walks.

Brodie Castle, Darnaway, Ballindalloch Castle and Towie Mill are but four of the historical attractions that offer a good quality visitor experience. The 48 miles of the Speyside Way, opened in 1981 as Scotland's second officially designated long distance footpath, various forestry attractions and the Glenlivet Estate offer, with other quiet areas, the opportunity to appreciate Moray's landscape and wildlife.

Our Museums Division operates the Falconer Museum and Nelsons Tower at Forres, the 200 year old Oldmills Watermill at Elgin, the Tugnet Ice House at the mouth of the Spey, the Peter Anson Gallery at Buckie, and Dufftown and Tomintoul Museums, both of these being combined with Tourist Information Centres. Private Museums include the Elgin Museum, its collections of national importance, The Moray Motor Museum, Fochabers Folk Museum and Lossiemouth Fisheries Museum. Local small scale heritage collections are at Findhorn and Buckie.

The Pictish stones around Forres, the ruined Elgin Cathedral, Duffus Castle, Lochindorb Castle and, now calm, Pluscarden Abbey give an insight into earlier more turbulent times. A series of planned towns and villages such as Cullen, Lossiemouth, Charlestown of Aberlour and Keith are important in the history of Scottish town planning. These are only a selection of the attractions available in our 850 square miles. On this impressive, yet under-promoted, range of visitor attractions, we plan to develop major new facilities to strengthen the tourism base of the area. The following pages deal with the strategy we have developed towards this goal.

EVOLUTION OF OUR STRATEGY

In concentrating on the District Council's contribution, I would in no way wish to undervalue the excellent work carried out by other organisations particularly in the private sector. Indeed, it is their vision, commitment to good quality, and expertise that have acted as a sound platform for the Council to emulate, not in isolation, but wherever possible, on a partnership basis. My story starts in 1988. Prior to this, decisions and planning tended to be carried out on an ad hoc and reactive basis rather than with a clear co-ordinated strategy in mind. During that year we produced a Museums Development Plan which echoed the national voice of concern about the proliferation of museums throughout the country, and identified that difficult decisions would require to be made locally as to which schemes should be supported by the District Council.

Subsequent to this the Council has evolved a policy confining support to registered independent museums, and a separate policy of financial and professional support for heritage developments dealing with a unique theme, which will increase tourist numbers and are able to demonstrate long term

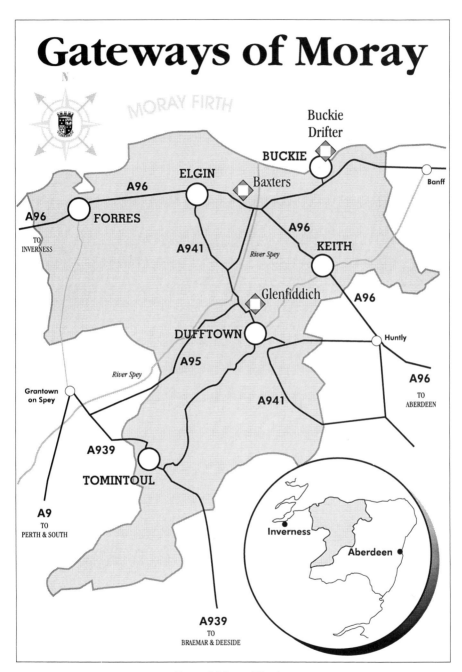

Figure 1 Moray District.

financial viability. Thus, in some small but effective way a quality threshold combined with an economic benchmark has now been established.

An exciting proposal in the 1988 Museums Development Plan was:

> ... to develop a large scale maritime/heritage centre covering all aspects of the sea and seafaring locally with exhibitions, audio visual displays, shop and restaurant ... Ideally this should be at the Buckie Harbour area to interpret the present and past, using the existing collections in the Buckie Maritime Museum with other items being borrowed.

At the same time as these developments were being proposed for the east coastal area of Moray, proposals were being developed for a MacBeth Heritage Centre in Forres, for which a feasibility study was carried out by Kit Campbell Associates. While the recommendations did not win universal approval, the data concerning potential markets proved particularly helpful, if somewhat sobering. Almost nine out of ten visitors to Moray District stayed for less than a week, with roughly two thirds staying for only one to three nights, implying that most tourists did not perceive Moray as a destination in its own right but as an area through which to pass. Moreover, visitors to Moray were mainly adult couples with no children.

The lesson was plain, Moray must seek to attract tourists who would stay longer in the area, and the way to do this was by developing a very much stronger range of things for tourists to do and see. Likewise, by increasing the range of choice through providing attractions of regional importance, the day trip market could be built up.

An important aspect of the Buckie proposals was that they had not evolved in isolation but owed their origins, in part, to Regional Interpretive Planning in Grampian, a strategy document which had emanated from the recommendations of a countryside interpretation workshop held in Aboyne in 1976. The report recognised the great danger of duplication which has been subsequently avoided. Gaps on the fishing theme were identified as: *Salmon Netting; Herring and the Steam Drifter; Whaling and Boat Building; Great Line and Small Line Fishing; the Overall Maritime Story of Trawling; and Oil.*

Seventeen years later, many of these proposals have come to fruition. Tugnet Ice House tells the story of salmon. The Buckie Drifter combines the scientific, social and technological story of the herring, while the whaling and boat building story is the basis for Peterhead's proposed maritime centre. Much of the approach to research and strategic themes emanated from the genius of Don Aldridge. Indeed, the components of the story of maritime heritage continue down the coast beyond Grampian, taking in the Signal Tower Museum at Arbroath and the Discovery at Dundee. This relative success reflects the strength of regional planning approaches in both Grampian and Tayside (1984).

The early proposals for Buckie were based on co-operation, discussion and a mutual will not to duplicate provision of facilities. So also is our current heritage strategy which has evolved from the experiences and research of the last five years. In essence, within its tourism and heritage strategy, The Council recognises the desirability of the provision of tourism flagships of regional importance in Buckie, Forres and Keith, sitting alongside private sector developments at Dufftown (Glenfiddich Distillery) and Fochabers (Baxters).

It also recognises the importance of further developing the museum and tourist information centre at Tomintoul as a key orientation point into the district. Such purpose-built, all-weather attractions should incorporate the latest interpretive techniques, retail, catering and toilet facilities, employ trained staff, and should offer the visitor a unique, good quality, value for money, visitor experience of between one to one and a half hours duration. The purpose of these major visitor centres is to *attract more visitors and tourists to Moray; direct visitors to the many other attractions in the district; encourage visitors to stay in Moray for a longer period of time; enable Moray to become established as a recognised good quality tourist destination; encourage increased visitor spending; create more jobs; broaden the tourist heritage structure within Moray and Grampian.*

All of these purposes sound rather mercenary, but they are necessary. I do believe, however, that they are insufficient by themselves. In the light of experience we must add that we want our visitors to experience the personality of the area, and we must establish a relevant continuum of time and space, so that visitors can, each in their own way, leave Moray feeling they have visited an important place which is worth returning to. Our aims in establishing these centres have been:

1. to provide a focus for visitors to the specific town and surrounding area which will assist in the economic regeneration of that town and its development as an important tourist destination;
2. to provide a community resource which will preserve, interpret and promote the heritage of that town and the area;
3. to guide visitors to the wider benefits of Moray District and Grampian Region thereby establishing the District and Region as recognised tourist destinations.

We are committed, wherever possible, to working closely with our neighbouring councils, eg Banff & Buchan District on our eastern flank. We are pursuing together the establishment of a network of major attractions, each different but which will equally appeal to the target market segment. These attractions must help pull discerning visitors into our corner of the North East and encourage them to stay for a longer period. Strategic links with coastal and other trails and linked attractions on a national basis will facilitate joint marketing and promotional activities. This way we have the opportunity to create the necessary critical mass of attractions that will benefit our special part of Scotland. A centre at Forres, a heritage park at

Keith, Baxters, Glenfiddich, the Buckie Drifter, Duff House in 1995, the possibility of Kinnaird Head, Fyvie Castle, Aden Country Park and the proposed Peterhead Maritime Heritage Centre provide an unrivalled series of complementary attractions that together can pull the visitor eastwards off the A9 and the A96.

This approach is in accord with the Grampian Tourism Strategy and its four strategic priorities: increased marketing, product development, enhanced customer care and service, and improved public and private sector teamwork. We also work closely with neighbours on our western flank where we recognise the great potential of the Spey Valley, Inverness and Nairn markets. In particular more cognisance must be taken of the family market if these visitors are to be wooed to Moray. These main magnet attractions, together with their satellite attractions, will be presented within an overall interpretation strategy which will ensure that all significant aspects of a region's character are being appropriately interpreted for the benefit of both residents and tourists.

THE BUCKIE DRIFTER

A feasibility study carried out by Cobham Resource Consultants in 1990 confirmed Buckie as an ideal base for a maritime heritage attraction with major tourism potential. The visitor potential in four key market segments was estimated as follows:

Day trips by local/regional residents	7,600	–	15,900
Buckie and local area chance visits	1,700	–	1,700
School parties	3,000	–	4,300
UK/overseas tourists	7,500	–	20,000
Total	19,800	–	41,900

In 1992, L & R Leisure was appointed by the District Council to take the project forward, together with input from the Kennedy Partnership, Don Aldridge and the MKW Design Partnership. The Council recognised that the project would best succeed by involving the local community and we formed The Buckie Drifter Company with eight directors drawn from the District Council and four other directors representing the RNLI, Buckie Fishing Heritage Society, Moray Badenoch and Strathspey Enterprise and the fishing industry. The capital investment of £940,000 has been funded by the District Council, the Scottish Tourist Board, Moray Badenoch & Strathspey Enterprise, Grampian Regional Council, Scottish Natural Heritage and community sponsorship.

The centre was opened on 16 June 1994 and it is anticipated that it will generate new visitor spending of some £190,000 and create up to twelve jobs. The Buckie Drifter is without doubt our most exciting, significant visitor attraction. It is a modern purpose-built facility incorporating a wide range of interpretive and display techniques and good quality retail and restaurant facilities. It will draw people into Buckie and encourage them, not only to spend time in the surrounding harbour area and town, but also to visit the fishing villages and other tourist attractions of the Moray Firth. It is of particular importance that they are encouraged to visit the immediate villages of Findochty, Portknockie and Cullen, each desperately in need of increased tourism trade.

Central to the whole experience is the story of the herring, not only told from the fishing communities involvement, but also portrayed by the evolution, development and decline of that fish. By focusing in on Buckie, once Scotland's premier herring port with 276 steam drifters, local experience is being used to tell a universal story. Don Aldridge's approach is to ensure that the apparently simple, strong, overriding theme which runs through the whole exposition will be different from maritime heritage treatments elsewhere; will educate and entertain; will be topical and robust; will tie in with other fishing and heritage facilities around Buckie; will reflect the natural heritage of the area and its people; and will relate to a number of sub-themes which may be introduced and varied over time. The concluding message is that the story has a wider relevance and is repeated all over the world whether the resource be coal, forestry or whatever.

The Buckie Drifter is designed to be different, incorporates a strong conservation theme, is determined to involve and reflect the local community, adopts a holistic approach to what is a multi-layered story, portrays that story in a logical order through a variety of experiences and adopts a scientifically based interpretation. The storyline has been thoroughly researched, the essential elements have been identified and selected, and the nature of the interpretation has been carefully thought out. The dramatic external experience of the centre has symbolic references to boat sails and the indigenous tarry boarded buildings of local fishing communities.

The ground floor of the centre uses appropriate sound effects, subdued lighting and an exciting mix of techniques to tell the story of herring and their exploitation by man with particular reference to the Buckie area. On entering the Museum area, one is faced by a five foot wide hemisphere model which illustrates the evolution of the North Atlantic. Through the use of fibre optics, the break up of the ice and the formation of the fishing grounds are stunningly told. Before reaching this part of the story are a selection of fossils, illustrating the first fish.

The *Life of the Herring* section uses a micrarium to allow a close look at micro-organisms, and then there is a video cartoon *Back to School* which tells the herring life story and the effects of increased fishing. A series of interpretive panels follows, tracing the story of fishing from the stone age to 1920s Buckie. *The Here Today* section uses touch computer screens, surrounded by stunning visual images, to bring together the more important factors which influence the size of North Sea herring stocks. The computer interplay is compelling and can be accessed at a variety of levels. The many variables are explored, explained and collated. Once can linger here for a few minutes or an hour.

Next is the human dimension, in particular the *Buckie Story*, which uses panels, artefacts and interplay to reflect the community's story, before the visitor climbs the stairs to be confronted in awe by a quayside and recreated Buckie steam drifter circa 1920 which can then be boarded. Projected on a wall is an eight minute selection of sequences from John Grierson's classic, *Drifters*, while large still images capture scenes of fishing ways. Live demonstrations of crafts and dioramas of the gutting and unloading the catch draw the visitor into a valid experience. A selection of Peter Anson maritime paintings concludes the story.

We believe that this experience, including restaurant, shop, RNLI room, exhibition room and lifeboat on external display, creates an affinity with the area and its heritage. It carries with it a sense of wonder, and should persuade the visitor to continue around the harbour, town and other neighbouring fishing villages. Indeed, in Buckie itself, the visitor will be able to participate in organised harbour tours, visit the local boatyard and seafood factory, before calling in to the Fishing Heritage Cottage, Peter Anson Gallery and Fisherman's Memorial.

MACBETH AND FORRES

Long before Shakespeare made it the setting for part of MacBeth, Forres was an established community. Its medieval street plan can still be made out. Forres has in recent years been consistently successful in the Britain in Bloom competition, while to the east of the town is Sueno's stone, arguably the most spectacular of all of Scotland's sculptured stones. The 1988 proposals by Kit Campbell for a visitor centre on the theme of MacBeth contained the following: *the interpretation of the real, and the Shakespeare, stories of MacBeth; the interpretation of the related twin themes of the making of Scotland and witchcraft in Moray; a new tourist information centre for West Moray; catering facilities; a gift and book shop.*

It was anticipated that the centre would attract some 80,000 to 110,000 visitors in total, would attract 25,000 to 35,000 tourists and would be used to promote Moray District under the banner of *MacBeth Country*. The estimated cost of the structure was £1.5 million, and it was concluded that the centre would require to be funded, at least initially, by the public sector. In 1991, L & R Leisure were asked to develop the proposals and concluded that, while the theme of MacBeth was acceptable, the development of the basic concept, its feasibility and implementation were less convincing. They defined in more detail the physical nature and content of the scheme and devised a possible implementation and funding strategy. The central idea of a trial scene remained, while the various sections of Sueno's Stone were to be used to illustrate the historical evidence. Regrettably, at that time the project could not proceed owing to lack of funding and the unavailability of the desired site.

With the recent awarding of Objective 1 Status to Forres, and the development of strong partnerships between the District Council and other funding bodies since 1991, it is now considered that the possibility of establishing a visitor attraction for Forres has been greatly strengthened. Moreover, the recent tourism survey carried out by TMS for the local enterprise company has clearly illustrated the critical importance of Forres and Dufftown as the gateways into Moray and Forres as a key gateway into Grampian. There is the danger that the existing tourism portfolio is so dominated by traditionally presented distillery tours and castles that potentially significant market segments such as young couples and families are inadequately catered for. Thus, this survey has confirmed the need to develop a family visitor market, and any revised proposals for Forres and, indeed, the rest of the District will incorporate these findings, while still ensuring that the existing main market of middle aged couples is properly catered for.

The District Council has recently indicated that the sole theme of MacBeth is possibly no longer appropriate for the Forres area and that there is merit in looking at widening the visitor experience to reflect the major attractions and heritage of Moray. There is also the necessity to review the central visitor experience given that a trial scene is not a unique enough attraction. Nonetheless, the name of MacBeth may well be the most suitable marketing theme.

Among possibilities to be considered is more effective exploitation of the Pictish and Medieval stories in order to retain visitors in the area and direct them to attractions such as Lochindorb Castle, Randolph's Leap, Brodie Castle, Burghead with its iron age fort and Pictish carvings, Elgin Cathedral, Pluscarden Abbey and on further to Buckie and Keith. At the centre of any Medieval story would be the story of Forres itself. In parallel with this, the centre should act as the unifying base to direct the visitor to the specific attractions of Forres, due regard being given to the town's established floral reputation. Whatever theme is selected, consideration will be given to ensuring that the visitor is pointed towards St Leonard's Church, the Falconer Museum, Grant Park, Nelson's Tower, the Witch's Stone, Sueno's Stone and any other relevant local attractions.

Should a major flagship not be developed within the next two to three years, there is still much merit in seeking to bring the existing attractions of Forres and its surrounding area together under one marketing theme, improving sign posting and publicity and achieving closer co-operation in regard to complementary opening periods and times.

THE KEITH AREA

In our proposals for the Keith area, diversity and flexibility of approach are further underlined. The basic strategic principle is to provide an attraction of regional importance, a nodal point, around which other attractions can be strengthened and jobs can be created, local characteristics can be promoted and interpreted, while the visitor is judiciously guided throughout Moray from one point to another. The cumulative effect of these nodal points is to create a critical mass of appeal at the local, district and regional levels, whereby visitors will arrive, wonder, stay longer and return again in the future.

Keith is in the eastern part of Moray, a small historic town of 4,700 people with an economy traditionally based on agriculture, textiles and whisky. It was a sizeable railway junction with its own locomotive workshops. The surrounding area is agricultural land. Grange to the north, for example, was farmed by the monks of Kinloss in medieval times. Keith's own industrial heritage of milling, textiles, tanning and distilling along the banks of the River Isla, spawned the development of a railway. Much of this is long gone, but the sites remain. The town of Keith is skirted by the A96, the potential visitor passing by with hardly a glance. Yet, there is a strong will within the community to see Keith and its area established as a visitor destination. Indeed, the Keith Initiative has evolved around a series of positive proposals. For example, Seagram Distillers, producers of Chivas Regal, have major plans to upgrade the Strathisla Distillery Visitor Centre and to create an exclusive visitor facility nearby, and the Keith-Dufftown Railway Association are bidding to run steam trains on the scenic eleven mile Keith-Dufftown railway which was closed in 1991.

The District Council is faced with a challenge in that Forres and Dufftown have been identified as the key gateways into Moray, and thus any attraction in Keith will require to be on a scale significant enough to attract visitors that bit further towards it. Yet, in realistic terms, the development of a major visitor attraction in Keith is unlikely to be attainable if funded solely by the District Council. While Moray is under-performing in tourism compared to its neighbours, Keith performs the least well and requires to develop its accommodation to a far higher degree. The solution to this dilemma lies in the fortunate coming together of a variety of plans and proposals which are now encouraging the District Council to consider the development of the concept of a Keith Heritage Park (this is the working title and has yet to be developed by the marketing people). The park can be built around the proposed restoration of the Dufftown-Keith rail link and the Glenfiddich and Strathisla Distilleries at either end of it. The rebuilding of the old Keith Station and development of a heritage centre, preferably using Keith's former tannery and surrounding buildings in the pleasant Hyde Park on the banks of the River Isla provide the core.

An essential prerequisite to this is the re-opening of the railway which provides the key novel ingredient of *The Whisky Train*. Such an attraction will persuade potential visitors to make the extra effort to visit Keith, and having arrived they will be presented with a series of unique, inter-related and good quality visitor experiences. Vital also is the coming together of individuals and groups in partnership, ensuring that the whole is greater than the sum of the parts.

The core of the Heritage Park will embrace the Hyde Park site and comprise three main components, the heritage centre, the station building and the outdoor areas. The old tannery could be fully restored and developed to illustrate the story of the whole tanning process, while a leatherware shop with a working craftsman might well be incorporated. The buildings adjacent to the tannery are on two floors, and might incorporate the information and orientation function and include a tourist information centre; retail area; interpretation of Keith and its local social and industrial heritage; an education room; and a coffee shop combining an indoor seating area and outdoor glazed courtyard overlooking the railway line and themed by using objects from the District Council's domestic agricultural collection.

Interpretive and orientation materials and methods would be of high quality, but relatively simple and sufficiently flexible to enable exhibition areas to convert to a range of community uses. Should these supporting buildings not prove adaptable they might be replaced by a purpose built structure. The old Keith Station might be re-instated as authentically as possible using a new built structure including ticket office, station master's office and waiting room, with this latter area telling the stories of the railway's golden era, distilling and the Whisky Trail.

Given its setting, attention to the outdoor elements of the Heritage Park would be vital and provision should include attractive landscaping; walkways and seating areas along the riverbank; effective signage to Keith landmarks; discreet car parking; and a play area for children. On-site buildings and the park environment should be developed to a high quality specification, thus relating to other nearby attractions and thereby creating a high visual impact and that critical mass with the potential of 40,000 visitors each year, provided the railway reopens. At the time of writing the proposals outlined above were still under consideration.

The establishment of Keith as a major visitor magnet can only be attained through partnership and not necessarily with the District Council providing the major funding. Rather, by working with other bodies, it can seek to facilitate the new Heritage Centre and the rebuilding of the railway station and thereby ensure the necessary keystone of a very attractive visitor package. These bodies might include the local enterprise company, Historic Scotland, Scottish Natural Heritage, North East of Scotland Heritage Trust, Keith Initiative, Moray Tourist Board, the Keith-Dufftown Railway Association, the local distilleries and community groups all of whom in turn would work together to create the stronger base for attracting European funding and for exploiting joint marketing opportunities. In seeking to implement its heritage strategy for the Keith area, the District Council has an excellent opportunity to provide that facilitating role that might serve as the model for the future.

THE ESSENCE OF OUR STRATEGY

There is still much to be achieved within the District Council's heritage strategy. The Buckie Drifter is in its infancy while the Forres and Keith proposals have yet to be implemented, but our strategy is clear in its aims and flexible to changing circumstances. It is based on an integrity and uniqueness of place and people at a local, district and regional level. It draws on the area's strong characteristics, its significant aspects and seeks to interpret them in a holistic manner that will instil an understanding together with a wish to find out more.

The strategy has not evolved in isolation but through co-operation, discussion and research, and it has been developed with a keen eye on what our neighbours are seeking to do and who we can attract to visit us. It identifies gateways to the area and develops proposals for significant attractions at these gateways that will provide platforms for communities on which to build. Our approach is based on partnerships, thereby seeking to ensure that the whole is greater than the sum of the parts. Our principal mission is to ensure that Moray District can deservedly become a nationally recognised destination worth visiting, discovering and rediscovering.

The Author

Alistair Campbell is Assistant Director (Libraries and Museums), Moray District Council. He worked closely with Don Aldridge to develop a district-wide interpretation strategy, including the Buckie Drifter project. He is also chairman of the North Branch of the Scottish Library Association, and is responsible for the building of a new library in Elgin.

References

Aldridge, D., *Environmental Awareness: Regional and National Interpretive Plans,* in The Museums Journal, Vol 73, No 3, Dec 1973

Aldridge, D., *Principles of Countryside Interpretation and Interpretive Planning,* HMSO, 1975

Aldridge, D., *The Monster Book of Environmental Education,* Council of Europe, 1981

Aldridge, D., *Dundee's Heritage: A Strategy for Interpretation: (Including Its Hinterland).*, Scottish Development Agency, 1984

Aldridge, D., *Interpretation and Resource Management in Scotland: A Retrospective View*, in *Our Place in Europe*, Association of Scottish Parks and Countryside Offices, 1992

Aldridge, D., *Site Interpretation: A Practical Guide*, Scottish Tourist Board, 1993

Banff & Buchan District Council, *Peterhead Maritime Heritage Centre*, Banff & Buchan District Council, 1993

Cobham Resource Consultants, *Buckie Maritime Centre*, Cobham Resource Consultants, 1990

Fladmark, J.M., *Discovering the Personality of a Region: Strategic Interpretation in Scotland*, in Heritage: Conservation, Interpretation and Enterprise, Donhead, 1993

Grampian Regional Council, *Regional Interpretive Planning in Grampian*, Grampian Regional Council and Countryside Commission for Scotland, 1977

Kit Campbell Associates, *MacBeth Centre Forres*, Kit Campbell Associates, 1988

L & R Leisure plc, *Discovering MacBeth: Prospectus for a Major New Highland Visitor Centre*, L & R Leisure, 1992

L & R Leisure plc and Aldridge, D., *The Herring Story: A New Fishing Heritage Attraction for Buckie*, L & R Leisure plc, 1992

McKean, C., *The District of Moray: An Illustrated Architectural Guide*, Scottish Academic Press Royal Incorporation of Architects in Scotland, 1987

Moray District Council, *A Development Plan for Museums in the Moray District*, 1988

Moray District Council, *Buckie Maritime Heritage Centre: Feasibility Study Brief*, 1990

Moray District Council, *Keith Heritage Centre: A Brief for Consultants*, 1993

Moray District Council, *Moray Heritage/Tourist Centre: A Brief for Consultants*, 1994

Sellar, W.D.H. (ed), *Moray: Province and People*, Scottish Society for Northern Studies, 1993

TMS, *Keith Heritage Park: Draft Final Report*, TMS, 1994

Figure 2 Proposed Macbeth Centre, Forres.

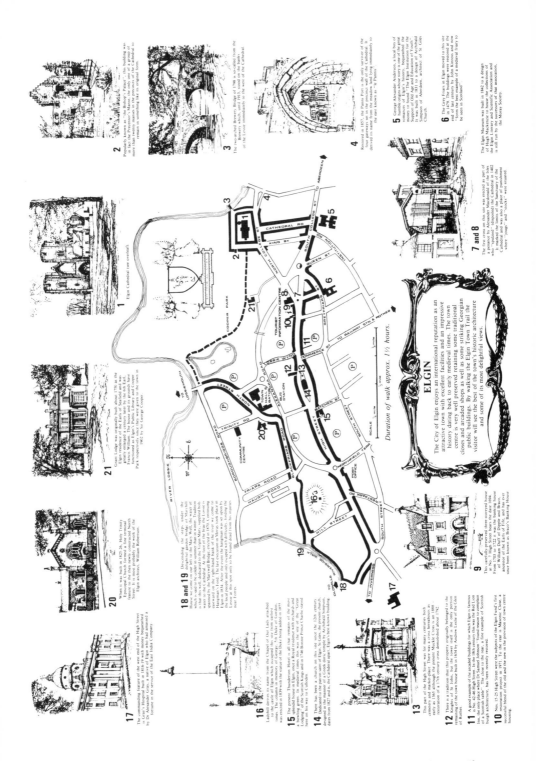

Elgin Town Trail, showing route map and illustrated points of interest from trail leaflet.

13

WHAT PRICE ACCESS?
Visitor Impact on Heritage in Trust

Trevor Croft

'We are not in the tourism business' is a phrase often heard from members of the National Trust for Scotland staff, especially those concerned primarily with the conservation and maintenance of its properties. However, with a total number of recorded visitors around the two million mark, an income of £1.1 million from admission fees, and trade in shops and tearooms of some £3 million, it is difficult to avoid the conclusion that tourism is exactly the business of the National Trust for Scotland.

Other buzz words heard frequently today include 'heritage tourism' and 'cultural tourism'. Culture is defined in Chambers Dictionary as 'to cultivate – to civilise or refine'. Culture is, in common parlance, the type or characteristics of a civilisation. Heritage is simply that which can be inherited. So what do we mean by these terms, and what is access to the cultural heritage or heritage in trust?

The Trust was founded in 1931 as a body which, in the words of Sir John Stirling Maxwell of Pollock, one of its founding fathers, 'serves the Nation as a cabinet into which it can put some of its valuable things, where they will be perfectly safe for all time ...' The Trust is commonly perceived as a government body but is in fact a charity, its powers legally established under the National Trust for Scotland Order Confirmation Act of 1935 and subsequent legislation. The Schedule to this Act records the Trust's purposes as being 'to promote for the benefit of the nation the permanent preservation of lands and buildings in Scotland of historic or architectural interest or natural beauty.'

The same Act gave the Trust the power to declare land inalienable: thus, giving security of ownership and freeing it from the threat of compulsory purchase or predatory developers. But what, one may ask, is the point of preserving properties if you cannot look at them? A later Order Confirmation Act of 1938, extends the powers to include the promotion of public access and enjoyment to its properties. Here we have the classical heritage dilemma.

How do we provide universal access whilst at the same time seeking to conserve something which is often incapable of withstanding great pressures?

The cultural heritage in our care might be loosely divided into buildings, furnishings, works of art and literature. Gardens are excluded here simply because this subject deserves a separate paper in its own right. The current guide to all our properties uses the following classification: *Castles and Large Houses, Countryside, Gardens, Historic Sites, Islands, Little Houses Improvement Scheme, Famous Scots, Museums,* and *Social and Industrial Heritage.*

The Trust owns many examples of buildings, but it is with its flagship castles such as Culzean or Fyvie that it is frequently most closely associated. However, this is only part of the story. Our built heritage includes not only the fine and the grand, but equally the artisans' houses that make up the largest part of our communities. One of the Trust's most successful acquisitions and presentations is the humble Tenement House in Glasgow. One of its most recent acquisitions is the Old Schoolhouse at Cottown in Perthshire: a simple dwelling with mud walls under a roof of Tayside reed, perhaps the original true vernacular building. Within these extremes there is a myriad of different examples including such 'designer' buildings as Charles Rennie Mackintosh's Hill House and Alexander 'Greek' Thomson's Holmwood, a 1994 acquisition.

The furnishings of all our houses, from the great castles to the humblest dwellings, are generally the work of craftsmen of one discipline or another. Chairs, tables and cabinets exhibit work of the very highest standards, painstakingly undertaken and often of great delicacy. Most buildings are enriched by works of art of different types. Many are noted for their fine collections of paintings, none more so than Fyvie Castle, with its excellent collection of portraits and landscapes, including works by Batoni, Raeburn and Millais, among others. Another new Trust property, Broughton House, is the former home of Edward Atkinson Hornel, one of the famous 'Glasgow Boys'. Now a gallery, it is dedicated to the display of his works, our first property dedicated to one artist.

Literature is featured in two ways. Many properties house important libraries. In addition to its paintings, Broughton House has one of the largest number of Burns' works in one collection, and that on Galloway is possibly the best of its type in existence. The family library in Brodie Castle is perhaps our finest, not simply in the collection of volumes, but because of the distinguished room in which it sits. Literature also features in the birthplaces of famous authors. Thomas Carlyle's in Ecclefechan, is perhaps a specialist taste. However, no one can deny the world-wide fame of James Matthew Barrie, famous everywhere for Peter Pan but born in the humble cottage at 9 Brechin Road in Kirriemuir. Here, Barrie listened to his mother's stories which were to influence his writings in later life. The importance of a property depends on what criteria we use, but by these standards Barrie's is more important than most.

These examples give some indication of the breadth of the cultural heritage resources in our care. They also indicate the wealth for the visitor to see, whether it be the majestic grace of a building, the refined skill of the craftsman, the deft touch of the artist's brush or the vivid imagination of the writer. So how do we balance the permanent preservation of all these with the need to promote access? Somewhere there must be a compromise. The basic principles are easy. Build a car park, employ the guides and open the doors. It sounds straightforward, but it is not as simple as this. Access means many different things. Do we look at objects; use them; listen to them; are they delicate or robust; big or small? The solid robust floors of a mediaeval castle can obviously withstand greater use than the delicate beams of a small cottage. Large buildings may be easy to get round, though equally they may have many narrow corridors and small rooms. Small buildings by definition cannot hold many people. So how do we achieve a balance, and perhaps most important, how do we pay for it all?

To find the answers it is helpful to look at some of the background to the Trust and the reason it has so many fine properties. Inalienability has been mentioned already. It is this which gives the Trust its primary strength. It inspires confidence in people to give properties to it, knowing that they will be safe for the future. Some 70% of our properties have come as gifts during people' s lifetime. Many others have come as bequests or negotiated deals with the government in lieu of death duties. Only very occasionally do we purchase on the open market, and usually then only if we are funded by others to do so. Such an example was Fyvie Castle, where a public outcry at the potential sale and dispersal of the contents led to support from the National Heritage Memorial Fund and Historic Scotland securing the property.

However, it is also a question of vision. One day in 1982 a young lady called Anna Davidson walked into Trust's Edinburgh Headquarters in Charlotte Square. An actress by profession, her uncle had been left a bequest of furniture in a tenement flat in Garnethill in Glasgow. Going with him to fetch the chairs, Anna discovered an Aladdin's Cave with seemingly nothing touched in years. Anna bought it and carefully put away the contents, the property of a Miss Agnes Toward who had died in hospital. Forced to sell, Anna wanted to see if the Trust could save it.

Faced with initial lack of interest, she was fortunate to meet Findlay McQuarrie, then a Deputy Director with the Trust. Findlay was a man of vision and, against much opposition, was able to persuade the Trust to buy the flat and its contents. The rest is now history but the Tenement Flat has done much to redress the accusation that we are only interested in castles or stately homes.

It was soon found that owning historic buildings is not a paying proposition, and we now have a policy of refusing to accept properties unless they are suitably endowed, breaching this only in exceptional cases of great national importance. Annual and running maintenance costs generally far exceed admissions and other revenue. The insurance bill for Fyvie Castle

1	Angus Folk Museum	56	Hutchesons' Hall
2	Arduaine Garden	57	Inveresk Lodge Garden
3	Bachelors' Club	58	Inverewe Garden
4	Balmacara Estate	59	Iona
5	Balmerino Abbey	60	Kellie Castle and Garden
6	Bannockburn	61	Killiecrankie
7	Barrie's Birthplace	62	Kintail and Morvich
8	Barry Mill	63	Leith Hall and Garden
9	Ben Lawers	64	Linn of Tummel
10	Ben Lomond	65	Malleny Garden
11	Blackhill	66	Pitmedden Garden
12	Boath Doocot	67	Preston Mill and Phantassie Doocot
13	Branklyn Garden	68	Priorwood Garden
14	Brodick Castle, Garden & Country Park	69	Rockcliffe
15	Goatfell	70	St Abb's Head
16	Brodie Castle	71	St Kilda
17	Broughton House	72	Shieldaig Island
18	Bruce's Stone	73	Robert Smail's Printing Works
19	Bucinch and Ceardach	74	Souter Johnnie's Cottage
20	Burg	75	Staffa
21	Caiy Stone	76	Strome Castle
22	Cameronians' Regimental Memorial	77	The Tenement House
23	Canna	78	Threave Garden and Estate
24	Carlyle's Birthplace	79	Tighnabruaich Viewpoint
25	Castle Fraser	80	Torridon
26	Corrieshalloch Gorge	81	Weaver's Cottage
27	Craigievar Castle	82	West Affric
28	Craigower	83	Antonine Wall
29	Crathes Castle, Garden and Estate	84	Castle Campbell
30	Culloden	85	Castlehill
31	Culross	86	Clava Cairns
32	Culzean Castle and Country Park	87	Crookston Castle
33	Cunninghame Graham Memorial	88	Dirleton Castle
34	Dollar Glen	89	Glenluce Abbey Glebe
35	Drum Castle	90	Hamilton House
36	Dunkeld	91	Lamb's House
37	Fair Isle	92	Parklea Farm
38	Falkland Palace, Garden and Old Burgh	93	The Pineapple
39	Falls of Glomach	94	Preston Tower
40	Finavon Doocot	95	Provan Hall
41	Fyvie Castle	96	Provost Ross's House (Aberdeen Maritime Museum)
42	Gatehouse of Fleet	97	Scotstarvit Tower
43	The Georgian House and Charlotte Square	98	Threave Castle
44	Gladstone's Land	99	Turret House
45	Glencoe and Dalness	100	Macquarie Mausoleum
46	Glenfinnan Monument	101	Menstrie Castle
47	Greenbank Garden	102	Abertarff House
48	Grey Mare's Tail	103	Geilston House and Garden
49	Haddo House	104	Kippen Smiddy
50	The Hermitage	105	Linlithgow Houses
51	The Hill House	106	The Old Granary
52	Hill of Tarvit Mansionhouse	107	Plewlands House
53	House of the Binns	108	Sailor's Walk
54	House of Dun	109	Stenhouse Mansion
55	Hugh Miller's Cottage		

71 St Kilda

♜ The National Trust for Scotland

Figure 1 Location map of National Trust for Scotland properties, 1994.

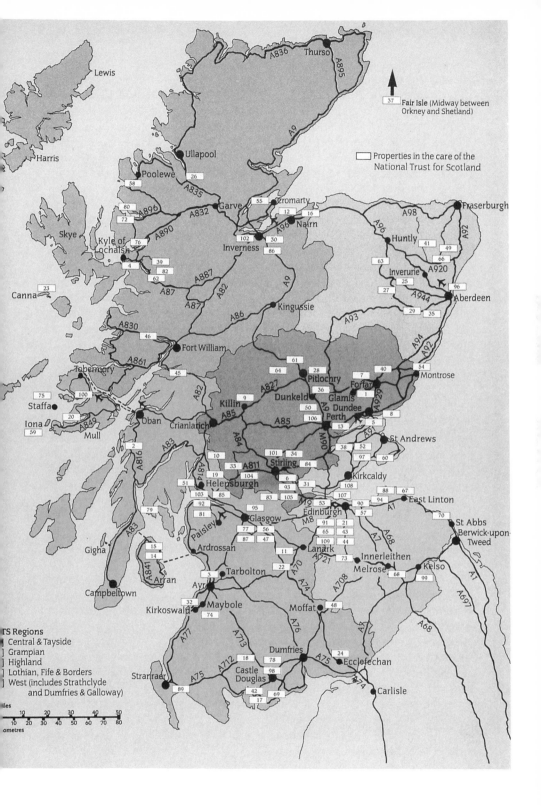

Lewis

Harris

Skye

Canna

Staffa

Iona
Mull

Gigha

Campbeltown

Ullapool
Poolewe 58
26

80 A896
72 A832 Garve 55 Cromarty
A890 76 12 16
Kyle of 30 Nairn A96 Huntly
Lochalsh 4 102 Inverness 86
39 A887 A82 A86 Kingussie
62
A830 46
Fort William
Tobermory A861
45
100
75
20
A849
59
Oban Crianlarich
2 A83
10
A816 A814 51 Helensburgh
79 103 85
92 95
81 Glasgow
Paisley 77 56
87 47
Ardrossan 11
15 Tarbolton 22
14
3
Arran Ayr
32 Maybole
Kirkoswald 74

Fair Isle (Midway between
Orkney and Shetland)

Properties in the care of the
National Trust for Scotland

A836 Thurso
A895

37

Fraserburgh
A98
A92
A96 41 49
63 66
Inverurie A920
25 96
27 A944 Aberdeen
29 35

A93
A94
A92
61 54
64 28 40 Montrose
Pitlochry 7 Forfar
36 A929
Dunkeld 1
50 Glamis Dundee
A85 106 Perth
13 5
38 52 St Andrews
101 34 97 60
Stirling 84
33 104
19 6
93 31
83 105 108
M9 53 107 88 67
Edinburgh 90 94 East Linton
M8 57 A1 70
91 21
65 43 St Abbs
109 44 Berwick-upon-
Lanark 73 Innerleithen Tweed
A21 Melrose Kelso
68 99

Kirkcaldy

A68

Moffat 48
A76
A77 A713
18 Dumfries 24 Ecclefechan
78 A75
A712 Castle 98
Stranraer A75 Douglas Carlisle
89 42 A74
17

TS Regions
Central & Tayside
Grampian
Highland
Lothian, Fife & Borders
West (includes Strathclyde
and Dumfries & Galloway)

iles
10 20 30 40 50
10 20 30 40 50 60 70 80
ometres

173

alone, for example, exceeds £25,000. Many private owners would hesitate fully to insure with sums like these. With the nation's heritage held in trust we do not have this option. The annual revenue deficit on the large houses is generally between £50,000 and £80,000. Even small properties run into five figures. Nor do these figures reflect fully the essential requirement for central advisory staff and regional administration. To the visitor at the property, they are irrelevant, the only people that matter are the staff that they meet. The central administration costs, however, cannot be ignored.

The most significant of our early acquisitions were countryside properties such as the Burg, Glencoe and Kintail. Others such as Crookston Castle and Culross Palace were either under, or were put under, guardianship of the Ministry of Works, and were accordingly not a problem to the Trust. Barrie's Birthplace in Kirriemuir was so small and remote that access was not a problem in 1937 when the property was gifted. It was only after the passing of fiscal legislation enabling tax benefits for families passing on properties to the nation that the so-called 'big houses' came on to the scene. The first of these was the House of the Binns in 1944, followed closely by Culzean a year later. Since then the numbers have multiplied.

In the early days, properties were 'developed' for access almost by rule of thumb. A few rooms would be opened one year, more the next and so on. Relatively few people had cars to get into the countryside where many of the finest buildings were located. Petrol rationing went on for several years after the Second World War, and visitor numbers were generally small. Access was not a problem. It was only in the 1960s, when what might be termed the recreation explosion started to take place, and coincidentally the number of Trust acquisitions rose substantially, that visitor numbers to our buildings started to rise significantly. It was then realised that the real problems with visitor access are really caused by pressure of numbers.

Today, the development of properties for access starts with the management plan. We have a dedicated team of planners working in the Policy Research Department with a programme to complete plans for each property over a five year period. The way that each property is used by the public is now fully and properly thought out. Many lessons can be learnt from past experience and put to good use for the future.

Our corporate plan identifies certain basic facilities which are necessary in order to open a property. At minimum, these would include a car park, necessary signposting and toilet facilities. This will often suffice for the smaller properties. Even here, however, it is necessary to provide some form of interpretation to enable visitors to get the best understanding of the property. Interpretive plans for properties are developed as part of the main management plan. In its simplest form, interpretation may be only a leaflet or guide book about the property. This might be called the strategy of least interference, where lack of labels or information boards leaves much to the individual imagination. Simple hand-held information boards, giving brief details of the room's contents, may be available. Most people, however, want more than this, and the development of exhibitions is almost a subject in itself.

On the basis that visitor pressure is the most difficult thing to deal with, there are two main approaches that can be made. The first is to restrict numbers which can be done in several ways. The best example of this is perhaps found at Craigievar Castle, possibly the finest example in our care of a traditional 'z-plan' tower house. Relatively unaltered over the years, it retains most of its fine architectural features which include many small rooms and narrow staircases. Such was its popularity that, over the years, visitor numbers rose to over 33,000. Everyone wanted to see this little Aberdeenshire jewel. Apart from the general unpleasantness of trying to look round a building crammed with people, it became apparent that some of the ceilings in the bedrooms were developing cracks, possibly from pressure of feet on the floors above. This was tackled by closing off the upper floor, removing access from rooms above those in greatest danger. Coach parties were banned, and numbers otherwise reduced by the simple expedient of cutting down drastically on advertising. Although it appears in our main guide book, there are now no special advertising leaflets, and it is not featured on regional advertising posters. The little take-away tea hut has also been removed, and numbers are down to a manageable 20,000 per year.

The sheer beauty and simplicity that had been the saving of Craigievar over the years also meant that there had not been extensive development of other buildings within the policies, such as are normally associated with large country houses. On bigger properties the key to management is spreading the visitors. Most individual houses, set in their policies, have a number of components, all of which can be attractive to visitors. There is usually the house itself, generally associated with a garden and often a courtyard or steading building. The House of Dun in Angus is a good example of this, and of the way in which we now tackle access at a new property.

A bequest to the Trust in 1980, it was formerly a hotel which finally closed in 1984. Subsequent years were taken up with extensive restoration, before it finally opened to the public in 1989. A courtyard on the west side of the house consisted of many outbuildings, including stables and coach-houses. These were restored first, providing space for displays, as well as commercial activities, including a tearoom and shop. This enabled people to visit the property whilst the main house and garden were being restored. Walks have been developed in the wider policies and it is now possible for visitors to spend three or four hours at the property exploring different aspects and finding quiet corners away from other visitors. Visitor numbers are still relatively low at around 25,000 per year, but the same management principles applied to busier properties, such as Crathes Castle, succeed in spreading the load around the property. Even at Culzean Castle and Country Park, with over 300,000 visitors a year, it is easy to spread people out within the 300 acre Country Park.

At the Tenement Flat pressure on space is acute. Here we have been able to purchase three other flats in the same block. One provides a home for our resident staff, whilst another gives valuable display space telling the story of the tenement. The third gives staff rest facilities and space for briefing school parties. Spreading the visitors in this way eases the pressure and makes for a more enjoyable and informative visit. At Barrie's Birthplace, another small property, an exhibition was created in an adjacent terraced house at No. 11 Brechin Road. In this way the scope of the property was extended, spreading the load and adding interest for children. Most importantly, the historical integrity of the original cottage was not prejudiced in any way.

So for better or worse, and for the benefit of the nation, the Trust opens its doors. The biggest single problem in opening a property is probably security, not simply from theft but also from damage to contents. We have all read about recent thefts from a number of stately homes in England and Scotland. There is little that can be done to prevent the really determined thief gaining access. A solid sledge hammer and will to defy the alarm system will get you into most buildings. And most properties, Trust and private, provide the courtesy of a handy guidebook, to say nothing of a guided tour, to identify valuable works of art. If the public are to get access to buildings, these are risks that have to be taken. Overall, greater dangers come from casual theft, particularly from prying fingers, and often from those who should know better. The occasional touch on delicate curtains or important needlework may not matter, but multiply this 5,000 times and the object of desire disintegrates before one's very eyes. Observation of furniture distressed over the years in normal use easily shows the damage which abuse can bring. We endeavour to present houses in the way they may have been lived in and avoid roping off areas. On occasions this may be unavoidable, but is the price to be paid when the threat of damage becomes too great to take a risk.

Another big problem is the sheer amount of dirt and dust which people inevitably bring into buildings. The impact of large numbers of people just breathing in and out can play havoc with environmental conditions and hundreds, indeed thousands, of feet pounding up and down on carpets grinding in pieces of grit leaves little to the imagination. The key here is conscientious cleaning. We now have a policy of introducing what is known as 'conservation cleaning' into properties in our care. Under this programme a rigorous but careful and gentle cleaning rota is put into being.

The programme started at Fyvie Castle where it is no coincidence that our residential representative has worked previously with our sister organisation south of the Border, the National Trust. We must admit that the National Trust is probably ahead of us in this work, largely because it has suffered a greater impact of visitors through sheer pressure of numbers. An invaluable book for anyone interested in this work is *The National Trust Manual of Housekeeping*. In it you will find details of how to look after anything from an ostrich egg to a rhinoceros hide. Careful cleaning not only maintains furnishings in good order, but also identifies early evidence of damage which may need careful conservation work to repair and restore. This programme will eventually spread to all our properties and emphasises that vigilance is the best way to protect our buildings.

Good interpretation, as well as explaining about properties and how they came into being, will also increase visitors' understanding of the need for conservation. On larger properties, where visitor numbers permit, additional funds will be spent on special displays related specifically to the property. This increase in understanding will enable the visitor to get more out of their stay as well as being a valuable management tool in spreading the load. Such displays are, however, expensive and the average life of each is around ten years, varying from property to property.

This introduces the biggest problem of all, finance. Extra visitor numbers mean more of everything. More guides, more security, bigger tearooms and shops. As well as being an important part of the visit for many people, such facilities bring in valuable income as long as we make sure that they give a commercial return on funds employed in their development. This income can contribute towards meeting the deficits already referred to.

Such is the cost today of opening major properties that we are unable to do this on our own. The partnership at Fyvie with National Heritage Memorial Fund and Historic Scotland has been mentioned above. The country parks in the policies of Culzean and Brodick Castles are run in association with the local authorities. Major fund-raising appeals bring support from commercial firms and charitable trusts. Our membership currently stands at 235,000, and our own Members' Centres and Groups also make valuable contributions. One simple way of reducing costs would be to reduce standards. However, the Trust's corporate plan insists that we must do things to the level of best current practice. This has to be right because as soon as we start to compromise standards will slip.

More and more the answer to the financial problem is a partnership with other bodies. The Old Schoolhouse at Cottown was in danger of collapse, but we could not take it on without an endowment. However, funding was not available for this and repair costs too. The problem was solved in an unusual way. A financial package from the National Heritage Memorial Fund, Perth and Kinross Heritage Trust and Historic Scotland provided for the purchase and repair of the building. Historic Scotland agreed to take the building into guardianship when the conservation repair is completed, and negotiations are being held to set up a local trust to run the building and open it to the public.

We are fortunate in that visitor pressure in Scotland has not generally reached the levels found at many National Trust properties south of the Border. Yet, constant vigilance and maintenance is necessary and the last message perhaps comes from the Trust's corporate plan. The first priority is conservation of its properties. Everything else comes second to this and, if the assessment is that damage may be done, restrictions will have to be made. We have not yet closed a property because of pressure of visitors, but the experience at Craigievar shows that numbers can be reduced and almost certainly this will happen again in the future. Visitor numbers are being monitored closely in a number of properties and action will be taken if necessary.

But there is no point in conserving buildings and contents for the benefit of the nation if people cannot have access to them. However, as visitor numbers increase, many difficult decisions will have to be made to adjust our policies for access so that they adhere to the principle of sustainability. Our primary duty is to ensure that the heritage we hold in trust is not irreparably damaged and remains intact for future generations to enjoy. This will require us to work closely with other providers of visitor attractions to develop a robust strategic framework for decisions about access and interpretation at national, regional and local levels of operation.

The Author

Trevor Croft is the Regional Director for Central and Tayside with the National Trust for Scotland. He was formerly their Head of Policy Research. Following a spell with the Countryside Commission for Scotland, he was responsible for establishing Lake Malawi National Park, now a World Heritage Site.

References

English Historic Towns Forum, *Getting It Right: A Guide to Visitor Management in Historic Towns*, EHTF, 1994

Hurd, R., *Scotland Under Trust: The Story of the National Trust for Scotland and Its Properties*, Adam & Charles Black, 1939

National Trust for Scotland, Property Guides, especially *Barrie's Birthplace, Craigievar Castle, Fyvie Castle, House of Dun, Tenement Home*, NTS, 1992

National Trust for Scotland, *Corporate Plan*, NTS, 1992 (unpublished)

National Trust for Scotland, *Guide to Over 100 Properties*, NTS, 1994

National Trust for Scotland Order Confirmation Acts, 1935 and 1938

Sandwith, S. and Stainton, S., *The National Trust Manual of Housekeeping*, Allen Lane, 1984

14

WHERE THE SHOE HURTS
The Ecological Impacts of Tourism

Thomas Huxley

It is a fact that the tourist industry has destroyed wild land habitats and thereby, either directly or indirectly, reduced biodiversity. Sir David Attenborough in *The First Eden* gives a vivid account of the impact of tourism on the Mediterranean. 'Huge, high-rise hotels were built like gargantuan palisades along the beaches. Swamps were drained to rid them of mosquitoes that might bite visitors unacceptably. Stretches of lonely dunes were bulldozed out of the way to create new building sites. Wide motorways were driven along the coast to link one resort to another.' And the visitors themselves inevitably took a toll from the countryside, 'wearing foot-paths down the bed-rock, trampling and uprooting wild flowers and carelessly setting fire to the dry summer forests.'

These words could describe many other parts of the world. Most of us have seen the same destruction, both as observers and as participants in this irreparable process because we all, at one time or another, become part of the millions of people who enjoy holidays in places that not so long ago had experienced little change over centuries. Indeed, one of the many reasons for visiting the countryside, along with fine scenery and nature generally, is to enjoy wildlife and, therefore, for our own pleasure as much as because of our responsibility to conserve wildlife for its own sake, we have to consider carefully where the shoe hurts.

Attenborough backs up his word picture with some statistics amassed by two hundred research stations now located around the Mediterranean by a United Nations Environment Programme begun in 1973. Into that enclosed sea were dumped each year 90 tons of pesticides, 800,000 tons of oil and 430 billion tons of domestic waste and sewage, 90% of it untreated. In recent years, action has been taken to improve this appalling situation. What is not made clear, however, is how much of the blame for this pollution can be assigned to the tourist industry. The coastal zone of the Mediterranean has attracted numerous other industries and cities whose economies are only

179

partially related to tourism. So there is an important distinction to be made between the impact of tourism on the environment and many other activities whose effects may be just as serious, possibly more so. There is a need for clarification; for more precision about where the shoe hurts and why. This paper begins by teasing out what is generally meant by ecological impacts and other relevant terms before examining their application to Scotland.

THE SHOE DEFINED

There are hard and soft meanings to ecology. In the hard sense, ecology is a branch of the earth and life sciences. It is a body of knowledge which describes the activities and relationships of whole organisms to each other and to their surroundings. Like other sciences, ecology has its own principles, concepts and unifying theories and ecological research is ultimately aimed at confirming and developing the truth of these principles. Much of the time, ecologists communicate only with each other, albeit bits of what they discover sometimes spill out into wider public discussion.

Soft ecology, however, is in no sense a discipline and has no structure, yet it is better known because it permeates the everyday language of green politics and media discussion of social and environmental issues. Bramwell uses the term ecologism: a political box for thinking about the environment. Bizarre phrases such as 'ecological footprint', defined as the impact Britain makes as a country on the world's natural resources, and 'drug ecology food chain' for the money which passes from the high street to main suppliers, occur in the newspapers and there are many combinations of the prefix 'eco' which convey an implication of environmental betterment. Examples are eco-labelling and eco-tourism, albeit some, such as eco-freak, can also have a pejorative connotation.

In this paper, I shall stick to hard ecology and the most important concept for the conservation of biodiversity, that populations of organisms are able to go on existing, generation after generation. For many reasons, numbers of organisms within a population may fluctuate widely over time, perhaps in a regular cyclic fashion, or there may be local extinction and replacement by inward migration from other neighbouring populations of the same species. The factors that regulate population numbers have preoccupied ecologists for over half a century. Thousands of papers in scientific journals and hundreds of books have been written on the subject and it makes sense, therefore, that ecologists rank the study of life history strategies among the top ten of the most important fifty concepts in ecology.

I have used the general word organism because, initially, one is thinking in an all embracing way about all forms of life: all kinds of animals, from mammals and birds to tiny insects, and all kinds of plants, from trees and shrubs to grasses and mosses. Later, I shall consider how limited to a few species ecological research on recreation impacts has been.

180

Another word currently much written and talked about is sustainability, which is about keeping things going continuously, and one can combine that idea with the concept of populations into a shorthand concept of sustainable populations. In the context of this article, what matters is that populations should be able to keep going continuously without becoming extinct. It is immaterial whether they can be easily seen, or whether they exist in what are deemed by us to be aesthetically beautiful surroundings. The scars of footpaths and access tracks on mountains or dumps of litter on beaches may for us be visual eyesores and detract from a feeling of wilderness. In the life history of a particular species, however, such factors may not matter for the sustainability of a population and the broader goal of conservation of biodiversity.

Tourism and associated activities also have to be defined. A tourist is someone on holiday who spends one or more bed nights away from home and much of the cash flow derived from the tourist industry comes from the supply of accommodation: from camping and caravan sites and bed and breakfast facilities to huge hotels. (This definition is intended to exclude nights spent away from home for business or other non-holiday reasons, although there may be activity overlap, eg people attending business conferences may also visit tourist attractions.)

Day visitors are people who venture into the countryside from home, mostly in their own cars or tour buses, which also carry tourists. The distinction between tourists and day visitors is of importance for people carrying out economic surveys. Once in the area being visited, however, there is no easy way to distinguish between a tourist and day visitor, other than by asking where the person stayed the previous night. As stated in a report published last year, although it was estimated that people resident in Scotland made some 85 million day trips per year, a large proportion was to areas and attractions also visited by tourists.

The important question, for the purpose of this paper, is in what activity the tourist or day visitor takes part. Unfortunately, although assigning activities into simply understood and mutually exclusive categories should be easy, in practice it is not. Although we may think of some activities mainly in relation to words such as sport, recreation or tourism (eg orienteering, skiing or canoeing as sports, informal walking as recreation and visiting stately homes as a tourist activity), there is considerable overlap between these major categories, in part because of the huge number of activities in which people nowadays engage in the countryside. For example, earlier this year a brochure was launched featuring 500 holidays in Britain covering more than fifty different kinds of activity holidays. Trends in behaviour also change over time. For example, although average numbers of recreational craft on Loch Lomond have remained fairly constant, the use of high powered craft has increased dramatically, indicating a change in the pattern of use from slow to high speed craft. In a general way, also, increased personal mobility by the use of private cars will continue to create impacts and problems requiring local, as well as national, management solutions.

In some respects the position is not made easier by the existence of organisations part of whose purpose is to oversee activities at a national level, such as the Scottish Sports Council, Scottish Tourist Board and Scottish Natural Heritage (having embraced the former Countryside Commission for Scotland and Nature Conservancy Council for Scotland) and, at the level of particular activities, a much larger number of governing bodies of individual sports, including the field sports of fishing and shooting. Within and between the national bodies there is continuous dialogue to avoid duplication of interests, particularly in relation to grants. Even so, it is not always easy to distinguish exactly what relates to tourism and what to numerous other countryside pursuits such as rambling and nature study which, although generally classified under recreation, are also included in lists of activities participated in by UK and overseas tourists on holiday trips to Scotland.

I have had to labour this difficulty of categorisation for the simple reason that most research in Britain on the impact of people on wildlife is associated with the key word recreation, whereas on a world scale it is associated with tourism. This may be because, at the larger geographical scale, our view is through tourist spectacles and we know little about locally generated recreation pressures, whereas in our own country, we perceive people pressure mainly in terms of recreation, while classifying much of the built infrastructure as tourism. Whether or not this is valid, for the purpose of this paper and notwithstanding its title (and the title of this volume) most of my examples will be drawn from the recreation literature.

Another generalisation about the difference between the ecological impacts of tourism in some other countries and in Scotland is that elsewhere tourist developments may occur in wild land where man's influence is minimal, whereas in Scotland there are few places which have not experienced centuries of land use change. This has a bearing on the conclusions to this paper.

Defining the nature of recreational impacts on organisms is even more complicated than classifying the impacts themselves. Perhaps the most helpful way to introduce this subject is to relate our own five senses (sight, sound, feel, smell and taste) to an organism that is not human but which we know reasonably well, for example, a pet dog or cat. Pet owners soon learn both the sharper and duller sensual acuity of their pets, compared to their own senses, and stimuli that lead to behavioural confusion. Our Border collie knows the front door bell but barks just the same when the noise is heard on the television. She can smell a grey squirrel long before we have seen it but an orange ball, when no longer moving, is often invisible. Low flying jet-planes justifiably scare her witless but her initial reaction is often the same when she hears high flying aeroplanes not followed by the same ear-piercing scream. Most people can give countless similar examples and can readily transfer that kind of experience to wild animals so as to imagine the range of stimuli that trigger a reaction. In a broad sense, the reaction is a kind of impact, considered in more detail in the next section.

Figure 1 Red Deer calf.

Figure 2 Ptarmigan hen with chick.

drawings by Freya Fladmark

Disturbance is an impact and it is a fact of common experience that when animals are disturbed they move away from the source of the disturbance. It is also well known that not all animals do so. Hedgehogs and pill woodlice roll into a ball, snails retreat into their shell and the young of some kinds of ground nesting birds crouch as low as their body form permits and trust in the camouflaging effect of feather coloration. For the first three days or so after being born, a red deer calf will freeze and lie deep in vegetation. Whatever the reaction, whether running or flying away, or curling into a ball, the important point is that at least the adult animal, if not also its young, is temporarily no longer doing whatever it was doing before being disturbed, which was probably feeding but might have been incubating or perhaps defending its territory. The upshot is that, however brief or extended the reaction period to the disturbance, during that time it will not be taking in nourishment or doing something else useful to itself or its young and it may also be consuming energy which has to be replaced. In the life history of many animals, such events will generally be of small importance. The individual's energy balance is programmed to cope.

We need to consider, therefore, in what ecological circumstances disturbance can be serious. To start with, a clear distinction can be made between kinds of animals that are widely distributed, often in more than one habitat, and those which are limited in their distribution to particular habitats, especially habitats which are also attractive for recreation. For the former, disturbance does not generally have any permanent effect on whole populations, even when it is lethal to the individual. For example, although little to do with recreation but usefully illustrative of something we all see, numbers of squished hedgehogs are directly related to the numbers generally in the countryside. But for animals which have a limited distribution, even a relatively low level of unintentional disturbance can seriously reduce breeding success, and consequently, if the national population is small, such disturbance can have a major impact on the population as a whole.

A combination of factors, such as sensitivity to disturbance and weather, may also be important, placing some species more at risk than others. For example, both golden eagles and divers leave their nests even when the cause of disturbance (such as a walker, perhaps unaware of the vicinity of the birds) may yet be some distance away. And because eagles nest early in the year when eggs are prone to chilling, such disturbance may result in the death of embryo chicks still in the egg. As to divers, their nests are so rudimentary that when unattended the eggs are readily exposed to passing predators, such as gulls or crows and the time lapse between the parent leaving the nest and predation can be quite short if predators are in the vicinity. Another example of a kind of bird sensitive to disturbance is the golden plover. Disturbance by passing walkers, while not shortening the lives of adult birds, can affect breeding success and so recruitment to the moorland population. If, however, there are surplus young from breeding

Figure 3 Little Terns.

Figure 4 Golden Plover.

185

pairs in undisturbed parts of the moor, the overall population level may be unaffected.

Most research on disturbance to animals from recreational activities has been done on birds and most of the evidence demonstrating impacts of importance for population sustainability is similar to the examples just given. Other examples of sensitive moorland birds are dotterel and ptarmigan and, among water birds, as well as divers, some species of grebes. The most critical stages in the organism's life history are related to incubation and protection of young and disturbance at these stages may allow a mortality factor to operate: the eggs get cold or are eaten by a predator, ditto the chicks. The Achilles heel is the sensitivity of the adult bird to the stimulus of disturbance, its immediate behavioural reaction, the time period before it returns to the nest or chicks and whether a lethal factor such as cold or predation is able to operate in that period. Probably the most clear cut example of the badly negative effect of recreation on birds is people walking through or near colonies of nesting terns, particularly Sandwich and Little terns, whose nests, furthermore, are so well camouflaged they can be trampled on inadvertently. In the case of tern colonies, however, no one can be unaware that they are causing disturbance because of the easily seen and heard panic reaction of birds taking flight and wheeling over the nesting area.

Anecdotal information and a little observational research has been assessed on disturbance by hill walkers (and cross country skiing) to deer, especially red deer, because disturbance can cause disruption of stalking and sometimes economic loss or inability to achieve desired numbers of culled animals. Related studies have been done on the long term effects of capturing animals for marking so as to learn about life histories, not only because of a concern for animal welfare but also to ensure that marking was not affecting survival of captured and marked animals. Disturbance of deer by hill walkers is much discussed because of continuing debate about access to hill country but the crucial conclusion, in relation to this article about ecological impacts, is that disturbance from most recreational activities does not affect the long term sustainability of deer populations. Possibly, and this is just my opinion, there is a deeper issue that if cull targets were to be greatly increased so as to reduce red deer numbers in Scotland by half, which some people advocate with the object of reducing grazing on native tree seedlings, such as Scots pine, then disturbance during the stalking season would have to be much reduced also; ie a major effort to reduce deer numbers might not be possible without an equivalent effort of self-control by hill walkers to enable the cull to be carried out effectively during the heavy cull period.

One of the by-products of studying disturbance to deer is the extent to which they can become accustomed to certain kinds of disturbance, people on footpaths but not ridge walks, certain vehicles but not when people get out of them and so on. As with our pets, however, there can be behavioural variation between and even within species. There are numerous examples world-wide where birds have never come to associate people with a need for avoidance reaction, for example in the Falkland Islands, and in Scotland visitors to Inchcolm or Handa may walk a few feet from nesting gulls without causing unacceptable disturbance. Nesting eiders at Montrose and the Ythan demonstrate a sit tight behaviour the reverse of run away and I have seen a great crested grebe nesting within easy lob of a pebble, below a much used public footbridge crossing a reservoir. Habituation to acceptable kinds of disturbance does happen, notably in sanctuaries and where disturbance is regular and predictable, but it is not to be relied upon. In summary, therefore, as well as the sensitivity of the animal and the sensitivity of the stage in its life history when disturbance occurs, the frequency of the disturbing stimulus and how long the disturbance lasts are also important. Such a lot of variables, however, make for difficult research.

I have concentrated on unintentional disturbance because it is the most difficult kind of impact to quantify and because we all cause some degree of disturbance when we go into the countryside, including bird watching, a popular growth activity sometimes listed as part of green tourism. Direct, intentional disturbance is much less common, albeit more serious in its effects. Egg collecting was in former times a fairly popular form of recreation but it has now largely stopped (it is against the law, as is the photographing of birds at the nest without a permit) although illegal egg collecting is still practised by a few die-hards for commercial purposes, along with the taking of young birds, mostly raptors. The business is deplorably damaging to some species but it is of relevance to this paper only in the context that if all such criminal action stopped and numbers of breeding raptors thereby increased, we might find that concerns about disturbance from informal recreation also increased because there would be more birds to disturb, notwithstanding that the particular species populations might be healthier than now. For example, in the last forty years or so, numbers of breeding pairs of osprey have increased from nothing to about one hundred but a consequence of this splendid gain is to have created a hundred places where there is now concern about potential disturbance.

World-wide, the impact of tourism on rare fauna has generally been much less than the impact of introduced species associated with man, such as goats and rats, which eat vegetation and destroy sensitive habitats or predate on easily killed animals. The once plentiful St Lucia lizard in the Caribbean was eradicated by introduced mongooses. We may not think of introductions as a problem in Scotland (although locally mink inadvertently released from fur farms have done much harm) but in the last decade, the ruffe has found its way into Loch Lomond and may endanger the survival of the powan, a locally endemic species that has survived in abundance since the last glaciation but whose future is possibly now at risk. It is believed that the ruffe was introduced by fisherman using it as live bait and throwing surplus fish into the loch at the end of a day's fishing. Whether the tourist industry embraces that kind of fisherman is for others to say but certainly fishing is included as an activity participated in by tourists. The management of fishing lochs has also, in some cases, greatly altered the natural fish fauna by the introduction of toxic chemicals to kill fish, prior to the introduction of quarry species.

Before concluding this section, it may be a prudent guard against criticism to recognise that this account is not comprehensive. For example, I have not mentioned otters who are on occasion disturbed by dogs but not much by people and whose overall numbers are much more seriously depleted by being at the top of a food chain poisoned by pesticides, by fluctuating water levels and canalisation of water courses. There is also concern about disturbance from noise and wash of speedboats affecting breeding water birds where zoning of activities has not provided for undisturbed sanctuary areas. Economies of space, however, preclude inclusion of examples of all kinds of animals whose numbers may at times be affected by recreational disturbance.

IMPACTS ON VEGETATION

Locally, the ecological impact of casual recreation on plant life is most readily seen on heavily used footpaths and, a decade or so ago, much research was done on what kinds of plants were damaged most readily by a measured amount of foot pressure, whether the damage was greater or less when walking up or down slope and ditto on the kinds of soil or rocky substrate and its drainage, and the conditions (including climate and altitude) which influenced the rate at which vegetation recovered, seasonally (when people were fewer) or longer term by blocking off footpaths for resting periods. Some of the results simply reinforced in a scientific form what was known from general experience: that dicotyledons with terminal growing tips were more easily killed than monocotyledons which have a basal form of growth (hence grass for mown lawns); that the vegetation of sand dunes and peaty soils with poor drainage are most easily damaged; and, probably less well recognised before the research was done, that damage to high altitude vegetation could take decades to recover or even be irreversible.

Most of the effort nowadays, in relation to footpath damage and erosion, concentrates on techniques for repair and maintenance. This is important work aimed at making hill walking more pleasant underfoot and reducing the visual detraction of footpath erosion. I have a particular interest in the subject having written one of the earliest Occasional Papers by the Countryside Commission for Scotland on footpaths in the countryside. The fact is, however, there is very little evidence that casual walking, including footpath wear and tear, actually causes loss of plant populations, including rare plants. Indeed, sometimes concentration on problems of erosion on footpaths has led to other causes, such as grazing on Ben Lawers, being overlooked as a much more serious factor in the loss of rare plant species.

Where damage by trampling can take place, for example in some of the important plant localities in the Breadalbane hills, it can generally be attributed to informed botanists and field study groups who, because there is nowhere else for them to walk safely, track along the base of cliffs or the top of screes precisely in the habitats of rare plants. Sometimes also, fired by enthusiasm to make a certain determination within a difficult species group, plants are dug up for laboratory examination. Like egg collecting, this is illegal, as is over-zealous gardening of the surroundings of plants for photography, which is also believed to be the cause of some rare plants becoming rarer.

In contrast to casual walking, mainly in narrow, linear patterns over the face of the countryside, where most damage is worse visually than ecologically, local concentrations of people engaged in recreation can do considerable ecological damage, sometimes with serious knock-on effects due to other causes. The most outstanding example of a type of situation where this can occur is close to water, both inland waters and the sea.

Loch Lomond has been the subject of several studies examining the effects of recreational pressures at its margins and in places the effects have been long-lasting, relatively large scale and, so far, irreversible. The sequence is as follows. People congregate on shores with a zonation from plants of the lower shore that withstand periodic inundation, to a middle zone of species that like their feet wet but their heads above water, to an inner zone that extends back to permanent dry land with tall trees. As a consequence of foot and bottom pressure on the lower shore in summer when loch levels are low, the most sensitive outer zone is damaged and, over repeated summers and with people pressure reinforced by various forms of wheeled transport, the protective vegetation cover is removed allowing wave action in winter storms to work at the unconsolidated shore substrate in such a way that it is removed into deeper water. An eroding step is thereby formed in the naturally gradual slope of the shore, and this cuts back until, as seen from the depth of exposed tree roots, there can be a loss of shore material, wedge shaped in profile, up to a metre high at its inner vertical edge and diminishing in height out into the loch for several metres. The weakened trees then fall over, helped sometimes by the exposed roots being hacked at for firewood. In this way, in too many places around the shores of Loch Lomond, because the places where people congregate are now so numerous and widespread, a protective community of plants (including several uncommon species) has been seriously damaged.

The same sequence can be seen around many other popular Scottish lochs, such as the south shore of Loch Earn and the east shore of Loch Morlich, albeit at the last named the much finer particle shore material makes for differences in the dynamics of shore erosion. Also, while it is fair comment to observe that management aimed at resolving problems at such sites is too often reactive rather than anticipatory, the sad fact is that such local erosion often has to become really serious before action is taken.

A somewhat similar sequence of events has taken place on many soft coasts, dunes and sandy beaches being particularly attractive for recreation. Following damage from people, cars and caravans acting on the protecting dune vegetation, both wind and water can then severely erode major parts of or even whole dune systems. A commonly occurring complicating factor, however, is the removal of sand (for building purposes or where lime rich for agriculture) from the intertidal beach. If enough of this is removed, the beach profile is steepened leading to undercutting of the dune face, slumping and erosion. The warrens of rabbits may also be a factor leading to weakening of the parts of the dune system. Another complication is that it is in the nature of soft coasts that they are dynamic: that processes of building and erosion are likely to be taking place whether or not they are used for recreation or mineral extraction. It is perhaps because of this that there may be a reluctance to recognise at a sufficiently early stage when recreation pressures and other land uses have to be managed.

IMPACTS BY BUILT STRUCTURES

I started by quoting David Attenborough's description of the impact of tourism on the Mediterranean coast and, in a much more modest way (such as caravan sites) the built structures of tourism have materialised on some greenfield sites around the coast of Scotland. Locally, these developments will have greatly altered communities of plants and animals. Habitats will have been destroyed, for example for the natterjack toad in parts of the inner Solway coast, but as yet the survival of species populations has rarely been put at risk because they have been able to survive elsewhere. In this context, tourism development is simply one of many kinds of development around our coast, the North Sea oil industry and power generation being other examples in recent decades. Just now the focus is on superquarries. In my view, whatever debate there may be about further development of the coast, about pollution of coastal waters and marine habitats, these are all mainly for consideration within the disciplines of planning and pollution control and are not a major issue for this paper. This is in no way to diminish their importance in other contexts and the heritage conservation organisations will rightly continue to examine all new developments carefully, not only on Scottish coasts but in all countryside.

There is, however, one facet of the tourist industry in Scotland where I suggest that there could be considerable room for improvement in a manner relevant to the amenity and local ecology of the countryside. Whereas in the short run it is the larger developments (hotels, marinas, golf courses etc) that initially cause the most obvious local damage to wildlife habitats, in the long run the penumbra of temporary destruction at up-market sites is generally made good and well maintained. What is not so satisfactory and sometimes downright awful are some smaller-scale developments, done on shoestring budgets, perhaps with shoestring grant, in locations where ecological sensitivity and interest is initially high but becomes degraded by sub-standard development and poor peripheral aftercare. Some parts of the crofting counties can be particularly unhappy in this respect and as they possess some of Scotland's richest wildlife habitats, there is a challenge here which should well repay a more concerted effort.

ACTION

Earlier this year, when launching the government's recent action programmes for sustainable development (at the same time as related programmes dealing with biodiversity, sustainable forestry and climate change) the Prime Minister rightly emphasised that everyone can contribute positively and that sustainable development requires changes in lifestyle for all of us. Among the many ways that we can play an active part in this highly desirable goal, one of the most accessible, because it involves most of us one way or another, is the way that we participate in countryside recreation, both as tourists and in day visits from home.

The providers of facilities for tourism and recreation are also crucial to achieving sustainable tourism, defined as the use and development of tourism resources in a way which allows enjoyment while, at the same time, ensuring that these resources will be preserved for use by future generations. The roles of participants and providers are of equal importance. Although the siting of facilities in locations carefully chosen to do least ecological harm is an obviously desirable aim, in practice the general location is sometimes determined by the fact that people are already congregating at a sensitive site. We have to recognise that sustainable tourism cannot always be achieved by total avoidance of environmental impact.

Action programmes can range from personal restraint, such as not searching for a golden plover's nest or resisting trying to photograph every kind of orchid (it has been done already), to multi-stage operations involving lots of people and perhaps lots of cash. In the latter case, deciding what to do will begin by finding out what has already been written on the subject and it will often save much effort if what has already been published is carefully read first. Publications and reports will generally fall into two groups. On the one hand, there are those aimed at setting out general principles and general prescriptions for good design and management, to codes of good practice dealing with specific activities, including a wide range of specific sports such as canoeing and climbing. On the other hand, there are publications which describe the results of research on impacts on animals and plants: what kinds of disturbance disrupt normal behaviour, when this is critical in an organism's life history, how much trampling on what kinds of soils leads to permanent damage and so on.

Generally speaking, the first group are all fairly readily obtained. They are quite often free or the retail price modest because subsidised. The main problem in their case is to know that they exist or, if received and filed away, to remember that they are already somewhere at hand and where. For example, in 1992 the Scottish Tourist Board produced on behalf of the Scottish Tourism Co-ordinating Group an excellent 32 page publication *Tourism and the Scottish Environment: A Sustainable Partnership*. It was prepared in consultation with about seventy departments of central and local government and related quangos, twelve tourist boards, forty federations, societies and similar bodies and twenty-four other bodies not readily grouped under the other categories.

By the date of writing this paper (March 1994), 5000 had been printed and 3000 distributed free. Nevertheless, I wonder how many people at the coal face of tourism and recreation provision, let alone among participants, have yet to absorb its analysis of intrusive activities and wider environmental disturbance and thought through the implication of one of the report's conclusions: that although impacts are widespread and a serious problem in a few localised areas, they can be overcome by careful management. One cannot put it better and it is excellent to report that, in April of this year, a newly appointed Tourism and Environment Manager started work, one of his tasks being to ensure that the Board's environmental publications are read by all the right people.

As well as the report just mentioned, dealing largely with principles, STB published two further reports in 1993: the first has the same main title of *Tourism and the Scottish Environment*, but is sub-titled *Guidelines for the Development of Tourism Development Programmes*. The second is *Going Green: Guidelines for the Scottish Tourism Industry*. Tourism Development Programmes (TMPs) focus attention at both national and local levels on the relationship between tourism and the environmental resource on which it depends, by the development of partnerships for support and advice. TMPs are also aimed at achieving wider publicity for environmental issues related to tourism and encouraging acceptance of responsibility for the environment throughout the industry. Six steps are recommended in carrying out TMPs, the last of which is monitoring by annual audits and progress reports; very important for ensuring that the initiative as a whole is sustained long-term and not limited to the initial start-up phase. *Going Green* casts its net wider by reminding tourism operators of a range of ways whereby to make the industry sustainable.

There are many other publications covering specific activities. For example, Scottish Natural Heritage has recently published a report detailing how to integrate the design and management of golf courses for the benefit of both golf and wildlife and several years ago the former Countryside Commission for Scotland produced publications about the management of skiing facilities, gardens open to the public, and coastal beaches, all of which gave guidance on recording or conservation of wildlife habitats. Many of the governing bodies of specific sports, such as rock climbing, off-road cycling, wildfowling, angling and sub-aqua diving, as well as other kinds of activities such as field studies, produce guidance notes for their members on caring for wildlife, along with other advice on reducing impacts on the environment.

For example, the virtual cessation of lead weights for fishing and thereby a reduction in lead poisoning of wildfowl, owes much to a campaign by fishing organisations at every level, including the manufacturers of fishing equipment. My impression, which may be challenged, is that if every publication, good practice guide and permit carrying specific prohibitions, was acted on rigorously by all the people to whom these bits of paper are directed, there would be less cause for concern about the ecological impacts of tourism and recreation.

Published primary source information about ecological impacts is, however, not only scarcer but also less readily available. Partly this is because few ecologists have judged the subject worth serious investigation (compared, say, to research about organisms unaffected by people). As mentioned earlier, a decade or so ago research about damage done to vegetation by trampling was quite a popular subject but this has mostly been superseded by practical manuals on how to manage such areas. Most research on disturbance to animals has been done on birds, especially species whose numbers are considered under threat or have an economic value such as grouse. Disturbance to deer has also been reviewed because of an economic interest. More than that there is little hard published data in British publications; rather more in North America.

Another problem for managers is that much of what has been published, including reviews of research on recreation, is to be found among the research reports and occasional papers of the bodies who commissioned the research. This is not a criticism of the bodies themselves. It is understandable that, when a body pays for problem-orientated research, it should want to publish the results under its own banner and edit it in a form which sits comfortably with that body's image. The drawback is that the publications can sometimes thereby have a limited shelf life, which is not the case if published in scientific journals, albeit that for some people these may be just as difficult to get hold of as individual research reports. The upshot is that one would have to be a very dedicated manager with a lot of spare time, which most managers do not have, to find out whether advice being given is based on well researched scientific study or is really opinion founded on casual observation.

I do not see an easy resolution of this problem. Fundamentally, this is because when ecologists look around at all the possible causes for impoverishment of biodiversity, studying recreation impacts takes a low priority compared to many other subjects, such as pollution and climate change, and land uses such as agriculture and forestry. Although locally, as we have seen, the impacts of tourism and recreation can be ecologically harmful, because resources for research are tight, the main effort has to be directed to understanding problems that have wide impact.

One somewhat unfortunate consequence of this in the actions of some of the bodies responsible for heritage conservation, is overmuch dependence on the precautionary principle. As an example of this, it is a fact that when a Site of Special Scientific Interest is notified and ticks put against the list of potentially damaging operations (PDOs), a tick is almost always placed against recreation, regardless of whether there is any real likelihood that recreation generally will be a threat to ecological sustainability. I have had the problem explained to me many times, that if a PDO is not ticked and it later becomes a threat, then under the relevant legislation there is no opportunity to comment. Well, so be it. Nevertheless, the issue still grates, and I recall several times advising recreation providers to get stuck in as quickly as possible before objections were raised from another quarter.

Overall, there has to be a balance and it can be achieved. A type of relevant example is the creation of country parks. Although their main purpose is recreation, in practice (because rangers who look after these places are committed to wildlife conservation) the management of country parks has generally well satisfied the needs of both people and wildlife. Culzean country park in Ayrshire received nearly 340,000 visitors last year and yet, although not classed as such, it also operates effectively as a nature reserve.

Another reason why country parks are generally well able to balance the needs of people and wildlife is because operations follow a carefully prepared management plan. Describing the preparation of such plans (or Tourism Management Programmes in STB terminology) would require another lecture; suffice it to say that most site problems arise because a plan has not been prepared, or inadequately thought through with sufficient foresight. The exceptionally large number of people received annually at Culzean, without damage to the sustainability of its many faceted heritage, is rooted in the very considerable effort made by many experts from different professions in the early planning and development stages of the park's development; that it continues to cope so well is because of a management structure responsive to changing needs. In the very different type of recreational activity of skiing and a much more intractable mountainous terrain, the skiing industry has made outstanding advances in sensitive land management, albeit at certain sites debate is likely to continue about possible ecological damage resulting from extending pistes into new areas.

In the context of forward planning, it may be thought remiss not to have referred to the concept of carrying capacity, about which much has been written, including definitions of different kinds of carrying capacity. I have not done so because this concept, while helpful to managers when thinking through objectives and deciding when enough becomes too much, can sometimes give a spurious gloss of precision to recommendations actually based on a mixture of common-sense and experience. This is not to knock the idea into history; just a suggestion that if it is introduced in debate, then ask exactly what is intended.

In concluding this section, here is a comment about costs. While it is true that some action programmes can be executed successfully on small budgets, or actual costs kept low by using voluntary labour, or by good forward planning before problems require major surgery, it is my experience that skimping on initial works too often means having to carry out later reconstructions, sometimes at considerably greater expense. For example, wooden raised walkways across marshy areas are an example of the kind of provision where economising on costs is always a poor investment. The idea is as old as the people who lived in crannogs and for them, an easily removed rough-sawn plank may have been an adequate solution for deterring intruders. Today, however, the aim is to secure access for large numbers of people, such that they do not need to step off the walkway onto sensitive terrain when passing or stopping to look. Many excellent such walkways have now been created in Britain, from nature reserves with a high water table in the Norfolk Broads, to peaty woodlands at the Landmark Centre, Carrbridge (among the first to be well done in Scotland) and the excellent quarter mile of wooden walkway beside the Clyde at the Scottish Wildlife Trust's reserve near New Lanark. Thankfully, people responsible for recreation provision in countryside are nowadays much more aware of the true costs of sensible investment than they were thirty years ago.

EDUCATION

Public education is an important element of managing land and water for recreation and in the past twenty-five years much effort and money has been expended on the creation of visitor centres, on ranger services and on raising standards for interpreting the environment. Culzean country park, referred to earlier as a type of tourism and recreation provision which copes well with large numbers of visitors, while at the same time being responsive to the park's ecological sensitivities, includes education as a crucial part of good site management. 20,000 school children participate in its educational programmes annually, the long-term aim being to increase awareness of the park's resources and by so doing encourage better behaviour. Education is therefore one of several ways whereby to reduce the ecological impacts of recreation and tourism by participants. Ecologically beneficial site management may also involve the careful siting of provisions such as hides for observing birds. Education and interpretation, however, are not only beyond my hands-on expertise, they would also require a paper to themselves to do these subjects justice.

The down side to knowledge is that it is sometimes the people who know what they are looking for who actually do the greatest harm. Impact-reducing messages have to be specific or they will be ignored and, in the long run, the security of a sustainable future for biodiversity will always much depend on individual restraint. Finally, on a rather different point, really more to do with training of people managing the tourist industry than education of participants, perhaps there is also a need for more understanding of ecological impacts amongst providers. To be effective, knowledge has to be shared!

CONCLUSIONS

In places world-wide, the ecological impacts of tourism and recreation have been damaging on a large scale. In Scotland impacts are mainly local as a serious cause of depletion of biodiversity, either directly (for example by reducing breeding success) or indirectly (by destroying habitats). For the most part, however, other impacts on the environment, such as pollution and climate change, are actually or potentially far more serious.

One of the problems for the providers of tourism and recreation, in trying to do the right thing, is that there is a scarcity of well researched information on what activities cause serious disturbance and sometimes the precautionary principle may be invoked where responsible enjoyment of the countryside will actually do little harm. An acceptable balance is possible, and where the creation of built structures is required, well resourced investments are generally able to provide more long lasting and environmentally sensitive results than when resources are skimped.

There is much useful written material advising on good practice for a wide range of tourism and recreation activities. Acting on this advice and good forward planning are the bases for developing co-operative working between the industry and conservation.

Dedication and Acknowledgements

This paper is dedicated to the late Dr W J Eggeling, one-time Director of the NCC in Scotland and later, for eight formative years, a Member of the Countryside Commission for Scotland. His outstanding knowledge as an ecologist and wildlife conservationist, combined with a keen recognition of the needs of people to enjoy the countryside, made his guidance uniquely valuable on balancing the demands of conservation and recreation.

It is a pleasure to thank Valerie Thom for an early discussion which directed my thinking in helpful ways. John Mackay was also invaluable in telling me about work currently being done for Scottish Natural Heritage and enabling me to see a draft of both Roger Sidaway's research review of recreation impacts and B W Staines' and D Scott's preliminary review of the issues relating to recreation and red deer. Both reports were of timely assistance but Sidaway's, because of its width of coverage, was particularly useful. Many of the examples and ideas were culled from his study. My thanks also go to Brian Brookes for some helpful thoughts about impacts on plants; to Peter Maitland for information about fish; to David Jenkins about otters; to the Scottish Tourist Board about their publications; to Gordon Riddle about Culzean; and to the Loch Lomond Park Officer for allowing me to include some information from a recent census of craft by C E Adams and R Tippett. I also thank BBC Publications for allowing me to quote from *The First Eden*, the editor for suggesting a neatly apposite title, Freya Fladmark for producing the drawings and my wife for proof reading.

To John Mackay, James McCarthy, Roger Sidaway and Valerie Thom, I am particularly grateful for having taken the time to read drafts and make many helpful suggestions. The good things are all due to them; the faults are mine.

The Author

Thomas Huxley came to Scotland in 1956 as a Regional Officer in the old Nature Conservancy, transferring in 1968 to the Countryside Commission for Scotland, where he became its Deputy Director. He served as Chairman of the UK Countryside Recreation Research Group, was a Vice-Chairman of the Scottish Wildlife Trust and is currently a member of the South West regional board of Scottish Natural Heritage. He also serves on the Loch Lomond Park Authority and, when the weather is kind, does field work on the distribution of snails and freshwater bugs.

References

Attenborough, D., *The First Eden*, Collins/BBC Books, 1987

Bramwell, A., *Ecology in the 20th Century: A History.* Yale University Press, 1989

Cherrett, J.M., *Key Concepts: The Results of a Survey of Our Members' Opinions*, in Proceedings of 29th Symposium British, Ecological Society, Blackwell Scientific Publications, 1989

Countryside Commission for Scotland, *Final Report of Highland Beach Management Project 1977–79*, CCS 1980

Huxley, T., *Footpaths in the Countryside*, Countryside Commission for Scotland, 1970

Royal Zoological Society of Scotland, *Ark File*, Vol.3, Spring 1994

Sidaway, R., *Recreation and the Natural Heritage: a Research Review*, Scottish Natural Heritage, 1994, in preparation

Scottish Natural Heritage, *Golf's Natural Heritage*, SNH, 1993

Scottish Tourism Co-ordinating Group, *Tourism and the Scottish Environment: A Sustainable Partnership*, Scottish Tourist Board, 1991

Staines, B.W. and Scott, D., *Recreation and Red Deer: A preliminary Review of the Issues*, Scottish Natural Heritage, 1994, in preparation

Talbot-Ponsonby, H., *Recreation and Wildlife: Working in Partnership*, Proceedings of the 1987 Countryside Recreation Conference, Countryside Recreation Research Advisory Group, 1987

Tourism and Environment Task Force, *Going Green: Guidelines for the Scottish Tourism Industry*, Scottish Tourist Board, 1993

Tourism and Environment Task Force, *Tourism and the Scottish Environment: Guidelines for the Development of Tourism Management Programmes*, Scottish Tourist Board, 1993

Department of the Environment et al, *Sustainable Development The UK Strategy*, (Summary Report), HMSO, 1994

Figure 5 Natterjack Toad.

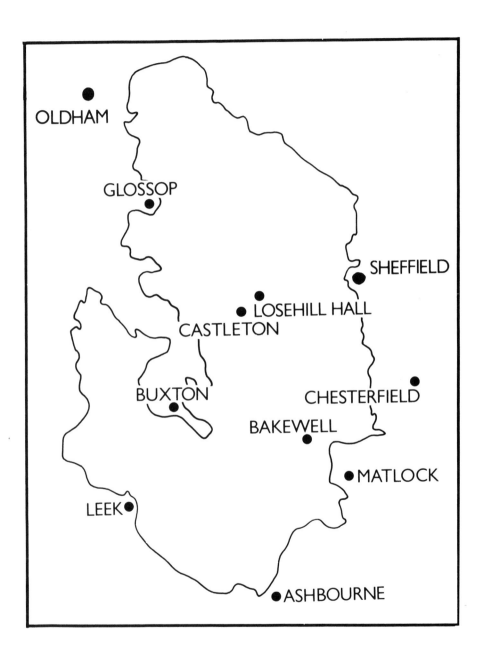

Figure 1 Peak National Park Designated Area.

15

LOVING THEM TO DEATH
Sustainable Tourism in National Parks

John Anfield

The land as we see it
is the product of human inter-action
with the natural world,
and all things are inter-linked.

Thus opened the volume of papers delivered at the University's 1993 Heritage Convention in Aberdeen, prefacing the section on cultural landscapes. Alongside this I would like to place the mission statement of my employer, the Peak National Park, which simply reads:

Caring for a Living Landscape.

It is indicative of the relevance of my paper to the theme of this volume that the meanings of these two quotations are so complementary. I also refer to the 1993 chapter on *Discovering the Personality of a Region* (Fladmark), which has an interesting historical report on the development of interpretation in the Peak National Park in the 1960s (we have come on quite a way since that time.) It traces the links of personalities and ideas between the Peak and Scotland.

NATIONAL PARKS OF ENGLAND AND WALES

There are ten National Parks in England and Wales. Additionally the Broads is a type of National Park and the New Forest in Hampshire is likely to have a quasi National Park status when the appropriate legislation is passed. You will note that there are no National Parks in Scotland. This is the result of the different history and politics of Scotland and could be the subject of a separate conference. I will not, therefore, make any further comment.

The National Parks south of the Border were established under the National Parks Act of 1949. The Peak National Park was the first to be established in 1951 with the other nine Parks following throughout the 1950s. With the addition of the Broads and the New Forest, just under 10% of the land area of England and Wales is covered by National Park designation.

As National Parks we are charged by Parliament with three main duties which can be simplified as:

1. To protect and enhance the natural beauty and other qualities of the National Park.
2. To provide for public enjoyment in a manner which is compatible with the conservation objective.
3. To have regard to the social and economic well-being of those who live and work in the National Park.

Legislation is likely to go through Parliament within the next year or two changing some aspects of national park administration and setting up free-standing national park boards.

For the purpose of this paper it is important to note that the British national parks are seen as part of local government with an accountable and mainly democratically elected board. They are not quangos. All meetings are held in public, except for a very few within clear legal guidelines. Members of the boards or committees are two-thirds elected councillors from the local authorities within the national park and one-third appointed by the Secretary of State for the Environment. The budgets of the national parks are provided with a 75% supplementary grant provided from the Department of the Environment or the Welsh Office. The remaining 25% is a call upon the counties and metropolitan districts within whose area a national park is situated. Additionally, national parks are encouraged to generate income themselves.

Thus, the total net budget for national parks for 1994/95 is about £25 million and that for my own Peak National Park is about £6 million. Needless to say, most national parks could argue effectively that they need to at least double this budget to effectively achieve their main duties.

APPROACH TO TOURISM IN THE PARKS

It will be seen that the conservation duty and the recreation duty can be in conflict. Government advice is quite clear that, where this is so, then the conservation duty has priority. This is particularly important when considering tourism in national parks. It is an easy reaction for a national park to say that tourism is a threat to conservation, and, therefore, the national park should not take any direct part in tourism. Crudely, that was the attitude of some of our national parks for many years. They argued that they were not in the business of promoting the national park, only in the business of managing the tourists and visitors that arrived.

With the massive growth in visitors to our national parks, around 100 million visits per year, this was seen as too narrow an approach. A major step forward was joint working with the English and Wales Tourist Boards which in the late 1980s produced a joint statement about tourism in National Parks. (Appendix 1.)

Of perhaps even greater significance was the publication *Tourism in National Parks – A Guide to Good Practice*. This was a very well-presented report which combined clear policy for tourism in national parks with an excellent series of case studies. The case studies were of the types of tourism which were felt to be suitable within national parks.

The joint working continues. There is a National Parks and Tourism Working Party which is chaired by the Dartmoor National Park Officer, Nick Atkinson and which has a number of representatives from national parks and tourist organisations and of which I am a member, (terms of reference in Appendix 2). I think it is indicative of the continued importance of working with tourist organisations, of focusing upon management techniques for tourism, and of learning together, that this working party continues and is seen to be important.

SUSTAINABLE TOURISM IN EUROPEAN PARKS

The Federation of Nature and National Parks of Europe is a non-political independent international voluntary body. It has approximately 200 members from 31 European countries. All the English and Welsh National Parks are members, and I am glad to know that the Robert Gordon University Heritage Unit is an academic member. It has a small staff based in Bavaria, Germany. The President until 1996 is a Scot, Aitken Clark, who is Chief Executive of the Broads Authority (National Park) in England. The main aims of the Federation are:

1. To encourage practical co-operation and exchange of information, experience and staff between national parks and nature parks and with other organisations and individuals responsible for nature conservation.
2. To promote international joint working to establish new parks and to improve the management of existing ones.
3. To disseminate information and technical knowledge on the management of natural and cultural heritage protected within the parks.

It is worth emphasising the words of *management* and *natural and cultural* heritage. Within a densely populated European context there are few areas which are not managed and where the centuries of occupation are not part of the cultural landscape which is being protected.

The European Federation recognises both the importance and the dangers of tourism for Europe's protected areas. It considered the topic so important that in 1991, it set up its first working group to look at sustainable tourism for protected areas in Europe. The project was supported by the European Commission (DGXXIII) Tourism Unit under its Rural and Cultural Tourism Programme. The project had four aims (Further details in Appendix 3):

1. To develop guidelines to help managers of protected areas and the tourism sector to take a new approach to tourism in and around protected areas.
2. To identify case studies illustrating how sustainable tourism is being developed for protected areas and to begin to produce a database of such information.
3. To report the current position of sustainable tourism related to protected areas in Europe.
4. To recommend the action required at international and national level and within the tourism sector to achieve sustainable tourism.

THE PEAK NATIONAL PARK

The Peak District National Park is situated in the North of England. It has an area of 143,800 hectares (555 square miles) and about 38,000 people live within the Park's designated area. About 17 million people live within 100 km of its boundaries. Most of the land in the Park remains in private ownership. There are still a few large estates (eg Chatsworth owned by the Duke of Devonshire), and there are 2,000 farms. About 15% of the land is owned by the recently privatised English Water Companies (Yorkshire Water, Severn Trent Water and North West Water plc). About 12% is owned by the National Trust, the very powerful private conservation body which has more than two million members in England and Wales. As a National Park Authority we only own 4%.

I would emphasise that by IUCN classifications none of the England and Wales areas are true national parks. Category 2 areas of the IUCN are state owned national parks. Our national parks are what is called Category 5 *protected landscapes* and are similar to areas known as *Nature or Regional Parks* in some countries.

As the Board's Director of Planning, it is not surprising that I would wish to emphasise the importance of the Peak Board being the sole planning authority for the Park. This means that the planning powers normally with counties and districts have all been given to the National Park Board. We are therefore responsible for preparing the *structure plan*, the *local plan* and dealing with more than 1,000 planning applications each year for development proposed within our designated area.

I would like to emphasise one or two wider points about the structure plan, as this is crucial for an understanding of the more specific management of tourism in the Park. There is a general strategic policy about development in the National Park which states:

1. 'All development will be controlled so that the valued characteristics of the Peak National Park can be conserved and enhanced, now and for future generations. To achieve this, development will not normally be permitted where:
   - it is incompatible with the policies in the Development Plan, or
   - it is incompatible with the twin statutory National Park purposes of conserving and enhancing the natural beauty of the National Park and promoting its public enjoyment, or with the Board's further statutory duty to have regard to the well-being of local communities. Where there is an irreconcilable conflict between these aims, the conservation of the National Park will normally take precedence.

2. Major development including that for which a national need is identified, will be subject to the most rigorous examination. Such development will not be permitted save in exceptional circumstances where there is no reasonable alternative and must be shown on balance to be in the overall public interest.'

The above is quoted in full as it applies to all proposals for development and is the over-arching conservation background to detailed policies in the following subject areas: conservation; housing, shops and community services; the economy; recreation and tourism; minerals and waste disposal; and transport.

This overall structure plan is now being followed up by a park-wide local plan which interprets these policies at the local level. What does this then mean for recreation and tourism? Our policies for tourism management are based on the underlying principle of *sustainable development*:

1. There is a presumption against proposals for recreation and tourism which are out of sympathy with the natural and physical qualities of the Park.
2. The scale, form and character of proposals must not spoil the Park. Proposals are assessed against factors which include:
   - The carrying capacity of the area;
   - the conservation of the area;
   - the impact upon road traffic and local communities;
   - any conflict with other existing recreation uses;
   - the potential for the proposal to be carried on outside the designated area of the Park, the policy assumption being similar to the question posed by the US National Parks Service for new tourist proposals: *is it necessary and appropriate?*
3. The Park is divided into five broad zones which set out how the different parts of the Park can accommodate different types of recreational development. They range from Zone 1 (where the only facilities permitted are footpaths and wildlife hides) to Zone 5 (where the major recreation uses and major tourist facilities can be accepted).
4. There is a hope that more visitors will stay overnight in the Park, as 90% are day visitors.

CURRENT ISSUES

With 22 million visits per year to the Park, it is the most visited national park in Europe, and is quoted as the second most visited in the world (after one in Japan). The pressures of development for tourism, the pressures of traffic and the pressures of erosion are the most intense in any of our national parks. At 15.00 hrs. on a busy summer afternoon, our research staff estimate that there are approximately one-third of a million visitors in the Park, 90% of whom have travelled by car.

Many people feel that too much traffic is the greatest threat to the conservation of the Park. The problems are familiar and are to do with traffic congestion, conflict with local residents, pressure for new car parks, erosion of footpaths adjoining the car parks, etc. It is not possible to cope with peak demands. To build sufficient car parks would (a) be very expensive, (b) damage the landscape, (c) attract even more cars. We therefore have a strategic transport and traffic policy for the Peak which is essential for coping with the visitor pressures:

1. Environmental quality will be the prime consideration in the design of any new road schemes.

2. No major improvements for the road system will be carried out, especially through the National Park linking Manchester and Sheffield.
3. Major financial support and sponsorship of recreational public transport services will be provided from the surrounding urban areas at weekends (approximately £140,000 a year).
4. Extra railway services into the National Park, especially linking with bus services and guided walks, will be provided.
5. There will be intensive marketing of these services.
6. Roads will be closed in very limited areas, with attractive transport provided by shuttle bus, with bicycles and with opportunities for walking.

I would emphasise the political will which is needed to carry out these policies. There has been television and media coverage this year about *closing national parks to traffic or charging for visitors to national parks* . It is difficult political territory to close roads to visitors, as these are also roads for local people. It is difficult both politically and in practical terms to work out methods of pricing entry to national parks. However, if the national parks are to be protected and if sufficient resources are to be generated for their conservation, then it is important that national park authorities should have the courage to experiment in these important areas. I have emphasised the need for management of traffic, as it is the most important aspect of visitor management.

We also give special attention to the extension and improvement of existing accommodation for visitors. Extensions are usually accepted, especially country house hotels or public houses with extra bedrooms. There is also emphasis on the improvement of caravan sites. People demand better sites with especially the ability to 'plug in'. These facilities are important for the local economy, as most facilities of this scale are locally owned so the benefits are retained locally. More than 50% of visitors who stay overnight use caravans or tents.

We give positive encouragement to farm-based tourism. There are almost 2000 farms in the Park, but there is a general decline in agriculture. However, farming is crucial for the maintenance of the traditional landscape and there is a strong desire to keep people living in the hills. Much of the Park enjoys Objective 5b status (European Union), which is for declining agricultural areas. I see the benefits of farm-based tourism as an opportunity for the conservation of redundant farm buildings, local income retained in the area, a chance for a shift in agriculture to multi-purpose industry: it is crucial to maintain this diversified base. We believe that a real countryside experience for visitors is through green tourism. There is a Peak District Farm Holiday Group of 40 members, which has been very successful in marketing farm holidays, increasing standards and developing training for its members.

We are trying to encourage the availability of local products which are so keenly sought by visitors. We have helped to form a Peak District Products Group. The income from these local products tends to be mainly retained in the area. This is part of the major benefit that tourist spending brings. If well managed, it can help to support many parts of the local economy.

We encourage walking, cycling, rock climbing etc, but there are dangers in excess. Green tourism can be inappropriate if its scale is excessive or if everyone wants to visit on the same day (eroded footpaths, weekend traffic congestion). The Pennine Way is a good example. This is a national trail which starts in the Peak National Park. The first 40 miles (64 kilometres) of the 270 miles (432 kilometres) are within the designated area of the Park, and are across some very difficult and wet peat bogs. The thousands of people who walk this route are all green tourists but the erosion they are causing is horrific and very expensive to repair. We discourage noisy activities like motor cycling, helicopter rides, and water ski-ing. Appendix 4 describes how we have dealt with visitor pressures in the Dovedale area of the Park.

CONCLUSIONS

I believe that much can be learned from studying the approach taken by park authorities throughout Europe, and in this paper I have sought to highlight how we have responded to the opportunities and the threats of intensive tourism to these nationally important areas. From my own experience in the Peak, I have learned that the following considerations are of fundamental importance:

1. The management of tourism is part of the long-term sustainable management of an area, and we must think long-term and not be tempted by short-term benefits.
2. A clear and up-to-date policy framework and strategy is essential for integrated management, the structure plan being particularly important as a basis for traffic control and management, which must be negotiated and agreed with the many other key partners who are involved with the management of an area.
3. This all costs money: national park authorities will have to maximise income from visitors to help pay for conservation measures, and political courage will be needed to charge for access to the most pressurised parts.
4. A key role of national park authorities is to influence how others promote and manage land and facilities within designated areas, and by fulfilling this role the parks will continue to succeed in their mission of *caring for a living landscape* that will be enjoyed by generations to come.

The Author

John Anfield is Director of Planning with the Peak National Park based at Bakewell, Derbyshire. Previous employment has included posts with Exmoor National Park and the Countryside Commission, and he was a member of the team from the Federation of Nature and National Parks of Europe which produced the report *Loving them to Death?* published in 1993. He has been an elected member of the Council of the National Trust since 1978, a large voluntary conservation organisation with more than two million members and a projected income of £90 million in 1994.

References

Fladmark, J. M. (ed)., *Heritage Conservation, Interpretation and Heritage*, Donhead, 1993 pp1

Fladmark, J. M., *Discovering the Personality of a Region: Strategic Interpretation in Scotland*, ibid. pp. 125–127.

Countryside Commission et al, *Tourism in National Parks: A Guide to Good Practice*, 1991

Federation of Nature and National Parks of Europe, *Loving them to Death? Sustainable Tourism in Europe's Nature and National Parks*, FNNPE, 1993

Peak District National Park, *Structure Plan 1994: Written Statement of Adopted Policies*, PDNP, 1994

Figure 2 Upper Derwent, Peak National Park.

APPENDIX 1

PRINCIPLES FOR TOURISM IN NATIONAL PARKS

Conservation

The tourism industry can help to protect the distinctive landscapes and wildlife of National Parks by supporting practical conservation measures. This can be achieved, for example, through joint initiatives involving the public, private and voluntary sectors.

Enjoyment

The activities and interests promoted by tourism should draw on the special character of the National Parks, with their many opportunities for quiet open air recreation and their distinctive beauty, culture, history and wildlife. Improved access for visitors should be sought where this is compatible with conservation requirements.

Rural Economy

The social and economic well-being of the residents of the National Parks is an essential consideration in achieving the statutory objectives of National Parks, and employment in the tourist and related service industries is an important part of the economy of the National Parks. The tourism industry should support the economy of local communities through, for example, using employees, products and services from the locality and by supporting the skills and economic activities which are traditional to National Parks.

Development

Appropriate facilities are needed to enable tourists to enjoy the National Parks. All tourism development must respect the quality of the landscape and environment in National Parks. Its scale, in particular, must always be appropriate to the setting. It should also recognise that some areas of National Parks are valued for being wild and remote. Proposals for development should always be tempered by the capacity of the immediate site and surrounding landscape to absorb visitors. Development can assist the purposes of conservation and recreation by, for example, bringing sympathetic new uses to historic buildings and derelict sites and opening up new opportunities for quiet open air recreation.

Design

The scale, siting, planning, design and management of new tourism developments should be in keeping with the landscape, and should seek to enhance it. The distinctive and highly valued character and landscapes of National Parks will continue to evolve through small scale changes. Major alterations to the landscape are unacceptable.

Marketing

The tourism industry should use publicity, information and marketing opportunities to deepen people's enjoyment, appreciation, understanding and concern for National Parks.

APPENDIX 2

NATIONAL PARKS AND TOURISM WORKING PARTY

Terms of Reference

1. To bring together the interests involved with tourism in national parks.

2. To consider matters of concern for the group including:

   – national tourism policy as it affects the environment in national parks;
   – visitor management projects in national parks;
   – monitoring the numbers and impact of visitors to national parks;
   – local mechanisms for co-operation between NPAs, regional tourist boards and the tourist industry.

3 In the short term (1991 – 1994), it will concentrate on work arising from:

   – the marketing and conservation audit;
   – the Edwards' Review Report;
   – the Tourism and the Environment Task Force;
   – the Guide to Good Practice.

4. To keep under review the 1989 Heads of Agreement and Principles for Tourism in National Parks.

5. To devise a work programme of research, seminars, publications, etc. and disseminating relevant information.

6. To keep under review the role and relevance of this group.

Membership

The membership currently comprises: Countryside Commission, Two Regional Tourist Board representatives, Two National Park Authority representatives, English Tourist Board, Rural Development Commission, Countryside Council for Wales, Wales Tourist Board, plus an National Park Officer nominated by the National Park Officers' Group.

LOVING THEM TO DEATH?

Sustainable Tourism in Europe's Nature and National Parks

The Working Group was Chaired by Norbert Heukemes from the Hautes Fagnes-Eifel Nature Park in Belgium. The Countryside Commission, England seconded Rosie Simpson to manage the project. A 14 member Working Group from 11 European countries was set up which included several managers of protected areas together with representatives from the tourism and research sectors and from private governmental and non government organisations. I was privileged to be a member of this group.

We had an interesting working method as we were attempting to use practical experience of tourist management in protected areas from many parts of Europe. We set up three workshops, held in:

1. The Broads, England (covering North West Europe).
2. Triglav National Park, Slovenia (covering the Mediterranean area).
3. The Tatra National Park, the Slovak Republic (covering Eastern Europe).

At these workshops were presented 40 case studies of sustainable tourism projects within the protected areas and 16 of these were used in the published report. We first had to decide what is sustainable tourism and our agreed definition was:

> When tourism is sustainable, the natural and cultural resources and the environmental, social and economic well-being of an area are maintained forever.

Tourism Trends in Europe.

These were summarised as follows:

1. a steady growth in tourism of 3 to 4.5% in Europe in the next 10 years;
2. tourism to the Mediterranean region is expected to double in the next 30 years;
3. a 45% increase in the number of cars in Europe in the next 20 years;
4. growing demand for holidays based on nature and outdoor activities and for cultural and educational tourism;
5. an increase in tourism that is environmentally friendly.

We then defined tourism activities which are general *compatible* with protected areas:
1. activities based on the areas' special character and quality: appreciating nature, cultural and educational tourism, as well as quiet, small scale or small group activities;
2. activities that cause no damage, disturbance or pollution.

In turn we looked at tourism activities generally *incompatible* with protected areas:

1. large scale facilities associated with organised or mass tourism, eg timeshare developments;
2. activities that are noisy, involve large numbers or that repeatedly disturb the wildlife, eg water skiing;
3. skiing and other large scale sports facilities and events, eg the impact of the 1992 Olympics on Vanoise National Park in France;
4. motorised recreational activities, eg motor rallies within national parks.

We realised that protected areas could not be looked at in isolation and that there was a need for *zones* for sustainable tourism in and around protected areas, which were defined as: a sanctuary zone; a quiet zone; a zone for compatible forms of tourism without further development; a zone for sustainable forms of tourism development; a zone immediately outside the protected area developed sustainably.

Guidelines In and Around Protected Areas

Apart from the case studies, this was the core of our report. We were acutely aware of the range of skills and experience within different protected areas, and we therefore set out a 15 step process for managers of protected areas:

1. State clear conservation aims.
2. Compile an inventory.
3. Work in partnership.
4. Identify the values and image on which to base sustainable tourism.
5. Assess carrying capacity and set standards that must be maintained.
6. Survey and analyse tourist markets and visitors needs and expectations.
7. Identify tourism activities that are compatible with the protected area.
8. Propose 'new tourism products' to be developed.
9. Assess the environmental impacts of proposals.
10. Specify visitor management required such as zoning and channelling, interpretation and education.
11. Propose traffic management systems.
12. Devise a communications and promotional strategy.
13. Establish a programme for monitoring and review.
14. Assess a resource and training needs.
15. Implement the plan.

Wider Action

Finally, we felt there was wider action needed for sustainable tourism in and around protected areas, and we recommended:

1. Stronger legislation and effective enforcement of controls.
2. National strategies and policies for sustainable tourism.
3. A European charter for sustainable tourism operation in and around protected areas.
4. A European action programme for sustainable tourism in and around protected areas.
5. Improved training.

CASE STUDY

The Dovedale Area Peak National Park

Dovedale in the south of the Peak National Park, first became famous 300 years ago after a well known local figure published a book on fishing. The River Dove winds through a series of magnificent limestone dales and then into a deep gorge. The area is tremendously popular, attracting over two million tourists each year, around three quarters of a million of whom walk the Dovedale footpath. As many as 2,000 people an hour use the famous Stepping Stones river crossing on busy Sundays in summer.

Most visitors were arriving by car and parking in a very visible car park. They were causing traffic congestion and parking problems as well as eroding footpaths and valley sides, in a nationally important wildlife and geological site. Visitors have been a mixed blessing for local people too. Owners of the car park and caravan site, and those providing tourist accommodation earn money from them. However, farmers have suffered in their every day work with problems from traffic jams, trespassers, disturbance to sheep and litter left by visitors.

Carrying Capacity

Park managers could see that the carrying capacity of the valley was being exceeded and that action was needed. Although the national park owns no land in Dovedale, it is responsible for working with landowners and other organisations to make sure that the landscape beauty is conserved.

A management plan was produced and was discussed with landowners, including the National Trust, visitors and local people. There was general agreement that action was needed to ease the problems, to improve visitor facilities, reduce pressure on the landscape and wildlife, enhance the dale and help the local community.

Elements of the plan have been implemented jointly by the national park, landowners and local councils. *Car parking within the dale has been reduced from 750 to 400 spaces* and new, smaller landscaped car parks have been built within three kilometres. A ten year scheme of footpath restoration was carried out. An all-weather path was created allowing visitors to enjoy the dale throughout the year without causing erosion. Only natural limestone has been used so that the path blends into the landscape. The work was carried out by local contractors and volunteers.

Traffic management was improved with a total ban on cars at the busiest times. Further improvements will be seen if current proposals are accepted to ban traffic on one stretch throughout the whole year. This will allow easy and safe year round access for walkers, families and people with disabilities. Other aspects of the project include improved ranger services, better public toilets and information for visitors, an environmental education service based at the nearby youth hostel and the restoration of eroded areas.

Outcome

The scheme has been successful in reducing the number of visitors to the area and in increasing the capacity of the footpath for walkers in a way that is sensitive to the environment. Traffic congestion has been reduced, local peoples' needs have been taken into account and the nature and landscape of Dovedale has benefited. The Dovedale project has also demonstrated the value of working in partnership, an approach that involves listening, understanding, discussion, negotiation and joint funding by all the partners concerned.

A number of key aspects are essential for success: a clear management plan is needed; the park authority must be able to act as a catalyst and co-ordinator for change; and the park or its partners must have the powers, negotiating skills and resources and will to implement the plan.

Park managers also had the confidence to enable them to reduce the capacity of the area and to restore it. Although only limited information was available on the visitors and ecology of the area, park managers used their professional judgement to take decisions. Sometimes action is needed urgently to make tourism use sustainable and to avoid further damage.

Figure 3 Dovedale, Peak National Park.

16

GREEN TOURISM AND FARMING

Richard Denman

This paper looks at certain aspects of the provision for tourism on farms, especially with relation to the environment and local communities. Much of the factual information presented comes from two studies we have carried out recently; one on farm tourism development in England's West Country in 1990[1] and the other a market research study across England in 1992[2].

A SUPPORTIVE RELATIONSHIP

'Green tourism' is a new phrase for a very old practice. It is not, as some would like to believe, a new phenomenon dreamt up by public sector agencies, but simply a form of labelling. However, as a label it has been most valuable in drawing attention to the positive relationship between tourism and the environment. It has earned respectability for tourism in heritage and countryside circles, amongst people with whom a few years ago tourism consultants had to tread warily and apologetically. Yet, there is still a lot of confusion about the labels and the concepts which have brought people together.

Such confusion is most apparent in rural areas. In some parts of Europe, noticeably France, green tourism or *tourisme vert* was simply a colour code for tourism in the countryside rather than in towns or seaside resorts. In Britain it is sometimes still used in this way, but more often it is used as a synonym for 'sustainable tourism'. This paper adopts this definition and so is about sustainable tourism in the countryside and its relationship with farming.

The dependence of tourism on the quality of the environment places it in a very special position in the whole debate about sustainable development. Unlike the situation in most other industries, to the tourism industry, concern for the environment need not be seen as a cost but an investment. It can be helpful to think of a simple model, which treats an attractive environment as *tourism capital* and income from tourism as supplying *environmental revenue*. Handled wisely, investment in environmental conservation, improvement and interpretation can lead to a greater return from tourism in the future; while income from tourism supplies one of the few forms of direct financial revenue to communities for caring for and conserving their environment. A policy to pursue sustainable tourism is not only about ensuring that the scale and type of tourism are appropriate to the long term needs of the environment and the community. It is also about encouraging this positive relationship of capital and revenue to flourish.

The importance of this relationship was specifically identified by IUCN, UNEP and WWF in their Strategy for Sustainable Living [3], recognising that 'tourism in protected areas may become a very effective instrument and source of finance for conservation.' The development of tourism on farms fits well with the concept of sustainable tourism, adding a special dimension to the way in which tourism can support not only the rural economy but increasingly the custodianship of the agricultural landscape and heritage in rural areas. Typically, such farm tourism includes bed and breakfast enterprises, self-catering cottages, bunkhouses, camping sites, catering and recreation facilities and farm attractions.

Certain criteria can be identified for sustainable tourism, and it is worth considering how well farm tourism is able to meet them. Sustainable tourism should involve:

1. **Sensitive development appropriate to the local environment.**
    The majority of farm tourism enterprises are based on existing traditional buildings. There are many examples where tourist accommodation has provided an economic use for disused barns which are important landscape features. Clearly, there are also problems with sizeable caravan sites and stark chalet developments on some farms, but these are a minority.

2. **Support for conservation.** At a time when farmers are being increasingly subsidised to support landscape and wildlife conservation, for example in Environmentally Sensitive Areas, there is potential for farm tourism enterprises to provide a further incentive for such custodianship. There is good evidence that visitors would respond well to this: two thirds of visitors staying on farms indicate that they would be interested in wildlife or conservation on the farms on which they are staying. Farmers have responded to some extent. In the West Country, one third of farmers with tourism enterprises had carried out some conservation activity on their farms, and half of these were influenced by visitor interest.

3. **Support for the economy at a very local level**, directly benefiting local residents and other indigenous enterprises. A special feature of farm tourism enterprises is that virtually by

definition they are developed by local people, with local control and profits retained in the community. Although few enterprises bring in staff, support for the farming families themselves is proving increasingly important. In the West Country in 1990, tourism was bringing in on average 36% of total farm income to those farms with a farm tourism enterprise. Across England, two thirds of farmers with tourism enterprises now believe them to be of vital importance to their ability to stay in business. The value to the local economy goes beyond this. For example, two thirds of visitors to farmhouse B&B use local pubs, restaurants and shops in a five mile radius, spending over £10 per head per night (1992 figures).

4. **Ecologically sound practice**, low energy consumption and non-polluting. Farm tourism has some weaknesses in this area. Over 96% of visitors come by car. As farms are so scattered it is difficult to see how public transport can relate to this form of tourism, although there is potential for more use by cyclists and walkers. There is little evidence of farms adopting energy conservation measures. In some parts of Europe and elsewhere, water use and sewerage dispersal creates a problem which needs to be tackled through training and assistance, collectively within the community or individually on each farm. Our survey of visitors showed considerable interest in organic farming and concern about animal welfare. There is a danger that by promoting farm tourism as 'green tourism' some more mechanised farms may not be delivering what this label implies.

5. **Providing visitors with a genuine appreciation of the area.** One of the special features of farm tourism is the opportunity it brings for visitors to meet local people. The chance to talk, for instance, over the breakfast table, is much valued by guests. Not only does this give visitors a feel and a flavour for the farm and the local community but also personal advice on how to enjoy their stay – first person interpretation in the true sense. This should be seen as a two-way benefit. Isolation is a well-known problem for farmers. 40% of those in our study said that companionship was an important reason for providing for visitors.

It is fair to conclude that, set against these criteria, farm tourism equates well with the concept of sustainable tourism.

SUPPLY AND DEMAND

Research on agricultural diversification suggests that around 15% of farms in Britain are providing some form of tourism enterprise. In certain areas this is far higher: for instance, in the West Country 23% of farms are doing so, rising to 35% in Cornwall.

Tourism on farms has been around for a long time. In Scotland way back in 1975, we found that 11% of farms and 10% of crofts were providing facilities for tourists[4]. Farm tourism businesses have a tendency to come and go, often for no other reason than fluctuations in the family life cycle as rooms and time become available. However, taking Britain as a whole, the number of new enterprises is striking. In the West Country we found that over a third had started in the previous five years. This growth, fuelled by the devastating decline in agricultural incomes, has led to concern about over supply. This is a problem in some areas but it is by no means universal.

The overall picture in England at the moment is of moderate levels of trading in farm B&B and self-catering enterprises, but with a considerable amount of spare capacity and with the majority of enterprises seeking more business. The priority is to strengthen marketing to fill this capacity rather than seek new development.

Our market research provides cause for some optimism. In the last three years only 5% of British people had used B&B on a farm. Yet, 46% expressed an interest in doing so, with 16% saying that they would be very interested. This interest is universal, showing up amongst all ages and socio-economic groups. Farm tourism is not simply the province of Guardian readers in sensible shoes.

The challenge is to determine how this apparent interest can be channelled into successful farm tourism businesses which show the characteristics of sustainable tourism outlined earlier. The remainder of this paper considers certain priorities and opportunities for the future, based partly on feedback from existing and potential visitors to farms.

TYPES OF ENTERPRISE

First, some issues relating to accommodation provision. A major component of farm tourism is farmhouse bed and breakfast. It can provide an opportunity for farmers with a shortage of capital to acquire a new cash flow with only modest investment, provided they have the right property and attitude. The call from visitors is for standards without standardisation. The basic need is for cleanliness, a comfortable bed and reliable hot water. There are still too many farms which do not reach even these standards. Beyond this, there is an opportunity to provide a wide range of quality standards. This could be reflected in a broader price spectrum rather than farmers sticking to 'the going rate'. The most recent issue concerns the provision of en suite baths or showers, now preferred by two thirds of farm visitors and bringing a better level of trading to those who have them. However, some fear that by following this trend there is a danger that farm B&B will slowly become like small hotels. At the end of the day, public response suggests that the character of the building must be preserved if farms are to retain their special appeal.

Character is also extremely important with self-catering accommodation. Careful, sympathetic conversions are good for business, as well as the environment. Visitors tell us that they prefer single cottages rather than large complexes of units, and there is little demand from existing farm visitors for the addition of leisure facilities. The appeal of chalets is considerably less than that of converted barns or farm cottages. In England, self-catering cottages continue to let very well. The problem is viability for the farmer, faced with high conversion costs.

The schemes to support the development of bunkhouses and camping barns on farms provide a good example of where the public sector has given leadership and an incentive to the farmer to use tourism to retain an important feature of the landscape. The schemes started in the Peak Park and the Yorkshire Dales and then spread through special projects to other parts of England, involving both capital grants and the essential ingredient of central marketing support. The barns can provide a good return on a small capital outlay, although total income earned in the year is usually quite small. Barns have been growing in popularity, especially for use by organised parties, though this creates a dilemma in that it can make them unavailable to the individual walker for whom they were originally intended.

Caravan and camping sites in the countryside have been a contentious issue for decades. It may be impossible to equate caravans with sustainable tourism, yet, their relative popularity has held up, especially during the recession. One sector of the market demands a high level of facility provision, meaning that some sites have to be large to be viable, but there is still a healthy demand for small, simple sites such as the caravan and camping clubs' Certificated Locations, which, when well sited, can have limited impact and provide a useful source of additional expenditure in local communities.

While farm accommodation in England has grown steadily, the growth in the provision of farm attractions in the last five years has been explosive. In the main these have been simple open farms with animals, farm machinery and a varying quality of interpretation. The market response has been strong, dominated by families with children. The main opportunity which visitors appear to be looking for, and to which they respond very positively, is for their children to see, touch and feed farm animals, especially baby ones. Handled well, with the right amount of personal attention, this can be a special experience for people, and farmers should be wary of allowing impersonal interpretation to stand in the way of this. Yet, we also detected a sentiment from visitors that some farms were becoming too much like cuddly zoos. The story told and the range of experiences offered, should be broadened to cater for the whole family (and by this we mean the adults). More could be made of local agricultural heritage, the processes of food production, and environmental issues.

THE SPECIAL INGREDIENT

More thought needs to be given to the special ingredient which farms can offer to people, to strengthen their commitment to and interest in this form of sustainable tourism and to deliver a more fulfilling experience of the countryside.

Part of our market research involved discussion groups with people who were interested but who had not necessarily stayed on farms before. This showed us that people have a romantic, rustic image of farms. Although often dated and unrealistic, they are looking for some of these images to be presented to them and to be fulfilled. To be attracted to farms, these people need more than simply a list of accommodation on a page and a standard guest house that happens to be in the countryside.

It is important to get the balance right. For the vast majority of people already staying on farms, the overwhelming requirement is for attractive countryside and peace and quiet. Many want little more than this, and to be left to their own devices. Yet, there are three elements which deserve particular attention.

The first is food. Visitors indicate that traditional farmhouse breakfasts are a special reason why they choose to stay on farms. Only half the visitors to farms in England are looking for an evening meal, but where they are there is significant interest in the use of fresh produce and dishes local to the area. Too little is still made of this aspect of our rural heritage, and it fits very well with farm tourism. It is a much more potent theme in the promotion of farm tourism in other European countries.

Making more of farm food need not be restricted to accommodation providers. Visitors to farm attractions indicated to us that the opportunity to buy and eat fresh food would be a popular part of their visit; many farm attractions appear to be missing an opportunity here. In France, a special identity is given to *Ferme Auberges* (farm restaurants) and *Fermes Gouters* (places to taste farm produce) and *Produits de la Ferme* (farm shops).

A second special element is the farm family. People value the interaction with their hosts. Clearly, this should not be too planned or formal, but there may be opportunities to make more of this. For example, self-catering is an increasingly important form of farm tourism, yet it provides less scope for natural interaction. This could be overcome by the opportunity to visit the host farm for a drink or a meal.

Finally, there is the farm itself. Research suggests that most visitors have only passing interest in farming, yet, for families, the possibility of seeing round the farm and participating in simple activities like egg collecting is appealing. Some farms make too little of this, especially those offering self-catering which is a much more popular form of accommodation for families.

ACTIVITIES AND EVENTS

An important aspect of the way farm tourism relates to the local environment and local communities is the activities which visitors can undertake in the local area and how they are presented to them.

Apart from general sightseeing, by far the main activity undertaken by people staying on farms in England is walking. People are looking for very local walks, often on the farm itself and in the neighbourhood. Some farmers have been very successful in identifying their own walking routes for visitors, using rights of way. There is no reason why this should not be done for cycling and longer excursions using public transport. Some groups of farms have looked at walking packages from farm to farm, as has been developed so successfully in Germany.

Much thought has been given to ways of involving local communities more in catering for visitors, interpreting aspects of their heritage both to them and to local residents. Farms and farm produce can have a role to play here too.

One example is from my home parishes in Herefordshire. This is orchard country. Our local apple farmers have joined with community groups such as the WIs and Village Hall Committees, to develop a series of special weekend events on the theme of apples. It is now one of the main sources of fund raising for these local organisations, hence providing an incentive for community involvement. By providing an event which attracts visitors from a distance, new money is brought in, and it also benefits our local pubs and B&B. Part of the objective is to raise awareness of the heritage of old apple varieties and orchards, amongst visitors and locals alike. Elements have included: displays of apple varieties, apple identification by local farmers, apple tasting, guided walks through orchards (led by farmers), farm gate sales of apples, farm visits, cookery demonstrations involving apples, painting exhibitions by professionals and school children from our two local primary schools, talks on growing old apple varieties and pruning demonstrations, and various cultural events such as an evening of folk songs and folk lore associated with apples. We take care to include more long-standing rural traditions: the events usually coincide with harvest festival in the parish churches and we have been able to include the local ploughing match as part of the rural farm-based experience offered to visitors.

In interpreting our rural heritage, more can be made of little events of this kind rather than set piece museums and attractions. A key is excellent, comprehensive information, well distributed and promoted. Too much packaging can sometimes be counter-productive and off-putting.

To conclude, farm tourism can provide many benefits to the local economy and a special way of conserving and interpreting our rural heritage to visitors. Yet, it needs nurturing and support, especially the raising of awareness. This is a challenge not only in Britain but across Europe, where all farmers and rural communities are facing hardship from economic decline in agriculture. Marketing is critically important. Where farms have joined together, in local co-operative groups and national movements, such as the UK Farm Holiday Bureau, much more has been achieved. In Britain we are some way off the high profile achieved by Gites de France. Many of us have a vision of a strong, co-operative, mutually supportive farm tourism movement across the whole of Europe, as a force for sustainable rural tourism. By linking together, national movements in each country can become much more recognisable, so visitors know where to go to find the kind of accommodation, welcome and experiences which can give a proper feel for local rural heritage.

The Author

Dr Richard Denman studied economics and natural science at Cambridge, and obtained his doctorate at the University of Edinburgh. He undertook a major study of recreation and farm tourism for the Scottish Tourist Board and the Highlands and Islands Development Board. In 1978 he became the Deputy Director of the Heart of England Tourist Board, and for the last five years he has been an independent tourism and recreation consultant, founding the Tourism Company Consultancy Co-operative in Ledbury, Herefordshire, of which he is a director. He is retained by the Countryside Commission for their Information and Marketing Advisory Service, and is a member of the Economic Advisory Panel of the Rural Development Commission.

References

[1] Denman R. and Denman J., *A Study of Farm Tourism in the West Country*, West Country Tourist Board (et al.), 1990
[2] Denman R. and Denman J., *The Farm Tourism Market*, Research report for English Tourist Board and other partners, 1993
[3] World Conservation Union (IUCN), *Caring for the Earth, A Strategy for Sustainable Living* , United Nations Environment Programme (UNEP), World Wide Fund for Nature (WWF), 1991
[4] Denman R, *Recreation and Tourism on Farms, Crofts and Estates*, Scottish Tourist Board, 1978

REALITY OR IMAGE
The Role of Heritage Interpretation

Reality and image
are different sides of the same coin
and both can be seen
by those who have the vision.

Figure 1 Dallas Dhu Distillery, Forres.

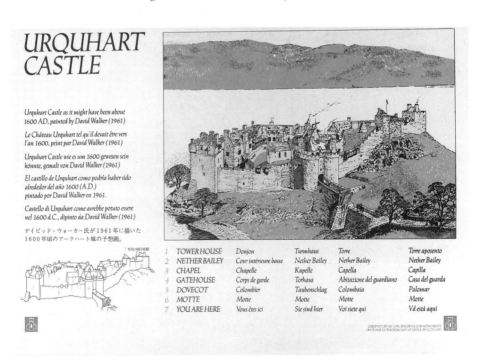

Figure 2 Multilingual Interpretation Boards at Urquhart Castle, Inverness.

17

PRESENTING HISTORIC SCOTLAND

Duncan Macniven

Historic Scotland is the part of The Scottish Office which is responsible for preserving and interpreting well over 300 historic properties which are in the care of the Secretary of State for Scotland. It is a very diverse estate. Geographically, it runs from Muness Castle in the most northerly of the Shetland Islands to Whithorn Priory and other sites associated with St Ninian in the south, and from Callanish Standing Stones in the west to part of St Machar's Cathedral in Aberdeen.

Our oldest property is probably the 6,000 year old houses on the Orkney island of Papa Westray; our newest, the distillery at Dallas Dhu near Forres which was built in 1898. Our properties run from palaces (such as Linlithgow Palace, or indeed the Palace of Holyroodhouse where we are responsible for maintenance but not for interpretation) to ordinary dwellings such as the neolithic village of Skara Brae in Orkney and the Black House at Arnol in Lewis. In between, we have a great many fine castles, churches, abbeys, prehistoric, Roman and other monuments. Our most famous properties are probably Edinburgh Castle (Scotland's main visitor attraction), Stirling Castle, Glasgow Cathedral and Skara Brae.

We paint on a wider canvas, too. We carry out the Secretary of State's job of giving legal protection to more important ancient monuments and historic buildings (through the statutory processes of scheduling ancient monuments and listing historic buildings, for example) and safeguarding them against damaging changes or demolition. We help to fund repair and conservation of the best of Scotland's built heritage, notably through historic building repair grant with a budget of over £11 million in 1994–95. We also help to fund archaeological excavation, and we give advice and assistance to others who are involved in giving a future to Scotland's built heritage.

So our task is a large one, when you take into account not only our own properties but also the far larger number of important buildings and monuments over which we have influence, ie more than 6,000 scheduled monuments, over 38,000 listed buildings and many other buildings in conservation areas. This paper considers both parts of our work, primarily our own work on our own properties but also the help and advice which we give to others.

Historic Scotland is what is called an 'executive agency' within The Scottish Office. Like other such agencies, we are directly answerable to Ministers rather than to a separate corporate body of members, as is the case with English Heritage, our counterpart south of the Border. But as an executive agency we have a high degree of delegated authority, within objectives set by Ministers, to get on with our distinct job. The day-to-day decisions are taken by ourselves rather than by Ministers, by the more bureaucratic parts of The Scottish Office or indeed in the dusty corridors of the Treasury Chambers in London. We have been an executive agency since April 1991, and have benefited a great deal from the greater independence of action, and distinct identity, which that status has brought. But we are still a government body ultimately responsible to Ministers to Parliament. We are not a free agent (but who is?), and we are not able (even if we wanted to) to retire inside our castle and do what we like without working together with others.

OUR INTERPRETATION POLICY

Our present policy for the interpretation of our own properties stems from a survey of visitors which we carried out in 1986, and which highlighted the need for more information on site. Our aim essentially is to provide our visitors, there are 2.4 million each year to our manned monuments alone, with a form of Tardis, allowing them to transport themselves back to the hey-days of the property they are visiting. That is relatively easy in places like Fort George or Glasgow Cathedral, where the building survives largely intact. It is a great deal more difficult with a ruined castle or a group of standing stones, or at places with complex evidence from more than one period. But we have nearly finished a programme of providing key information, in the form of durable interpretation boards, normally including reconstruction drawings, at all but an unsuitable handful of our properties. Wherever possible, our boards encourage readers to visit other similar sites or museums with apposite collections. At key sites, we provide information in foreign languages, eg Japanese at Urquhart Castle, Norwegian at the Viking sites in the Northern Isles and Gaelic in Gaeldom.

Around 70 of our properties justify more extensive interpretation at the property itself. First, we staff all but a few of these monuments with custodians who are carefully recruited and trained to welcome visitors. At all these monuments, we provide a guidebook, and we are steadily improving the text and presentation of these guidebooks, to make them more attractive and readable. At Skara Brae, for example, we now sell a full-colour guidebook as a *walk through time*, linked to viewing points around the prehistoric village. We also publish a series of books linking together our

Figure 3 St Andrews Castle Visitor Centre, Fife.

Figure 4 Duff House, Banff.

properties in a particular part of Scotland or monuments of a particular kind, such as *Scottish Castles* and *Scotland BC*. Most importantly, our custodians and encouraged to chat to visitors, to answer their questions and, where possible, offer guided tours.

Next, in the hierarchy of interpretation, come our interpretative centres. Some are small, as in the case of Tolquhon Castle, a forgotten gem near Old Meldrum in Aberdeenshire, or Edzell Castle. Others are quite large purpose-built visitor centres such as that at Jedburgh Abbey and at St Andrews Castle.

At major monuments, of course, we can do a great deal more. At Fort George and at Dallas Dhu Distillery, for example, it is relatively easy to recreate the atmosphere of the building's hey-day. At Duff House, near Banff, we are recreating a country house gallery, which was the original intention of the Earl of Fife who built it, in a joint exercise involving also the National Galleries of Scotland, Grampian Regional Council, Banff and Buchan District Council and Grampian Enterprise. At Edinburgh Castle and Stirling Castle, we are making good progress with major projects which both enhance the conservation of the buildings and greatly improve interpretation for visitors. Our new permanent exhibition of the Honours of Scotland, Scotland's Crown Jewels, at Edinburgh Castle was opened by Her Majesty The Queen at the end of June 1993; an exciting introductory display at Stirling Castle opened in April 1994. This work is on a scale not previously undertaken in Scotland.

That is not the whole story. Our education service, and the events which we arrange at certain of our properties, are among the other ways in which we help visitors understand what they see, and enjoy what they understand. But it will suffice as background for the rest of this paper, which deals with the following key themes: *partnership, strategic planning and sustainability*.

PARTNERSHIP

First and certainly the most important, is the theme of partnership. In Historic Scotland, we are experts on the 'built heritage'. Our interest, and that of most visitors, starts with our properties. In their own right, they are often very complex, evocative and exciting to explore. But it would be naive of us, and very misleading for people who visit historic properties, to assume that the built heritage is the only thing which interests visitors. I do not think that it is possible to interpret a society, and that is part of what we are aiming for, simply through its surviving buildings. Buildings are, after all, set in an environment which is part natural and part man-made.

Often the environment in which we see the buildings today is radically different from the environment at the time they were built. While there are many of our visitors who like to admire the buildings themselves as an art form, most people are interested in understanding their historical, social and geographical context, not simply the buildings alone. The setting of sites was of course often crucial to the original purpose, eg defence (as castles or hill forts), livelihood (as Skara Brae) or natural resources (Bonawe Iron Furnace). Our interpretation has always stressed that angle, and the human side too, because buildings were used by people and most of today's visitors are acutely interested in that. And of course the inhabitants of these old buildings had their own oral tradition (of words spoken or sung), and lived a life which can be illustrated by the things they left behind them, like the fine Roman-period dragonesque brooch which was unearthed in the excavations which preceded our recent improvements to Edinburgh Castle.

Historic Scotland may be the expert on buildings and their history, and to a lesser extent the history of the people who lived in them. As I have explained, we are happy to share that expertise, as we always have been. We have a certain amount of knowledge in other fields. But there are others who are far more knowledgeable, and it is vital that we act in partnership with them when we are interpreting our monuments or encouraging others to interpret theirs. In the past and today, we have been active in fostering that kind of link.

We have always had a close relationship with what is now the National Museums of Scotland and with local museums. I am glad to say that, since the creation of Scottish Natural Heritage a little over a year ago, we have built up very good partnerships there too. One of the fruits of this is a new accent which we are putting on the interpretation of nature conservation at our properties in care, eg at Tantallon Castle in East Lothian. There are plenty other examples of ways in which partnership can improve the quality of interpretation.

It can also, of course, improve the quantity. Our resources, like everyone else's, are limited. By working with others, we are able to 'double our money'. One example of this is at Callanish in the Western Isles, where we have long wanted to improve the interpretation of an internationally-important group of standing stones which is in our care. A visitor centre and car park is being provided near, but not too near, the stones. It is funded by the European Community, the Islands Council, the Local Enterprise Company, Scottish Natural Heritage and Historic Scotland, and it has the support of the local landowner and the local community. I emphasise the local community particularly, because there are big gains for a national organisation like Historic Scotland in pooling efforts and ideas with people who live nearby. For the first time, visitors to Callanish will have proper information about the significance of the stones and about the landscape in which they were set. At the same time, the immediate surroundings of the stones will be greatly improved by the removal of cars and signs.

These projects are important to the economies of some of Scotland's most fragile rural areas. But in urban areas, too, our work helps economic regeneration and attracts support from others as well. At Dumbarton Castle, for example, we have made improvements in interpretation as part of a programme of other work to attract visitors, supported by Dunbartonshire Enterprise, the Area Tourist Board and Dumbarton District Council. And our improvements at Stirling Castle are a vital part of the Stirling Initiative partnership which aims to revitalise the town as a place to live, work and visit.

I have dealt so far with partnership involving our own properties. But we are very happy to help others as well, with strategic advice, and with practical help and sometimes funding for individual projects. Historic Scotland helped create Banff and Buchan District Council's excellent Agricultural Heritage Centre at Aden, both by grant-aiding the repair of the buildings in which it is housed and by giving advice on the vernacular architecture which it portrays. Further north, my colleagues have been giving advice to those responsible for interpretation of the prehistory of Dunbeath and Helmsdale. We have of course very close links with the National Trust for Scotland, again contributing grant finance and advice to the wonderful buildings in the Trust's care, including the Castles of Mar, which are such a delight, in the hinterland of Aberdeen.

STRATEGIC PLANNING

But there is a limit to the scope of these kind of partnerships. I am very happy indeed with the pooling of information so that we do not all have to become experts in each others' fields. But I am not entirely happy about the thought that partnership should avoid 'unnecessary competition and duplication.' Certainly, at a time when resources are limited (and when are they not?), we must use them wisely. We must avoid, for example, concentrating on the interpretation of mediaeval castles and the nobility who inhabited them, while ignoring prehistoric sites, vernacular buildings or industrial monuments. But frankly, I think that duplication is virtually impossible because each building is unique. For example, I am very glad indeed that the National Trust for Scotland did not refuse to take an interest in Castle Fraser, Haddo House and Drum Castle on the grounds that these were all Castles of Mar and they had one already.

There are two reasons why I think that this kind of duplication is positively desirable. First, competition puts us all on our mettle. My colleagues and I look very carefully at the number of visitors calling at properties which are comparable to ours, to see whether there is some secret of marketing success which we have missed. Similarly, we have learned a lot, directly or through the medium of consultants, by studying others' ideas on interpretation, and I hope that others have learned from our efforts too. Secondly, I think that such duplication is desirable because properties like the Castles of Mar are complementary to each other rather than being in competition. While some people will have time or energy to visit only one, there are others who are positively attracted to 'collecting' all the Castles of Mar, or all Historic Scotland properties. And we know that people who visit Historic Scotland's properties go on to visit similar properties in other ownership, and vice versa. Be they local residents or visitors, people want a variety of things to see and to do, and two castles, or better still a castle and another form of historic building, are better than one.

That is not to say that there is no place for strategic planning for interpretation, to ensure that at least a representative selection of monuments and buildings survive for future generations. Although Historic Scotland takes a strong national-scale view on which historic buildings and ancient monuments should be preserved, we have no ambitions to do the same on interpretation.

We are, of course, conscious of other historic buildings as we interpret our own, and that gives a good chance to emphasise to visitors the family or architectural links between them. With an eye to the value of interpreting as many different types of monument as possible, we are also conscious of gaps in interpretation. For instance, it is far more difficult nowadays to visit a lighthouse than it was before so many of them became automatic and we have long wanted to find a way of giving access to a well-explained lighthouse. To that end, we are co-operating with the local authorities and with the Northern Lighthouse Board to do just that at Kinnaird Head Lighthouse, at Fraserburgh.

So we are happy to co-operate with others in filling gaps. But we exercise no central control, nor are there formal arrangements to fill gaps. Personally, I think that it would be quite wrong for central government to try to control in a centralist way, because I am sure that it would stultify initiative more than it would rationalise the use of resources. But I would be interested to hear what people think about how Historic Scotland might help, in identifying gaps in the interpretation of the built heritage, and in bringing together people who might fill them.

While I think that it would not be productive for central government to try to impose a planning framework on the interpretation of Scotland's heritage, I am very happy indeed to co-operate with local authorities when they seek to do so, because it is an exercise more likely to be successful at local level and seems to me entirely consistent with local authorities' role as planning authorities. For that reason, my colleagues and I have had a number of very helpful discussions with Highland Regional Council as they put together an interpretation policy for the Highlands. As operators of important heritage properties in that region, we are happy to be influenced by the Council's views. As experts in the built heritage, we are glad that they are willing to be influenced by our views. Gordon District Council has done similar work in our field. And we talk very frequently to other local authorities, to local enterprise companies and to area tourist boards who are, in a similar way to Highland Regional Council, interested in integrating action in their areas.

Sometimes, we take the initiative. The current project to create a country house gallery at Duff House grew out of steps which we took to encourage joint action, and there are many other examples. We now make no significant improvement in the interpretation of our properties without speaking beforehand at least to the local authority and to the Area Tourist Board, and to anybody else locally whom we identify as having an interest, to check that it fits in with other plans of which they are aware. Sometimes, of course, we act on the initiative of others. The very important proposal for a visitor centre at Callanish, for example, grew in its present form out of a study of historical interpretation initiated by the Islands Council, although of course we had long wanted to improve our interpretation at Callanish.

STRENGTHS AND WEAKNESSES

So what are the strengths and weaknesses of the system we have in place at the moment? I hope I am not being complacent when I say that I think it has many strengths. First, it produces, generally speaking, very high quality interpretation. Rome is still being built, of course, and we need to get the average up to the level of the best. But, by comparison with other countries which my colleagues and I know, I think we do very well. We achieve that high quality, partly because we are a relatively small community where good partnerships are relatively easy to foster. For instance, I strongly suspect that Historic Scotland's links with Scottish Natural Heritage are much closer than English Heritage's links with English Nature. That is paralleled in other heritage fields. And it is helped by easier arrangements for strategic planning. The Scottish Office Minister plays a pivotal role since he is responsible both for the natural environment and for the built heritage. So he can, if necessary, ensure that the priorities of different bodies do not get out of line.

But it would be naive to suggest that there are not weaknesses. The main weakness, frankly, is that there are not enough hours in the day or reapers in the field. In Historic Scotland, we have achieved a tremendous amount in the years since we became an executive agency. But the gleams in the eye still exceed the goods on the ground, even though our resources have been augmented and we have tried to 'double our money' through partnership.

The second weakness of our partnership arrangements is that it can be difficult to get schemes off the ground, because all parties (and not just one) need to assent. However strong the good will, and it is normally very strong, the reality of budgets and staffing sometimes limits co-operation. I think this is an inevitable price to pay for the benefits of working in partnership on the larger and more important schemes.

Third, not all local authorities or Area Tourist Boards or Local Enterprise Companies are as interested in 'heritage' as the more enthusiastic of their fellows. That is not a complaint: there may be other priorities in the area and the 'main chance' in terms of jobs or visitor interest may lie elsewhere. But it inevitably slows things down, by depriving us of the benefits of full partnership.

Lastly, successful partnership needs to be accompanied by selectivity, because people can be overwhelmed and the environment damaged by a visitor centre which tries to interpret everything. In Historic Scotland, we need to be ready to subordinate the archaeological or architectural end of things, to give proper place to for the nature conservation aspect, if that is the real focus of interest at a particular site, and vice versa. Compromise is important, if the great potential of action in partnership is to be realised.

SUSTAINABILITY

Sustainability is a very important issue for us, because our main business is to ensure that the ancient monuments, which we enjoy today, survive for future generations. In my book, interpretation can help that process. Formerly, Historic Scotland's predecessors were famous for their 'keep off the grass' attitude to visitors. Our experience now, at Callanish and elsewhere, is that people will keep off the grass far more willingly and readily if they know that that will help preserve the monument for the future. We regard our very successful scheme of free visits for organised school parties, and the educational materials which we produce to fit in with the school curriculum, as a good investment for the future because that helps the children appreciate that the survival of their local monuments depends on them and their friends.

Nonetheless, there are potential problems. The pressure of visitors can destroy the fabric or, less tangibly, the atmosphere of what they come to visit. Interpretation boards are very worthy but they can be obtrusive in photographs and need to be carefully sited. The more so do visitor centres. I do not actually think that our record on this is bad, in the heritage field in Scotland. And the sites which are overloaded with visitors are, fortunately, few and far between at the moment. But we need to keep it so, in the face of an increasing interest in heritage generally and the built heritage in particular. It needs very careful management in places like Orkney, where we restrict visitors to the tomb at Maes Howe to twelve at a time, and where the protective sward at the Ring of Brodgar can be severely damaged by summer peaks of visitors. So Historic Scotland is a full participant in the Tourism and the Environment Working Party, set up by Scottish Office Ministers under the chairmanship of the Scottish Tourist Board, to encourage people to recognise problems and to disseminate information and experience about how they can be avoided and managed. The new visitor centre at Callanish is one of the demonstration projects adopted by the Working Party.

CONCLUSION

In this short paper I have tried to underline the importance of partnership, which we in Historic Scotland embrace wholeheartedly. I firmly believe that partnership is the key to improving both the quality and the quantity of interpretation. I have also pointed out one or two of its limitations: the need for all to be in agreement before the full benefits are realised, the possibility that not all the potential partners are fully committed, and the potential problem that the quantity and diversity of any proposed interpretation must not be allowed to become overwhelming.

Communication is a central part of encouraging and supporting collaboration. Conferences such as the heritage conventions organised by The Robert Gordon University represent an important practical forum in which potential partnerships can be formed and cemented. Through published papers we can share deeper insights into how our organisations operate. From this paper, you will hopefully have a better idea of what makes Historic Scotland tick and where to find relevant points of contact. By sharing information and meeting together in this way, I think we can develop more systematic strategies for identifying what I have called gaps in interpretation, and shaping partnerships which can fill them.

The Author

Duncan Macniven is Director of Properties in Care at Historic Scotland. After graduating in history from Aberdeen University, he joined the Scottish Office in 1973 and worked for periods in Industrial and Economic Development and in the management of the Health Service before joining Historic Scotland in 1990. He is responsible for all aspects of preservation and interpretation of the 300-plus historic properties which are in the care of the Secretary of State for Scotland. These include Edinburgh and Stirling Castles, the Border Abbeys, Glasgow Cathedral, Fort George, Dallas Dhu Distillery, and a wealth of prehistoric sites such as Callanish Standing Stones in Lewis and Skara Brae in Orkney.

References

Ambrose, T. (ed.), *Presenting Scotland's Story*, Scottish Museums Council, 1989

Baldwin, J., *Exploring Scotland's Heritage: Lothian and the Borders*, RCAHMS, 1985

Breeze, D. and Donaldson, G., *A Queen's Progress*, HS, 1987

Cavers, K., *A Vision of Scotland: The Nation Observed by John Slezer 1671–1717*, National Library of Scotland, 1993

Close-Brooks, J., *Exploring Scotland's Heritage: The Highlands*, RCAHMS, 1986

Dunbar, J.G. and Fisher I., *Iona*, RCAHMS, 1983

Fawcett, R., *Scottish Medieval Churches*, HS, 1985

Fojut, N. et al, *The Ancient Monuments of the Western Isles*, HS et al, 1994

Fojut, N. and Pringle, P., *The Ancient Monuments of Shetland*, HS, 1993

Hay, G.D. and Stell, G.P., *Monuments of Industry*, HS, 1986

Historic Buildings Council for Scotland, *Historic Buildings Council for Scotland Annual Report 1992–1993*, HMSO, 1993

Historic Scotland, *Arbroath Abbey*, HS

Historic Scotland, *Balvenie Castle*, HS
Historic Scotland, *Beauly Priory*, HS
Historic Scotland, *Bishops and Earls Palace*, HS
Historic Scotland, *Blackness Castle*, HS
Historic Scotland, *Bonawe Iron Furnace*, HS
Historic Scotland, *Brough of Birsay*, HS
Historic Scotland, *Cærlaverock Castle*, HS
Historic Scotland, *Cairnpapple Hill*, HS
Historic Scotland, *Craigmillar Castle*, HS
Historic Scotland, *Crichton Castle*, HS
Historic Scotland, *Crossraguel*, HS
Historic Scotland, *Dirleton Castle*, HS
Historic Scotland, *Doune Castle*, HS
Historic Scotland, *Dryburgh Abbey*, HS
Historic Scotland, *Dumbarton Castle*, HS
Historic Scotland, *Dundrennan Abbey*, HS
Historic Scotland, *Dunstaffnage Castle*, HS
Historic Scotland, *Edinburgh Castle*, HS
Historic Scotland, *Elgin Cathedral*, HS
Historic Scotland, *Fort George*, HS
Historic Scotland, *Hermitage Castle*, HS
Historic Scotland, *Historic Scotland*, HS, 1994
Historic Scotland, *Historic Scotland Annual Report 1993 – 1994*, HS, 1994
Historic Scotland, *Historic Scotland Corporate Plan 1994*, HS, 1994
Historic Scotland, *Huntingtower*, HS
Historic Scotland, *Inchcolm Abbey and Island*, HS
Historic Scotland, *Inchmahome Priory*, HS
Historic Scotland, *The Island Blackhouse*, HS
Historic Scotland, *Jedburgh Abbey*, HS
Historic Scotland, *Kildrummy Castle*, HS
Historic Scotland, *Linlithgow Palace*, HS
Historic Scotland, *Lochleven Castle*, HS
Historic Scotland, *Maes Howe*, HS
Historic Scotland, *Melrose Abbey*, HS
Historic Scotland, *Memorandum on Listed Buildings and Conservation Areas 1993*, HS, 1993
Historic Scotland, *Orkney Monuments*, HS
Historic Scotland, *Rothesay Castle*, HS
Historic Scotland, *Scotland's Listed Buildings: A Guide to their Protection*, 2nd ed., HS, 1993
Historic Scotland, *Stirling Castle*, HS
Historic Scotland, *Sweetheart Abbey*, HS
Historic Scotland, *Tantallon Castle*, HS
Historic Scotland, *Withhorn Priory*, HS
Horsey, M., *Tenements and Towers: Glasgow Working-Class Housing 1890–1990*, RCAHMS, 1990
Ritchie, G. and Harman, M., *Exploring Scotland's Heritage: Argyll and the Western Isles*, RCAHMS, 1985
Ritchie, A., *Exploring Scotland's Heritage: Orkney and Shetland*, RCAHMS, 1985
Ritchie A., *Picts*, HS, 1989

Ritchie, A., *Scotland BC*, HS, 1988

Ritchie A. and Breeze, D., *Invaders of Scotland*, HS, 1991

Royal Commission on the Ancient and Historical Monuments of Scotland, *Argyll Inventories, Volumes 2–7*, RCAHMS, 1975–92

Royal Commission on the Ancient and Historical Monuments of Scotland, *Dundee on Record: Images of the Past*, RCAHMS, 1992

Royal Commission on the Ancient and Historical Monuments of Scotland, *Images of Scotland*, RCAHMS, 1993

Royal Commission on the Ancient and Historical Monuments of Scotland, *North-East Perth: An Archaeological Landscape*, RCAHMS, 1990

Shepherd, I., *Exploring Scotland's Heritage: Grampian*, RCAHMS, 1986

Stell, G., *Buildings of St Kilda*, RCAHMS, 1988

Stell, G., *Exploring Scotland's Heritage: Dumfries and Galloway*, RCAHMS, 1986

Stevenson, J., *Exploring Scotland's Heritage: The Clyde Estuary and Central Region*, RCAHMS, 1985

Tabraham, C., *Scottish Castles and Fortifications*, HS, 1986

Walker, B. and Ritchie, G., *Exploring Scotland's Heritage: Fife and Tayside*, RCAHMS, 1985

18

MARKETING OUR PAST

David J Breeze

A report to a ICOMOS UK meeting in 1990 by the administrator of Notre-Dame, M Francois Girard, highlighted the problems of over-visiting for a popular historic building (Girard, 1990). Notre-Dame receives 10½ million visitors a year, of which 2¼ million go to make devotionals, this is in comparison to about one million visitors to Edinburgh Castle and Stonehenge and two million to York Minster.

The Cathedral authorities of Notre-Dame have attempted to deal with the visitors in several ways. Visitors have been forbidden access during services, but that merely created disruption as worshippers tried to get through the throng of tourists and the guides outside tried to tell their parties about the building. Visitors are therefore allowed in even during services but encouraged to follow the same circular route. Controlled tours have been attempted and abandoned. Pollution, from people inside, the vapour given off by respiration and the soot from candles lit by visitors, and the fumes from coaches outside, is another major problem. Consider also that most visitors spend less than 18 minutes in this great Cathedral, which has an effect on how the Cathedral is interpreted. Notre-Dame typifies the complexity of the problems and the variety of possible management schemes for monuments under visitor pressure.

The erosion effect of visitors at British monuments is experienced from Stonehenge in Wiltshire to Maeshowe in Orkney. The problems at Stonehenge are well known. At Maeshowe, Historic Scotland for many years has had to restrict the number of visitors entering the burial chamber at any one time to 12 because of the problems caused by the human breath, and in 1991 a new access path had to be laid as a result of erosion along the approach through the earthworks. Elsewhere north of the Border, the National Trust for Scotland has taken a well-publicised decision to restrict the amount of advertising given to certain sites which it feels are at risk.

In 1989, there were 127 million tourist trips in Britain, 86% by British residents (English Tourist Board, 1991, p7). These British made an estimated 630 million leisure day trips in 1989. Historic buildings in England alone attracted 140 million visits. Overseas tourism to Britain has grown by 39% in the last decade and is expected to increase by 34% over the next five years. The figures for Scotland are nine million tourist trips a year and 80 million day trips (Scottish Tourist Board, 1992, p2).

In the face of increasing visitor numbers it is essential that we should be considering now the potential impact of such numbers on our historic monuments and buildings. The existence of tensions between tourism and conservation, and the likelihood of these tensions increasing, has been appreciated by the Government. Working parties were established in 1990 to examine the relationship between tourism and conservation, both of which have reported (English Tourist Board, 1991, Scottish Tourist Board, 1992), and further consideration is now being given to the subject.

Cultural resource managers have an important part to play in the debate which is now in progress. The debate is not simply about how to achieve the right balance between conservation and tourism, or, in extreme cases, how to protect our sites from overvisiting; it also encompasses how we present these sites to the public.

As a responsible heritage organisation, Historic Scotland is concerned to achieve an appropriate balance between tourism and conservation. This is clearly stated in our corporate plan which gives primacy to conservation (Historic Scotland, 1994). Historic Scotland is a full member of the group which is looking at ways in which environmentally friendly tourism can be encouraged in Scotland. We have not always been successful in achieving the best balance between tourism and conservation ourselves and some of the examples I will cite are our own mistakes, from which we have tried to learn.

Let me say first of all that I am emphatically in favour of people visiting ancient monuments and historic buildings. I love such sites and I enjoy visiting them. I wish others to have the same degree of enjoyment, develop the same affection, and I encourage visitors by leading parties myself. I participate actively in marketing historic properties and interpreting them, for example, through the writing of guide-books. Visitors are positively beneficial to our work as cultural resource managers. We have the chance during visitors' tours of our sites to educate them and excite their interest not just in a particular monument, but in wider fields too, including conservation and management, as well as encouraging an environmentally responsible attitude to monuments.

Many people's first contact with archaeology is a visit to one of Historic Scotland's properties and it is important that we get the level of interpretation right, through appropriate guide-books and information boards, so that they will go on to visit other sites, monuments or museums. Greater numbers of visitors should allow us to undertake more conservation, as well as produce better guide-books. Clearly there is a limit on the number of visitors our monuments can tolerate, although we do not yet perceive a real problem at other than a few sites at present levels of visiting.

The heritage is big business. Many heritage organisations are seeking to increase their income and therefore encourage more and more people to visit

Figure 1 The Maeshowe Dragon, Orkney. While all observers are agreed that this carving is deteriorating, exact measurements are difficult to achieve owing to the different levels of lighting operating when photographing the carving.

© *Historic Scotland.*

Figure 2 Skara Brae, Orkney. The delicate features within the houses are protected by restricting visitors to the wall-tops. This in turn, however, places pressure on the walls themselves.   © *Historic Scotland.*

their ancient monuments and historic buildings, but that has a cost: the gradual destruction of the fragile resource which the visitors come to see and which it is the aim of bodies such as Historic Scotland to protect. It is important for us to have an idea of how many visitors a monument might tolerate without resulting damage. Each monument requires a visitor profile, by which I mean an appreciation of the numbers of visitors each monument can tolerate and how those visitors should be spread across the year, around the monument, and within each day (English Tourist Board, 1991, p49). Few sites yet have such visitor profiles. Historic Scotland is preparing management plans for its own properties which will encompass all aspects of management, including visitors.

It is obviously sensible that the protection of the resource itself be given the sort of primacy enshrined in Historic Scotland's Corporate Plan, ie we seek a balance between our wish to encourage to encourage more people to visit our monuments and the necessity of protecting the resource. One particular problem is exemplified by Skara Brae in Orkney. A visit here is a must for the parties travelling on the cruise liners. Visitors walk round on the wall heads, yet we have an incomplete understanding of how well the monument can tolerate the weight of visitors on the wall tops in the long-term. We are, therefore, now looking at ways in which we can address the particular challenge of presenting this world-class monument to those who understandably wish to visit it while ensuring its long-term preservation in which we have invested so heavily in the past.

Another potential danger of tourism which we must guard against is over-concentration on the earning power of the archaeological heritage. This could lead to those monuments which cannot bring in money being ignored and gradually deteriorating. This, of course, would not merely be bad for those monuments, but would lead to even more pressure being placed on the paying sites. Such an approach is emphatically not the policy of Historic Scotland, where our programme of conservation work does not distinguish in this way and where we are committed to the same high standard of conservation throughout our estate. Nevertheless, the very pressure of visitors at Edinburgh Castle and their expectations are such that it receives considerable allocation of staff and financial resources within Historic Scotland in order to meet that demand and to continue to raise income.

At the other end of the spectrum, however, we ought to be prepared to accept that some archaeological sites, perhaps even some museums, will always be an acquired taste. This is certainly true of the Antonine Wall, which, even for those with a powerful imagination, is not a patch on the most famous sections of Hadrian's Wall. Historic Scotland has long adopted a policy of low-key signposting of the Antonine Wall. Thus, only visitors who really want to find it reach the monument, expectations are not raised unduly, while the low-key approach also helps to protect a very fragile monument.

It is also worth noting that increased mobility has brought many more visitors in recent years to sites where no admission is charged. There is

Figure 3 The west gate of the Roman fort at South Shields, built in 1989. The gate sits exactly on the original Roman foundations.

© *Tyne and Wear Museums.*

Figure 4 Roman buildings at Aquincum. The line of dark plaster marks the distinction between original (but consolidated) masonry below and new build above.

© *David J Breeze.*

undoubtedly a greatly increased demand from car-borne tourists for things to do and places to visit. Within our own estate there is strong anecdotal evidence for increased numbers at sites, such as Callanish, Clava Cairns, Ruthven Barracks and Glenbuchat Castle where there is no commercial pressure.

The expectations of the visitors increases too. Shops, tearooms, floodlighting are all now almost de rigeur. Yet each carries a potential penalty in the necessary adaption of an existing building or the insertion of below ground cabling which might affect archaeological remains. Castles were built to keep people out, yet we want to encourage them in. Thus, at Edinburgh Castle, a tunnel has been driven through the rock to allow access for maintenance and other traffic and keep vehicles away from the tourists.

The tranquillity of some of our most elegant ruins is perhaps another factor to consider. We would all accept, I suspect, that some sites require quiet respect to best understand and appreciate them. No modern techniques could improve on the natural setting of such monuments. Low-key interpretation is all that is required: once the basic facts are provided, such monuments speak for themselves.

A relatively few years ago, this was regarded in many quarters as the best approach to the interpretation of all ancient monuments. It was assumed that many people wished to have the experience of learning about monuments themselves and, of course, in a Christian country we assumed they understood how church buildings were designed in response to particular forms of worship. Thus, little on-site interpretation was provided. Few would contest that today more is required in most cases and Historic Scotland is now coming to the end of a programme to place at least one modern interpretative panel at every property in its care. Wherever appropriate, each board includes a reconstruction drawing and uses appropriate foreign languages. Yet, pressure increasingly grows for something more. Drawings are not enough, goes the argument, visitors can really only understand a building if it is physically reconstructed.

After a long pause since earlier attempts, there has been a spate of reconstructions recently, in particular of Roman sites, including the Lunt, the Manchester gate, the South Shields gate. The last spawned an interesting and wide-ranging discussion at a local public enquiry, in the report of which the inspector, Sir Alexander Waddell, stated that the rebuilding of this gate in situ was a special case and was 'experimental and for the results to be evaluated in practical, educational and archaeological terms before considering the extension of the technique to other scheduled monuments. In short the claims for Arbeia [South Shields] would need to be proved in practice before any kind of precedent is set' (HSD 9/2/01, para 11.27). Yet, now there is a proposal to reconstruct another building at South Shields.

It is important to emphasise that I am not against replicas per se; I am only against reconstructions in situ. And for very good reasons. These reasons were carefully considered by UNESCO and led to the Venice Charter which stated that there should be no reconstructions in situ (ICOMOS 1966, Articles

Figure 5 The cross-hall of the headquarters building of the Roman fort at Saalburg, built between 1898 and 1907 on the actual Roman foundations. The hall was reconstructed as an open hall, but all authorities now agree that it would have been covered (Baatz 1971, 7). © *David J Breeze.*

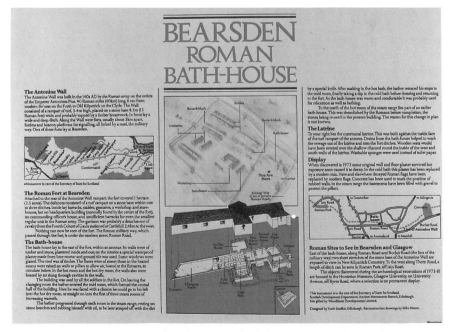

Figure 6 The information board at the Roman bath-house at Bearsden on the Antonine Wall. © *Historic Scotland.*

9, 12 and 15). There are several points to be considered in any discussion on reconstruction or restoration. The rules concerning restoration were laid down in the 19th century and are still largely accepted in Britain (Thompson 1981, 20). Reconstruction in situ ought not to destroy the original masonry, should be identified, reversible and should only be undertaken in order to help preserve fragile elements of the historic fabric: in the words of Frank Baines, the Commissioner of Works Architect in 1913, 'restoration as commonly understood ... will only be permitted ... in those cases where the safety of the building absolutely demands such treatment' (Baines, 1913, p103, para 12).

At some sites it might be considered that re-roofing would act as a beneficial conservation measure, although such re-roofings are rarely as simple as they might seem at first sight as there are often problems with fenestration, doorways and other fittings or simply knowing all the details of the original building. In Scotland, we have placed concrete domes over cairns as a protective measure and I would regard this as acceptable as it is reversible: it also helps the visitor appreciate the monument much better.

The reconstruction of certain monuments, however, could destroy what many see as the attraction of those monuments today, such as the beauty or tranquillity of their current appearance. We have grown to appreciate certain buildings as ruins and to change them would be deeply upsetting to many people. Another major constraint is the fact that we can seldom know exactly what the building we are reconstructing really looked like. We know now that the Roman fort which Kaiser Wilhelm had partially reconstructed at the Saalburg is wrong, but the builders 100 years ago thought it right. Indeed, if we have learnt anything from the history of building reconstructions it is that the next generation will prove us wrong.

The present stewardship policy, which entails consolidating but not reconstructing what we have inherited, has much to commend it. It offers an obvious line at which to stop. Once that line has been crossed, it is not easy to see where to cease. Should we stop, as at Aquincum, the Roman Budapest, at partial rebuilding of the walls; or rebuild only the interesting sections as at the Roman baths at Weissenburg in Germany; or go towards complete reconstruction as at the Saalburg. A better approach would be to preserve our irreplaceable archaeological sites inviolate, not restoring in situ but building replicas on different sites as at Beaune in France or, adopting the Jorvik approach. This approach is now becoming more widespread, especially with the growth of theme parks.

Reconstructions have enormous educational value, but they also have limitations in that they tend to establish a particular and static representation of how a monument might have looked. Although different options can be reconstructed and changes can be made, these are more difficult and expensive than altering two-dimensional images, or even models. As certainty is never possible in this area, alternative artists' impressions, or computer graphics can be more challenging, flexible and cost effective.

Moreover, historic sites are often more complex than those who interpret them are sometimes prepared to accept. Or rather they have alternative histories. For the modern druid, Stonehenge has a particular significance which many archaeologists would prefer to ignore (Chippindale, 1990). In the past, modern 'intrusions' at a monument have been swept away in order to focus on a particular phase in its history or to aid interpretation. Guide-books may ignore the later history of a monument. Historic Scotland's guide-book to Edzell Castle until recently contained no reference to the reconstruction of its famous walled garden (compare Simpson 1987 with 1989, p22 – 25).

It is important that all the information we impart is appropriate to the monument and as accurate as it can be at the time, that it is not deliberately laundered in order to suit the preconceptions of the audience, nor to patronise them. If we do this, we risk trivialising our subject. We have an ever present danger of just this with advertising which naturally seeks to simplify, and in doing that can present a misleading picture, although no doubt unintentionally. While presenting our product, the monument or museum, in the best light we should take care not to over-sell it for that could be counter-productive and perhaps put people off visiting other sites. Only if we pitch our information and marketing at the right levels, though these may vary, can we retain respect for ourselves and our subject and gain the support of others. In fact, of course, we want to provide information for visitors so that we interest them in ancient monuments and historic buildings and thereby gain support for the work of protecting the built heritage: we want our visitors to think, not merely pay. In short, we must present the material as honestly as we can, recognising that it may need to be altered as information and the needs of visitors changes.

There is, in fact, scope for many different approaches to presenting our heritage. The museum world reacted badly to Jorvik, although it is not a challenge to traditional museums. I find it difficult to find anything to complain about with Jorvik because it is impeccably researched, with the evidence as accurately presented as it could be and with no one claiming more for the visitor centre than that it is one type of presentation. The only problem, I believe, comes if we view Jorvik as an ideal for us all to aim for. For me, it is merely one of a whole range of types of heritage sites for visitors to see and enjoy. The Jorvik treatment is very relevant to archaeological sites where the remains are not able to speak for themselves. This is not true for ancient monuments and historic buildings, where it is but one of the several methods of interpretation which could be used, for the essential difference here is that the structure survives to speak for itself. In choosing which method of interpretation to use, the needs of the individual monument must be paramount.

All too often we see our monuments as if divorced from their wider surroundings. Yet of course, they are not. The setting of Dryburgh Abbey, for example, is as much a part of the monument as the Abbey itself. However, in recognising this, the next step of trying to integrate interpretation of the monument with its wider setting is rarely taken. We consciously do try to do this in Historic Scotland. The board at the Roman bath-house at Bearsden, for example, advises visitors where to see the best surviving sections of the Antonine Wall, the adjacent sections and the museum where the finds are on display. In my view there should be more such linking of sites and museums. It has been a constant disappointment to me how rarely cultural heritage organisations are prepared to advertise each other's wares, and thereby help each other out while helping the visitor to achieve a fuller and more rounded appreciation of a historic period through related buildings and artefacts.

Moreover, an appreciation of the wider setting of monuments and their relationship to geography and natural history is crucially important at some sites. We can hardly understand the reasons for the location of Bonawe Iron Furnace on the shore of Loch Etive without an appreciation of the local vegetation, the trees which provided the charcoal, to which we draw attention on our interpretative panels. At other sites nature conservation interests have a different relevance: Tantallon Castle is one of several monuments in the care of Historic Scotland which sits in a SSSI and our interpretation identifies the natural heritage interest as well as the historic.

Several organisations, including English Heritage, Historic Scotland and the National Trust for Scotland, have commissioned reports on the natural history of their sites as part of a move to learn more about other dimensions of our heritage. This perception of our cultural heritage as a part of the wider environment is, I believe, an important step forward. Co-operation between all bodies involved in tourism and the heritage in order to protect the resource is one of the main recommendations of the reports on tourism and the environment (English Tourist Board, 1991, p38–43; Scottish Tourist Board, 1992, p24).

The ways we present our monuments are always improving, but we need to monitor the consequences of each change as we move forward. New techniques offer new and exciting challenges. I return to the point I made at the beginning: my wish is to engender in the public my own love of our historic monuments and buildings. Balancing the desire, indeed the need, to encourage visitors with the protection of the fragile archaeological resource is the principal challenge facing heritage managers today. Marketing should not be allowed to override the proper protection of our monuments. If we can achieve this, the task will be made easier and more rewarding for tomorrow's managers.

The Author

David J Breeze is Chief Inspector of Ancient Monuments in Historic Scotland and a past President of the Society of Antiquaries of Scotland. He is an acknowledged expert on Roman archaeology and, in particular, Hadrian's Wall on which he has published several books. Dr Breeze would like to thank Mr Graeme Munro and colleagues in Historic Scotland, particularly Mr P.J. Ashmore, Mrs D. Grove, Dr R. Fawcett, Dr L. Macinnes and Mr C.J. Tabraham, for their comments on this paper.

References

Baatz, D., *Saalburg Roman Fort*, 1971

Baines, F., *General Instructions to Foremen in Charge of the Works of Preservation*, in Peers, C. R., *Ancient Monuments and Historic Buildings*, Report of the Inspector of Ancient Monuments for the Year ending 31st March 1913, HMSO, 1913, pp 102–117

Chippindale, C., *Who Owns Stonehenge?* London, 1990

English Tourist Board, *Tourism and the Environment. Maintaining the Balance*, ETB, 1991

Girard, F., *The Cathedral of Notre Dame de Paris*, lecture text to ICOMOS UK Heritage and Tourism Conference, Canterbury, 1990

Historic Scotland, *Corporate Plan* 1994

HSD 9/2/01, Public Local Enquiry into an application for scheduled monument consent for the proposed reconstruction of the west gate, sections of the west walls, bridge and ditches of the South Shields Roman fort, 27–30, November 1984

ICOMOS, *International Charter for the Conservation and Restoration of Monuments and Sites* (The Venice Charter), 1966

Scottish Tourist Board, *Tourism and the Scottish Environment: A Sustainable Partnership*, STB, 1992

Scottish Tourist Board, *Going Green: Guidelines for the Scottish Tourism Industry*, STB, 1993

Simpson, W.D., *Edzell Castle*, HMSO, 1987, revised by Richard Fawcett

Simpson, W.D., *Edzell Castle*, HMSO, 1989, revised by Richard Fawcett

Thompson, M.W., *Ruins: Their Preservation and Display*, London, 1981

HIGHLAND FOLK PARK

19

INTERPRETATION IN THE HIGHLANDS

William McDermott and Ross Noble

Highland Region has some of the most outstanding landscapes, wildlife and cultural heritage within North West Europe, and much of the Region's economy is dependent upon using the natural resources through the primary industries and tourism sector. These activities are estimated to account directly for some 35–40% of total employment within the Region, while downstream processing of resources, for example through the food manufacturing and textile sectors, accounts for a further 5% of employment.

During the 1980s there was an increasing public awareness of the impact of man's activities on the environment. The Brundtland Report in 1987 and subsequent work by David Pearce and colleagues explored the issues of sustainable development in some depth and laid particular emphasis on the polluter pays principle, a principle now embodied in the European Commission's environmental policy. In Highland Region, debate on these issues has led to a formal recognition by the main public sector agencies that economic growth should be based on sound environmental principles, and in particular that new approaches are needed to encourage the sustainable use of natural resources.

Against this background, a joint study, *Development Opportunities In The Natural Environment*, explored ways to generate employment and business opportunities through enhanced conservation and interpretation of the natural environment. This innovative work adopted an integrated approach to conservation and development. The study sponsors comprised: Highland Regional Council; Highlands and Islands Enterprise, the Nature Conservancy Council for Scotland and the Countryside Commission for Scotland (now combined to form Scottish Natural Heritage), and the Scottish Office. The wide backing given to the study at the time, and subsequently in progressing the study's recommendations, demonstrates an increased awareness by these agencies of the need for:

1.   informed debate and consideration of environmental issues;
2.   a balanced approach to achieving economic development and

environmental objectives; and

3. co-operation between agencies in formulating an integrated policy and in developing and implementing practical projects.

In the course of a single study it was not possible to explore fully all aspects of the economic use of resources. The work focused its effort in the two areas of land management and tourism development. Developing an Interpretive Strategy has implications for both of these areas, and some key factors in each are important for understanding the relevant background and how the Strategy itself was formulated.

LAND MANAGEMENT ISSUES

Consideration of current land management practices in the study identified the following key issues:

1. continuing deterioration of natural woodlands because of the deer management policies adopted by sporting estates, in particular the reduction of Caledonian pine forests which are recognised as a priority species;

2. poor muirburn practices and overstocking of moorland by sporting estates has led to a reduction in heather cover and reduced soil fertility;

3. negative environmental effects caused by intensive sheep farming and commercial forestry, in particular a reduction in natural woodland, but also a general reduction in the diversity of species and habitats;

4. negative views by landowners and managers regarding public access to land due to:
    – the disturbance to other activities, particularly sporting activities, which arises if public access is not strictly controlled; and
    – the costs associated with maintaining footpaths and other infrastructure if this is subjected to high levels of public use;
    – erosion of hillsides and other vegetation, including the habitats of priority species;
    – disturbance to wildlife caused by a lack of public understanding;

5. negative attitudes to tourism due to:
    – pollution, mainly from litter and sewage, but also from increased noise levels; and
    – a reduction in visual landscape quality as a result of poor design and location of tourist facilities.

250

These issues provide an excellent illustration of the conflicts which can exist between environmental and economic interests. Generally speaking, much of the conflict is based on the different perspectives of the protagonists, particularly in terms of time scale. In the past the negative effects have been intensified through lack of an integrated approach by the various bodies concerned: landowners and managers; conservation bodies; statutory planning authorities; and economic development organisations.

TOURISM DEVELOPMENT

Tourism is recognised as a key sector within the economy of Highland Region, generating expenditure in excess of £400 million per annum and supporting in the region of 20,000 (full time equivalent) jobs. It is crucially important that tourist operators receive support in developing the sector further, but that such development is achieved in a way which is consistent with the principles of sound environmental management and with maintaining the quality of life for those people who are permanently living and working in the rural communities of the Highlands. This is what we understand by the terms sustainable tourism .

The Study helped to identify the type of development opportunities which could generate additional local employment and income within the tourism sector, whilst at the same time increasing levels of awareness and understanding of environmental issues. Whilst these opportunities relate mainly to tourism, they are also targeted at local residents in context of the part they have to play in land management (for example through agricultural practices) and in maintaining the quality of the natural environment at the local level.

Development proposals include the following: presentation and interpretation of the environmental and cultural heritage of the Highlands; initiatives to increase the amount of time which visitors spend in rural communities and enhance the interaction which takes place between the two groups; the development of value-added services based on natural resources; tourism management initiatives; and restoration, conservation and maintenance of natural resources.

Underlying all of the development proposals are a number of strategic policies for sustainable development. These policies were articulated through the Development Opportunities study and have been formally adopted by the sponsoring organisations. The policies are based on five key principles:

1. sustainable development requires a shift from short-term to long-term objectives;
2. the maintenance, management and restoration of resources should go hand in hand with their development;
3. there is a complex interdependence between economic activity

and environmental quality which must be recognised;

4. local involvement in planning, decision making, developing and managing projects should be a specific goal; and

5. decisions regarding the utilisation and development of natural resources should be made on the basis of informed choices.

PRODUCING AN INTERPRETIVE STRATEGY

The art of explaining the significance of sites to the public should be a central plank of any sustainable development policy for the Highlands, both from a fundamental understanding of its philosophy and purpose, and as a way of creating tourism attractions and as a visitor management/conservation tool. Interpretation of the natural, historical and cultural environment of the different parts of Highland Region can provide a mixture of benefits for those that provide the facilities and services, for local people and visitors. These can be summarised as follows:

1. For the provider of facilities and services:
    – encourages careful research, survey and analysis of the resource being interpreted;
    – provides a justification to the public for conservation policies and expenditure;
    – provides a framework for managing visitors; and
    – provides an economic benefit through charging/selling goods.

2. For local people/communities:
    – provides a framework for other development opportunities, such as redevelopment and economic regeneration;
    – can enhance the quality of life in a community through encouraging participation in planning and managing facilities and services;
    – can act as an inspiration for local policy makers;
    – gives local people a stake in welcoming visitors;
    – provides an income in some cases; and
    – generates a pride and sense of place.

3. For visitors:
    – gives an opportunity to see at first hand and to appreciate sites of natural, historic and cultural significance;
    – aids individual exploration and discovery;
    – provides attractive, interesting and enjoyable facilities and services; and
    – gives a sense of place and identity to the visitor, but it is important to co-ordinate the development and

implementation of interpretive projects to avoid duplication of facilities and to ensure that the most appropriate themes and sites are used.

When the time came to develop the Interpretive Strategy it was clear that it would be impossible to prepare a detailed prescriptive plan for the entire 10,000 square miles of Highland Region. The Strategy needed to have the blessing of local communities which meant in effect recognising their separateness; and yet also allowing the expression of an overall Highland identity. The Strategy therefore set out the following objectives:

1. Clarify the important characteristics of the Highland Region in terms of its culture, landscape and natural history so as to provide an overall unifying picture of the area.
2. Outline a possible framework of interpretive provision through partnership or individually by the Steering Group of Agencies.
3. Produce a set of principles of good practice for providers of interpretation to avoid duplication of themes and to encourage imaginative ways of communicating interpretive messages.
4. As part of good practice , encourage the production of local detailed interpretive plans which set the context for interpretation at a local level.
5. Seek community involvement, where possible in the provision of interpretation.

The idea of a Highland Heritage Network was developed to foster good practice and a sense of cohesion and partnership in all those who provide interpretive facilities. It should also help maintain high standards of presentation. Facilities on the Network would be identified, initially, in Gateway Centres or Orientation Centres at points of entry into the Region. Only those fulfilling specifications and standards of good practice would be allowed into the Network. It would allow for the development of themed trails or linked marketing of specific interests across the Region.

Detailed interpretive prescriptions will only arise at the local planning level, in a way similar to the division between Structure Plans and Local Plans in the statutory planning system. Local Interpretive Plans should operate at community level with help and advice from professional interpreters, knowledgeable about the different communities and skilled in negotiations with all the different interests. Clearly that calls for adequate resourcing and a consistent approach across the Region.

Few attempts to develop a planned system of interpretation across large geographical areas have been successful. In fact, the evidence suggests the initial enthusiasm usually fades as staff are pulled on to other work when the start-up capital has disappeared. A laissez-faire approach to implementing the Strategy will quickly see the whole effort run out of steam. It is important to build up momentum through a dedicated unit of interpretive staff, working region-wide with communities, supplying a service, setting standards and creating good quality jobs which diversify into related resource based activities. Jobs and the local economy are key words in a Highland context. With 60% of the economic activity of some parts of the Highlands tied up in tourism, there is every chance that the Strategy can be made to work.

THE STRATEGY IN PRACTICE: the Highland Folk Park

Many of the elements of the Interpretive Strategy have been part of Highland Regional Council's plan to develop a Highland Folk Park at Newtonmore in the heart of the Central Highlands. It has been viewed by elected members and officials alike as one of the most important projects embarked upon by the Department of Libraries and Leisure Services. In parallel with the Interpretive Strategy it deals with land management issues and has a clear contribution to tourism development. It is a flagship project aimed at creating a 'leisure and learning' experience for a new millennium, embracing such concepts as sustainable tourism, learning by participation, integration of a living environment with living history. All the environmental management principles are involved: detailed research and planning by the provider, strong community links and well thought out interpretation strategies for visitors.

In philosophical terms, the concept is firmly rooted in the 'open-air museum' tradition which began in Scandinavia a century ago and in the more recent eco-museum concepts of George Henri Riviere. Pragmatically, it has developed out of the changing role of the Highland Folk Museum in Kingussie, Britain's first specialist folk and open-air museum opened in 1935, which has evolved from being a last sanctuary for the material remains of traditional Highland culture to a focus for the integration of traditional lore and skills into modern Highland life.

The 'Heritage in Action' programme at the Highland Folk Museum takes as its starting-point the belief that the past is not something dead, which can be attractively but safely interred in glass coffins, but is an essential element in a fulfilling present, and a major contributor to a sustainable future. Thus, the museum has become a venue for over 100 'live' events annually, where demonstrators not only present the richness and complexities of traditional crafts and activities, and allow public (and particularly school) participation in the event, but highlight the relevance of their activity for modern man. However, the constraints of a six acre site and a collection of culturally important buildings and artefacts has limited the full development of the Heritage in Action programme.

The Highland Folk Park development will remove these constraints. The site comprises 80 acres of mixed terrain: farm land, water, heath, water meadow, pine woods and deciduous woodland. Only the 19th century Aultlarie farm steading and a possible neolithic chambered cairn require recognition as cultural monuments. Any further additions to these, in terms of buildings or artefacts, will only be introduced in accordance with the management plan. Otherwise, replicas, archaeological reconstructions and modern buildings can be used to create the setting and the landscapes, which will meet the aims and objectives of the Park, which are:

> To raise awareness of the heritage and culture of the Highlands : to create opportunities for people to gain a deeper understanding and appreciation of past traditions and practices, and of the need for their conservation: to do so in a development which is sensitive to, and compatible with, the economic and environmental needs of the wider area.

In these three short clauses are encapsulated the three-fold objectives of the Park: *Interpretation, Education, Community Development.*

INTERPRETATION

Raising awareness, increasing enjoyment and promoting the conservation of the Highlands and its culture will be achieved through several different techniques. It will be done fundamentally through a series of imaginative reconstructions of historic Highland settlements enhanced by displays, live demonstrations and visitor participation in traditional practices. Re-introducing traditional breeds of farm animals and older varieties of crops will highlight biodiversity and also help in practical terms to establish a gene-bank. The continuing operational need for traditional craft skills in the Park will underline both their importance and their aesthetic value.

To focus the visitor's mind on the interpretive experience, the reception building will take the form of an 18th century inn. Here the visitor takes the role of traveller and is encouraged to explore, in time as well as space, reconstructions ranging from the Stone Age to the twentieth century. The interplay of modern buildings, preserved cultural properties and theatrical (though academically sound) settings, will be itself a means for the interpretation of the built environment and its interaction with the natural landscape. However, it will be made clear, that this is not site interpretation, and that the visitor should follow up the Park experience with visits to site-specific attractions elsewhere in the Highlands.

EDUCATION

The Highland Folk Park is an educational resource. It does not simply contain such resources or provide opportunities for formal or informal learning processes. It is itself the vehicle for education. Schools, colleges and universities have been involved from the start in planning and developing the Park. Participation in the creation of a new form of heritage interpretation is one of the most important contributions the Park can make to the present generation and those to follow.

The Park may not yet be 'open' to the public, but already student projects relating to heather management, soil seed-bank sampling, wind power, and interpretive techniques are underway. School children have taken a keen interest in the 'Victorian Croft' development. The local primary school has adopted a field, and will be involved in crop rotation. This year they planted potatoes and made scarecrows to protect their crops.

The very nature of the Park, in which buildings and structures will age and decay, and replica artefacts will be used to destruction, means that even in the longer term there will be a need for continuing work by craftsmen with traditional skills. This again offers a rich educational opportunity. Training courses and perhaps even apprenticeships in traditional crafts are a logical extension of this aspect of the Park's development. A woodland management course has already begun, through Employment Training, and a dry-stone walling course took place in 1993. In the future, furniture-making, textile crafts, basketry and a host of other crafts and skills will be on offer as short-term classes.

The site is large enough for parts of it to be made available to teachers and students as locations for practical social history experiments, and for environmental studies outwith those offered by the Park's teaching staff. Replica buildings might be made available for experiences in 'historic living' over a weekend or longer. The Park, in conjunction with its parent body, the Highland Folk Museum, will also house information, archival material, research collections, which will be a major resource for schools, colleges and open-learning students. Thus, the traditional role of the museum will not be lost in the drive towards innovation.

COMMUNITY DEVELOPMENT

The Park aims to be an integrated part of the wider community in several ways and on several levels. Obviously, it will provide local employment and, unlike many tourist-related facilities in the Central Highlands, many jobs will be attractive to young men. It is hoped too that some of the Park's workforce will be drawn from the local crofting community, so that its way of life will be underpinned rather than undermined by the development. The Park in its function as visitor attraction will create economic spin-offs for local business: new visitors will be drawn into the local communities and existing visitors encouraged to stay longer in the area. The potential for hosting academic conferences and short-term courses in the Park could help to fill accommodation during the shoulder months between the summer and winter seasons.

The role of the Park as a supporter and employer of local craftspeople will bring a welcome spotlight on the whole range of crafts carried on in the Highlands, and can be used to raise awareness of regional arts and crafts guilds and societies. Moreover, the work of creating replicas or experimenting with 'lost' techniques could bring about new uses, new products and new demand for traditional skills. Positively encouraging the involvement of local groups such as, children, elderly and disabled people, and the unemployed, will foster co-operation, mutual support and a pride in their Park which will strengthen community links and its sense of well-being.

Newtonmore is still, in feature and outlook, a traditional Highland village. Kingussie is similarly a small Highland town. It is hoped that, as part of the conservation initiative within the Park, both will be seen as continuing parts of the story: present day extensions of the settlements portrayed in the Park. If this is achieved, local pride in the physical appearance of these communities may increase and encourage local resistance to the pressures of architectural fashion and expediency. In time this effect might diffuse into the wider Highland area as a whole. The Park's intention is to heighten awareness of the rich cultural and natural landscapes of the region, and to deepen the sense of identity and sense of place among natives, incomers and passing visitors alike.

At the strategic level, the Park is intends to be a tourist attraction of international importance, drawing people to the Highlands and encouraging them to stay longer and explore further. Most importantly, it will offer Highland tourism operators an example of best practice in management and sustainability.

As stated earlier, the Highland Folk Museum draws its inspiration from the European Open-Air Museum Movement, which is now a century old. Through membership of the Association of European Open-Air Museums, Park staff have been fortunate enough to visit a large number of institutions in both Western and Eastern Europe. Many of the specific ideas for the Park have been inspired by examples of best practice in other museums, especially some of the recent attempts at establishing gene-banks or preserving skills.

The term 'Folk Park' has been chosen for the Newtonmore project quite deliberately to distinguish it from the open-air museum. There is a fundamental difference in concept. In an open-air museum, the buildings or other large man-made structures are the focal points, the objects of attention and study. The landscaping, often brilliantly executed, and the demonstrations in an open-air museum are intended as an experience designed to raise ones awareness of the buildings. In the Folk Park, on the other hand the buildings and other man-made objects are intended to provide a setting which raises ones awareness of the experience.

By using mainly replica structures, there is no need to preserve the buildings in a museum-like state of conservation. Repair and disrepair will be a continuous feature of the experience. Buildings, vehicles, implements will be seen in new and pristine condition rather than as preserved relics. The provision of space within the Park for open-air museum activities, the preservation of historic structures, in situ or translocated, will mean that visitors will doubly experience the time continuum of the cultural landscape: firstly, in their own 'real time' sense of old and new buildings, and, secondly, in the Park's artificially created time capsules.

The Park Management Plan, which is currently being prepared, places as strong an emphasis on land-use issues as it does on museology or visitor management. This is not surprising, given the objectives of environmental awareness and sustainability. But the plan goes beyond mere conservation of the site and postulates that the Park can become a training centre for traditional countryside skills: dyking, ditching, vermin control, woodland management. Thus, the Park is intended to spearhead the creation of a new skilled workforce which will be available, throughout the Highlands and beyond. Given the growing interest in environmental control and protection, often seen as in opposition to exploitation for the benefit of visitors, this workforce can rightly be seen as a necessary prerequisite for the wide-spread introduction of green tourism concepts in the Highlands.

The establishment of the Highland Folk Park, as described, is a daunting task from the perspective of its originators. It will not be the overnight creation of a visitor attraction. By their very nature, some of the processes involved in building the Park will be measured in years. For example, it has been estimated that to create the 17th century 'Highland Township' element in the Park, some 15 – 20 buildings, all constructed from timber frames and turf walls, with an associated 'runrig' farming system and summer shieling settlement, will take 10 men at least four years to complete. The breeding programmes, which hopefully can be carried out in partnership with the neighbouring Highland Wildlife Park, an offshoot of Edinburgh Zoo, and the plant protection programmes will be even longer term projects.

The Park can only succeed if it gains and retains the commitment of the local authority which funds it, the staff which develop and operate it, and the local community who must perceive their basic ownership of the concept. It must also provide acceptable levels of entertainment, interpretation and education for its customers, who are the key element in the funding package.

The Authors

William McDermott is Depute Director of the Libraries and Leisure Service of Highland Regional Council where he has particular responsibility for the Heritage and Interpretation Division. With a training in ecology and land agency, he has held previous appointments as Assistant National Park Officer with the Peak District National Park Authority and Assistant Director of Merseyside County Museum (now the National Museum and Galleries on Merseyside).

Ross Noble has been Curator of the Highland Folk Museum, and Regional Curator for the Museums Service of Highland Regional Council since 1976. He pioneered the concept of 'travelling curator' with the Scottish Countrylife Museums Trust, assisted by the Carnegie UK Trust. He helped to develop Auchindrain Museum in Argyll, and to write the interpretive plan for Biggar Museum Trust. During the late 1980s at the Highland Folk Museum, he developed the concept of 'Heritage in Action' programmes, where traditional crafts, skills and music become a daily part of the museum's interpretive techniques. Ross Noble is a member of the Association of European Open-Air Museums, and is currently President of the Society of Folk Life Studies.

References

ASH Partnership and Cousins Stephens, *Development Opportunities in the Natural Environment*, Highland Regional Council, 1992

McDermott, W.G., *An Interpretive Strategy for Highland Region*, Highland Regional Council (unpublished), 1993

Pearce, D.W., Markandya, A., and Barbier, E.B., *Blueprint for – Green Economy*, Earthscan, 1989

World Commission on Environment and Development, *Our Common Future (The Bruntland Report)*, Oxford University Press, 1987

Figure 1 The Highland Folk Park Reception Complex, Kingussie.

Figure 1 The new 'standard map' of St Andrews.

20

INTERPRETING ST ANDREWS

Michael H Glen

The subject of this paper is a scheme for visitor orientation and interpretation in St Andrews. The client was a consortium which brought together Fife Enterprise, North East Fife District Council, the Area Tourist Board for St Andrews and North East Fife and the Scottish Tourist Board under whose overall aegis it was established. The implementation of proposals is being steered by the St Andrews Tourism Management Plan's project executive, Alison Butcher.

The contractor was also a team, convened in the first instance by Douglas Sampson of the Derek Lovejoy Partnership in Edinburgh and including Bremner & Orr Design Consultants of Tetbury and our own consultancy, Touchstone, more properly called Derek Lovejoy Touchstone to reflect our close association with the Partnership. As the project evolved, we took over leadership during the study and Bremner & Orr were the main contractors for its implementation.

A BALANCING ACT

Throughout our advisory and implementation work we attempt to maintain our corporate ethos of supporting the real and organic, that which grows from its locus, in preference to the synthetic and imposed, that which owes little to its location. This ethos was very much to the fore in our work for St Andrews and, as a general rule, it demands that we seek to achieve a number of balances. These balances lie, for example, between:

- *clients' aspirations and visitors' expectations*: between the demands of the producer and the needs of the consumer;
- *development opportunities and conservation needs*: between the demands of the promoter and the needs of resource;
- *economic benefits and long term sustainability*: between the demands of the present and the needs of the future;

- *sponsors' wishes and community interests*: between the demands of the investor and the needs of the neighbourhood;
- *the appeal of the project and market realities*: between the demands of the seller and the needs of the buyer; and
- *entertainment and integrity*: between the demands of the ephemeral and the needs of the substantial.

That is what we set out to achieve, but is this ambition realistic? Is this holier-than-thou approach appropriate in today's climate of investment appraisal, cost benefit analysis, competition for business and market forces? Well, we believe it is and, insofar as it is practical to stand our ground, we do so. We are not purists, however, nor blind to the need to stay in business.

While we side with the angels, we are not, and can not afford to be, heavenly purists. While we bow to the Tabernacle of Tilden and the Altar of Aldridge, we are bowed by 25 years' experience of, and involvement in, interpretation and many other communications media. We carry our own torch, our touchstone, if that is not a mix of metaphors.

THE MECHANISM AND PLAN OF INTERPRETATION

Interpretation forms, or should form, a fundamental part of the presentation of a destination. It should, of course, be closely linked to the marketing strategy and it also has a bearing on the improvement of facilities. It is therefore a vital consideration in tourism management and promotion. However, interpretation and the allied functions of communication, orientation, information, personal guiding, publications and marketing can not themselves minimise adverse effects of tourism, but they can create greater understanding of surroundings, awareness and concern and, through this, changed behaviour. This quality stems from the early work of Freeman Tilden and his colleagues and their use, in the US National Parks, of interpretation as a management tool to achieve conservation aims as much as to establish visitor satisfaction. The two are, of course, inextricably linked. (Tilden, 1957).

Interpretation is not an end in itself: it is a powerful mechanism, a means of benefiting visitors to places and the places they visit. Its original meaning, embodying revelation and provocation, has been extended in recent years, to the dismay of the purists, to embody information. In this context, I fear that much of what we have done in St Andrews falls somewhere between presenting information simply, comprehensibly and relevantly, and interpreting that information to reveal connections and provoke enquiry. It will, we believe, provide a basis for person-to-person interpretation to go into greater depth, to forge further links in visitors' minds and to generate greater interest.

The background to our work in St Andrews included two linked elements. One of these was the Scottish Tourist Board's programme called *Tourism and the Scottish Environment*. This programme was designed to set up schemes which manage tourism and visitors in a way that minimises any adverse effect on the physical and cultural environment. It is, unequivocally, a measure under the sustainable tourism banner.

Another element stemmed directly from the STB programme and was the St Andrews Tourism Study, undertaken by the Pieda consultancy. They produced a good report which recommended, inter alia, that an interpretation plan should be prepared for the town and the surrounding area of North East Fife as part of overall improvements to tourism facilities, presentation and marketing. This in itself was not a novel suggestion, we have made the same recommendation many times, but it was given weight by the findings of the report which indicated that little was done to help visitors to the area to find their way around, to discover its less apparent attractions and to appreciate it in greater depth.

The original brief asked us to consider St Andrews in considerable detail and three areas of North East Fife in lesser detail: the Tay coast, the central area and the East Neuk. In the event, we concentrated substantially on the town of St Andrews itself and treated the Tay coast, from Newburgh to Newport, and the central area, broadly the Howe of Fife, as one entity in presentational terms. Apart from key points like Falkland, Auchtermuchty (now because of its Dr Finlay connections), Ceres and Cupar, the area was not heavily visited.

We also felt that, as much work was already under way in presenting and interpreting the East Neuk, any further detailed proposals for that outstanding area could confuse rather than help. Our views were based on getting the plan right for St Andrews and, in effect, allowing proposals for the hinterland to follow.

We began by undertaking a heritage and tourism audit of St Andrews. The town is unique for six reasons, the first being the combination of the other five, the whole being greater than the sum of the parts:

- *history*: it has a formidable place in the political and religious heritage of Scotland and played a major role in the Reformation;
- *trade*: it is remarkable survivor of a medieval market town in its harbour, central area street pattern and many of its buildings and, for North East Fife, it remains the market town to this day;
- *education*: it boasts Scotland's oldest university which itself has recorded a series of firsts in a number of ways, together with two highly regarded schools;

- *golf*: it is the undisputed home of golf and this has given it international standing in terms both of the courses and of the administrative headquarters, the Royal and Ancient Golf Club;
- *landscape*: it is set in an outstanding coastal and countryside environment with considerable natural history interest and recreational facilities, and has become a place of resort for thousands of families.

Together with other attributes, this combination of architectural, commercial, cultural, educational, historical, natural and recreational heritage forms a kaleidoscope of dynamic and inter-related forces which provided the basis of our plan. However, the audit presented us with a series of other considerations. These included:

- *market*: the nature of the present and potential audience, whether enquiring visitor, student, local resident, leisure seeker, golfer or business visitor;
- *cars*: the major conflicts which had arisen in terms of traffic management, an ill-considered parking scheme and a plethora of uncoordinated road and pedestrian signing;
- *advice*: the lack of orientation to visitors on arrival, very patchy help and guidance in the form of publications available, and disparate information sources (but an excellent tourist information centre); and
- *tourism*: the north coast of North East Fife was little visited, had few developed attractions and yet offered opportunities for exploration, augmenting a visit to St Andrews itself.

Lastly, and crucially, we had to consider the vulnerability of the town to visitor pressures, to the introduction of new signs and information points and to superficiality of message through the need to convey information concisely.

OUR RECOMMENDATIONS

Our deliberations were much helped by consultation with a considerable number of people in and around St Andrews and the guidance of our client group. In association with our colleagues, we recommended a substantial series of measures which we believed would help to make a visit to St Andrews even more fulfilling than that already enjoyed by, as Pieda calculated, two million people a year.

Many, but not all, of our proposals were related to physical manifestations: signage, informational infrastructure, printed material and so on, and it is these on which this paper concentrates. But we also set out a philosophical and design-based approach to guide longer term interpretive provision. And we looked at the relationships between the interests and aspirations of various organisations with concerns of one kind or another for the visitor.

These included the University (almost all of whose students come first as visitors, as do their families), the Merchants' Association (many of whose members welcome visitors to their retail premises), the St Andrews Preservation Trust (whose museum attracts many visitors) and the operators of attractions from the Castle to the Byre Theatre, the Sea Life Centre to the Botanic Gardens. Our report suggested linkages and interaction for these and more.

THE INTERPRETIVE THEMES

Although I have considerable reservations over what is called *themeing*, often an over-simplistic and contrived vehicle, we based our recommendations for St Andrews on a thematic approach at two levels. The first, the abstract level, stemmed from the kaleidoscope, which was invented (possibly in Edinburgh) by Professor David Brewster who became a distinguished principal of the University. The kaleidoscope's principle, of presenting a simple series of different and constantly re-aligning *shapes* within a set framework, seemed to us to embody the nature of St Andrews whose key characteristics formed and reformed in different patterns as you went about the town: golf mingling with nature, the University with life in the town, history with everything.

We used this philosophical approach to suggest that each of the five themes we chose should be identified on signs and in printed material by a simple shape and colour, a red triangle for university connections, a white circle for golf and so on. The exigencies of printing costs etc will, I fear, consign this idea to the text books. Not so the kaleidoscope itself, which has been used as a linking graphic mechanism on many of the interpretive media, or the themes which we defined, based upon our original audit of the town's qualities:

- *The Coast and Countryside*: the natural heritage, as a backdrop to other themes as well as a theme in itself, but including parks and gardens.
- *The Inspiration of St Andrew:* the political and religious heritage with emphasis on the cardinal role of the town and the significance of its cathedral and castle.
- *A Place of Learning and Invention*: the University, with special reference to the town's continuing role as a place of teaching and innovation.
- *The Fair Ways of the Golfer:* golf (or the *gowff*, as many Scots call it), primarily in terms of the institution and its influence in St Andrews and worldwide.

265

- *Ancient and Royal:* the market town (or, as we preferred, *the mercat toun*), particularly in terms of its medieval heritage, the fabric of the buildings and its continuing to thrive as a retailing centre.

Importantly, all but the first of these are as much about today as they are about yesterday; in a sense, the historical is a part of today as well, through the influences it has had and the changes it wrought. St Andrews is a live, thriving community. There was no way in which we wished to see an interpretive aspic descend upon the place.

In our report, we expanded considerably on the content of each of the themes in order to take account of the many facets of St Andrews which might appear to have been overlooked in presenting five titles. Such greater detail covered such topics as the establishment of the religious settlement at Kilrymont, the long list of famous names associated with the town in a variety of ways, the local and international golfing heroes, the now-departing fishing industry, local characters and children's traditions.

In the wider context of North East Fife, we chose similar themes to those pertinent to St Andrews: the natural heritage, the political and religious history, agriculture and fishing, and the social and cultural heritage of the area. We suggested that these themes could best be evoked as a series of tales: the Farmer's Tale, the Pilgrim's Tale, the Mason's Tale and the Airman's Tale, for example, the last bringing in 20th century heritage.

ACTION ON THE GROUND

When it came to practical recommendations, in other words, what should be done on the ground, we provided our clients with a considerable list; this was costed and scheduled in detail in order to provide for an initial programme and for continued implementation after the first year. The key elements of the programme were:

- *presentational mechanisms,* including thematic and geographical approaches, design criteria and graphic devices;
- *revised and new signposting,* both for drivers and for pedestrians;
- *orientation points,* to be provided at key arrival and decision making locations;
- *interpretive devices,* from maps, panels, plaques and leaflets to person-to-person interpretation and events.

Rather than go through the detail of each and every proposal, I should like to highlight a number which reflect the approach and could transfer to other towns and villages, which was part of the point of our study in the first place. It was seen as a pilot for other places in Scotland and we were delighted when our recommendations were accepted and, now, substantially implemented.

It was at the later stages of the study, once the audit and theory had been completed, that the landscape planners and the graphic designers came into their own and the final proposals reflected this team approach. The use of *we* should be taken to include all three practices, where appropriate, throughout this paper. It was not a solo performance by Touchstone by any means.

SIGNPOSTING

If you cannot find your way to, or around, a destination, your day out gets off to a bad start. While road signing in and around St Andrews was up to standard in terms of basic information, it lacked cohesion and displayed all the problems of accretive rather than co-ordinated signing.

We proposed a complete revision of traffic signposting in the town including the improvement of the town centre parking scheme and, in particular, the removal of intrusive and excessive signs. The parking voucher system was characterised by a rash of signposting of epidemic proportions which, I am delighted to say, is no more. We were told it was only temporary, but our voice with many others seems to have foreshortened the temporary period.

St Andrews, for all its qualities, has a certain Scottish reserve about it; visitors are received with what we described as less than overt enthusiasm. While we will not change people much, we did recommend the use of highly illustrative town boundary *welcome signs* for St Andrews and all the towns of North East Fife. These have not yet been incorporated in the implementation plan, but will give a local flavour to the approach to each community within a district-wide design approach.

The town, despite its long history, has nevertheless lost some of its linguistic character, evidenced in street names. The creeping disease of anglicisation (for largely specious reasons) has resulted in the disappearance of *Mercatgait*, for example, and the arrival of Market Street. In addition, many of the old carved street name signs have been lost to the ravages of time, or name changes. We strongly recommended the replacement of street name signs, where appropriate, with incised-letter signs, and the re-introduction of old street names.

The use of Scots was a question we had been asked to tackle and I will come back to the point below. It is something I care about deeply and can get quite passionate about.

There is streak in the mapmaker which, if not mischievous or malevolent, is anarchic. Whether it is the decision to join Ordnance Survey maps at crucial points in order to sell two instead of one, or being so slavish to compass points that all logic is defied, the cartographer holds the whip pen. St Andrews has a street pattern of four thoroughfares leading eastwards (as it happens) towards Castle and Cathedral. This is not a whim, it was designed that way to create processional routes.

The visitor to St Andrews arrives, in the main, at the west end of the town centre. All sightlines lead east; so the mapmakers tend to turn logic around by 90 degrees to suit the compass. We disagreed with this approach and agreed with the sensible maverick who had had the courage to make a map of St Andrews look like St Andrews. None of the existing maps, however, had enough to commend them as the principal map for visitors.

We recommended, therefore, that a completely new base map of the town should be devised and produced, and that it should act as the *standard map* for use on introductory leaflets, information panels, publications etc. Our design colleagues got to work and produced an illustrated map which reflects the shape of historic St Andrews and its medieval street layout as well as alluding to the town's heritage through illustrations. This map is now in use and forms the basis of a new map-leaflet which we compiled for the burgh.

ORIENTATION POINTS AND PEDESTRIAN SIGNBOARDS

Perhaps the single most important proposals was for a series of *orientation points* to be set up at key arrival areas such as major car parks and the bus station, pedestrian nodal or decision points and a strictly limited number of town centre locations. Each orientation point was designed to have three vertical panels attached, in triangular formation, to a central post. In car parks and open spaces, that post would be a flag pole, to mark clearly the location of the orientation point and to add additional movement and colour through flying the *Saltire* flag whose design is, of course, that of St Andrew's cross. In the town centre, the orientation points would be attached to existing street furniture but with a distinguishing pennant flying above. A number of orientation points have now been erected and each incorporates, using the separate panels:

- a *town map*, with a message of welcome and introduction to St Andrews;
- a *more detailed précis* of the town based upon the five themes which I referred to earlier; and

Figure 2 Car park orientation point.

Figure 3 Proposed welcome sign for roadside.

- *specific information* and interpretation about the immediate locality and its attractions, eg at the junction of Golf Place and The Scores, the panel refers to the Royal and Ancient Club House, the Golf Museum, the Sea Life Centre, the beach and coast and the Castle.

An element which we and the designers are most pleased about is the unusual design of the panels themselves which, uniquely, incorporate a crow-stepped top, which evokes the dominant feature of the townscape of St Andrews and other Fife towns, particularly when the three panels are seen as a composite trio.

We proposed an innovative scheme of pedestrian signboards for use in place of the multifarious finger posts and similar signs which were springing up in profusion. The method we recommended avoided further street-edge furniture and was inspired by a system used in some European countries which employs a series of pictograms and arrows in vertical formation and placed at obvious points around a town or village.

Our approach employed a single, composite, direction panel, rather than a stack of individual panels, and would use illustrations of destinations and arrows on a single slim vertical panel. The panel would be set at the back of the pavement, usually placed against a building wall at each of a number of key street junctions. The shape and style of the signboards echoed that of the orientation panels, which maintained the strict design control which is essential in any such overall signposting scheme. This vertical signboard design has not been used in Britain, as far as we know, and may take time to be accepted. It has not yet been approved for St Andrews.

INTERPRETIVE PANELS

We proposed the carefully controlled use of low-level *interpretive panels* at key locations such as the site of St Mary of the Rock, the original church in the town, and at the often-forgotten harbour, overlooking St Andrews Bay, and at other places where there was a story to tell which might not be immediately obvious. The design of the panels was conventional, using an unobtrusive (but clearly seen) lectern panel of 'landscape' shape.

The interpretive panels were intended, as far as possible, to rely on illustration to make their point rather than simply on words. In the event, however, I suspect that the word has scored something of a victory because explanation can never be done without setting parameters based on visitors' own knowledge. A number of panels have now been designed and put in place.

As a support mechanism to full-scale interpretive panels, we recommended that the existing, and rather unimaginative, plaques near a number of buildings with historic connections should be replaced by a more evocative style of *marker plaque* which echoed in physical style the heavily framed stone plaques used on buildings to show coats of arms, the initials of owners and so on. These could be created in modern materials indistinguishable to all but detailed examination from stone.

The proposals for orientation points, interpretive panels and marker plaques were equally applicable to such places as Ceres, Cupar, Falkland and the East Neuk communities, but their introduction there will be in a later phase.

OTHER INTERPRETIVE MEDIA

We did not want interpretive media to be limited simply to panels and, as I have indicated, we were concerned that there should be controlled provision of panels to avoid intrusion and visual indigestion. We were helped in our original thinking on this score by the guidance of our Lovejoy Partnership colleagues and also by the streetscaping scheme for St Andrews proposed by Anderson Jeffrey Associates in a study which also followed the Pieda Report with which he had been involved. We proposed, therefore, that much of the meat of the interpretation should be in the form of other media:

- *a map leaflet,* which would use the standard map accompanied by sufficient text to provide pointers to areas and sites of interest and which, by its *followability* would help to minimise the need for on street signposting;
- *a more detailed introductory leaflet,* setting out thematically the story of St Andrews and its many qualities; this leaflet would also include *taster* information on the hinterland of the Tay Coast, the Howe and the Neuk;
- *thematic leaflets,* which would deal with specific topics in greater detail, whether they be the maritime heritage, the medieval townscape, the development of the university or whatever;
- *a self-guided walking trail,* using existing *markers* and an accompanying leaflet, would highlight places of particular interest and explain how they contributed to, or fitted in with, the story of St Andrews; we were not keen to recommend *Walkman-style* tours, although they have been successful in places like Linlithgow and many historic properties;
- *a children's trail,* which would aim to present the story of St Andrews in terms which young people would relate to and understand;
- *programmes of guided walks,* building on the existing provision and other elements of person-to-person interpretation which has always proved to be the most lasting and successful means

of conveying stories about places, and is equally applicable to countryside as to town locations;

- *street-theatre* as part of a series of events and happenings which would draw visitors into the spirit of the place; some events exist already, like the Kate Kennedy Procession, but more are needed throughout the year to give St Andrews a much greater sense of liveliness and colour if it is to succeed in earning a substantial part of its income from tourism.

LANGUAGES

We are not good at speaking others' languages in Scotland; equally, multilingual signboards and leaflets are off-putting and difficult to design well, if other than minimal information is to be included. Our recommendations were to provide translated leaflets in key languages and to provide summary leaflets to relate to the content of the principal orientation and interpretive media. We made a number of other supportive proposals.

One question we were asked to address, and to which I referred earlier, was the use of the Scots language and how it could or should be incorporated into our interpretive material. This is actually a much more difficult question than it appears, but it was timely, given the considerable current interest in lowland Scots, perhaps spurred on by the successful campaign by the Gaels for greater recognition of their language.

Many Scots words are in current use in Fife as they are across Scotland; some are local to Fife. However, their appearance in written form often appears contrived unless they are in proper context or shown as quotations within the normal medium for public interpretation which is standard English, ie unless the whole text is in Scots, which is a largely unfamiliar medium to most people in Scotland, even those who speak the Scots tongue, or versions of it, all the time. I am not going to fall prey to the temptation to deliver a polemic on the use, abuse, misuse and no-longer use of Scots; that is for another paper.

Furthermore, because Scots are Scots, interpretation written wholly in Scots would arouse conflicting opinions among experts and would also confuse visitors unfamiliar with the language and its variants. However, St Andrews has a long history and much of what was spoken and written in or about the town, up till the 18th century, was written in Scots (when it wasn't written in Latin or French).

We recommended, therefore, that a legitimate and appealing way of bringing Scots into written and spoken interpretation, and introducing it to visitors who did not understand its place in Scots society, was to provide quotations from the past and by using the Scots names of places, trades and the like, where feasible. It could also be used to good effect in person-to-person interpretation and street theatre, where it could also be explained, compared and contrasted. Many Scots words are onomatopoeic, entertaining to hear and to get one's tongue round, and infinitely more expressive than standard English.

We suggested that trails and walks be given titles in Scots, where apposite. Overall, our recommendation was that Scots words should be used in context, and only where self-consciousness or introspection could be avoided. Words like *kirk* are obvious; *gowff* was rejected on what I personally felt were quite erroneous grounds, but that is life for an interpreter.

WELCOME TO ST ANDREWS

In summary, then, our interpretive plan was accepted in October 1993 by our client group, and by representatives of local people, after considerable internal and public consultation. The *Standard Map* has been drawn, publications have been prepared, and the first *Orientation Points* and *Interpretive Panels* are being put in place at the time this paper was written in May 1994. We await with interest the reaction from visitors, and from fellow professionals.

The Author

Michael Glen is Managing Director of Derek Lovejoy Touchstone Ltd, a consultancy which advises on the wise use and creative presentation of heritage resources. His professional career and personal pursuits have been largely concerned with all facets of communication, principally the use of the written word and its relationship to graphic media.

References

Aldridge, D., *Site interpretation: A practical guide*, Scottish Tourist Board, 1993
Aldridge, D., *Guide to countryside interpretation, part one: principles of countryside interpretation and interpretive planning*, HMSO, 1975
Balnaves, A. (Ed), *St Andrews Tourism Study*, PIEDA plc for Fife Enterprise and others, 1992 (limited circulation)
Glen, M. H (Ed), *St Andrews Interpretation Plan: report*, Derek Lovejoy Touchstone Ltd for Fife Enterprise and others, 1993 (limited circulation)
Jeffrey, A. (Ed), *Townscape Vision*, Anderson Jeffrey Associates for Fife Enterprise, unpublished, February 1992
McCarthy, J. and Aldridge, D., *Heritage Signs in Scotland: assessment of potential in North East Fife*, unpublished 1992 (limited circulation)
Tilden, F., *Interpreting our heritage*, University of North Carolina Press, 1957

Figure 1 The Braes of Glenlivet.

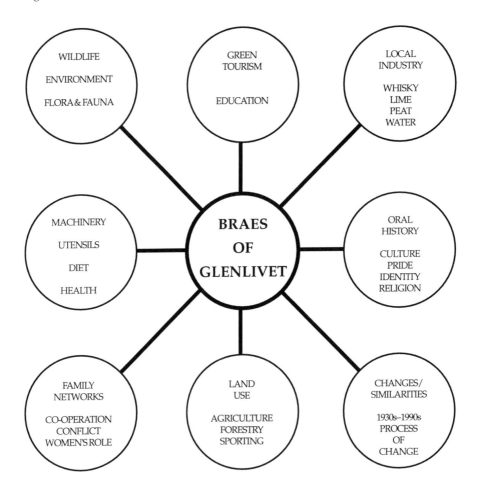

WILDLIFE

ENVIRONMENT

FLORA & FAUNA

GREEN
TOURISM

EDUCATION

LOCAL
INDUSTRY

WHISKY
LIME
PEAT
WATER

MACHINERY

UTENSILS

DIET

HEALTH

**BRAES
OF
GLENLIVET**

ORAL
HISTORY

CULTURE
PRIDE
IDENTITY
RELIGION

FAMILY
NETWORKS

CO-OPERATION
CONFLICT
WOMEN'S ROLE

LAND
USE

AGRICULTURE
FORESTRY
SPORTING

CHANGES/
SIMILARITIES

1930s–1990s
PROCESS
OF
CHANGE

Figure 2 Framework for Glenlivet Study.

21

THE BRAES OF GLENLIVET
A Study in Oral History

Priscilla Gordon-Duff

Glenlivet Estate covers about 23,000 hectares of the southern part of Moray District in Grampian Region. It is the largest agricultural property belonging to the Crown Estate. Much of it lies above 300 metres, but the gentle, rolling hills and fertile soils make cultivation possible. Indeed there have been settlements here since at least the Bronze Age. Today, the average farm size is about 310 hectares, of which some 70 hectares is usually arable. In addition, there are common grazings. Most of the farms are leased from the Estate and are family run.

From the 16th century the Estate was a Gordon, latterly Richmond and Gordon, property. In 1937 it was acquired by the Crown Estate. As tenancies were given up, the Estate's policy was to amalgamate farms in order to retain viable units and to allow effective investment in new buildings. However, by the mid 1980s, there were increasing concerns about the future of upland farming. The Crown Estate Commissioners agreed to adopt a more positive role than that of traditional landlord and actively encourage a wide range of economic activity in order to sustain a healthy rural economy. A new approach was required. The Glenlivet Development Project was set up to actively encourage rural economic development including diversification on let farms, improved provisions for visitors and promotion of the Estate as an area to visit. As a result, Glenlivet Estate began emphasising its identity, making use of many traditional farm buildings which had become redundant and proactively assisting the development of small businesses.

As the Estate began to promote itself as a quiet, unspoilt area to visit, a ranger service was developed to offer access to the countryside through the provision of walking routes, estate tours, explanatory leaflets and evening talks by the ranger in local hotels. An interpretive map was produced in 1993 with help from Scottish Natural Heritage, entitled *Discover Glenlivet: A Landscape to Explore*. One of the walking routes runs through the Braes of Glenlivet, a well-defined and rather isolated area of high ground centred on

Chapeltown in the south east of the Estate a few miles from Tomintoul. The Glenlivet Development Committee recognised that this area's particular strength was in its long-settled population and their very definite sense of belonging to the Braes. The Committee wanted to acknowledge this by recording the memories of those who had lived and worked there for the past sixty years or more, and financial support was sought from the Moray Badenoch & Strathspey Enterprise Company for a study on the oral traditions of the area.

At this time, I was employed as a Trainee Land Agent by Smiths Gore, the firm which manages the Estate on behalf of the Commissioners. Someone remembered that, as a rather less mature student, I had trained as an anthropologist. When the Local Enterprise Company granted the funding, I was asked to take on the study. I was delighted to find myself spending many a pleasant morning away from my theodolite, drinking tea and listening to tales of life in the 1930s. It was as well that I was offered nothing stronger than tea, for I needed all my concentration to tell which Grant family was which and whether we were talking about Stuarts or Stewarts. It was all crystal clear to those telling the tales: they had lived all their lives with the complicated genealogies of their families and neighbours.

What I did find difficult was how to formulate an approach for my study which would enable me to gather relevant and meaningful information for my report to the Committee, while at the same time allowing interviewees to relate information relevant and important to them. Rather than listing different aspects of life under separate headings, I chose to start with the area of the Braes of Glenlivet as a whole and consider what radiated from it, as shown in the diagram. When I first met the interviewees I explained the purpose of my visit and showed them the graphic illustration as a starting point. I did not structure my questions, but used this illustration as a framework. I recorded the interviews in the same way.

The Braes of Glenlivet are part of the Parish of Inveraven. They have an identity recognised by the people who live there and by those who live outside. The bowl-shaped area of the Braes is approached through a narrow opening beneath The Bochel Hill and was originally used as summer grazings, or *shealings*, by farmers lower down in the Parish. *Sgalan*, like the word *bothy*, is Gaelic for a dwelling in the hills. These names are retained in Scalan and in Tom a Voan or *Tom a'bhothain*, the Hill of the Bothies. By the 18th century, with the pressure of population, an improving landlord and the availability of well manured ground, these temporary grazings became permanent settlements. Eskemulloch was such a place, originally part of the Tombae grazings, it was first listed as a separate holding in 1748 when it was taken in by John McRobie. Often the new settlements were subdivided and a 'new town' or 'Bellno' (Gaelic, *Baile nuadh*) formed. Some of these new towns have come full circle, being absorbed back into a larger holding: the Belno of Tomnalienan is now part of Calier.

Figure 3 Bill Grant's father, fee'd at Auchorachan early this century.

Photograph by courtesy of Bill Grant.

Figure 4 School pupils and teachers in the Braes of Glenlivet, 1927.

Photograph by courtesy of Bill Grant.

During the 1930s and 1940s, the time in which I was particularly interested, the land was used intensively. Cultivated fields produced oats and turnips for human consumption and animal feed. Milk cows provided dairy produce and hens provided eggs and meat. The horse was used for pulling power. Apart from cattle and sheep raised as cash crops to pay the rent, the area was mainly self sufficient, even waste being recycled on the farm midden. Litter was not a problem. According to the Valuation Rolls of 1931 there were 21 inhabited farms and 43 crofts, 29 with houses and 14 without. In 1993 there were 7 let farms. Achnascraw was a farm of 69 acres arable, a little rough ground and common grazings in 1939. By 1993 it encompassed the ground of 14 former crofts in an area of 370 acres with access to 3000 acres of common grazing. The land has become summer grazings again, there are no milk cows, very few hens and many modern efficient farm buildings and machinery. Unlike the 18th century when the animals and their human keepers could only spend the summer there, now there is an all year round population, albeit diminishing in numbers.

It is the winters that are long, dark and lonely. Perhaps this is why many of the remaining crofts are summer residences or weekend retreats for people using the hills, not to graze their stock, but to recharge their own batteries away from the city hustle. Many of these holiday homes are owned and used by people who have an association with the Braes, who perhaps lived there once and now return as visitors. Many are a younger generation of former inhabitants who make their living elsewhere, but are pleased to retain their connection with this particular place. This is welcomed by those who live there permanently, for it reinforces their sense of belonging, the sense of the specialness of the area and it provides company and stimulus. Most important, it enables the year-round residents to show their warm welcome and the generous hospitality for which they are well known.

Indeed, many of those I interviewed looked back to a time when every house in the Braes was full, when neighbours would call in, when threshing, harvesting and peat cutting were social events and when one could rely on neighbours at a time of need. Gaggles of children no longer meander along the road to school nor do lines of lights wend their way to the dances on a Friday night in the village hall. They were saddened by the changes, feeling those were happier times. At the same time they were under no illusion about the hard work and problems of former times. Many had to leave the area to find work, or walk long distances to supplement the farm income by working in a distillery or on another farm. Conversely, men arrived or 'walked in' looking for work in the Braes and even to eventually marry and settle in the area. There was always coming and going.

Although much of the labour was family labour, there would frequently be times when a hired help, male or female, was necessary. This, of course, depleted the profit of the farm, so children were encouraged to leave school as soon as possible and work at home for little more than their board and lodging. Many children were granted an exemption from school to enable them to help with the harvest or grouse beating. The latter work was preferable, because, unlike home, there was an actual payment, and a good one, of seven shillings and sixpence (37p) a day. Farm work, even when paid, could not compete at three shillings and sixpence (17p) a day. A bicycle was the best way of getting to work, but, of course, you had to have a job to raise the cash to buy one. However, it was possible, and when you had enough cash saved, you bought your bike in the Braes from Russell and Robertson who ran the village shop. These two enterprising men, one of whom had returned from America to the home of his father who had been the local tailor, imported cases of tea into the Braes by motor bike and acted as the selling agent for Elswick cycles. Diversification is not new.

The shop was a great meeting place, open until seven or eight on Saturday nights with a different van delivering every day of the week. Of course, there were no estate ranger paths and bridges in those days, and tracks that were too rough for a horse and cart meant that the rider might have to push his bike some way. Jimmy Stuart solved the problem in winter by using the frozen Crombie River as a cycle path, an easier route than the snow-rutted track.

By going to other farms to work, young people from farms might be paid but there was no flexibility in the comings and goings. It was the bigger farms of Clashnoir, Lettoch and Calier where men were *fee'd* all year round. Willie Rattray of Clashnoir would stand with his watch in his hand, ensuring everyone kept to time. at these large farms the men were fee'd for six months and slept in a bothy or *chaulmer*, rather than the casual, neighbourly help given on the smaller farms and crofts. At Lettoch and Clashnoir the men ate in the kitchen whilst the farmer and family ate through the house. Elsewhere everyone ate together.

The farm household would also supplement its income by ploughing for the small crofters who did not have a horse of their own. This was the major difference between a croft and a farm. Crofters would win their ground from the rough grazing by trenching two feet deep with spades and subsequently hire a farmer and his horses to plough the ground. It was all very labour intensive and payment was given in money or deferred in return for some help at a busy time in the future. A farmer's field, by comparison, might be four acres or so, larger than many a croft.

Poaching was another activity which added to the farm income. This seemed perfectly fair when the grouse were being fed by the neat stooks in the parks. The gamekeeper chose to live on the more fertile side of the Braes, but he and the two *watchers* employed from August to October would have seen more on the Crombie side. It required much patience and skill to snare the grouse which were feeding on the oat stooks, an occupation which sustained the local Post Office as hampers were sent off to London with postal orders received by return.

I was particularly interested to know about the role of women, and was very pleased to talk with Irene Grant and Jessie Robb. Mrs. Grant was brought up in Aberdeen but spent her childhood holidays with her Granny at the Bochel and eventually married and settled in the Braes. Jessie Robb was born in the Braes in 1902 and only lived elsewhere for a few years in her twenties. She went to Glenrinnes as a housemaid but returned to care for her mother. If the men's working day seemed arduous, the women's day was both arduous and never ending. Men worked six days a week, starting at 5.30 a.m. each day to feed the horses and ending at 8 p.m. after they had been groomed. There was feeding to be done on Sundays. Men's work was outside, women worked everywhere. They helped with the farm work, particularly at the busy times of peat cutting and harvest but this was additional to the day to day domestic tasks, and at these busy times there were many more mouths to feed. Mrs. Robb remembers working on one farm where there were 18 men and 16 women to feed. All the water had to be carried from the well, only the Priest's house had water at that time. In order to be able to cook the meals a large supply of peats had to be at hand.

Domestic tasks which are now automated would take a whole day. There would be a day for washing, when the fire would have to be well stoked to boil water in a big black pot for the whites. The next day would be for ironing, again the necessity for a good fire in which to heat the heaters in the Box Irons. Then there would be a day for baking, again a plentiful supply of peats required. Oats were the staple diet for horses and people, but for the people they had to be milled and then baked or cooked. Mr Grant has fond memories of returning from school hoping to be in time for a warm oatcake, fired on the sway above the peat open fire and set on edge against the bricks to dry out. Broken into a bowl of milk, this treat was called 'snap and rattle'.

Besides these day-to-day requirements inside the house there were day-to-day tasks outside. The hens and milk cow were domestic responsibilities so they had to be fed and cleaned out. Eggs had to be collected, the milking had to be done, and the cows' udders washed and kept free of disease. Butter was made and kept in stone jars, cheese was wrapped in muslin. *Croods* and *yirned milk* went well with oatcakes. Excess butter and milk needed to be taken to the shop or vans, the proceeds supplementing the household budget. Comrie Stuart remembers walking the five mile round trip along the cart track, carrying the heavy jars. And in between times there was always the gardening to be done, kale and cabbage supplementing the diet of meal, milk and tatties.

In the autumn and spring when the large, steam powered threshing mills came round it was time to change the beds. After the thrashing winnowing removes the chaff, the outer covering of the oat kernel. The chaff was then used to stuff the cotton covers to make mattresses. Any chaff left over went to the pigs and hens for bedding, and in return the hens provided feathers with which to stuff the pillows.

Children would be expected to help with the tasks as soon as they were able. Bill Grant was hoeing neeps as soon as he was big enough to hold a hoe. Jessie Robb was on the hill in the summer gathering cranberries and blaeberries. Then there was jam to make, the surplus berries being sold in the shop for 1 shilling (5p) a pound. And there were a number of children to help. One way of supplementing the farm income was to take in foster children from Glasgow and Edinburgh. This was arranged by the Church and meant a monetary income, but it also meant more mouths to feed and beds to make so their help with the work was essential. Most boys seemed keen, or felt obliged, to leave school as soon as possible to help on the farm. There was an 'exemption' allowing children to stay away from school in order to go grouse beating and to help with the harvest and at the age of 14 many left completely. It was the girls who chose to remain longer at school and enter careers such as nursing and teaching rather than to work at home scrubbing flagstones and wooden tables and knitting socks at the end of the long day.

From every account it is clear how closely people lived and worked with their environment. Natural resources such as clean water (although the iron rich water at Fuerandarg or The Red Well would turn the whites red during washing), fertile soil, lime for fertiliser, peat for fuel together provided the opportunity for cultivation and the development of a culture. The landscape itself is the coldest area of Inveraven Parish. According to the Third Statistical Account of 1845 'snow prevented field operations and hindered communications'. Yet, one of the enduring advantages of the Braes has been its 'hindered communications'. The large number of hill tracks over the Feith Musach, the Ladder Hills, and along the Crombie Water, all lead to low ground and certainly hindered those who did not know them. For those who knew them well they provided access to secluded areas in which to train and hide priests, distil whisky illegally and to poach grouse and deer. Lack of a familiarity with these routes frequently prevented the powers that be from interrupting such farm diversification schemes and enterprise.

The Estate's policy is now to encourage access along clearly defined routes. Some of the information I collected during the course of my study may come to be used in connection with such walking routes. The intention is to extend the Scalan walk to include the ruined crofts of Fuerandearg and Larryvarry which still clearly show the pattern of land holding with long strips of land giving each croft a share of poorer and better ground. The walk will be waymarked and a booklet for visitors is planned to help them understand the land they are walking in. It will explain, in a readable and stimulating way, the connections between people and landscape. It will also include interpretations of Gaelic names, poems and personal narrative. An accompanying map will illustrate this connection of people to the land by indicating vernacular buildings and the use of resources such as water (springs and dams), lime (lime-kilns), pastures (sheep folds) and how extensive grazing has resulted in a varied flora.

The interviewees will, of course, be consulted during the booklet's preparation. For example, Sandy Mathieson lives at Scalan and it is important that he in particular is involved in this proposal which will affect him directly. It is hoped that the Estate and local people may continue to work together in this way, responding further to a changing world with appropriate developments which allow the use but not the exhaustion of local resources together with community involvement. Rather than being swamped by modern methods the people of the Braes have always responded to new challenges and adapted to change. Through working together, the spirit of partnership can be rekindled and the present level of population maintained. At the same time the landscape will not be 'preserved', but will go on being worked, as well as being enjoyed, respected and understood by residents and visitors alike.

The Author

From her home at Drummuir Castle, Priscilla Gordon-Duff has combined being mother of four children, restoring the Castle and a water mill with a tea room and craft shop, running an organic farm, and rehabilitating a Walled Garden on an estate that has been Duff property since 1621. She is a social anthropologist with qualifications in land economy, and a member of the Royal Institution of Chartered Surveyors. She recently became a governor of Gordonstoun School, and her work on the oral history of the Braes of Glenlivet will soon be published.

References

Banffshire, *Valuation Rolls 1931/2 and 1938/9*, in Elgin Library

Carter, I., *Farm Life in North East Scotland 1840–1914*, John Donald, 1979

Crown Estate, *Discovering Glenlivet: A Landscape to Explore*, Glenlivet Estate and Scottish Natural Heritage, 1993

Fenton, A. *Scottish Country Life*, John Donald, 1976

Fladmark, J.M. (ed), *Heritage: Conservation, Interpretation and Enterprise*, Donhead, 1993

Glenlivet Estate, *Glenlivet Estate Archives*, in Scottish Record Office

Glenlivet Estate, *The Present of the Past*, booklet in the Estate Office, Tomintoul

Jamieson, L. and Toynbee, C., *Country Bairns, Growing Up 1900–1930*, Edinburgh University Press, 1992

Ordnance Survey, *Ordnance Survey Map 1904*, held by Smiths Gore, Fochabers

Scottish Office Agriculture & Fisheries Department, *Agricultural Statistics 1931*, SOAFD

Scottish Office Agriculture & Fisheries Department, *Agricultural Statistics 1992*, SOAFD

Smout, T. C., *A Century of the Scottish People 1830 – 1950*, Fontana, 1986

Third Statistical Account for Scotland, 1845, in Elgin Library

22

THE WHISKY EXPERIENCE
Interpretation and Brand Identity

Ann Miller

Visitor centres at Whisky distilleries are have a special purpose, ie that of adding to the value of the brand of Scotch whisky produced at the distillery. They are part of the marketing strategy for the brand as a whole. Within the visitor attraction sector in Scotland, the whisky experience is exceptional in its aims and realisation.

In this paper I discuss the different approaches required to cover what I see as two distinctly different branches of interpretation: the site specific and the marketing specific as related to the whisky experience. I had considered using the familiar jargon of product led and market led. However, I feel, like Peter Rumble in his essay, *The Built and Historic Environment,* that:

> Interpretation has been defined as the attempt to create understanding. I agree, provided 'understanding' is seen to have an active quality. There should be a positive educational element in what we do. We should offer the means of understanding and a springboard for further study.

This *active quality* presupposes an audience. Don Aldridge also makes clear the importance of visitors: 'site interpretation is the art of explaining the significance of a site to the people who visit, with a view to pointing a conservation message.' I cannot agree that conservation is the only valid message to be conveyed by interpretation. In his introduction to the second volume of *Heritage Interpretation,* the editor, David Uzzell, considers the scope of the definition of interpretation as follows: 'It is possible to identify four principal uses to which interpretation has been put:

1. Interpretation as 'soft' visitor management
2. Interpretation as 'hard' visitor management
3. Interpretation as propaganda
4. Interpretation as a value added product of the tourism industry.

My concern is mainly with definitions (3) and (4) above. Uzzell continues and expands his definition of *interpretation as propaganda* as follows:

> To this category one might also add the kind of interpretation that is provided as an adjunct to industrial tourism. The interpretation of 'extinct' industry is commonplace. However thriving industry has also seen an opportunity to promote itself through interpretation. The heritage of the product – its constituent properties and its manufacturing process, along with the philosophy and ethos of the company and the industry – are increasingly regarded as marketable commodities like the product itself. The funding for this interpretation is likely to come under public relations, marketing and advertising budgets.

Clearly this is part of the purpose of distillery visitor centres, but I will demonstrate that the whisky visitor experience amounts to more than mere propaganda. It will be obvious to the casual visitor that the major aim of organisations like The National Trust for Scotland and Historic Scotland is to interpret specific sites. Occasionally, they have wider educational aims, for example at Glencoe and Ben Lawers, but on the whole Skara Brae is Skara Brae.

In fact, Historic Scotland has a distillery visitor centre of its own at Dallas Dhu, which it uses to illustrate the history and techniques of whisky making, as well as the architectural features associated with the industry. Such a centre, however, with all due respect to Historic Scotland, would not interest visitors were it repeated thirty times at centres throughout Scotland. Yet, beyond the Malt Whisky Trail in Speyside, there are another thirty or so distilleries which welcome visitors. Why do people visit them, and why do their owners invest in them?

On the whole whisky companies have no great interest in interpreting the site itself; the buildings in which Scotch whisky is made are after all functional and fairly similar. The characteristics which distinguish them from other buildings, like pagodas, are features common to distilleries.

The aims of whisky companies in providing distillery visitor centres extend beyond propaganda to the creation of a value added experience which contributes to the overall marketing strategy and the creation of a brand identity. Here I feel it is important to consider what a brand is and how it differs from a commodity.

Brands differ from commodities or products in that they are unique and sought after repeatedly by consumers by name. A successful brand endures whilst commodities may become out dated. Examples of commodities are soft drinks, rainwear, coffee and scotch whisky. The corresponding brands would be Coca Cola, Burberry, Nescafe and Chivas Regal. Let us consider how a commodity becomes a brand. A brand was originally the Trade Mark or symbol that manufacturers put on their products to distinguish them from those of their competitors. Today, it is the unique combination of basic commodity and added values, a blend of functional and emotional values. A brand is a product for which the consumers are prepared to pay a bit more now and in the future, particularly because of what they feel about it. Communication is an important driving force behind a brand. A brand is a unique asset, essential to a company's future.

The elements which people perceive in a brand, beyond its value as a naked product, service or commodity, are those which set it apart from similar products. Some elements are functional improvements in the way the brand performs or what it contains compared with competitors. Some are emotional: aspects of design, style and associations.

Although a brand satisfies more than a simple function in terms of the value that the purchaser perceives, there are also very real differences between brands of the same type of product. When we promote Scotch Whisky, we seek to emphasise these points of difference, the intrinsic unique selling points of each brand, in order to distinguish our own products from others in the market place. Whisky companies seek to segment the market and create appropriate brand images for each brand which have been carefully researched to meet the perceived needs of the market. All activities associated with the marketing of a Scotch whisky brand, including its packaging, advertising, promotion, distribution and selling, aim to reinforce that specific brand image.

Now, having considered the building and marketing of a brand, let us turn to its application to the whisky experience. Distillery visitor centres are part of the overall brand marketing strategy. Their purpose is to add value to the brand image by inviting consumers to visit and identify with the quality, traditions and craftsmanship of whisky making. These developments have been mirrored by a growing trend to use the heritage values of tradition and craftsmanship in advertising, as well as direct mail, promotional and public relations campaigns.

Increasing restrictions on the traditional marketing of alcoholic drinks mean new techniques are required to communicate with consumers. Heritage can be an effective means of transmitting the brand message to the consumer. The increasing diversity of media available makes targeting consumers accurately more difficult and less cost effective.

More and more consumers are seeking brands which exemplify authentic values, which possess indisputable quality and a pedigree with which they, the consumers can establish long term personal bonds. The origins and traditions inherent in the distilleries are powerful tools with which to convey the brand's integral values directly to consumers on a personal basis. Heritage can underpin and substantiate these brand values as well as communicating the emotions to which consumers can respond.

At the Chivas and Glenlivet Group, we have three distilleries which we invite consumers to visit, ie The Glenlivet, Strathisla and Glen Grant. Our objective is to enhance and reinforce the quality image and core values of the group's Scotch whisky brands by providing hospitality and education for visitors. This in turn motivates the drinks trade in the marketing and the public in the consumption of Scotch whisky in general, and The Chivas and

Glenlivet Group's brands in particular. It is useful to note the importance to the industry of the trade visitors who come from markets of all shapes and sizes and who are invited to attend intensive product knowledge courses and who return home more motivated to sell our brands.

It is important to the group that our facilities should be among the best in Scotland, so we have embarked upon an ambitious five year refurbishment programme. We will make a multi million pound investment in the group's whisky heritage, renovating key malt whisky distilleries and creating homes for our portfolio of Scotch whisky brands. This is a long-term commitment which will have benefits for tourism and the local economy as well as bringing about considerable environmental improvements. A great deal of archival research and archaeological investigation have been undertaken in its support.

Established in 1786, Strathisla Distillery is the oldest working distillery in the Highlands, and is arguably the most picturesque and memorable. Its 12 year old malt has long been acknowledged as *The Heart of Chivas Regal*, which is the leading brand of premium Scotch whisky in the world. It is a brand which epitomises success, achievement, good taste and status, transcending all barriers with style and sophistication, that is, a brand to which people aspire.

The refurbishment of Strathisla, the home and the heart of Chivas Regal, needs to reflect and embody these important qualities, to provide an identifiable provenance for the Chivas Regal brand to which it has always made a significant contribution, whilst creating a living heritage. Our objectives are to enhance and strengthen the quality image and distinctive core values of Chivas Regal with the aim of instilling a greater awareness and appreciation of the authenticity and credibility inherent in the brand.

The strategy is to create a physical and spiritual home for Chivas Regal at Strathisla which defines and communicates its roots, history, tradition and integrity. At the same time we intend to develop a unique experience which will attract, satisfy and motivate visitors ensuring that the production values of quality, skills, craftsmanship and loving care are clearly recognised and acknowledged as being central to the premium aspirational image and status of Chivas Regal.

Hospitality will be experienced as a warm and genuine personal welcome. Visitors, or rather guests, will discover the distillery, its heritage, production processes and products in a more direct, effective and personal manner than was the case hitherto. A carefully developed self guided tour of discovery will engender an appreciation for and an understanding of the inherent qualities and traditions of the whisky produced at Strathisla, the home and heart of Chivas Regal.

The design will complement and expand the historical and architectural quality inherent in the distillery. At the same time it will achieve an atmosphere which speaks clearly of the history, location, heritage and style of Strathisla. Careful layering of appropriate decorative treatments and quality furnishings will create an environment which appears to have evolved naturally over the years. All relevant information about Strathisla distillery, its malt whisky and Chivas Regal will be conveyed tastefully and unobtrusively.

Strathisla distillery will epitomise the 'value added' version of interpretation for the visitor or guest who will receive a gift of a quality souvenir brochure before departing.

The refurbishment of the distillery visitor centres at The Glenlivet and Glen Grant will be accomplished with the same attention to quality and effective presentation of the brand values of each of these very different whiskies.

The Glenlivet was the first distillery in the Highlands to be granted a licence under the Excise Act of 1823. Since then it has become the number one 12-year old malt whisky world-wide, and is the foremost malt whisky brand in the United States. The recently launched 18-year old *The Glenlivet* has been very well received and, together with the 21 year old, they must count among the finest Scotch whiskies in the world.

Visitors to the refurbished Glenlivet Distillery will discover the story of its establishment by George Smith in 1824 as the first to be licensed in the Highlands, the earlier involvement of the family in illicit distilling and the subsequent growth and success of the brand. Modern multi-media techniques will be amongst those used to convey the fascinating and meticulously researched story. However, our aim will be to welcome people to the home of The Glenlivet and never to allow modern technical interpretive techniques to intrude between the consumer and the brand.

Glen Grant by contrast, is a light fragrant malt whisky, until recently known and appreciated mainly in Italy where it is the brand which leads the entire whisky market, malts and blends. It is now increasingly available in the rest of Europe. With the by-line, *Different by Tradition*, the interpretation planned for Glen Grant Distillery will be light, airy and sophisticated. The story of the founding of the distillery and its subsequent success will be *narrated* by the late Major Grant, son and nephew of the two brothers who founded the Distillery in 1840.

Glen Grant is also known as the distillery set in a garden. These wonderful woodland gardens, originally laid out in the 19th century by Major Grant, are being restored to their original glory. With substantial replanting, the rebuilding and relaying of original bridges and paths, and even a whisky safe set into the rock face above a running stream, the gardens present an idyllic insight into the Victorian vision to capture the rugged romance of the Highlands. This is indeed an example of providing added value for visitors to a distillery.

So we observe that the marketing message to be conveyed by a distillery visitor centre is not generic or even an amalgam of the company's brands, but a specific exercise related to a single brand. That these developments have occurred at the same time as the growth of sales of malt whiskies is no accident. The two have grown hand in hand. The identification with the vision of the brands has reinforced its marketing success.

The strong concentration on brand building and the clear marketing and merchandising policies required pose interesting questions about the roles of Dallas Dhu and the Scotch Whisky Heritage Centre. Dallas Dhu, operated by Historic Scotland, encapsulates the history of distilling in the Speyside area, and has created its own brand from the maturing stock of malt whisky acquired with the distillery.

The Scotch Whisky Heritage Centre was opened in Edinburgh in 1988 in order that visitors to Scotland, mainly from overseas, who had neither the opportunity nor the time to visit the major areas of Whisky distilling, might nonetheless find out more about Scotland's national drink. Conceived from the start as a joint venture by brand companies who each bought shares in the venture, there was a conflict of interest implicit between the different aims of brand marketing and generic promotion.

There was to be no specific focus on brands which changed places regularly in the shop in order that none should be perceived to gain an advantage. This difficulty in creating generic promotion for branded products was perhaps best symbolised by the reluctance of the directors to accede to visitor demand to taste Scotch Whisky. After all how could they provide a taste, except anonymously and without upsetting each brand owner? And how could they offer an anonymous taste without equally upsetting the brand owner? Happily the brands now rotate on a weekly basis and visitors can enjoy a dram of whisky at the end of their tour.

It would appear that the drinks industry leads the way in using interpretation as a marketing tool. Other examples within Seagram companies can be found in Cognac, where Martell has a successful centre which combines to meet the needs of visitors and the drinks trade, and at Champagne Mumm, as well as at other wineries and distilleries in North America.

The same interpretative tools could be appropriate to other luxury goods. However, we need to distinguish between the value added interpretation of the whisky industry and interpretation used to support retail selling which we see regularly at woollen centres, potteries and crystal factories. They hope to increase direct sales to the consumer. The whisky industry aims above all to reinforce its brand image and establish an emotional response in the consumer.

However, a major feature of the whisky distillery visitor centres is merchandising in the shops. Originally these were an addition to the basic distillery experience but increasingly they are a carefully researched part of the brand building effort. The income shops can generate makes a useful contribution to the running costs but, unlike many other visitor centres, this is only part of the story. Merchandise is carefully selected, not only on the basis of whether it will sell but, more importantly, because of the contribution it can make to the building of the brand image. Opinions diverge here. At Glenturret, every item is branded, whether it is made with the malt whisky or not. Other companies, including United Distillers, promote their branded malt whisky above all and where they sell other consistent products eg jam, marmalade, honey, chocolate, fudge they are unbranded provided they support the general brand image.

I have dwelt on the value added aspects of marketing a brand through a visitor centre, but it is also appropriate to consider the marketing of the centres themselves. Once again we perceive a marked difference from the general visitor attraction. Unlike Edinburgh Zoo which needs high visitor numbers to feed the animals and fund research, or Deep Sea World which needs high visitor numbers to pay off its capital debts and provide the return on investment promised to its investors, or even the Scotch Whisky Heritage Centre which needs high visitor numbers to meet its running costs, the whisky visitor centre owners are not simply interested in a high volume of visitors for its own sake.

The marketing of distillery visitor centres is increasingly targeted towards those most likely to identify with the brand image: to existing and potential consumers. It is counter-productive to attract too many inappropriate visitors, as they would diminish the brand exclusivity, and reduce the effectiveness of the message to those who were most receptive to it. It would be wasted marketing effort to attract to Strathisla those who could not aspire to a bottle of Chivas Regal.

Visitor centres can also be used as the source of a range of marketing messages, direct mail campaigns, club membership affiliate schemes etc, which reinforce image and gain consumer loyalty. For example, committed consumers can be invited on an exclusive visit to the distillery through a range of mechanisms.

In summary, the whisky experience takes all the interpreter's tools and uses them in an extremely conscious and focused way to convey a message which is part of the brand marketing strategy. We seek to associate a brand with dedication to quality, hospitality and customer care so that it adds value to the visitors' experience. The brand's value to consumer and trade visitor is likewise enhanced in the process. The brand companies derive added value by creating a powerful and emotional pedigree for their brands which supports their differentiation from competitors' brands and enhances their values.

The Author and Acknowledgements

Ann Miller's professional career has included being Marketing Manager of the Scotch Whisky Heritage Centre in Edinburgh and launching Deep-Sea World in Fife, before becoming Hospitality and Public Relations Manager for The Chivas and Glenlivet Group in 1994. Based in Keith, she is responsible for their Heritage Programme and the Chivas Regal Academy.

Thanks are due to Tom Band, Senior Advisor to The Robert Gordon University Heritage Unit, for his help in developing the concept on which this paper is based, and for pointing me in the direction of suitable reference material.

References

Aldridge, D., *Site Interpretation: A Practical Guide*, Scottish Tourist Board, 1993

Jones, P., *Management in Service Industries*, Pitman, 1989

Kutler, P., *Marketing Management: Analysis, Planning, Implementation and Control*, Eaglewood Heights, 1988

Rumble, P., *Interpreting the Built and Historic Environment*, in Heritage Interpretation, Vol 1, Uzzell, D. (ed), Belhaven Press,1989

Uzzell, D., *Introduction*, in Heritage Interpretation, Vol 2, Uzzell, D. (ed), Belhaven Press,1989

Williams, K. C., *Behavioural Aspects of Marketing*, Heinemann, 1982

23

WHISKY HERITAGE OR HERESY?

Michael Moss

Imagine, if you will, the year 2,200. The use of cannabis and other soft drugs have been legal for many years, following the advice of Interpol in the 1990s. An industry has developed with intense competition to attract custom and each firm is keen to promote the distinctiveness of its product. Many firms had their origins in the illicit trade which burgeoned in the 1960s and use their history to help promote their business. Some have opened cannabis heritage centres in university towns, or on the coast where drug running was commonplace, the Mull of Kintyre for example. Here can be seen sanitised versions of gun fights between the Customs and Excise and smugglers and accounts of the development of individual brands; accurately researched, I hasten to say, by historians and archivists. Is this fanciful nonsense or not far removed from contemporary whisky visitor and heritage centres?

What I want to do in this paper is to step back a little from the presentations of the industry representatives and consider what archivists, historians and museum professionals can contribute, if anything, to the interpretation of the history of an industry, which in its time had all the ingredients of modern drugs running. This is not an easy task, particularly, as the industry is consciously trying to distance itself from the social problems caused by over-consumption of alcohol by reference to the apparently beneficial effects of moderate use. However, the fact remains that a very large percentage, possibly more than fifty per cent, of accident and emergency cases in our hospitals are alcohol related and alcohol is a powerfully addictive narcotic, as the supporters of decriminalising soft drugs point out.

Since brand promotion began in the middle of the nineteenth century, history has been used to promote whisky. At a time when Scotland was being made popular as a romantic tourist attraction, as a result of the novels of Walter Scott and the enthusiasm of Queen Victoria and Prince Albert, whisky makers joined the bandwagon by associating their products with the romantic heroes of Scottish History like Rob Roy and highland scenery. Labels showed brawny claymore-wielding kilted highlanders standing against a backdrop of misty mountains. Names like Roderick Dhu and Old Cantyre evoked a nostalgia for the traditional highland way of life, particularly amongst Scottish emigrants in the colonies where an increasing volume of whisky was sold. In the twentieth century, history has continued to be used as a selling device as the drinks market has become internationalised and more competitive. A long history, however tenuous, is used to endow a product or a supplier with respectability and reputation. The trend has increased in recent years with the renewal in popularity of single malts which command a premium price in the market, justified by the long maturation periods and quality supported by tradition and history.

Integral to the development of the market for single malts, has been the creation of heritage centres at distilleries and elsewhere. These attempt to do two things: educate the visitors as to how whisky (mostly malt whisky) is made and tell something of the history of the industry and of individual distilleries. The distilleries and their heritage in turn form important ingredients in promotion and marketing. Packaging often takes the form of attractive images of white-painted distilleries with pagoda roofs over long-disused malt kilns dominating a sunlit landscape of sea and mountains. The accompanying leaflet will explain that the distinctive flavour is linked to the craft of an illicit distiller and the water drawn from some improbably named burn or well. The impression is of a continuum: the modern dram is apparently not far removed from the whisky of yester year. Nothing could be further from the truth.

The Scots whisky industry, as we all know, is five hundred years old this year or, more correctly, this is the five hundredth anniversary of the first documentary reference to the distillation of spirit from a malt mash. It probably does not date back much earlier than this, as the technology to produce an alcoholic distillate was not available in Europe until the late thirteenth or early fourteenth century. The manufacture of *aqua vitae* then spread rapidly throughout northern Europe, largely because of its remarkable restorative qualities. By the seventeenth century, Scotland had a cottage industry spread throughout the country with considerable domestic production in the bigger houses of the lairds and merchants. There were a few large public distilleries usually supported by one of the great estates like the Forbes family's distillery at Culloden.

The first excise duty was imposed temporarily during the Civil War, reintroduced in the 1690s and increased almost unremittingly thereafter. The industry expanded during the mid-eighteenth century with the establishment of several large distilleries in the bigger towns. Much of the *aqua vitae* or whisky produced at this period was harsh and consumed straight from the still, only made palatable by the addition of herbs and other flavourings. Consumption was formidable, particularly at weddings and funerals. The government first interfered directly in the industry in 1757 when, following a disastrous crop failure, all distilling was banned. Some domestic distillers flouted the rules and made whisky for sale. Others began

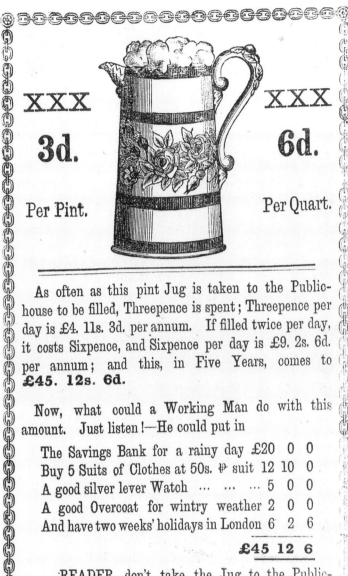

XXX   XXX

3d.   **6d.**

Per Pint.   Per Quart.

As often as this pint Jug is taken to the Public-house to be filled, Threepence is spent; Threepence per day is £4. 11s. 3d. per annum. If filled twice per day, it costs Sixpence, and Sixpence per day is £9. 2s. 6d. per annum; and this, in Five Years, comes to **£45. 12s. 6d.**

Now, what could a Working Man do with this amount. Just listen!—He could put in

The Savings Bank for a rainy day	£20	0	0
Buy 5 Suits of Clothes at 50s. ℔ suit	12	10	0
A good silver lever Watch ··· ··· ···	5	0	0
A good Overcoat for wintry weather	2	0	0
And have two weeks' holidays in London	6	2	6
	£45	**12**	**6**

READER, don't take the Jug to the Public-house any more, but save the THREEPENCES and SIXPENCES and "Go in" for good clothes, silver watch, and two weeks' holidays.

W.

Liverpool Temperance & Band of Hope Union, 42, Renshaw-st., Liverpool.
4d. per 100, 3s. per 1000.

Figure 1 A typical nineteenth century temperance poster.

distilling illegally. As a result, when the ban was lifted, the licensed or *entered* distillers found it hard to recapture their market. The government tried, unsuccessfully, to stamp out the illicit trade in the 1770s by imposing tougher controls.

By 1779, in Edinburgh alone, there were reputedly 400 illicit stills. Nevertheless, legal output began to climb chiefly because the entered (licensed) distillers used their productive capacity to force down the price, making it hard for the illicit distillers to compete. The Excise authorities for their part were given wider powers to combat illicit distilling and smuggling and private distillation was prohibited. During this period, several very large distilleries were constructed in Central Scotland to supply not only the local market but also more importantly the London market. These distilleries, largely controlled by the Stein and Haig families, soon became engaged in a price war with their London counterparts which they ultimately lost. At the same time, disastrous harvests in the Highlands led to further bans on production and punitive increases in duty aimed at slashing consumption. Further legislation in 1784 was designed to encourage licensed distilling in the Highlands. Defeated in their price war, six of the great distilleries, led by the Stein and Haig families, were driven into bankruptcy in 1788, flooding the Scottish market with cheap unpalatable spirit.

A glutted market, combined with a massive increase in duty in 1793 to pay for the war with revolutionary France, drove more of the trade underground. As hostilities intensified, duty spiralled upwards and, with Britain deprived of food imports, distilling was periodically banned until Napoleon's final defeat at Waterloo in 1815. In the circumstances it is not surprising that illicit distilling and smuggling flourished and licensed concerns found it difficult to keep going without themselves stretching or even breaking the rules. The most common method was to work off the pot stills rapidly, as duty was calculated not on output but on still capacity. The resulting whisky was often burnt and full of unpleasant congeners guaranteed to produce a headache. Consequently, smuggled whisky, illicitly distilled slowly in the Highlands, became popular, particularly in the large towns and cities.

Whisky, of course, was only a part of a huge trade in contraband goods during these years in, for example, tea, sugar, wines, brandies and salt, mostly smuggled from mainland Europe. Smugglers were well-organised, transporting their illegal goods in large well armed bands, sometimes of as many as fifty to one hundred and fifty horses moving audaciously during daylight. Landowners, who as magistrates, were responsible for maintaining the law, regularly turned a blind eye to the activities of the smugglers and illicit distillers, principally because it was the income from illicit whisky that helped their tenants to pay their rents. When cases were brought, sentences were invariably lenient to the dismay of the Excise service and the licensed distillers. It is hardly surprising, when excise men travelled in fear of their lives, that many made common cause with the smugglers.

The government was not unaware of the problem, and a Parliamentary inquiry was launched in 1797 to investigate the distilleries in Scotland. The Lowland distillers constantly clamoured for effective measures to stamp out the illicit trade, which they believed passionately was undermining their business. Much of their evidence was highly charged and exaggerated. The Excise service was strengthened and measures taken to improve quality by outlawing rapid distillation. This, coupled with the demand for spirits from the army and navy, encouraged a revival in the industry and the re-opening of the Stein and Haig families 'great distilleries' to serve the English market.

The smugglers were badly hit by poor harvests at the turn of the century which persuaded some landowners to adopt a tougher stance towards illicit distillers, even evicting them from their property. Such repressive measures were short-lived; after the threat of famine passed, illicit distilling re-emerged on an even greater scale. However, the strengthened Excise began to achieve much higher detection rates, which were still not accompanied by adequate punishments. Such licensed producers who remained at work in the Highlands had to struggle against almost impossible odds. The recession that followed the end of the Napoleonic Wars, coupled with further changes in Excise regulations, spelled disaster for those that survived. By 1816 there were just twelve registered distilleries operating in the Highlands.

In the face of a sharp fall in receipts from duty on whisky, the Scottish Excise launched an inquiry. All were agreed that the way to eradicate illicit distilling and smuggling was to reduce duty sharply and impose severe penalties on those caught making or selling whisky illegally. With the government no longer in need of such large revenues, duty was reduced by about a third in 1816 and measures introduced to stimulate legal output in the Highlands. Although these reforms matched expectations at the outset, they failed to provide a long-term solution because they lacked the support of the landowners. During the next four years, after some violent exchanges between smugglers and the Excise, opinion changed in response to the more settled economic and political climate.

Some landowners themselves, keen to increase their income, built distilleries on their property, making it clear that they were no longer willing to tolerate illicit distilling or smuggling. The Illicit Distillation (Scotland) Act of 1822 greatly increased the powers of the Excise in dealing with illicit distillers and smugglers and imposed severe mandatory fines for those brought to justice. The Excise Act of the following year reduced duty and actively encouraged licensed distilling by providing much more straightforward regulations and permitting duty-free warehousing. These two pieces of legislation had the intended effect. Over the next two years more than 150 new distilleries were founded and smuggling was eclipsed.

It is from this heroic period from 1750 to 1828 that the stories of illicit distilling and smuggling derive. The brief account I have provided I hope illustrates that this is a complex story and simple representations, beloved of marketing men, that cast the gaugers (excise men) as baddies and the smugglers and illicit distillers as goodies are misleading. Tied up in the tale is famine in the Highlands at times almost in Third World terms and criminality and violence on a wide scale. To present the history of this period in visitor centres in a manner that is accessible to a general public, whose first language may not be English, is difficult. It is hard not to over-dramatise the illicit distillers and the smuggler, very largely because popular perceptions of smuggling are romantically coloured by a great deal of popular literature and drama. We may decry contemporary drug smugglers and believe those caught red-handed in Far Eastern countries deserve their harsh sentences; we happily condone smugglers of the past, believing that they must have been dealing in the *real cratur*. Such legends overlook the crucial fact that until recently whisky was consumed straight from the still and, therefore, would, by its very nature, be very different from the well-matured single malts on the market today. It also ignores the pernicious effect of dram-taking in the Highlands at the time. Elizabeth Grant of Rothiemurchus, looking back at her childhood in the early 1820s, remembered how a dram and cheese was offered to anyone who came to the house, morning, noon or night. She singled out dram taking as the bane of Highland life at the time.

Equally problematic is the link between the licensed distilleries established after 1823 with smugglers and illicit distillers. Licensed distillers, at least from the time Alfred Barnard wrote his *The Whisky Distilleries of the United Kingdom* in 1887, were keen to enhance their legitimacy by claiming direct lineal descent from illicit distilling at a time when malt whisky was being challenged by patent still grain whisky and its sister blended whisky. Such lineages were often dubious and sometimes wholly fictitious. Their currency derived from the fact that landowners' anxious to establish distilleries in the wake of the 1823 legislation had sometimes turned to illicit distillers to help them. A view of the history of whisky-making based around these powerful myths in turn accentuates the importance of the pot still and malt in the evolution of the modern dram. This is also misleading. The whisky we enjoy today is mostly blend which is a skilful combination of grain and malt whisky. In the heroic period of the industry, grain whisky was made in large quantities entirely by the great licensed distillers in the Lowlands. Almost certainly most of the whisky consumed by most people at the time was grain whisky, which curiously enough, straight from the still, is smoother and less sharp than malt.

After the 1820s reforms, despite the establishment of a large number of pot stills making malt spirit in the Highlands, the trade continued to be dominated by the large Lowland grain distillers making a style of spirit not that dissimilar to that made in Ireland. Pot still production of spirit on an industrial scale is very inefficient. After each distillation, the stills have to be cleaned out before the process can start again. The Lowland grain distillers brought the process to a peak of perfection by adopting very large stills and a system of using bells to indicate when the various stages in production had been completed. It is possible to see such a still dating from the early nineteenth century at the Irish Distillers Heritage centre at Middleton, not far from Cork in the Republic of Ireland. The purpose of the large bell hanging above the gigantic still is not explained.

Ideally the great distillers wanted to be able to manufacture whisky continuously. Experiments began in the late eighteenth century but it was not until 1827 that Robert Stein of the Kilbagie Distillery in Fife perfected a still which was shaped as a column, divided into a series of small chambers by haircloth diaphragms. Before his still could be widely adopted, Aneas Coffey, the retired Inspector-General of the Excise in Dublin, perfected in 1830 an improved continuous or *patent* still for the continuous production of grain whisky. Over the next decade patent stills were installed by a number of distillers in the Lowlands, Ireland and England capable of producing vast quantities of grain spirit.

At about this time, both malt and grain whiskies began to be matured for a period in casks. This practice was familiar to wine and spirit merchants used to dealing in clarets, sherries, ports and brandies and the whiskies were usually filled into casks in which other wines and spirits had been shipped. Wine and spirit merchants also knew that many imported wines and spirits were blends of the produce of different vineyards and different vintages, it is not surprising therefore that they began to use grain whisky to cover the stronger flavoured malts or in some cases simply to adulterate them to earn a higher margin. The practice of blending was certainly well established by the mid-nineteenth century and Andrew Usher, often accredited with producing the first blend *Old Vatted Glenlivet*, was just one amongst many producers.

By the middle of the nineteenth century it was possible for Scottish wine and spirit merchants, who effectively controlled the distribution of whiskies, to exploit a much larger market for their domestic product. The railway network throughout Britain was more or less complete and colonial markets were now served by regular steamer sailings. Developments in bottle-making technology and mass-production of whisky made it possible to distribute blends of roughly uniform consistency in standard packaging. Advances in printing later in the century, allowed for the mass-marketing of whiskies, particularly blends, throughout the world in common with many other products. Some malt distillers like the Smiths of Glenlivet and the Mackenzies of Dalmore, also, began selling their whiskies on the world market.

Whisky became popular in the late nineteenth century due in part to serious setbacks to continental wine and spirit producers following the devastation of grape harvests by odium in the 1850s and then from the mid 1860s the destruction of vineyards by the phylloxera aphid, which in Charante alone obliterated well over half the acreage under vines. Denied access to quality French and Spanish brandies and with the continent flooded with adulterated spirit made by mixing brandy with patent still spirits made mostly from sugar, British wine and spirit merchants, who controlled the world wine trade, looked to whisky. This is still not to say that the blends being sold in the late nineteenth century were the same as those sold today.

They cannot have been because the character of the ingredients was different. Malt whisky was much peatier than would be acceptable to most modern palates and the whisky was probably not being matured for as long and the barrels used would have been mostly sherry or brandy wood.

The Scotch whisky trade has difficulty in explaining these fundamental developments in its history to visitors. Most heritage centres are in pot distilleries where the emphasis is on the single malt, even though the bulk of production of any single malt distillery goes into blend. Patent grain distilleries are large industrial units which on the whole are not very attractive. If you visit Middleton outside Cork, you see a magnificent late eighteenth early nineteenth century plant on the scale of the finest industrial buildings of the period. Through the trees you glimpse a massive stainless steel column where it is explained with a wave of the hand that all Irish Distillers whiskies are made. Afterwards you are invited to taste the modern dram, and very good it is too; but the impression is that it has been hand-crafted in much the same way as it was hundred years ago. Irish Distillers are also unusual in having their distillery in a lovely rural market town with a high street full of appealing traditional pubs. Most grain distilleries are in unappealing settings in the midst of large towns. Bottling halls have little visitor appeal and anyway it is difficult to integrate visitor attractions with large scale mass production. The Scotch Whisky Heritage Centre in Edinburgh's Royal Mile credibly bridges the gap between malt and grain; achieving a more balanced picture of the history of the trade.

From the beginning of the twentieth century until after the Second World War whisky distillers and blenders experienced a long period of decline in common with the whole world trade in alcoholic drinks. This was due in part to the prevalence of anti-drink sentiment and to the world-wide economic slump of the inter-war years. The temperance and abstinence movements traced their origins in Scotland to the 1820s. Spirits had always been singled out as more injurious to health and family budgets than beer. There is no doubt that over-consumption of alcohol was a serious problem in the early nineteenth century, not just because factory owners wished to optimise production. Social reformers constantly clamoured against the evil effect of drink. Posters and melodramas illustrated dramatically the effect of over-indulgence on domestic economy and the beneficial effects of sobriety and thrift.

When the Liberal government came to power in 1905, Lloyd George, a confirmed abstainer, taxed drink heavily to pay for new social programmes. Taxation continued to be increased during the First World War and production and sales controlled in the widely held belief that drink was sapping the moral fibre of the Allies. In response to this onslaught whisky distillers agreed to minimum maturation periods as it was widely believed that spirit straight from the still was dangerous. In a disastrous error of judgement the Russian government banned drinking altogether for the duration of hostilities. After the war the world, gripped by moral fervour, adopted further measures to reduce consumption, notoriously so in the USA where the sale of alcohol was *Prohibited*. Whisky producers, faced with a collapse in demand, connived to circumvent Prohibition either legally through the sale of whisky as a medicine or illicitly by shipping in large quantities for bootleggers to offshore markets, particularly in the Caribbean. However misguided American policy was thought to have been, this illicit trade was associated with gangsters and wide spread law breaking, as it had been in the past in Scotland. Nonetheless, the smugglers and gangsters of the 1920s have now also entered folklore, becoming sort of heroes in popular perception. Some firms even use photographs of whisky running to promote their product.

In the late twentieth century, it is difficult for us to understand the popular appeal of abstinence. Much of the rhetoric of thrift was undermined by inflation in the 1970s and 1980s and since the second world war in western economies, most people have enjoyed relatively high standards of living, making it possible for them to afford alcohol on a scale that was not possible before. This does not mean that any objective history of whisky should ignore this subject. It is hard to know how the events after the 1911 budget can be explained without reference to temperance. It is not enough simply to dismiss Prohibition in the USA as an aberration. Such views are still widely held by a significant section of American opinion and temperance attitudes are becoming more prevalent in Europe. The industry has always been ambivalent about how it should respond to alcohol abuse and temperance. Recently, much emphasis has been placed on the social use of alcohol and the beneficial effects of moderate consumption. The industry has also been shielded by the seemingly far more serious problem of drug abuse.

What I have sought to show, is that the heritage of whisky is beset by ambiguities and issues that cannot be ignored in any objective account of its development. I believe the trade is brave and responsible enough to address them without glamorising the illegality of past activities. It is easy, when in doubt, to blame the marketing men for taking liberties with its history, claiming associations with illicit distillers that never existed or casting smugglers of whatever age as goodies and law enforcement agents as baddies. However, it is up to the historians and archivists, working both within and outside the industry, to ensure that the heritage displayed is balanced and as far as possible accurate. I do not believe that such whisky heritage attractions are misconceived in the same way that I would not be opposed, if I were alive, to a cannabis heritage centre opening in the year 2,200 to mark the centenary of its legal sale. Whisky is part and parcel for good or ill of the Scottish way of life. We should be proud of it, but not unaware of the problems that accompany the use of any drug.

The Author

Michael S Moss was educated at Worcester College Oxford and has been Archivist with the University of Glasgow since 1974, where he is also responsible for the Business Record Centre which contains the records of several distilling companies along with the Scottish Brewing Archive. Publications include (with John Hume) *The Making of Scotch Whisky – A History of the Scotch Whisky Distilling Industry* 1981, 'Scotch Whisky 1933–1988' in M Chick (ed) *Government Industries and Markets – Aspects of government-industry relations in the UK, Japan, West Germany and the USA since 1945* 1991, and (with NJ Morgan) 'The Marketing of Scotch' in R Tedlow and G Jones (eds) *The Rise and Fall of Mass Marketing* 1993.

References

Bruce-Lockhart, Sir R., *Scotch*, London, 1959, reprinted Putnam, 1974

Barnard, A., *The Whisky Distilleries of the United Kingdom*, London, 1887, reprinted Lochar, 1987

Craig, C., *The Scotch Whisky Reference Book*, Scotch Whisky Association, (forthcoming) 1994

Daiches, D., *Scotch Whisky – Its Past and Present*, André Deutsch, 1970

McDowall, R.J.S., and revised by Waugh, William, *The Whiskies of Scotland*, John Murray, 1986

Moss, M. & Hume, J.R., *The Making of Scotch Whisky – A History of the Scotch Whisky Distilling Industry*, James and James, 1981

Sillett, S.W., *Illicit Scotch*, Aberdeen University Press, 1965

Wilson, R., *Scotch: Its History and Romance*, David and Charles, 1974

24

THE ROLE OF
THE MUSEUM IN INTERPRETATION
The Problem of Context

Colin Thompson

Interpretation is a slippery word, and let me say at once that the difference between museum and site interpretation has come up more than once in my discussions with Don Aldridge, one of our masters of site interpretation, and I have benefited considerably from his comments on an early draft of this paper.

The dictionary defines interpretation as 'explaining the meaning or significance of a thing', and Freeman Tilden proposed three stages in site interpretation: 'Through interpretation, understanding; through understanding, appreciation; through appreciation, protection.' These stages must already have been gone through for objects in museums, since they are already protected, but the first two stages hold good for the ordinary museum visitor.

It seems to me that if you have a heritage site, all you have to do is decide what interpretation is about and then get on and do it. The site will not go away. The trouble with things in museums is that somebody put them there. And this raises two questions: what are they doing there and where did they come from? You may think this is a minor matter, but I hope to convince you that, on the contrary, it is crucial not only to the way the things are interpreted, but to a clear understanding of the relationship between our national and local museums, and between museum collections and heritage sites.

NATIONAL VERSUS LOCAL: A FALSE POLARITY

The only principle I have ever heard advanced, to guide decisions on where things should be, is that if a thing is of national importance its place is in the capital city. The clear implication is that we are dealing with a polarity, *national* versus *local*, and that this is associated with places, the capital city (Edinburgh or London, in Scotland it is never very clear which) and somewhere other than Edinburgh or London. The reality is that, while *local importance* does attach to a specific place, the concept of *national importance* does not refer to place at all but is no more than a vague value judgement, presumably capped by *international importance*.

What is at issue is the significance of the object: its importance to the heritage. In an object of great beauty or rarity, we may recognise an intrinsic or inherent importance, that is an interest unaffected by association or context. An object of importance to the heritage may have little or no intrinsic value, but it will have an importance that comes from association, often in more than one context. Perhaps the commonest context is either the place with which a thing is associated or its original environment, and there is an important difference between the two.

For instance, Walter Scott's desk has no great inherent interest as a piece of furniture, but in the environment of Scott's study at Abbotsford its value is incalculable. By contrast, when a Charles Rennie Macintosh desk was being sold, the French were keen to acquire it for the Musée d' Orsay in Paris, so its inherent importance is clearly international. It is now in Glasgow, where it has an additional significance as the work of a local architect, although it is in the Hunterian Art Gallery and not in its original environment, wherever that was.

The chairs in the *firehoose* at Kirbuster[1] on Orkney are an integral part of that environment. Similar Orkney chairs are important to the display of types of Highland chair at the Highland Folk Museum at Kingussie. Does this make the ones at Kirbuster of national importance, or regional (a new category), or do they remain of only local value?

A large hoard of iron nails was found in a Roman camp at Inchtutil in Perthshire. They have great importance as evidence of conditions under the Romans, therefore national. In proof of this, you will find nails from Inchtutil in a number of museums in Britain. In these museums their association with Perthshire is irrelevant (they could be from any of the Roman camps), but this does not diminish the importance of their local association when you see them in the museum in Perth.

National interest of a rather different kind attaches to the first bicycle, not for the light it throws on Victorian culture, but because we have all of us ridden more recent models. But it still has a particularly strong association with the blacksmith who made it near Dumfries.

In short, heritage objects vary widely both in their inherent value and in the associations that give them their special significance. But one thing stands out: the several elements, inherent or associative, are not mutually exclusive. On the contrary, they reinforce each other. By the same token, therefore, the idea of a national, local polarity is false.

CONTEXT AND INTERPRETATION

As for the effect of context on interpretation, an almost unique demonstration is provided by the new St Mungo Museum in Glasgow. The principle followed in setting up the displays was to bring together objects from the several Glasgow collections that related to the new theme: 'an exploration of the role of religion in human life'. So you meet things here that you could have seen before in the People's Palace, in the Burrell Collection or at Kelvingrove in the fine art section, and above all in the ethnography section. But you now see them not as works of art or craft or as ethnographical specimens, but in their religious connection, and this alters the way you look at them. The change with ethnography particularly is from a rather specialised museum category to an aspect of life that affects us all. And it is noticeable how attentively visitors look at the exhibits.

One exhibit prominent in the section on religion in Scotland is a painting, *The Covenanters' Wedding*. In fact it is an imaginary scene painted long afterwards, in 1842. This is a particular aspect of context that is offered only by pictures, because besides being objects in their own right, they usually interpret some other object, person or event, real or imagined.

Over the mantelpiece in the sitting room at the Earl of Rosebery's Dalmeny House near Edinburgh is a large group portrait by Alexander Nasmyth of the Third Earl and his family in the grounds of nearby Barnbougle Castle. The painting's history and what it represents tell us a great deal about life and ideas in the late 18th and early 19th century in Scotland. But the painting would also be valuable in the context of a number of exhibitions: of the work of Nasmyth; of Scottish conversation pieces; of landscaping round country houses; or indeed landscape painting in general; of the history of the Rosebery family; and so on. Each new context will tend to focus our attention on a different aspect of the painting, and we will see it, and remember it, slightly differently.

It should perhaps be said in passing that contexts vary in their significance. The Portrait Gallery in London was recently asked to lend the centre-piece of one of their rooms, a double portrait of the Old Pretender and his sister with their pet dog, for an exhibition of dog collars. And I think it was Dorothy Parker who said when she saw the Parthenon: 'Beige, just my colour.'

There is yet another aspect of paintings that distinguishes them from arrowheads and steam hammers: they are subject to aesthetic judgment, and for this reason the way we look at them changes from one generation to the next. One of the most fascinating aspects of art history is the way in which people at all periods suffer from a kind of myopia which always makes them see paintings of the past, quite subconsciously, in terms of their present aesthetic prejudices. For us now, when everything is being recorded in photographic images of some kind, this myopia causes us to see representational paintings, whether of the present or the past, in the light of our experience of photographs.

This has, I believe, a particular relevance to the discussion now going on about the establishment of a National Gallery of Scottish Art and History, part of whose function has been described as 'telling the story of Scottish life and history.'[2] The very notion of using paintings as historical illustrations clearly springs from our contemporary myopia. So the danger is that a gallery so arranged is likely to be seen as a regrettably incomplete set of very unreliable photographs.

For those of us who were brought up with lofty ideas of spiritual nourishment from paintings akin to listening to music, history provides some consolation: whatever the aesthetic prejudices of this generation, they are certain to be overturned by the next.

INTERPRETATION FOR WHOM?

To return to the problem of context, I drew a distinction between the actual environment in which a thing properly belongs, like the Nasmyth picture at Dalmeny, or Walter Scott's desk at Abbotsford, and the place with which a thing is associated, like Glasgow for the Rennie Macintosh desk or Dumfries for the first bicycle.

The ideal may be to keep a thing in its original environment. But what do you do when this original environment is irrecoverable? Take the case of the Trinity Altarpiece, painted by Hugo van der Goes for the Chapel of Trinity College in Edinburgh in the 1470s. The chapel was demolished in 1848 to make way for the Waverley Station. Does it matter that the nearest place of safety for the two surviving panels is the National Gallery in Edinburgh?[3]

I think the question we need to ask is: to whom does it matter? The altarpiece is of enormous inherent significance for its sheer quality as a work of art. As such, it would certainly be treated as a prime object in any museum from here to Malibu. It is also of great significance in the contexts of Netherlandish painting and of 15th century Scotland. This means, does it not, that people who are well versed in these subjects will be interested in the altarpiece and will recognise its significance, and I doubt if such people will be strongly affected by the place or the context in which they see it.

But such people are a very small minority. Those who are less well informed must also have some way of *relating* to it (in that useful modern sense of the word), if they are to take any real interest in it. That is to say that the interest of a heritage object for any particular visitor depends as much on the knowledge or experience that the visitor brings to the encounter as it does on the accepted significance of the object itself.

It follows that a lack of prior knowledge in the visitor needs to be replaced by some kind of explanation or demonstration, by interpretation in the usual sense. How much prior knowledge can be assumed in the visitor? Or to put it in the way that confronts the museum curator: what is the lowest common denominator among visitors who cannot be assumed to have any prior knowledge?

I believe this can be of two kinds. It may be the comparison with objects we use ourselves with a similar purpose, as in the case of the first bicycle. But the proper study of mankind, as Alexander Pope observed with a fine disregard for sexism, is man, which has much to do with the way visitors to the St Mungo Museum look at ethnographical specimens. And the closest that objects from the past get to 'man' is via the people who made them or used them. And the closest we can get to the makers and users of these objects is usually at the place where they lived and worked. If you think of it, this is a fact that people were sufficiently convinced of in the middle ages to undertake long and hazardous pilgrimages. Today's tourists may not be so strongly motivated to visit our heritage sites, but then getting there is slightly easier.

REPLICAS VERSUS THE REAL THING

In the case of the Trinity Panels, their importance to Edinburgh was acknowledged, and Queen Victoria had them moved from Hampton Court to Holyrood in response to a petition of 1857 and they are now in the National Gallery in Edinburgh. Another of Scotland's prime heritage objects, the St Ninian's Isle Treasure[4], is also in Edinburgh, but in these two cases Edinburgh means two different things. The Trinity Panels were coming back there, and the Scottish National Gallery is the local museum, in preference to the UK capital, London, where the panels had been since the 17th century. The Pictish hoard discovered in 1955 on St Ninian's Isle off the Shetland mainland was restored in London and brought to Edinburgh as the capital city of Scotland, presumably for the first time in its long history.

With the locality goes local loyalty and local pride. Edinburgh people take some pride in the Trinity Panels. The people who take pride in the St Ninian's Isle Treasure are on Shetland. What you see in the museum in Lerwick is a set of electrotype replicas, and replicas are often so good as to be deceptive. Does it matter if you ca not tell the difference?

Not so long ago, I dare not ask if it is still true, visitors to the Albertina Collection in Vienna were shown into a special room housing what were stated to be the famous Dürer drawings and water-colours. But to save the originals from the damaging effects of light, what they actually saw were facsimiles. No indication of this was given, and it is not hard to see why: so many people would protest, having come specially to see the Dürers, to find they were being fobbed off with a bunch of fakes.

So it is not a matter of being able to tell the difference. The pilgrims were content to go a long way to visit the thighbone of their patron saint, although it quite often was not visible inside the reliquary that contained it. But they would not have crossed the road to see a fibreglass replica. The fact that we cannot rationalise the hold that real presence or real place has on us, does not diminish its power. Things that survive from the past are a tangible link, a way we have of keeping our sense of continuity: 'This stone was carved by a Pict 1500 years ago' and 'Walter Scott wrote his novels sitting at that desk.'

But replicas have their place. Their value is in showing what a thing looks like. In 1879 Viollet-le-Duc founded a museum in Paris, now called the Musée des Monuments Français and currently being revitalised, which assembled casts of Gothic and Romanesque cathedral portals from all over France. The National Museum (Queen Street) in Edinburgh exhibits replicas of Pictish stones that are still in place. In both cases they serve exactly the purpose for which they were intended, to enable comparisons to be made. And it is not accidental that they carry the bonus for tourism of inciting people to go to see the real things in their original environment.

NATIONAL VERSUS LOCAL MUSEUMS

But the allocation of the St Ninian's Isle Treasure to Edinburgh is a matter of history. Thirty-eight years ago when the treasure was discovered, there was no museum on Shetland where it could be lodged with any safety, and no provision has ever been made to revise the allocation of Treasure Trove when there is a material change in the circumstances that determined it.

This is a timely reminder that, while the interpretation of heritage sites is hardly more than forty years old and official recognition of the need to preserve the sites themselves just over a century, in this country museums go back to the Ark: to be precise, *Tradescant's Ark*, opened in Lambeth in 1628.

The museum was always the centre for keeping things safe: safe from deterioration, safe from theft, safe from sheer ignorance. In about 1817, when members of the Society of Antiquaries of Scotland learned about a Pictish silver hoard that had been found at Norrie's Law at Largo in Fife, a good deal of it had already been melted down, and they were only able to save what survived by bringing it in to Edinburgh.

And bringing like objects of uncertain use together in one place facilitated their comparison, and hence their interpretation. When one of the first curators of the Ashmolean Museum, Edward Lhuyd, visited Scotland in 1699, the Highlanders showed him stone arrowheads which they said were made by the fairies. 'But', said Lhuyd, 'these are just the same chipped flints the natives of New England head their arrows with at this day.'[5]

So the big central museum brought the objects together, to preserve them and to make them available to scholars, allowing anyone else who knew enough to be interested to come and see, so long as they wiped their feet and did not make a noise.

And for the ordinary visitor the first thing about being in a big museum is that you are in a museum that is big. This is unquestionably a reassurance for many people, the feeling that you have come to 'the place where it's all at'.

On the other hand, the claim that ten times as many people *see* an object in a museum that attracts 300,000 visits a year than in one that attracts only 30,000 makes the remarkable assumption that every visitor to the British Museum or the Victoria and Albert looks at every single object on display there. But it is true that a big central museum offers more opportunities to more people than a smaller outlying museum.

Nevertheless, carrying off archaeological objects from the place where they were found meant that a great deal of contextual information about the site was lost for ever. One of the first men to recognise this was General Pitt Rivers, himself a distinguished museum curator, who introduced a system of detailed records and plans of his excavations. And we are now realising that this alienation also has the effect of impoverishing the objects themselves. Not so much for the trained archaeologist, as we have seen, as for people who lack their background of knowledge. And this can happen with any objects that are removed from their original environment, whether or not their new context makes up for the loss.

THE END OF THE PERMANENT DISPLAY

General Pitt Rivers became our first Inspector of Ancient Monuments in Britain. That was in 1882, and I take this as the start of the movement of site preservation, leading in due course to site interpretation. Since then we have been seeing the increasing ease of transport, promotion of tourism and appreciation that for many children real places and real things mean more than logarithms and the square root of two. These changes have led to a spate of new museums and refurbishment of old ones throughout Scotland, museums run by professional curators, fit to house valuable heritage objects.

This has gone side by side with the development of heritage sites; side by side, too, with the National Trust for Scotland, founded as recently as 1931, which has consistently held to the principle of keeping objects together as aspects of a whole environment.

Historic Scotland, the direct descendants of General Pitt Rivers, have followed the same principle, keeping the objects in their care as near as possible to the sites they come from, as with the marvellous collection of Pictish stones in the old schoolhouse at Meigle, 13 miles north of Dundee, which magically illuminates the history of the flat ground of the surrounding valley by their presence. This is a significant break with the national museum habit: the fact is that younger bodies recognise and respond more easily to present needs.

Meanwhile, the big central museums have been going through a transformation. The leading article in the Museums Journal for May 1993 begins: 'Museums should be more than stores of objects. They must educate and communicate. A fundamental concept...' Quite so, but we need to remember that this 'fundamental concept' would have gained only patchy support among museum curators as little as forty years ago.

The change came with the big loan exhibitions. And these temporary exhibitions, when they are designed to illuminate aspects of our own culture, can be a valuable counterpart to site interpretation. Admittedly they are evanescent, but by the same token they are always a response to a present interest, presented with current exhibition techniques, not the interests and techniques of an earlier generation.

From there, it was only a small step to reconsider the most vivid and informative way of presenting permanent collections. After all, for people visiting a town for the first and often only time, the permanent display in the museum there is in effect a temporary exhibition, which *closes* the day after they leave the town. We owe some brilliant presentations to this thinking, like the ethnography display in the Anthropological Museum here in Aberdeen. And museums now tend to think in terms of semi-permanent displays which are not expected to last more than 15 or 20 years. Moving pictures around is easier, and the regular re-hanging of the permanent collection is now built into the programme of the Tate Gallery.

On the other hand a presentation, once and for all, of the whole of Scottish land, life and history is a different matter.[6] This objective, which is quite unrealisable, grew out of one of the two principal aspects of *The Museum of Scotland*, as it was first envisaged by the Williams Committee in their report of 1981.[7]

A MUSEUM OF SCOTLAND?

The Committee imagined the extensive permanent collections all displayed and interpreted along contemporary lines. Now, twelve years on, I think we can see that they were confusing the Victorian idea of a comprehensive permanent collection, presented objectively, with recent theme exhibitions, which by their nature can never be either objective or comprehensive.

In point of fact, the notion of a comprehensive display was undermined from the outset by the Committee itself in recommending a quite separate Museum of Industry,[8] probably in Glasgow. Obviously, this would have divorced the presentation of Scotland's industries, a crucial aspect at least of the past 200 years, from displays of the natural resources they relied on and of the changes in living conditions they brought about.

In the event, a quite different pattern was already beginning to emerge before the ink on the report was dry, which would effectively supersede the Museum of Industry altogether.[9] This was the development, principally during the 1980s, of a number of independent industrial museum trusts. New Lanark led the field in 1975, followed principally by the Museum of Lead Mining at Wanlockhead, Dundee Industrial Heritage, the Scottish Maritime Museum at Irvine, the Scottish Mining Museum at Newtongrange, the

Scottish Railway Presentation Society at Bo'ness, Summerlee Heritage Trust at Coatbridge, the Dalmellington Conservation Trust. A great part of the national responsibility for presenting an account of Scottish industry has in effect been absorbed by these trusts and, since they are all first and foremost heritage sites, they illustrate perfectly the trend I have been describing and, in doing so, raise issues that are outside the scope of this paper.

At the same time, this development has brought into sharper focus the second aspect of the Williams Committee's concept of the Museum of Scotland. They saw it as the centre of a network[10] for the whole of Scotland: a centre for museum research and information; the centre of a network of smaller linked museums; a centre for conservation and curatorial advice; and as making use of its collections to initiate temporary thematic displays, loans and travelling exhibitions. It was then also seen that the museum was well placed to act as a *synoptic centre*, at which visitors to Edinburgh could learn about other places in Scotland, particularly the industrial heritage sites, in the same way as replicas in a central museum invite travel to see the originals.

This aspect of the Museum of Scotland idea, far from looking backwards into the past, looks more like a blueprint for the future, in which the central and local museums and the heritage sites all contribute in their several ways to the national pattern. Co-operation on this scale is no easy thing to achieve, and a much clearer commitment to it on the part of central government is needed, but at least we are far closer to achieving it in Scotland than they are in the south.

BUT THE VICTORIAN DRAGON LINGERS

Can we, I wonder, finally lay to rest that superannuated Victorian maxim about *national importance*? If a thing is of national importance, its place is where it can best serve the nation. And this is likely to be in the context that best permits its interpretation, or that best allows it to contribute to the interpretation of some wider aspect of the heritage.

But we do no service to the heritage by pretending that there is not sometimes an irreconcilable conflict of interests.[11] Perhaps on occasion it may be resolved by the fact that we are dealing with objects that are movable, subject always to their resistance to the hazards of travel. A permanent home for an object in an outlying area, when this is the best context for it, need not preclude it from being shown from time to time in the different context of temporary exhibitions at the centre.

And we need to recognise, too, that whatever decisions we take on display or interpretation is bound to have a limited life, because they are, inevitably, subjective. The art historian Max Friedlaender said of the assessment of paintings: 'Without a point of view, no judgement; with a point of view, no objective judgement.' And I would say: Without context, no interpretation; with context, no objective interpretation.

309

The Author

Colin Thompson CBE was born in 1919. He attended Sedbergh School and King's College Cambridge (Modern Languages) before going to Chelsea Polytechnic School of Art. He worked at GCHQ 1941–45, before becoming a lecturer at Bath Academy of Art 1948–54. He joined the National Gallery of Scotland in 1954, and was Director of the National Galleries of Scotland 1977–84. He was a member of the Scottish Arts Council 1976–83 and Edinburgh Festival Council 1979–82. Chairmanships have included the Scottish Museums Council 1984–87, and the Board of Governors, Edinburgh College of Art 1989–91. He has been Chairman of Judges, Scottish Museum of the Year Awards since 1988, and became Chairman of the Scottish Mining Museum Trust in 1993.

References

1　Details of this and most other Scottish museums and sites referred to will be found in Thompson, C., *Exploring Museums (Scotland)*, HMSO, 1990

2　The whole project has been sent back for reconsideration. The last description, and also the most detailed, given by the Director of the National Galleries of Scotland on 18 January 1994, referred to it as 'a proper social history of a proud nation'

3　For the history of the panels see Thompson, C. and Campbell, L., *Hugo van der Goes and the Trinity Panels in Edinburgh*, National Galleries of Scotland, 1974

4　Close-Brooks, J., *St Ninian's Isle Treasure*, HMSO, 1981

5　Murray, D., *Museums: their history and their use*, 1904, vol. I p 241

6　The project is discussed in some detail in *A New Museum for Scotland*, National Museums of Scotland, 1990, pp 37–46: 'Meeting the public needs?' by Anderson R.

7　Williams, A. et al, *A Heritage for Scotland, Scotland's National Museums and Galleries: the next 25 years, Report of a Committee appointed by the Secretary of State for Scotland*, HMSO, 1981

8　op. cit. paras 2.8 and 9

9　Progressive stages can be followed in:
(i) Miles, H. et al, *Museums in Scotland: Report by a Working Party of the Museums and Galleries Commission*, HMSO 1986, Chapter 9: 'Industrial Museums and Industrial Heritage Sites';
(ii) The Marquess of Bute et al, *Report to the Secretary of State for Scotland by the Museums Advisory Board*, SED 1985, paras 4.20 – 4.30): 'Museum of Industry'; and
(iii)*A New Head of Steam*, Scottish Museums Council, 1990, pp 13 – 18: 'Industrial museums in Scotland: heritage sites, visitor attractions or national network?' by Thompson C.

10　loc. cit. Chapter 8

11　For illustrations of this conflict, including the allocation of the St Ninian's Isle Treasure, and for the unquestioned acceptance of the conventional view of 'national importance', see Cheape, H., *Collecting on a National Scale*, Museums Journal, December 1990, pp 34 – 37

25

TELLING THE STORY IN MUSEUMS

Richard Harrison

I have worked in museums for over 35 years, but it is only since I became a consultant during the last six years that I have had the opportunity of extending that experience into the more general heritage and tourism field. In the context of my role as an interpretive planner this has been invaluable and it seemed appropriate within the context of this volume for me to consider some of the benefits that interpretive planning as a technique can bring to museums.

After all, the theme of the 1993 Robert Gordon Heritage Convention, for which I originally wrote this paper was: *making the ordinary seem extraordinary through interpretation*. That event, and many of the papers in this volume, could have been designed for a wholly museum audience. Successful interpretation depends a great deal on the nature of the resource to be interpreted, whether it be an historic site, a nature reserve, an industrial process or a museum collection of objects made out of wood which represent a wide and fascinating range of human endeavour, such as *The Collection of Treen* in Birmingham Museum and Art Gallery.

In his paper, *The Role of the Museum in Interpretation* on a similar theme, Colin Thompson has quoted a number of examples which illustrate that in resource terms museums have a richness unequalled, I would suggest, in any other field. My purpose is to discuss how the interpretive planning process can make the most of this.

Thompson's paper also gives me a number of other useful reference points. He considers at some length context and illustrates this in a number of ways and the emphasis in the title of my paper on the story derives much from the value of giving the museum visitor or user a sense of context particularly as the artefacts (the resource) are frequently in a museum which is itself a considerable distance from their source in time as well as space. Thompson also refers to the degree of knowledge that a visitor or user brings to a museum experience. Knowledge and awareness of this is crucial to the interpretive planning process.

THE INTERPRETIVE PLAN

Let me start by defining the interpretive planning process as I, and others, whom I have worked closely with over the past ten years or so, see it. It also figures to a large extent in the chapter written by Professor Brian Goodey on *Interpretive Planning* to be included in the *Manual of Heritage Management* sponsored by the Association of Independent Museums to be published by Butterworth Heinemann in the autumn of 1994. It has four key elements:

1. understanding the nature of the audience: the market;
2. identifying the themes and stories to be told;
3. identifying the resources to be used in interpreting these themes and stories;
4. considering the most appropriate and effective media to be used in the context of the above three elements.

UNDERSTANDING YOUR MARKET

The first step in the process has not always ranked as a top priority among museum professionals, but increased competition and greater emphasis on marketing and customer care has changed this. The purpose of the exercise is to obtain information which enables you to construct profiles of market segments. It should provide answers to the following questions:

1. What geographical area will visitors and users come from, including estimated travel time?
2. How many people live there?
3. What is their age and socio-economic structure?
4. What is their propensity to visit an 'x' type of museum?

But in the context of an interpretive plan, it should go a great deal further:

1. Are there sectors of this market that should be specifically targeted and, if so, these should be reflected in the interpretive plan?
2. What is their likely level of experience and pre-knowledge and how should this be reflected in any interpretive brief, eg their level of comprehension (reading level)?
3. Identifying the specific needs of special groups of visitors and users: families, school groups, disabled, special interest groups etc.

IDENTIFYING THE THEMES AND STORIES

To me the essence of good interpretation is 'a good story well told'. I find this simpler and in some ways more helpful than the Tildman definition. It is of course very easy for this approach to become hackneyed and devalued as has happened in some of the more commercial heritage enterprises. Goodey describes it thus:

> Themes are the broad concepts containing the significant elements which define a unique local history and topography: a means by which fact and personality-strewn academic and popular knowledge can be organised for presentation within the contemporary value systems. Stories are the specific strands which may be drawn from each theme in order to highlight the role of buildings, sites features or individuals (or in the context of this paper collections). They also imply an attractive structuring of evidence to involve the visitor and resident.

It is essential that the identification of appropriate themes is supported by detailed, scholarly research that respects the integrity of the subject.

IDENTIFYING THE RESOURCES

These can vary significantly depending on the nature of the project, but what is so often overlooked is the range that is available. In the case of an historic castle, the structure itself is a key resource and can be used to illustrate the development of the castle over many hundreds of years, but if the identification of themes calls for the interpretation of life in the castle, or of the people who lived there, then a wide range of additional resource opportunities should be considered: archives, artefacts, pictures of all kinds, published descriptions etc. All of these can be used to ensure that the interpretation of a particular theme or story responds to the identified visitor market.

Equally important is the human resources needed to ensure that the interpretive plan meets its objectives; be they market analysts, researchers, curators, designers, script writers, media specialists or interpreters.

IDENTIFYING APPROPRIATE MEDIA

This is becoming increasingly important. The range of media now available means that it is essential that consideration of appropriate media should form part of an interpretive plan. As peoples' horizons are widened, particularly through travel and television, their expectations are becoming greater. No longer will badly designed, poorly researched, dull interpretation suffice.

At the other extreme, technology is all too often taking over from effective interpretation. This is encouraged by the increasing pace of development of new technologies and the view 'I must have one of those'. One example is the ride, absolutely right for Yorkvik, but attempts to repeat its success have been less effective. A high tech multi-media programme costing a quarter of a million pounds is of little value if it fails to respond to needs of the interpretive plan.

Available funding can also have an important influence, although an expensive solution does not necessarily ensure success. Many times a simple, low-cost solution, well executed and which responds well to the interpretive plan can be much more successful.

MUSEUMS AND INTERPRETATION

With a number of notable exceptions, the track record of museums in the UK in effective interpretation is not good, although it is probably better than in many other countries. I suggest there are a number of reasons for this. Museums have a range of key objectives and traditionally greater resources have gone into collections management: the collecting, documentation, care and study of frequently very large collections of artefacts. This extends to the recruitment of skills, priority being given to those skills required for collections management, ie curatorship. The implications of this are very much to the fore in the current financial climate. Museums with large collections to manage, but with a comparatively poor record of high quality provision for visitors and users, are having to re-examine their priorities.

Another factor is that, until comparatively recently, the majority of museums were in the public sector, normally local government. This has meant competing for resources against a whole host of services and priorities. As a result, all too often museum budgets have been disproportionately overloaded with staff costs and the cost of managing and maintaining buildings which are frequently themselves part of the heritage in their own right: castles, historic houses etc. Nor has there been any great incentive to respond to the needs and interests of the visitors. However, this is changing very rapidly in a climate where management by objectives, cost effectiveness, value for money and awareness of visitor needs are very much to the fore.

As Director of the Museums Service in Portsmouth in the late 1970s with six museums and a budget of over one million pounds, but less than 10% available for funding a service to visitors and users, I am well aware of the dilemma.

A phenomenon of the 70s and 80s was the growth of the independent museum, largely dependant on visitors for income. Their priorities in terms of effective use of scarce resources has been quite different to the traditional public sector museum. Whilst many of them are low cost operations, they nevertheless reflect a need to understand their audience and to respond effectively to their interests and expectations.

Another factor has been the museums reliance on their artefact collections as a primary interpretive resource, which has meant that artefacts have dominated their presentations to the visitor. This is often to the detriment of any interpretation, other than at a very basic level, and largely unrelated to the visitors interests, level of pre-knowledge or background. We are all too familiar with display cases packed with artefacts with either little or no interpretation or alternatively endless texts which take hours to read even if we understand the language being used.

Admittedly it is some years ago now, but I well remember visiting a number of German museums, new buildings, outstanding collections, displayed beautifully, but with hardly any interpretation, and very few casual visitors.

At the other end of the scale there has been the significant number of new displays in museums, where the interpretation has been secondary to the design, and where lighting, colour, layout and the use of inappropriate media has dominated, together with the misuse of resources, notably artefacts. A photograph tilted to give symmetry to a design is to my mind bad interpretation. Similarly, captions with both margins justified may look very tidy but are difficult to read.

At the other extreme, is the use of just one or two artefacts when, in reality, to understand the particular theme being interpreted, a range of examples is required. There has also been the temptation to create an 'oo-ah' experience rather than an educational, recreational or inspirational one which should be the aim of all good interpretation. Examples include the mega exhibitions staged in London in the 1960s and 70s, in contrast to some of the new galleries in the Natural History Museum of London.

In the field of slide- and audio-visual programmes, all too often it is the number of projectors used that is paramount, rather than the effective use of this media as an interpretive tool. The reliance on artefacts and the sometimes extreme commitment to authenticity, accuracy and integrity by curators has frequently led to media opportunities being missed, eg the use of reconstructions, figures, animated or not, replicas, sound and light and interactive displays of all kinds. However, this is another area in which attitudes are changing.

UNDERSTANDING THE AUDIENCE

Many museums serve specific geographical areas or communities and in general terms aim to provide a service to everybody. This should not preclude the need to understand this audience and to use this knowledge effectively. The majority of museums tend to provide primarily for the interests and needs of the middle class sectors of their community, but there are exceptions, for example, the Springburn Museum in Glasgow. There are also encouraging signs that those museums that have analysed their audience and targeted sections that have not hitherto used the museum are having some success, the Museum of Science and Industry at Manchester for one.

Knowing the structure of the audience is one thing, assessing their level of knowledge and likely interest is another. This cannot easily be achieved at the interpretive planning stage unless the information already exists. However, by using, over a period of time, quantitative and qualitative techniques, a picture can be built up, based on the evaluation of the effectiveness of each new exhibit during its development and after it has been completed.

Most of the pioneer work in this field has been done in the United States, I saw some in the 1960s. It is now coming to the fore in the UK as evidenced by two conferences held in 1993, one organised jointly by the Society for the Interpretation of Britain's Heritage and the Centre for Environmental Interpretation in Edinburgh the other, entitled Research and Evaluation in Interpretation at the Science Museum in London. An assessment of the following can be used to validate an interpretive project as it passes through the concept, design and implementation stages.

1. the response by a particular market sector;
2. the level of understanding reflected in all aspects of the interpretation;
3. whether the interpretation is meeting the objectives of the brief;
4. the effectiveness of the display in conveying the story line.

IDENTIFYING THE MOST APPROPRIATE THEMES AND STORIES

The essence of effective interpretation is the message: this may be philosophical, ie issues of conversation, protection or inspiration. In the museum context it is more likely to be the story derived from an overall theme. However, the very organisation of museums by discipline and by collections has encouraged an approach which says: we have a collection of Roman artefacts, or of 18th century musical instruments, the contents of a wheelwright's shop, or a collection of mounted birds we should display. The result is often of little interest to the average visitor.

This same visitor is likely to be or is an avid TV watcher who loves the nature programmes and historical plays, has been to see *Jurassic Park*, has travelled and seen Disneyland, has participated in guided walks in his nearest historical town, has used a tape tour, or better still an Infra-Red or Induction Loop system at his local castle, has enjoyed the tape-slide show and interpretive panels at his local nature reserve and expects to find the same approach in his local museum. All of these experiences will have been themed, and museums must learn to respond to this level of expectation.

Figure 1 The Hardware Department in the Co-operative Store at Beamish. A reconstructed shop using a mixture of original artefacts and replicas. *All illustrations reproduced by kind permission of the North of England Open Air Museum Beamish.*

Figure 2 Cheesemaking in the Dairy at the Home Farm, Beamish, where demonstrating a process using the original artefacts is a way of successfully interpreting otherwise rather uninteresting exhibits.

It is equally important that it is not done in isolation. Museums are increasingly developing thematic displays but all too frequently these are still collections led and take little account of the market. It is vital that selecting and adequately researching the appropriate themes and stories is part of an interpretive planning exercise in the museum context.

IDENTIFYING THE RESOURCES

One of the benefits of the *market, themes and resources approach* is the way each element leads on to the next. In a non-museum situation this element of the interpretive planning process would examine all the options including artefacts but also archives, originated graphics, pictures, reminiscences, music and other audio material etc. A museum must do the same.

A museum has the advantage that its resources are unique and first-hand. This has led to them being either used exclusively or having a dominating role. This is understandable. When I was involved in the development of the Mary Rose Exhibition at Portsmouth, the artefact resource was so special, so unique, that there was a temptation to rely on it exclusively. This was resisted eg contemporary paintings were used to illustrate the Tudor context, as were drawings and contemporary descriptions, to the benefit of the visitor experience and in meeting interpretive objectives.

This reliance on artefacts also leads to museums into not interpreting certain themes just because they are not represented in their collections or the additional resources required are not to hand. As a result some local history museums tell a disjointed story. A good example is the *Story of the High Peak* at Buxton Museum; an excellent piece of themed interpretation, but where the whole of the mediaeval period gets scant attention because the museum has few artefacts from this period.

The choice of themes must be audience and story led and relevant resources must then be found, whether by loan of original material or replicating material from other sources or using photographs and archive material.

THE APPROPRIATE MEDIA

A number of Museums have adopted the interpretive planning process and, as a result, have had considerable success using media which reflects the market, themes and resources approach. One such museum is Beamish, the North of England Open Air Museum. As an open air museum, it has little use for the more formal type of display, but has taken full advantage of many other forms of media available for interpreting the complex themes relating to life in the North East.

Figure 3 Reconstructed buildings in the turn-of-the-century Town at Beamish, furnished with artefacts, replicate life at that time.

Figure 4 Lessons in the Board School in the Colliery Village at Beamish. First person interpretation effectively recreates the atmosphere of school in Victorian times.

However, the developments at Beamish do underline the potential conflict between collections as primary evidence and their use as an interpretive resource. Many artefacts are too important as primary evidence, too rare, too sensitive to environmental change, too valuable or too attractive to thieves to be used in some of the ways employed by Beamish. Even collections of this kind, which by necessity have to be shown behind glass, can be supported by other kinds of interpretive media. This can make them to be more accessible to various market sectors, as well as effective in interpreting their various themes. A number of recent multi-disciplinary exhibitions organised by the Tyne and Wear Museum Service illustrate this point very well.

This was certainly my approach in interpreting the Mary Rose story. The artefacts, mainly highly sensitive organic objects, had to be shown in air-conditioned display cases. By using high quality graphics, visual presentations with a minimum of words, film and slide material, diagrams, models, reconstructions, replicas and human figures, it was possible to interpret the story very successfully to a wide audience.

The need to sustain visitor interest is also an important factor in choosing appropriate media. Most people have a quite limited attention span and varied graphic and audio-visual displays offer changing perspectives to retain interest through even very complex stories. Equally important is smoothing the flow of visitors through a particular exhibition area. The use of varied media can both sustain interest and ease visitor flow while, at the same time ensuring clear communication which is educational, inspiring and, above all, fun.

Visitor participation becomes increasingly important in this context. Science centres have led the way in designing *hands-on* exhibits, and advances in computer technology are placing such innovations within reach of other intrepretive facilities. Compact Disc technologies are capable of packaging graphics, audio and cross-indexed information for passive display or interactive access by the single user. The *tape tour* uses computer technology to allow the visitor individual access through a handset to interpretive sound material. The visitor has the freedom to choose what interests them. The interpreter has the opportunity to offer a much wider range of material in a single display, to aim it different audiences offering choices of language and levels of detail, complexity and perspective to match their interest and stamina.

The Author

Richard Harrison's distinguished career in the museums service has included posts in both local government and the private sector, and he established himself as an independent consultant in 1988. He spent ten years with two area museum councils, five years as Director of a major provincial museum, and nine years as Executive

Director and subsequently Museum Director of the Mary Rose Trust. His primary interest has been with the provision of services to the visitor. Both in these museums where he has worked, and as a director of area councils, he has strived with some success to make museums more visitor friendly. He was a Churchill Fellow in 1967, and has travelled widely in the USA, Canada, Sweden, Germany and Holland to study interpretation in museums. He is a founder member and currently Treasurer of the Society for the Interpretation of Britain's Heritage.

References

Alderson, W.T. and Low, S., *Interpretation of Historic Sites, Nashville*, American Association for State and Local History, l976

Alfrey, J. and Putnam, T., *The Industrial Heritage*: *Managing Resources and Uses*, Routledge, l992

Ambrose, T. (ed), *Museums are for People*, Scottish Museums Council and HMSO, 1985

Ambrose, T. and Runyard, S., *Forward Planning*, Routledge, 1991

Belcher, M., *Exhibitions in Museums*, Leicester University Press, 1991

Chadwick, A., *The Role of the Museum and Art Gallery in Community Education*, Department of Adult Education, University of Nottingham, 1980

Cossons, N. (ed), *The Management of Change in Museums*, National Maritime Museum, 1985

Falk, J. and Dierking, L., *The Museum Experience*, Whalesback Books, 1992

Foundation of France/ICOM, *Museums without Barriers*: *A new deal for disabled people*, ICOM in association with Routledge, 1991

Harrison, R.F. (ed), *Manual of Heritage Management*, Butterworth Heineman (forthcoming)

Goodey, B. and Parkin, I., *Urban Interpretation*, (2 Vols), Oxford Polytechnic School of Planning (now Oxford Brookes University)

Hooper-Greenhill, E. *Museums and the Shaping of Knowledge*, Routledge, 1992

Jensen, K.B. and Janowski, N.W. (eds), *A Handbook of Qualitative Methodologies for Mass Communication Research*, Routledge, 1991

Kavanagh, G., *Museum Languages: Objects and Texts*, Leicester University Press, 1991

Lord, G.D. and Lord B., *The Manual of Museum Planning*, HMSO, 1991

Middleton, V., *New Visions for Independent Museums in the UK*, Association of Independent Museums, 1990

Miles, R.S. et al, *The Design of Educational Exhibits*, Allen & Unwin, 1982

Royal Ontario Museum, *Communicating with the Museum Visitor*, Royal Ontario Museum, 1976

Runyard, S., *The Museum Marketing Handbook*, HMSO, 1994

Touchstone Associates, *Quiet Nature and Kinder Climate: Presentation Plan for Ilfracombe, Bristol/Stroud*, Touchstone Associates for the Civic Trust, 1987

Thompson, J.H. (ed), *Manual of Curatorship*, Butterworth Heinemann, 1992

Uzzell, D. (ed), *Heritage Interpretation*, (Vols. 1 and 2), Belhaven Press, 1989

There are a wide range of articles on the subject in the following Journals: *Museums Journal; Environmental Interpretation; Curator; Museum Development; Journal of Interpretation; Museum Studies in Material Culture;* and *International Journal of Museum Management.*

26

VISUAL COMPLEXITY
Are we cleaning our heritage to death?

Christopher Andrew

Why do tourists choose to visit historic towns and cities? What expectations and conceptions do they bring with them and to what extent are these reinforced or changed as a result of the architectural heritage which they experience? The answers to these questions are inextricably linked with the policies adopted towards our urban architectural heritage. These policies often vary depending on the age or architectural significance of individual historic buildings. Yet, it is the 'gestalt' or whole of the urban environment that contributes towards the visitor's experience of the urban environment. Lynch (1972) suggest that 'Under the banner of historical preservation, we have saved many isolated buildings of doubtful significance or present quality, which are out of context with their surroundings.'

In recent years the debate about urban conservation and preservation policy has become more fervent as the rate of urban renewal and regeneration programmes increases. The formation of an architectural heritage policy has to be conducted within the context of an understanding of the meaning which architecture has for individuals as they move through the urban landscape. This meaning can be analyses at a number of different levels. Most empirical research has concentrated on how urban areas are conceptualised in essentially spatial and relational terms, with relatively little attention being paid to the emotional appeal of places or temporal cues so important to the heritage experience.

A significant landmark in this discussion was Lynch's book (1972) *What time is this place?* The central theme of Lynch's work was how external signals of time within the environment fit with internal experience. Lynch argues that the quality of the personal image of time is crucial for individual well-being, as well as for success in managing environmental change. The external physical environment plays a role in building and supporting that image of time. Lynch goes further and suggests that to effectively preserve the past, 'we must know for what the past is being retained, and for whom.'

However, all to often conservation decisions are made on an ad hoc and subjective basis.

McWilliam (1975) has argued that conservation of the built heritage is characterised by 'a general failure to define policies and objectives, either in discussion or in practice.' Even Lowenthal (1981) who has been one of the most prolific writers in this areas suggests that little is know about the philosophy or psychology of conservation. Similarly, Kain (1981) argues that exactly what the built heritage contributes to the physical and spiritual well being of man has not been adequately addressed. Even if a policy towards our built heritage could be developed out of an understanding of the meaning which it has, there is always pressure to adapt and change the urban landscape for modern usage, and therein often lies a larger problem.

REGENERATION AND AUTHENTICITY

Lynch (1972) argues that many economically advanced countries retain fragments of obsolete physical environments as emotional relics of times gone by. This retention of old buildings can take a number of forms. They can simply be saved from destruction and retained in their present day condition, although the extent to which it is possible, or desirable, to attempt to freeze buildings in time is another question. Many architectural conservationists favour this position, arguing that by doing this the buildings authentic history is retained, adding a true historic sense to the environment, as well as giving a temporal dimension to the onlooker. This may be a possibility for historic buildings which would be retained under any circumstances. However, there is more doubt over historic buildings of lesser significance. These may have some measure of architectural merit, but may not be considered sufficiently important by urban planners to preserve in an unrestored condition. This situation is quite common in large areas of the urban landscape, particularly in cities which have had a prosperous past, the legacy of which has been their buildings. Keeping these buildings almost always involves repairs, restoration and often complete refurbishment.

In many industrial cities, refurbishment often entails giving the building a 'facelift', usually involving exterior facade cleaning. Sometimes all that remains of the original buildings are the outer walls, all else is demolished. It could be argued that without the wholesale redevelopment of these buildings, they would simply be knocked down anyway, leaving no trace of their existence. While in many cases accepting this argument, some conservationists and others involved in heritage interpretation, suggest that in attempting to bring them into useful life by alteration and restoration, this leads to a false sense of history and a distorted interpretation of the past.

There is evidence that the age of historic buildings is consistently underestimated, and that cleaning and restoration compounds this error further (Andrew, 1992). A question which then might be posed is: would it be better to make an honest statement about the present, by building from new in a contemporary style, or appear to distort the past by the wholesale changing of buildings while still presenting them as old? What effect these changes have on the perception of our historic urban areas by visitors poses another question. The challenge for planners is to adapt the built heritage of the past to fulfil present day needs, while at the same time maintaining an authentic sense of the past.

AESTHETICS AND MEANING

Scruton (1979) suggests that 'to take an aesthetic interest in a building is to attend to it in all its completeness, to see it, not in terms of narrow or predetermined functions, but in terms of every visual significance that it will bear.' It could be further argued that a full appreciate our architectural heritage must involve an understanding of its emotional and cognitive, as well as visual appeal. All too often the emotional and temporal meanings which old building create in the minds of onlookers is not considered, or is ignored in favour of some presumed visual improvement.

Typical of this deterministic approach are the extensive facade cleaning programmes which have been undertaken in many historic cities. The assumed visual benefits of this activity has tended, until recently, to obscure any discussion of its potential damage, both in terms of the building fabric being cleaned and the change in character brought about by cleaning. If the heritage experience of urban areas is to be maintained, then planning needs to maintain the integrity and unity of the urban environment.

In many historic urban situations a unity exists between buildings and between streets which gives an identity to whole areas of cities and towns. In some situations, particularly those where buildings are constructed of similar materials, the uniformity of building form and facade condition adds to the overall sense of place of the region, distinguishing it from its neighbours. Some good examples of where this unity appears to operate are selected areas of Edinburgh New Town, where facade cleaning has been restricted. The result has been that these areas have maintained, with their weathered facades, a degree of uniformity and retained an unbroken linkage with the past. Other areas of Edinburgh and other historic cities have undergone extensive facade cleaning programmes resulting in a brighter, and some would argue more agreeable urban environment. Which of these presents to the visitor the more authentic heritage experience is open to question, and the issue presents an invitation to researchers.

DECAY AS ENRICHED HERITAGE

Piper (1947) in an essay entitled, *Pleasing decay*, discusses the theme that as buildings age they may, particularly if forethought has been given to the original design, develop a pleasing attractiveness which is enhanced by the ageing process. Good town planning, according to Piper, will incorporate 'present decay as well as possible future decay'. Decay may not only be pleasing in itself, but it also provides relief and contrast. Decay is not a fixed condition, but a growing and continuing process which eventually effects all building. The environmental planner might then wish to consider how aesthetically pleasing a particular decayed building is, whether to arrest or even cultivate the decay, or perhaps the degree to which it should be returned to its former condition.

Piper suggests that 'the natural weathering of the surface of a building is beautiful, and its loss disastrous. Old buildings are loved for what they stand for rather than for what they look like.' Piper remarks that 'it is usually only after an old building has been permed, and had its eyebrows plucked, that we notice that its whole character has been changed.' Buildings, even every surface, need to be taken on their individual merits and regarded as possibly having virtue or charm in their decayed or weathered state. The pleasure to be derived from weathered or decayed buildings is, in Pipers view, a sophisticated pleasure and one which the eye has to become accustomed to.

There may well be a case for a policy of minimal intervention in some historic districts to preserve a genuine sense of place and time, perhaps more consistent with visitors preconceptions. The question is not only one of authenticity but also of the aesthetic feel of urban environments. Congruity, complexity, mystery and surprise are all elements which need to be considered in historic urban spaces. Any sense that the visitor feels that by chance they have come upon an area which is genuinely untouched by urban regeneration or artificially manipulated for their own supposed benefit is to be valued and adds to their experience.

RETAINING UNITY AND AUTHENTICITY

Weathering affects all buildings and all building materials. The effects of weathering on buildings and hence their visual appearance is dependent on the interaction of a range of factors which include the building material, patterns of wetting and drying, architectural features which influence the run off of rainwater and the deposition of atmospheric dirt and pollution. The type or category of a building influence the acceptability and aesthetic value of any weathering on its facade. The expectation for some buildings is that they will be weathered, and that this weathering is part of their character. Many castles, for example, may be in this category.

In the past, some of the worse damage in terms of the detrimental visual effects of facade restoration has been to streetscapes. In essence, the problem stems from owners of individual properties in terraces, circles, crescents and squares cleaning their properties in isolation. These architectural forms were built with unity of storey height, fenestration, detailing and building material and were clearly designed to be read as a whole. If only some of these buildings undergo facade cleaning, the unity is invariably destroyed. Individual properties in terraces, cleaned over an extended period, enter the resoiling cycle at different times and inevitably the quality of the architectural experience is reduced.

The exterior of buildings pass through a cycle of change as soiling accumulates on the surface. The speed of this change may vary considerably. Materials vary in their susceptibility to the influence of weathering, but every material and so ever facade alters in appearance after long exposure to wind and rain. Many modern buildings, for example, those with precast concrete exteriors or harled surfaces, quickly develop patterns of staining through rainwater run-off which are unrelated to any underlying architectural feature and may look unkempt after only a few years, while many old buildings which have developed large accumulations of soiling over centuries may display an aesthetic quality which enhances the visual appearance of the building. Carrie and Morel (1975) illustrate this neatly in their example of the porch of the church of St Margaret at Westminster. Many perceive the facade, weathered through years of exposure to wind and rain, as an example of the displeasing soiling which covers many European cities. Others argue that the moderate accumulations of soiling add to the building's visual quality and is part of the buildings heritage.

TO CLEAN OR NOT TO CLEAN

The past decade has seen large-scale facade cleaning programmes in many of our major cities, so much so that it is difficult now to move through large areas of cities such as Edinburgh and Glasgow and see historic buildings which have not been subjected to facade 'improvement' schemes. The value of these programmes has been the subject of much debate (Webster, 1992), but what does seem to emerge from the arguments, both for and against facade cleaning, is a tendency for those involved to adopt extreme positions on the issue. For example, The Architectural Heritage Society of Scotland consistently opposes any application for stone cleaning referred to them. By the same token, many historic buildings which do not need planning permission for cleaning, have been permanently damaged by inappropriate cleaning seemingly undertaken without knowledge of the complex issues involved (Andrew et al. 1994).

In Scotland much of the early cleaning of sandstone buildings used physical or abrasive techniques, principally grit blasting. These techniques work by removing a layer of grains from the surface of the stone and with it the outer soiled layer. Commercial pressures to clean buildings can lead to misuse of the technique, by for example increasing blasting pressures. The result has been that architectural details, such as arises, tooling marks and stone carvings, etc, on historic facades have been irreparably damaged. Abrasive techniques can also remove the built up of patina on the stone, often developed over decades, exposing the stone to potentially accelerated rates of decay. As a result of these concerns there has been a move towards the use of chemical cleaning techniques. Problems have arisen with these techniques as well, particularly the retention in sandstone of significant percentages of the applied chemicals. The longer term detrimental effects of these chemicals on historic buildings has still to be fully assessed, and yet chemical cleaning agents continue to be applied to our built architectural heritage. The arguments on both sides of the stonecleaning debate have recently come to a head with the controversy over the cleaning of the Sir Walter Scott Monument in Edinburgh, where Historic Scotland has opposed the cleaning of the monument.

One possible way of looking at the issue is to draw on the concept of visual complexity (Andrew 1992). Initially, light soiling on surfaces which have uneven texture (eg rock faced and tooled stone) lodges mainly on horizontal and outermost surfaces of the stone. Similarly, light soiling around architectural detail adds to the visual complexity of a building by increasing contrast and shadowing effects.

Verhoef (1988) argues that in northerly cities of Europe, soiling can emphasise architectural designs which for much of the year would be lacking definition due to the absence of sharp, well defined shadows. However, as the build up of soiling continues this eventually leads to a complete blackening of the surface of the building, which reduces the visual information provided by architectural details and completely obscures colour, texture and any shadowing effects. In effect, the visual complexity of the building is reduced by the very heavy soiling on the building facade. Entire buildings may progress through this pattern of soiling in a relatively consistent way.

Alternatively, parts of facades may soil at different rates. A strategy which could be adopted by planning authorities would be to permit limited restoration and facade cleaning where visual complexity has been reduced to a minimum by the complete blackening of surfaces. Less damaging restoration and cleaning techniques are now available which will remove some, but not all accumulations of soiling from buildings. Approaches to historic facade cleaning which take into consideration the complexity provided by weathered surfaces provide a framework for planning which moves away from a merely subjective view. Some would argue that this approach represents simply another way of manipulating our architectural heritage to create a false sense of history, and that all weathering and soiling should be retained as evidence of a building's history. However, with pressures for urban redevelopment as they are, it is often a case of refurbishment or removal. In this situation limited facade cleaning may be the lesser of two evils.

It remains to be seen whether the move towards the cleaning of historic buildings has been simply a passing fashion, and one which has been detrimental to the physical fabric of much of our built heritage. If we value this heritage we should consider now what future generations will make of the recent drive to remove the evidence of passing of time. Greater priority should be given to finding out what image is most valued by local communities and tourists alike. We also need to be culturally alert to the fact that what is considered of little value today may be highly fashionable at some time in the future. Therefore, any historic building should be treated with respect.

The Author

Dr Christopher Andrew graduated with degrees in psychology from the Universities of London and Surrey. An Associate Fellow of the British Psychological Society, he has been engaged in teaching and research in Aberdeen since 1980, and obtained his PhD from St Andrews University in 1994 on the subject of urban architectural aesthetics based on his contribution to a major study for Historic Scotland on masonry conservation. Other research has included perceptual aspects of tourism promotion and rural housing, and he acts as adviser to the Robert Gordon University Heritage Unit. He won a 1993 Carnegie Trust travel scholarship for study in Scandinavia, and was awarded a 1994 Churchill Memorial Travel Fellowship to research building conservation in South East Asia.

References

Andrew, C. *Towards an aesthetic theory of building soiling,* in Webster, R.G.M. (ed), 'Stone Cleaning and the nature soiling and decay mechanisms of stone', Donhead, 1992

Andrew, C. , Young, M. and Tonge, K., *Stonecleaning: A guide for practitioners.* Historic Scotland, 1994

Carrie and Morel, in Verhoef, L.G.W. (ed), *Rilem Report: soiling and cleaning of building facades,* Chapman Hall, 1975

Kain, R., *Planning for conservation,* Maxwell, 1981

Lowenthal, D., and Binney, M., *Our past before us,* Temple Smith, 1981

Lynch, K., *What time is this place?* MIT Press, 1972

McWilliam, C., *Scottish Townscape,* Collins, 1975

Piper, J., *Pleasing decay,* in Architects Journal, Vol 179, pp 87–89, 1947 (reprinted 1984)

Scruton, R., *The aesthetics of architecture,* Methueun & Co., 1979

Verhoef, L.G.W. (ed), *Rilem Report: soiling and cleaning of building facades*, Chapman Hall, 1975

Webster, R.G.M. (ed), *Stone Cleaning and the nature soiling and decay mechanisms of stone*, Donhead, 1992

Figure 1 The unity of architectural appearance has been maintained by restrictions on cleaning in this view of the New Town District, Edinburgh.

CULTURAL SUSTENANCE
Making a Meal of Our Heritage

The past is the recipe
from which today is prepared
and tomorrow is the feast to come.

Figure 1 The fine towers of Fyvie Castle, Turriff, dates back to the 13th century and is one of the finest examples of Scottish Baronial architecture.

27

SCOTTISHNESS IN ARCHITECTURE
Towards a Theory of Regional Interpretation

Charles McKean

If you agree with Charles Rennie Mackintosh that architecture is the world's history in stone, then you can interpret that history at regional and local level by a close study of what is built. This brief guide interprets that against five essential factors, of which the last, changing social patterns, is the most significant.

Earliest building, created by artisans, locals or by community effort, (and later, builders), forms the vast bulk of what is commonly, but incorrectly, described as vernacular: ie pre-industrial everyday building. Basic building materials and construction were broadly similar throughout Europe with variations based on national, regional and local cultural traditions, geology, climate, transport and trade.

Architecture, created by master masons, master wrights, and architects, was not essentially different, in terms of construction, from artisan buildings. It was built with the same technology and materials, in the same way, but by skilled rather than unskilled people, increasingly with broader knowledge of architecture and Europe. The difference lies in the use of more developed ideas of planning, structure and style, based on knowledge of architectural theory and practice in other societies (Baltic States, Holland, France, Italy England etc). This may have been learnt through travel or books (now magazines) or through the arrival of foreign architects, craftsmen or artists (French masons, English joiners, Swiss/Italian plasterers etc) .

GEOGRAPHY AND ECONOMY

The better worked the building, the more expensive and time consuming it was to build. You can determine from such a simple item as the presence of expensively dressed stone, or the use of rare long span timber, the substance of the occupants. Dressed stone implies the cost of a quality stonemason, and long-span timber would generally have had to be imported. Building equals money. Little was wasted. The cast-offs: the chippings, rough material and rejected stone of the hewers as they dressed ashlar would be re-used by the builders as rubble, wall-core filling, pinnings and in, for example, cherry-cocking.

Money derived from agriculture, fish or trade. More elaborate buildings are almost always located either in fertile districts or where a good trade was to be had. The poorer you were, the only choice was to build solely with materials to hand. Imported material (even if only imported from around the coast) was more expensive and patterns of distribution by river, sea or pack horse often explain the presence of materials.

For example, slate was expensive and therefore rare in places where quarries were distant; whereas commonly used near the quarries. Local stone slates were much used in Angus. Even when thatch was used, reasonably widespread in Scotland as much as for substantial homes in towns like Jedburgh or Dunblane as for rural cottages, there were class differences between reed thatch, straw, heather etc. What grew or could be quarried locally, was most used, until transport reduced cost.

Equally, where good building stone was scarce, and good clay present, the structure was adapted, and clay-walled buildings constructed in techniques, later developed for no-fines concrete, as in Erroll, or mixed with boulders, as at Garmouth in Moray. Good clay provided the opportunity, rare in Scotland, for facing brick, as in the Montrose region. Good local clay may also account for the presence of pantiles; and appears to have been widely used as mortar.

Coal was important as a source of income and employment. One reason why old Hamilton Palace had enormous chimneys on the Venetian model was to boast the existence of coal. It paid for much of Scotland's elaborate architecture, and was the cause of much of its disappearance through mining subsidence, eg Hamilton Palace and Balbardie House.

With the arrival of mass communications, first sea, then rail, then road, these traditional patterns became strangely inverted. It may now be cheaper to deploy some pre-packaged building material even if manufactured in Korea; just as it was for Australians to buy prefabricated and crated metal buildings from Scotland in the 19th century.

The continuation of local identity is threatened by the fact that, with current ownership patterns, virtually nothing can be *taken as found*, and therefore without cost. The first issue is the extent to which builder or client could realise their intentions within existing technology and local materials, or whether importation was required.

Scotland saw nothing unusual, save expense, in import (normally afforded for finishing materials such as Memel pine). Scots colonies and trading posts existed throughout the Baltic and there were strong West Coast links with southern France and Spain. The roof timbers of Sir James Hamilton of Finnart's royal palace came from Estonia and the proportions and detail of James VI's chapel at Stirling bear a remarkable similarity to those of the

Figure 2 Urquhart Village, Moray showing typical stone architecture of the countryside circa 1900, slated roofs on the right having replaced traditional thatch still seen on the left.

Figure 3 The Smithy at Greenskares, by Gamrie, Banffshire is typical of much rural architecture as it survived into this century with thatched roof and walls of part stone and part clay, sometimes rendered and whitewashed when funds permitted.

Senate Room in Krakow's Jagellonian University. The old cloistral buildings of King' College, Aberdeen, had onion dorres similar to 16th century Danish Churches, whereas proportion and detail in both Heriot's Hospital, Edinburgh and the 17th century north wing at Linlithgow bear remarkable similarities to the Kronenborg and Frederiksborg Palaces in Denmark. The continent was a major source of timber, horses, guns, inventions, and clothing. Scottish building forms are intelligible only within a northern European context.

Geographical factors bear much more on the poorer end of the scale (for example, the efficient way that black houses of the 18th and 19th centuries tackled wind, weather and insulation) and socio-cultural factors on the wealthier end (11th-century Romanesque, 16th-century chateaux, 18th-century Palladianism and 19th-century eclecticism). That some periods have been much more international than others (13th, 16th and 18th centuries), and others more provincial (15th and late 17th centuries), probably reflects periods of peace and prosperity as opposed to war and poverty.

CLIMATE

Climate imposes upon architecture physically and aesthetically. Scottish winds are ferocious, and exposure to wind driven rain is 300% worse in central Scotland than in Buckinghamshire. Variations of over 100% can exist even between the Firths of Clyde and Tay; and in some parts of Scotland, notably at Carradale, wind-driven rain comes not just horizontally, but upwards. Early constructors would do their best to use landscape forms or trees as shelter for buildings. Although brochs, duns and early castles seemed, perversely, to be perched on the most exposed site, almost certainly coated, outside or in, against the howling wind, they were invariably located for easy access to drinking water.

During the Middle Ages, Scottish country mansions were built up in the form of a tower for reasons of passive defence. During the Renaissance, it remained important to build high, tall and flamboyantly visible for cultural or dynastic reasons, but the Scottish climate demanded a limit to the number of entry points into a building through which the weather could squirrel.

That is the origin of the seemingly defensive appearance of so many Scottish buildings: solid walls with fairly small windows punched through them, although the openings were often splayed for maximum light. To compensate, however, some sported external timber galleries from which to take the air; although long, stone high-windowed galleries soon replaced them. Only in protected town centres with their own microclimates, such as Renaissance Edinburgh or Dundee, could different patterns prevail and risk be taken with large, glorious windows.

Coating of buildings is also a consequence of climate. Thick-walled rubble buildings provided good protection against the weather, particularly where

Figure 4 Fordyce, Banffshire showing the informal harmony of roofscape, landscape and architecture where building has responded to changing requirements over time.

Figure 5 Old Deer, Buchan, where the architecture of several vintages and styles makes up a restrained townscape so typical of rural Scotland positively punctuated by the Improvement Kirk.

337

given a middle lining of earth, clay, sand or whatever, In Ardkinglass, Robert Lorimer used slate. For both aesthetic and for functional reasons, it became customary to coat poorly jointed rubble with a plaster or rough harling coat, or limewash, in a different colour, over the dressed stone. These coatings prevented the joints being scoured out by the weather, and concealed from view the fact that some lairds were not sufficiently wealthy to afford a complete facade of dressed stone. It was also a matter of fashion. Wealthy aristocrats, who could afford whatever ashlar they wished, used harled rubble by preference up to the late 17th century, particularly for the lower storeys or plinth. The colour of the harl was a matter of choice. Pigments could be bought from the continent in any one of eight primary colours and then mixed; although the natural coloration in the local sand was probably as much the preferred colour as imported pigment. The resulting contrasts formed a key feature of native Scottish architecture.

Another consequence of climate was the 16th/17th-century fashion for tall, steep-pitched roofs, which became shallower as time passed. It is still possible to gauge the date of a building from the pitch of its roof.

GEOLOGY

Scotland is a stone country, and its architecture is the product of innumerable quarries which worked many stones in many different ways. Since the early Middle Ages, preponderantly it has lacked long-span timber for building (much burnt for charcoal). Apart from the localised exceptions of buildings near woods, such as Forests of Drum, Abernethy and Cadzow, the structure of Scottish building until the mid 18th century remained, generally, that of the stone vault. That also governed their width, and explains the particular development of building plan which took the form of adding wings as self-contained structures to a central lodging.

Possibly uniquely in Europe, Scotland had no significant tradition of framed structures outside the few forest areas until the mid 19th century. The walls were the structure: and Scottish architecture grew out of the structure itself, rather than something superimposed upon it. Once (iron) framing arrived in the 19th century, a debate arose over whether structure was the servant of architecture, or whether architecture was merely decorated structure. There were many who came to believe that the erection of a simple frame was architecture in itself provided it was done with sufficient delicacy.

RELIGION AND POLITICS

It is through architecture that, in contrast to the history we were taught, we discover that Catholicism, with its particular liturgical requirement, was never extinguished in Scotland, but lingered in Moray. Episcopalianism, with

Figure 6 The Gartur Stables, Stirlingshire, is typical of the Palladian design approach to Improvement farm steadings at the turn of the 18th and 19th centuries.

Figure 7 Lodge and Gates at Keir House, Stirlingshire, shows the fondness for a classical theme when the money was available, circa 1820.

its different liturgical requirement, persisted steadfastly in North-East Scotland, until it became respectable and came out in the 19th century. It is through architecture that we can perceive the difference between the non-hierarchical Celtic society, and the hierarchical Lowland society. Lowland castles generally followed the pattern set by the Normans with a hierarchy of gatehouse, hall and principal tower; whereas in the *gaeltachd*, castles take the form of a simple stone curtain-walled enclosure, with buildings placed evenly on the inside.

CHANGING SOCIAL PATTERNS

Architecture provides a wonderful lexicon of how social patterns have evolved in Scotland under the following influences:

a) The change from a vertical living form (the tower) into a horizontal living form (the chateau), in which one room opens into another in an increasing procession of privacy, begun in the early 16th century. Multi-function rooms, like the medieval hall, began to be superseded by a sequence of chambers with a unitary function.

b) Only once great wealth was present, predominantly in the 19th century, did Scots destroy the past, and rebuild. It had been much more customary to add, adapt, reface and extend. By studying the stonework of buildings in places as diverse as Dunfermline to St Combs, you can trace how the original large bouldered cottage went gradually upmarket as the finances of the owners permitted. It was a display of economic escalation. In sequence of the centuries, that cottage would gain a dressed stone pediment, new windows, an attic storey, a full second storey, then a complete refronting in ashlar, a rear wing and perhaps a porch. Of course, to extend upwards was the principal means of increasing accommodation without increasing floor area. Many a seemingly 18th century building in central St Andrews, both large and small, is a refronted medieval structure. Dating buildings of such mixed parentage used to be problematic. It is now possible to deduce the history of a building by examining the thickness of its walls.

c) The agricultural improvements of the late 18th century led to population increase as agriculture was able to sustain a larger population. That led to two principal building types: the new Improvement kirk, and the Improvement farmhouse. The former was built on to or replaced a medieval kirk and was usually identified as a God box with large round-headed windows. A distinguishing characteristic is the span of its roof,

Figure 8 Mill workers' cottages at Deanston Mill, Perthshire.

Figure 9 Tenement housing in Park Circus, Glasgow.

up to three times that of its predecessors, and three times or maybe more higher. It was this factor that permitted much larger kirks, which catered not only for the rising rural population, but for the amalgamation of parishes (and consequent saving in Ministers' stipends).

The Improvement farmhouse was generally three bays, two storeys, varying seemingly only in the elaboration around the doorway. Whereas wealthier farmhouses might have a basement, be two rooms deep, with a pavilion roof, simple versions, one room deep, might not even be able to afford adequate dressed stone for margins, angles and doors. Improvement farmhouses also vary substantially in projecting wings, adjacent courtyards or steadings.

d) Rural wealth paid for new settlements, particularly in the North East, village improvement, turnpike roads through the countryside, and new farm steadings. Financed as a result of the 1792 Montgomery Act, the improved estates transformed the landscape with new or refronted mansions, formal planted approach routes, contrived vistas, monuments, temples and statues, and carefully deployed lodges, gates, farm cottages, imposing steadings, grandiose stables, exhibition home farms, dairies, bridges and shelter belts of trees.

e) There were two concomitants of this massive change in Scottish society 1780– 1820. The first was enclosure of previously open ground, as lairds sought to maximise their return. The second was sufficient money to finance the great age of Scottish urbanism, the building of splendid New Towns adjacent to Ayr, Perth, Aberdeen, Glasgow and Edinburgh, adding classical new schools and academies to even the smallest of communities. Although, (save in Edinburgh) Scots cities were razed and utterly rebuilt, the ancient town plan and plot size (that of the rig) proved remarkably resilient. It is recognisable in Dundee, Glasgow, and Aberdeen. Rural enclosure, however, led to the abandonment of the rural rig pattern, and the start of the decline in the thirlage to local materials and techniques had begun.

f) It was about this time that many of the Renaissance chateaux, that had remained as the homes of minor lairds or their factors, tacksmen or chief tenants, were finally abandoned for more modern houses; ending a process that had begun with the forfeitures after 1715, and accelerated by those after 1745.

g) The arrival of the railway from about 1840, offered rural industries access to markets eg the Moray whisky industry, previously with no market. Remote areas could now buy fashionable building materials and household goods relatively cheaply. The Highlands became easily accessible by rail for all new forms of tourism. The Great Exhibition of 1851, and the subsequent Scottish Exhibitions, ensured that knowledge of new products (and the desire to possess them) left few parts of Scotland unscathed, now that access had been made easier.

SUMMARY

Artisan architecture, at the *popular* end of the scale, is Scots because, like language and music, it embodies and expresses genuine Scottish culture and character, forged from a combination of genetic factors, foreign influence, historical memory and environment. As you might expect, eighteenth century burgh architecture of important burghs like Wick, Inveraray and Haddington blends national characteristics with distinct regional ones in even measure, whereas local features predominate in the vernacular houses of Orkney, Angus or Tiree.

So, through architecture we can sense the ebb and flow of the economy, the influx of foreign influence, and the changing patterns of lifestyle as one form dies and gives way to the next. Differing as it does from region to region, district to district, it provides an exact record of man's occupation of the land and expression of culture through building.

Our only problem is how to interpret it. For too long, we have ignored the evidence, and have tried to fit the economic and social history of the country to patterns imposed from the outside. Since what you see often offers a distorted perception of what was really built, an understanding of how buildings have changed over time is necessary for a full understanding. Architecture is a fundamental corrective to mythology and ignorance, but only if you can read it correctly.

The Author

Charles McKean is Secretary and Treasurer, of the Royal Incorporation of Architects in Scotland. A prolific author, he is founder and series editor of the popular RIAS/Landmark Trust illustrated architectural guides to Scotland, several written by him. He has contributed chapters to Glasgow– the Making of a City, The Scottish Country House and the forthcoming volume about Alexander 'Greek' Thomson. Other works include The Scottish Thirties (1987), Architectural Contributions to Scottish Society since 1840 (1990) and Edinburgh: Portrait of a City (1991). Grateful thanks for helpful advice is extended to Ingval Maxwell, David Walker, and James Simpson.

References

Buxbaum, T., *Scottish Garden Buildings*, Mainstream 1989

Dunbar, J., *The Historic Architecture of Scotland*, Batsford 1966

Fenton, A. and Walker, B., *The Rural Architecture of Scotland*, John Donald 1981

Fladmark, J. M., Mulvagh, G. Y. and Evans, B. M., *Tomorrow's Architectural Heritage*, Mainstream 1991

Gifford, J., *William Adam 1689 – 1748*, Mainstream 1989

Howard, D. (Ed), *The Architecture of the Scottish Renaissance*, RIAS 1990

McKean, C., *The Scottish Thirties*, Scottish Academic Press 1987

McWilliam, C., *Scottish Townscape*, Collins 1975

Petzsch, H., *Architecture in Scotland*, Longman 1971

RIAS/Landmark Trust illustrated architectural guides to Scotland:
Brogden, W., A. *Aberdeen*, Beaton, E., *Ross and Cromarty*, Close, R., *Ayrshire*, McKean, C., *Banff & Buchan*, McKean, C., *Edinburgh*, McKean, C., *Moray*, McKean, C., *Stirling & The Trossachs*, McKean, C., and Walker, D., *Dundee*, McKean, Walker and Walker, *Central Glasgow*, Pride, G., *Fife*, Sinclair, F. and Walker, F., *North Clyde Estuary*, Swan, A., *Clackmannan*, Walker, F. A., *South Clyde Estuary*

Robertson, P. (Ed), *Charles Rennie Mackintosh: The Mackintosh Papers*, MIT Press 1990

Sinclair, F. (Ed), *Scotstyle: 150 Years of Scottish Architecture*, RIAS, 1984

Figure 10 Gamrie, Banffshire, as it looked in 1890 with the gable ends stepped into the hillside facing the sea, the sheltered stepped passage for access being a typical response to a severe climate. Note the use of stones from the beach laid as paving to form an artful pattern.

28

IMAGINATION IN ARCHITECTURE
Art and Technology in the Context of Place

Robin Webster

> Engineering, medicine, business, architecture and painting
> are concerned not with the necessary but with the contingent
> – not with how things are but how they might be
> – in short, with design.
>
> *Herbert Simon*

The nature of architectural forms speak for any culture. Wherever we go throughout the world, the form of buildings old and new are a significant indicator of a country's past and present ambitions. The question that must engage architects and society in Scotland today is what should generate architectural form here, at the end of the twentieth century?

Architectural students, encouraged by critics and journalists, search for new architectural forms from all quarters of the globe, and international 'designer' architects like Frank Gehry or Zaha Hadid are creating buildings in different cities throughout the world which owe more to their own personal artistic development than to any geographical imperative. I would prefer to leave it to others to define exactly what it means to be a Scot today in our society of plural values, where we are all part of the global village, but it is true that all who live here have a shared experience of our particular environment and of our particular architecture. I believe that we can accept therefore that there may be some shared cultural requirements and expectations of architecture.

The notion of the architect as a 'universal man' is not currently fashionable, but it is vital that architects and their buildings should not only address a specialised minority. In the past, the Age of Enlightenment represented a convergence of ideas and interests in all the arts and sciences. However, the arrival of specialist professionals over the last 150 years has largely destroyed this spirit of convergence, but architecture is an area where such interdisciplinary convergence might still happen. It is clear that our society must have an architecture which addresses its needs, and that architectural form must evolve through an increased understanding of these needs and a continually developing technology which allows us to meet them more fully, possibly to an extent undreamt of before. This evolution of architectural form is generated by a reiterative process in which engineering, business and social concerns are critically brought to bear on forms which are created and generated by the artist/architect.

If there is no creative leap in making the new form, then there is no evolution. If there is no critical analysis relating the form to its use, then the form can not be more than a tomb or a monument, and can have no more significance to society as a whole than a folly. Our heritage of past architectural form is a legitimate starting point for the new, and the study of any of our great Scottish architects such as Mackintosh, Thomson, or Lorimer will show this. It is, however, the point of departure only, and our admiration for past success should not stifle our need to develop an architecture of our own time, as all of these architects did. It is in the nature of a healthy society that it can embrace and deal with new opportunities in ways not tried before. Everyone in society may be legitimately engaged in the speculation of how things might be better in the future, and this speculation should not be unduly fettered.

NAIVE FUNCTIONALISM

The functionalist tradition in architectural design, promoted in the 19th century as *Form follows function* by Louis Sullivan and others, taken up by the Werkbund in Germany, and adopted as orthodoxy by CIAM in the 1920s, appears to relegate art to a secondary role in the generation of architectural form. The grain stores and ocean liners which are eulogised in Le Corbusier's polemic *Vers une architecture* of 1919 owe nothing to art or artistic theories, but are the product of engineers dealing with the forces of physical loads, which determine its form. This functionalist and 'unconscious' design tradition may not account for all legitimate architectural form, but it is a powerful and significant generator of forms which in time become accepted as culturally important.

An example of this in Scotland is the vernacular black house, *tigh dubh*, of the Western Isles, where the nature of the materials to hand, stones, turf, heather, grass, and a very limited amount of timber, shaped the form of the buildings, together with the extreme demands of the climate and the available skills and traditions of a people constrained by the seasonal requirements of subsistence farming and fishing. Aesthetic theories did not feature strongly in the design of these buildings, but they are extremely sophisticated in technical detail, which is the result of a gradual evolution, and the buildings which quite recently used to be described as hovels, are now seen to be charming. They have the compactness of an egg, and the snugness of a tea cosy, are greatly enjoyed as holiday cottages, and appear on postcards and dishtowels as illustrations of our cultural heritage.

There are many examples of engineering structures in Scotland which have transcended their original utilitarian purpose and have become culturally significant, or at least perceived as attractive by the population at large, and not just by architects and engineers. The Forth Railway Bridge is a good example, which is a design generated by a structural idea about balanced cantilevers and the process of construction. It now has a cultural significance for Scotland similar to that of the Eiffel Tower in Paris (Barthes), which reaches far beyond its original function of spanning the Forth.

It is interesting to note that eminent architectural critics of the day, such as John Ruskin, refused to accept Paxton's Crystal Palace as being architecture: its form was seen as being purely utilitarian, and architecture was an art and seen as being something different. Paxton's design offered a brilliant technical solution to the need for large spans and maximum daylight penetration. It might have appealed to a champion of gothic architecture like Ruskin, one would have thought, had he not been so concerned for the individual contribution of craftsmen, although why the hard physical labour of the stonemason should be seen as being preferable to the skills of the steelworker is unclear.

The technology and environmental qualities of the Crystal Palace led to the development of a new railway architecture, Captain Fowler's Main Hall at the Royal Scottish Museum, and John Kibble's Palace at the Botanic Gardens in Glasgow, to name a couple of much loved buildings whose form was similarly generated by the technical solution to the need for large spans and natural daylight. Today we have comparable instances of engineers creating unprecedented forms: Sir Norman Foster greatly admires the jumbo jet, an exceptionally beautiful design like many aircraft, which has arisen not as a complete and intact conception from an artistic genius, but has evolved from an original idea that has been tested and refined by the painstaking calculations of many nameless aeronautical engineers. It could be said to meet many of the requirements of architecture, such as firmness, commodity and delight, in addition to being able to fly across the Atlantic.

Other architects like Nicholas Grimshaw, Richard Horden, and Jan Kaplicky have lifted some of this engineering technology and incorporated it into their buildings, which do not fly of course, but may raise issues regarding the relationship between their form and their use, as well as their compatibility with their surroundings. This superficial technology transfer seems to me to be highly suspect, and I would not classify such buildings as properly belonging to the functionalist tradition.

Important developments in architectural form should surely come from an evolution of building technique and performance expectations. Since Darwin, it has become more and more difficult to accept the generation of form as a wilful and God-like act. Our understanding and analysis of the underlying reasons for form in nature, as described by D'Arcy Thompson, F. Stevens and others more recently, together with the discovery of the significance of the gene and its capability for the generation of form, as described by Richard Dawkins, have reinforced this. If we wish that a form should have any validity and significance beyond itself, it has to be seen as the result of an evolution, where conflicting needs and requirements are resolved. Otherwise, the form is no more than a folly. It would seem that the personal signature of an individual designer on a building is now as inappropriate and unhelpful as attributing the form of a leaf to the finger of God.

If we consider the performance of a mammal's skin, in particular the human skin, we can observe that it consists of a highly sophisticated technology which achieves a robust interface between the external environment and the internal requirements of the human body. This skin has an enormous range of qualities: it is wind and waterproof, yet porous, it is pressure sensitive, thermally self regulating, will transmit messages by changes of colour, texture and smell, and is self healing. If we consider the skin of a building, and compare its qualities, we can see immediately that it is relatively inert, and that its evolution has a very long way to go before it begins to approach such sophistication.

We do not even understand fully how this inert skin functions. Douglas Cawthorne is carrying out SERC funded research at the moment, at The Robert Gordon University School of Architecture in Aberdeen, into the porosity and permeability of different forms of wall construction, as our knowledge and understanding of this is limited and superficial. This research was prompted by the interest generated by the so-called 'breathing wall' in the traditional construction of rural Norwegian buildings. The way in which a building skin might be expected to perform if the human skin was taken as a paradigm would have enormous implications on the quality, operation and maintenance of the internal environment, and on the potential quality of life for the building's occupants.

Examples of buildings with responsive skins do in fact already exist, for example the Hooker building at Niagara in Canada, or the solar dairy near Oslo in Norway. The need for passive environmental control, which avoids the huge energy costs of heating and cooling buildings, and the subsequent overproduction of CO_2, means that various forms of responsive skins will become increasingly common, and more and more sophisticated. If full advantage is to be taken of solar radiation when it is available here in Scotland, the emissivity of the buildings surfaces will have to change according to the weather, and so will the appearance, varying according to the season and the time of day. Technical advances in glazing, where excellent insulation values are now possible, and where the level of transparency can be controlled at will, suggest that the concept of something called a window may be anachronistic in certain circumstances. Consequently, the idea that an architectural composition of an elevation reflects the permanent positioning and ordering of solids and voids may no longer be tenable as the only scenario available when designing this sort of environmentally responsive building.

Reaction to such a building form may be that it is inappropriate to our existing environment, but when we obstruct the introduction of something unfamiliar but which is genuinely based on performance advantages, we are in danger of emulating those who decreed that motor vehicles be preceded by a man with a flag. We may be forced to reinterpret our understanding of the nature of architecture, and the functional tradition which I have been discussing would define the meaning and significance of architectural form as relating to its use.

IMAGINATION AS GENERATOR

Naive functionalism, (which is a term used by Aldo Rossi to describe the Cartesian approach to design such as that popularised by Hannes Meyer at the Bauhaus) does not result in architecture on its own, unless the original formal proposal (which is generated by the architect to be tested against the functional requirements) is inspired in some way, and evolved by an element of visual play or game. This is where the creative and artistic imagination is essential, as suggested by Wilson:

> The design process is not simply the clapping of solution on to problem, like a snuffer on a candle, but is the interaction of two agents in a reiterative process of discovery. This exchange of energies has no parallel in any other art, and it is the reason why there can be no such thing as 'autonomous architecture'. Unless it be born out of this dialogue (between the appetite and its satisfaction) no work can ever achieve the status of architecture: it can only be a folly.

If we accept Aristotle's and St Thomas Aquinas's definition of art as being 'The right way of going about things ', it is clear that the necessary dialogue that Wilson refers to is what he believes to be the right way of going about architectural design, and therefore qualifies as an art. Wilson gives examples of the 'exchange of energies' in the form of sketches by Alvar Aalto for his library at Viipuri, which illustrate the way in which different forms were played with in relation to the functional need for a high standard of daylight for the library users. Other examples of this process are developmental sketches of the central rotunda for the Stadtsgallerie at Stuttgart by James Stirling where the original imaginative leap is being explored and tested in a fertile manner.

Louis Kahn's search for 'What the building wants to be' led him to create deliberately vague fuzzy but formally suggestive drawings, which helped him to make the synthesising leap which resolved the differing functional requirements. This need for imprecision at an early stage in a design is important if the opportunity for making creative moves is not to be stifled. This has been picked up by researchers at the Martin Centre at Cambridge, led by Paul Richens, who have discovered that the precision of computer

349

aided drawings is extremely inhibiting at an early stage of design. They have developed a number of methods to combat this, starting with the 'wobbly pen' plotter, where a loosely held pen in the machine produces slightly wrinkled lines, and the drawings contain sufficient ambiguity to allow different options in interpretation, preventing an enquiry to be closed down too fast. Some of these drawings and other techniques are indistinguishable from hand drawn sketches, while others offer rather different approaches to the suggestion of form, which may stretch the imagination in unexpected ways.

Other approaches to stimulate the imagination in architectural composition are to incorporate a familiar existing form at an unexpected scale in a drawing or model, and then to test it against its functional requirements, making positive use of our capacity for *post hoc* rationalisation. The sculptor Claes Oldenberg has probably gone furthest in this area, and has collaborated with Frank Gehry in various proposals for a grand piano lid as an office block at the Arsenale in Venice, a coiled snake as a fire station, a giant fish as a restaurant, and having actually completed an enormous pair of binoculars as an entrance foyer to an office block in Venice California. While Gehry and Oldenberg wish to retain the identity of the object in the final design, other architects may commonly use an assortment of found objects in a model or montage, which may help a speedy consideration of different strategies, but where the original identity of the objects is finally lost in more conventional architectural forms.

We have been running a small experiment at The Robert Gordon University School of Architecture for the past six years, where we invite talented designers to design a small building for us in half an hour. We give them an outline brief of the accommodation required, and show them the site, and then we record them designing by video. We record what they say and what they draw. We call the programme *The Sweatbox*, as it can be pretty intensive. What is clear in every case, is that the process involves the generation of forms and a running commentary of rationalising explanation. Time is short and a form of improvisation may ensue, rather like a jazz musician, where possible new interpretations of forms may be generated by the dialogue, or new ways of thinking about certain prescribed functions may be spontaneously suggested by the nature of the forms. Neither the form nor the rational dialogue can be categorically stated to come first: they are mutually interdependent.

The principles of the Werkbund, which I believe many architects would still subscribe to, suggests a much more linear approach to the generation of form. According to Mies van der Rohe:

> Form as an end in itself inevitably results in mere formalism. This effort is directed only to the exterior. But only what has life on the inside has a living exterior... The un-formed is no worse than the over-formed. The former is nothing; the latter is mere appearance. Real form presupposes real life... This is our criterion: we should judge not so much by the results

350

as by the creative process. For it is just this that reveals whether the form is derived from life or invented for its own sake...

I understand this to mean that imaginative invention has no place in the process of architectural design, even as a stimulus to get the juices going, and very regretfully I have to part company with Mies on this point. Of course I agree that forms have to be subjected to rational analysis, and I have made clear my respect for the functional tradition, but I hope that it is also clear from the illustrations above that I do not think that rational analysis on its own can ever be the whole story in the initial generation of architectural ideas.

Four out of the six architectural schools in Scotland are closely related to art schools, in contrast to England, where this is the exception. One might expect this to lead to a different approach by Scottish students, but I can not say that I have detected this. It may even operate against creativity, where the architectural students perceive themselves as being more 'responsible' and professionally orientated than the art students, and are thus more inclined to employ Cartesian approaches to design in deliberate contrast to the more liberal and open approach of the art students. If this is the case, it is most unsatisfactory, and we wish to work more closely with sculptors in particular, as we find that many of them are able to generate three dimensional ideas and manipulate them in a way which would be of huge advantage to our students, an approach much favoured by Ralph Erskine in Sweden. We have recently validated a new course in Interior Architecture which we hope will give the opportunity for both schools to work together in generating designs for the immediate interface between the building user and the environment, and by working sometimes at full scale, placing the architectural student directly alongside the sculptor.

THREE EXAMPLES

I wish to clarify the points I have made by reference to three buildings in Scotland, two of which have been recently completed and the third is still to be built. The first is the pair of residential towers designed by Jeremy Dixon and Edward Jones for The Robert Gordon University at Garthdee in Aberdeen, the second is the conversion of the Fruitmarket Gallery in Edinburgh by Richard Murphy, and the third is the design for a proposed house in the outskirts of Aberdeen by myself.

The development of the form of the two towers at Garthdee exhibits the use of play in architectural design particularly well. The general site strategy was established at an early stage: the architects proposed two alternatives, a low courtyard building dug into the slope, or a couple of towers along the edge of the escarpment which drops steeply southwards to the River Dee. The latter strategy was preferred, in recognition of the nature and quality of the existing landscape, which suggested that the spaces between the

351

buildings should be left intact. The architects already had photographs of tower houses which might be an appropriate departure point for the designs, as well as illustrations of a recent building at Princeton University, which suggested a more contemporary language for the building skin. Time was short, and the planning application drawings were prepared when the internal arrangements of the buildings were defined, but the final forms of the roofs remained to be completed.

The subsequent development of these forms can be seen in the sketches by David Naessens, who was largely responsible for this stage of the design, and they indicate pretty well the playful but serious manipulation of the volumes to meet the functional requirements of the building plan, and the alternatives that were explored to meet the need to achieve a tower like appearance from the North, where the square tower is actually quite a squat building. This process seems to me to illustrate the need for an artist in the architect, and this modelling, cutting and shaping the tower can not be far from the activities and sensitivities which one might normally associate with a sculptor. The difference between the initial drawings and the final version is quite startling, where the early drawing now looks feeble in comparison.

The second building shows how Richard Murphy exploited the geometry of the new roof at the Fruitmarket gallery, where an orthogonal layout made constructional sense, and sets this against the geometry of the original masonry walls, which follow the line of the street. This elegant solution which helps to clarify what is old and what is new was only arrived at after a considerable amount of three dimensional studies of the building, and examination of alternatives. Murphy is a leading authority on Carlo Scarpa and his buildings, and the way in which he has opened up the original masonry box with neat incisions, where views can be directed towards the significant surrounding Edinburgh buildings, demonstrates a deep understanding of the Italian master's work. This is a building which may take the past as its point of departure, but is clearly looking to the future.

The third building is my own proposal for a house to be located on a very narrow strip of land which slopes steeply down to the flood plain of the river Dee. It combines two themes of place and technology. The idea of the long continuous staircase is to ensure that the nature of the landscape is felt throughout the design, and in this I know that I am indebted to some designs by Luigi Snozzi in Ticino, although I could not point to any one building in particular. It also refers to the long narrow passages that one finds running down from the High street in Edinburgh, and also in Aberdeen. The house also has evolved from my steel framed house which I built in London in 1980, where we had a large flat glazed roof through which you could look at the stars. Both Robin Spence and Michael Wigginton, who teach at the school with me, are also developing glass houses, and I have referred above to some of the exciting possibilities which are offered by new developments in glazing technology and insulating louvres. This design responds to what exists: a granite wall and a landscape, but I hope it also points clearly to 'what might be' in the future.

The Author and Acknowledgements

Professor Robin Webster is head of The Robert Gordon University Scott Sutherland School of Architecture, and a member of the Royal Fine Art Commission for Scotland. A winner of two international design competitions with wide experience in private practice, he has lectured at several other UK schools of architecture and in USA. The Author is grateful to the Editor for finding time to give helpful advice and make constructive suggestions in the course of writing this paper.

References

Barthes, R., *The Eiffel Tower*, Hill & Wang, 1979

Celant, G., *A Bottle of Notes and Some Journeys: Claes Oldenburg/Coosje van Bruggen*, Northern Centre for Contemporary Art and The Henry Moore Centre for the Study of Sculpture, 1988

Clark, K., *Ruskin Today*, Harmondsworth, 1967

Le Corbusier, *Toward a New Architecture*, Butterworth, 1989

Dawkins, R., *The Blind Watchmaker*, Longman, 1986

Johnson, P., *Mies van der Rohe*, Secker and Warburg, 1978, who quotes Mies's letter to Dr Reizler, which was published in *Die Form*, 1927, under the title *Rundschau: zum neuen jahrgang (an Dr Reizler)*

Knight, R.P., *An Analytical Inquiry into the Principles of Taste* First ed, 1805, who makes reference to Aristotelian philosophical Scholasticism applied to the analysis of Gothic Architecture), Facs repr, 1972)

Loos, A., *Ornament is Crime* XXX

March, L. and Steadman, P., *The Geometry of the Environment*, Harvester Wheatsheaf, 1981

Martin, J., *Art and Scholasticism*, Sheed and Ward, 1947, who quote definition of Art by St Thomas Aquinas

Nakamura, T., *Louis I. Khan: Conception and Meaning*, A & U Publishing, 1983

Simon, H.A., *Sciences of the Artificial*, Massachusetts Institute of Technology, 1981

St John Wilson, C., *Architectural Reflections*, Butterworth, 1992

Thompson, D'A., *On Growth and Form*, Cambridge University Press edition, 1961

Watkin, D., *Morality and Architecture*, Clarendon Press, 1977, who quotes Adolf Loos: 'The lower the standard of a people, the more lavish are its ornaments.'

Figure 1 Proposed house at Cults by Robin Webster.

29

THE SCOTS LANGUAGE
European Roots and Local Destiny

Sheila Douglas

In the North of Europe there is a family of languages all of which bear certain resemblances to one another. They have been subject to each other's influences, as well as those of other languages and they are all consequently of a mixed character, as many languages are. These are the Germanic languages, which in turn are only one of the groups of languages that form the Indo-European language map. English and Scots are two of these Germanic languages, as are, for example, German and Dutch, Norwegian and Danish. No one argues against the separate existence of any of these languages, except for Scots.

What are the grounds for this argument? The most common one is that Scots is just a dialect of English. To anyone who knows anything at all about Scots, or about language in general, this is manifestly absurd. First of all, Scots is not one dialect, but several. Put a man from Wick, another from Aberdeen, a third from Perth, in a room with a Fifer, a Glaswegian and a Borderer, and see if they all speak the same dialect. They are just as distinct from one another as a Scouse, a Cockney, a Geordie, a man from Avon, Dorset or Devon would be. Yet, Scots is the name applied to the way people speak everywhere north of the Tweed, which would seem in itself an admission that this is a separate language. Certainly it has all the characteristics of one: it has a variety of forms, it has a long history and it has a literature. In fact this important difference between all the English dialects and Scots, is pointed out in the introduction to the Concise Scots Dictionary: 'in England the only dialect which can match Scots in possessing its own separate and well-documented history is Standard English itself. And only England as a whole can compare with Lowland Scotland for dialect variety.' The Dictionary recognises no fewer than 42 dialect areas in Scotland and Ulster, where Scots is also spoken.

Certainly it was not until the 15th century that the term Scottis was used for the language by Gavin Douglas and by that he meant the literary Scots he helped to forge out of the spoken language of the majority of the population, along with the other Mediaeval Makars, who, like Geoffrey Chaucer in England, raised the status of the language they spoke to the position hitherto occupied by Latin. It had of course existed along with Norman French for some time, until the barons gave it up in favour of what had become the majority language. In calling it Scottis, Gavin Douglas was appropriating a term that earlier had been used for the Gaelic of Scotland and Ireland. In an age of growing nationalism and the feeling of being one nation, however diverse within itself, one can see why Gavin Douglas chose to call his language by a name that the whole country had come to apply to itself. He obviously felt it was different from the language spoken over the Border in the country from which Scots under Bruce and Wallace had fought to free themselves two centuries earlier.

In fact, the Lowland tongue had been called Inglis and was derived from the Northumbrian dialect of the Anglo-Saxons heavily influenced by the Norse of the Vikings. In Scottis that influence was retained and can be demonstrated to this day, while in England it existed only in the North and did not last to the same extent. This Norse-influenced Inglis formed the basis of the language later to become known as Scots. But, as languages always do, in different places, it developed in a different way, was subject to different influences and was used to create a quite distinctive literature. For example, there was a strong Gaelic influence on Scots vocabulary which English did not receive. To be a separate language, related to English, as well as to Danish and German, makes Scots no different from other Germanic languages.

Of course nowadays there is no Standard Scots, in the same way as there is Standard English; there is no standard Scots spelling, just a series of allowable alternatives, based on dialectal variation. Efforts to recreate a literary Scots have not met with conspicuous success; the Lallans devised by writers of the 20th century Renaissance, some of them great poets, all too often seems artificial and full of affectation to most Scots readers. It suffers from what I like to call the *ettle to jalouse* syndrome; that is the determination to use old Scots words at all costs, whether they sound natural or effective or not.

However, this may just be a characteristic of an early stage of development. For one thing is sure: you can not create a literary language in a short space of time, any more than you can bring a standard language into being by passing a law. It has to evolve and it may well be doing so, in spite of the drawbacks noted. If Scots were to be used by the media, not all the time, but regularly, as a normal practice; if schools and colleges were to treat Scots as an acceptable form of expression; if people in everyday life were to feel able to express themselves in Scots without feeling ashamed of it for any reason, then we might see the emergence of a Standard Scots. The fact that it does not exist at the moment is not an argument against bringing it about.

There is also the equally mistaken theory that Scots is a *corrupted* form of English. This word carries with it a suggestion of inferiority, that can not quite be reconciled with the fact that our so called corrupted language has from very early times produced a literature of the very highest quality, from the Mediaeval Makars to Hugh McDiarmid and beyond. The people who hold this viewpoint can never explain how the language came to be corrupted or even what exactly they mean by the word and why that makes it inferior. In linguistic terms of course it is meaningless; but of course linguistic terms are not what these critics have in mind. What they are expressing are social and political prejudices that come from their blinkered view of their country in its European context. It is noteworthy that those who claim Scots is just a form of English are often the same people who say they can not understand anyone who speaks Scots, even if it is only Scots-accented English. If it isn't all that different, why is it so hard to understand? If they can not understand it, perhaps it is because it has, for example, so many words in it still shared with Danish. I shall return to this point in due course.

First, I want to denounce the poisonous racism inherent in the system by which generations of Scots have been taught to reject their own language. 'Speak properly,' has long meant for Scottish school-children, 'Speak English'. This is a monstrous piece of the linguistic equivalent of ethnic cleansing and something I am glad to report our Universities and schools are beginning to banish from their curricula. To speak of the two I know about (there may be others) Professor Graham Caie of Glasgow University, who significantly has experience of living and working in Denmark, devotes a considerable amount of time to teaching Scots, as does Professor Charles Jones of Edinburgh University, which means we are likely to get more language teachers in our schools who know something about Scots.

The Scots which students in these two Universities bring with them is accepted and studied, instead of being regarded as something to be eliminated. But as I know from experience, those teachers who at present try to teach Scots language and literature in our schools are still up against barriers of prejudice and ignorance among teachers and parents. Often the work with pupils is made more difficult by the influence of the home, as well as the ethos of the school, which are resolutely opposed to Scots. During my teaching career, I had to disabuse quite a lot of my pupils of the idea that Scots is some kind of slang, and I experienced more than once the use of Scots intended as a form of insolence. These were quite easy things to deal with. One can easily explain the difference between slang and dialect, show the long history of the usage of Scots in literature and defuse attempts at making speaking Scots a way of giving cheek by switching the conversation into Scots.

But to get people to understand that Scots is a living language, to be proud of, one has to try to help them to grasp the nature of language itself, which is not so easy to do. Present day Scots is often described as *eroded* or *diluted*, as if there were something unnatural about this. But it is part of a natural process, akin to that which affects the landscape. To say Scots is different from what it was one or two hundred years ago is of course true: a living language does not stay the same; it changes constantly, and you can not put the clock back or stop it. All languages evolve, losing words that are no longer needed and acquiring words for new ideas, inventions or purposes.

On the other hand, it is true that Scots has suffered heavy blows to its development, from the publication of the Authorised Version of the Bible in English, to the moving of the royal court to London in 1603, to the Union of the Parliaments in 1707, since when Scots has been actively discouraged for political and social reasons, since it is no longer the language of law and government or of the more pretentious sections of society. The trouble is that the establishment has tried to disguise these political and social reasons as educational and linguistic ones.

Scots have been given the impression by their teachers that there is something inherently wrong or inferior about their *mither tongue*, and consequently it has had to be confined to the playground, the pub and the tartan variety show, the back lanes of Scottish life, rather than the main street. Fortunately, this has not been fatal to it, but it did upset the continuity of our cultural development until someone like MacDiarmid came along to raise it to the heights once more. In the meantime, Scots have had to become bilingual, which is not in itself either unusual or disadvantageous. The trouble is that Scots have also lost a sense of identity and the confidence that goes with it: that is what has been taken from us by the pernicious system that seeks to trample on the Scots language.

In the political situation we are in today, with the majority of Scots virtually disenfranchised by a bankrupt system based on a Union foisted on our people in the most undemocratic fashion possible, a fact that not enough Scots are aware of, drastic action is called for not only in constitutional change, but in education and in every branch of Scottish culture. The modest changes taking place in education as regards language, literature and history have to be stepped up. It is not good enough for anything Scottish to be just an option that pupils or teachers can choose if they like or if they have time.

In what other country of Europe would you find such a state of affairs? It is all the more tragic when we have had such a wonderful literature, that it should be so neglected. Look through the bookstores of Scottish schools and see how much Scots literature, prose or poetry you will find among the English authors. The fact that we have had this century a poetic renaissance of world-shattering proportions seems to have passed the majority of our population by. Most of us have been brought up to write off our own language, our literature and our history as so much lumber from the past, something to be discarded as of no value, only of interest to antiquarians and nutty folklorists. Scots language in particular is to be avoided at all costs.

Do other Europeans think like this? Certainly not in Denmark or Germany. In Switzerland, which has four languages, it's quite normal for people to speak at least two of them, as well as English, for their vital tourist trade. In

Scotland, which was a European country on good terms with countries like France, Spain and Holland, when England was fighting them, we must stop thinking as if we were under colonial rule and start living in a way more in keeping with our European roots.

To return to the link I referred to between Danish and Scots, it might well open a few eyes if I were to give some illustration of the extent to which these two languages share a vocabulary. I am not a linguistic expert and anyway to go into deep academic waters into which many people reading this would be unable to follow would serve no purpose. But I would ask for the following sample to be considered as proof of the fact that Scots is not merely some variation of English or any kind of aberration by a whole population over a period of centuries. It is a language with European roots and connections. The words in this list are pronounced the exactly same or almost exactly the same in Danish as in Scots and of course have the same meaning:

Scots	Danish	Scots	Danish
alane	alene	kirk	kirke
bairn	barn	lang	lang
bane	ben	ligg	ligge
blae	bleg	lirk	lirke
blad	blad	lowe	lue
brent	braende	mair	mer
claith	klaide	moose	mus
clart	klatte	oot	ud
coo	ko	reek	røg
cruik	krykke	rowan	røn
cruisie	kruse	saip	saepe
dook	dykke	sark	saerk
drucken	drukken	sang	sang
efter	efter	seck	saek
forbye	forbi	seik	syg
fremmit	fremmed	siccar	sikker
gang	gang	skaith	skade
gavel	gavl	skellum	skaelm
greet	graede	skelly	skele
grey-hairit	graharet	smaa	sma
grue	gru	smiddy	smedje
grund	grund	smool	smugle
hals	hals	smit	smitte
het	hed	soor	syre
hoose	hus	starn, stern	stjerne
ken	kunne, kende	stane	sten
kilt	kilte		

This list is not exhaustive: a Danish friend who visited Scotland some years ago for about ten days, made a list, even in that short time, of over three hundred words common to both languages and pronounced the same or almost the same. What conclusions can we draw from these examples? The Danish words, like the Scots words, have a common ancestor in Old Norse, as had Anglo-Saxon, but the fact that these words exist in parallel in the present day, while their English equivalents, where they did once exist, do not, points to the divergent paths these languages have followed. Can we therefore say that English is just a dialect or just a corrupt form of the original? I think not. In the same way it is just as wrong to say Scots is just a dialect or a corruption of English. This comparison of Scots and Danish, superficial though it may seem, is surely sufficient to show that Scots has strong European roots and is not just an off-shoot of English.

Other links can be made with other languages, such as French, through words that exist in Scots but not in English. This reflects the Auld Alliance and the fact that there were links between the royal houses of both countries, rather than the effects of conquest or takeover:

Scots	French
arles	arles
ashet	assiette
aumry	armoire
bien	bien
braw	brave
douce	doux, douce
dour	dur
fash	fâcher
gigot	gigot
tassie	tasse

Dr J. Derrick McClure in his excellent book *Why Scots Matters* also points out the list of words Scots has acquired from Dutch, including the following, some of which will have a familiar ring to anyone from the North-East:

craig, cuit, dowp, bucht, farrow, heck, owsen, callant, doit, howff, redd and scone.

Similarities between Scots and German and Scots and Norwegian can also be shown, including the famous *stursuker* [phonetic spelling] for vacuum cleaner. Scots of course also has words that have come into it from our country's other language, Gaelic. Many place names and surnames show this connection as well as words such as the following brief selection:

glen, ben, loch, strath, clachan, kyle, ceilidh, banshee and boorach

Although Gaelic is now spoken only by 2% of the population as a first language, it now being learned by many other Scots, keen to enrich themselves culturally. Gaelic is also a language with European roots, linked to other languages like Irish, Welsh, Breton, Galician and Catalonian. In this present day, when the European community is drawing together, part of its attraction is not the uniformity so many people dread as a consequence of centralisation, but the rich variety of cultures that is one of the means by which one country learns to respect another. If countries are to retain their own identity, they must retain their languages. Thus a plea for recognition of the Scots language as a medium for Scots culture is not an attempt to hang on to something that is outdated, but a way of affirming ourselves as twentieth first century Scots, a people with European roots.

The Author

Dr Sheila Douglas is an active performer and an author of several books. She has been a leading campaigner to revive Scottish folk music. An Honorary Member and former Chairman of the Traditional Music and Song Society, she has been Secretary of the Scots Language Society. Her books include *The Sang's the Thing (1992)*.

References

McLure, J.D., *Why Scots Matters,* The Saltire Society and Scots Language Society, 1988
Kay, B., *The Mither Tongue,* Alloway Publishing, 1993
Murison, D., *The Guid Scots Tongue,* The Mercat Press, 1977

Figure 1 Sir Walter Scott.

30

THE IMAGE OF SCOTLAND IN LITERATURE

Paul H Scott

Samuel Johnson said in the Preface to his Dictionary: 'The chief glory of every people arises from its authors.'[1] Ford Madox Ford had a similar thought when he said that 'Henry James was the greatest writer of my time and therefore the greatest man.'[2] David Hume went even further when he wrote in his *History of England*: 'Such a superiority do the pursuits of literature possess above every other occupation, that even he who attains but a mediocrity in them, merits the pre-eminence above those that excel the most in the common and vulgar professions.'[3] Few people today, I imagine, would be willing to expose their intellectual snobbery quite so nakedly.

Johnson and Hume, of course, were using the words 'literature' and 'authors' in a wide sense to cover books of almost every kind. When Hume in a letter to Elliot of Minto said of the Scots that we were the people 'most distinguished for literature in Europe',[4] he was thinking mainly of history and philosophy, of the classic texts of the Scottish Enlightenment, of the works of Robertson, Smith, Ferguson and, of course, his own. Hume was not indulging in outrageous exaggeration. He was speaking of a time when Scotland led the world in ideas and scientific discovery. The ideas of Adam Smith, to take only one example, led to the doctrines of both capitalism and marxism. Buckle said of Smith's book, *The Wealth of Nations* that 'it was probably the most important book which has ever been written whether we consider the amount of original thought which it contains, or its practical influence.' [5] (He was writing long before Margaret Thatcher appealed to Smith as an authority in ways which revealed that she had little idea of what he had actually written.) The historian, Christopher Harvie, said in a recent book: 'The peculiar history of the Scots has meant that, man for man, they have probably done more to create the modern world that any other nation.'[6] He had in mind, I think, the influence principally of Scottish literature in the sense in which Hume used the word.

Nowadays 'literature' and even 'writer' tend to have a much narrower meaning. Perhaps under the influence of university departments of literature, the words are increasingly applied only to what they call 'creative' or 'imaginative' writing in the sense mainly of fiction, poetry and plays. When Ford said that James was the greatest writer of his time, he meant the greatest novelist. The word 'literature' is also used by businessmen and scientists in senses which need not detain us; by the first of these to mean printed publicity or explanatory material, and by the latter for writings on their own speciality.

Whatever definition of literature you take, I do not suppose that everyone would agree spontaneously with the notion that writers are of pre-eminent importance. I find it hard to understand, but I am told that a great many people hardly ever open a book after they leave school and never enter a bookshop. Edward Gibbon said in his *Autobiography* that his 'numerous and select library' was the foundation of his works and the best comfort of his life both at home and abroad.[7] Many of us, I am sure, feel the same, but we are apparently in a minority. Even so, whether people read or not, whether they are conscious of it or not, they can hardly avoid the influence of books. Their education derives from them. Most of what they see on television or in films was first of all written. Their lives are affected at every turn by ideas, techniques and technology preserved and disseminated by books. We all live in a climate of opinion of which books are a major component.

My present intention is to confine myself to the influence of literature in the narrower sense of fiction, poetry and plays. Partly this is because it is now the normal usage, but more because this is the kind of writing which has most effect on the idea or image of a nation. I think that we have to distinguish between the image of a nation in the eyes of its own people and the image which it projects to other countries. They are not necessarily the same. I look first at the external image.

THE IMAGE OF SCOTLAND IN OTHER COUNTRIES.

In earlier times it was the Scottish philosophers and scholars, rather than the poets and story tellers, who had an important influence outside Scotland. I do know of any evidence that even the great mediaeval makars, Henryson, Dunbar and Douglas, or that powerful play, *Ane Satyre of the Thrie Estaites*, were known outside Scotland at all. Of course, at that time, and especially before printing was invented and became wide-spread, people, ideas and writings travelled rarely, little and slowly. An exception were the philosophers and scholars, and many Scots among them, who travelled from one university to another, using Latin as a universal language. Between its foundation and the Reformation the University of Paris had seventeen or eighteen Scottish rectors.[8] Many of these Scottish scholars had a European-wide reputation, Michael Scott, Duns Scotus, John Ireland, John Mair.

Towards the end of this period, when Latin was beginning to be displaced by the vernacular languages, George Buchannan (1506–1582) was regarded as the prince of poets and his plays were performed all over Europe for at least a century. He was one of the teachers of Montaigne as well as of Mary, Queen of Scots, and of James VI. His historical and constitutional writing on Scotland had an important influence on Scottish opinion on these matters; but most of his poetry and all of his plays had no relation to Scotland and can hardly have affected the image of the country at all.

In fact, the first Scottish writer to have a major effect on our image abroad, some two hundred years later, was a very unlikely one, now little read and generally regarded with disapproval. This was James Macpherson who between 1760 and 1763 published what he claimed to be translations from ancient Gaelic poetry, and particularly the *Works of Ossian, the Son of Fingal*. Macpherson was born near Kingussie in 1736 and was closely related to the clan chief, the Macpherson of Cluny who played a prominent part in the '45. James was a student in Aberdeen at a time when a Greek scholar, Thomas Blackwell, was Principal of Marischall College. His book, *Enquiry into the Life and Writings of Homer* argued that great epic poetry could only be written in a heroic and uncorrupt age. Eighteenth century opinion was receptive to the idea that heroic virtue, and therefore great poetry, might also be found in the Highlands of Scotland. Macpherson, as a patriotic endeavour, undertook the discovery and translation of the texts. He found only a few scraps and supplied the rest from his imagination.[9]

At first, Macpherson's *Ossian* was received in Scotland with enthusiasm. For example, when Tobias Smollett was back in Scotland in 1766, he drew on his experiences for his novel, *Humphrey Clinker*. One of his characters remarks that the poems of the 'divine bard', Ossian, 'are in every mouth'.[10] This enthusiasm did not last in Scotland itself when it became apparent that Macpherson could not produce the original Gaelic. He is perhaps the only man in the history of literature who has been condemned because his work was his own and not a translation.

In other countries Macpherson, or rather his creation Ossian, had a remarkable success. Although his first and most virulent detractors were in England, Hazlitt placed him on a par with Dante and Blake, saying that he was 'an admirer of Ossian equally with any poet whatever'. It was in continental Europe that enthusiasm for Ossian reached its greatest height. He was Napoleon's favourite poet and he carried a copy on his campaigns. Goethe, Schiller and Lessing were among those who accepted him as the equal of Homer. Beethoven said that Ossian and Homer were among his favourite poets and this was one of the reasons why he was eager to write settings for Scottish songs.[11]

These two influences, Macpherson's *Ossian* and the prolific literary and musical heritage of Scottish song created a strong image of Scotland throughout Europe, at least among educated people. The effect of this is very clear in European music. An Englishman, Roger Fiske, made a study of this and recorded his conclusions in a book, *Scotland's Music*, published in 1983. He showed that every major European composer for about 200 years, and especially Schubert, Mendelssohn, Bruch, Haydn, Beethoven, Chopin and Schumann wrote music with Scotland in mind. It was a Scotland that was largely imaginary, a land of noble Ossianic heroes, but sometimes the real flavour of Scotland came through in passages adapted from Scottish melodies. The idea became established that Scotland was a special place, close to ancient virtues long lost elsewhere, with a history that merited a pilgrimage, even if the pilgrims had only the vaguest ideas about it. This is an attitude which persists to this day and you can find it, not only among European, but also among American and Japanese tourists. It is one of the ironies of literary history that Macpherson, despised at home as an impostor, has been one of the most influential of all writers in creating an image of his country.

Robert Burns was born 21 years later than Macpherson, but they both died in 1796. Burns played a part in this external influence through music because he wrote or collected the words of many of the songs which were given new settings by Beethoven, Haydn and others. His political and social satires are another matter, but they too are a powerful influence, often in translation, especially the Russian. Their image of Scotland is as remote as possible from Ossian's; but they co-exist, just as Burns himself could be both Jacobite and Jacobin.

Hugh MacDiarmid, forgetting Burns for a moment, once wrote that three Scottish writers were among the most influential in almost all civilised countries, Macpherson, Walter Scott and Byron.[12] Of these Byron, outside Scotland, is often thought to be English, although he said himself that he 'was born half a Scot and bred a whole one'.[13] He had a strong influence on European romanticism, but the setting of most of his poetry is Mediterranean and it cannot be said to have affected the image of Scotland. Scott, on the other hand, followed the impact of Ossian with a more historical vision of the Scottish past which was an overwhelming force all over Europe and beyond for more than a century. Novelists everywhere, Balzac, Manzoni, Tolstoy and hundreds of others imitated him. There are innumerable operas, plays and paintings based on his work. He created a new attitude towards the past. Also, because so many of his narrative poems and novels, in fact the best of them, were set in Scotland, they reinforced the Ossianic curiosity about Scotland and a disposition to regard it as a place of special interest and enchantment.

Let me give you just two examples. A former Napoleonic soldier, Gabriel Surenne, said in a letter to Scott in 1827 that before his novels the French had been little acquainted with the customs, laws and manners of Scotland; but 'now there is a thirst for everything concerning the Scots, as a Parisian would be disgraced in society, were he to appear less familiar with Scottish affairs and places than with French ones'.[14] Before Jules Verne began the long series of novels like *Twenty Thousand Leagues Under the Sea* or *Around the World in*

Figure 2 Robert Burns.

Eighty Days, his first book was *Voyage en Angleterre et en Ecosse* which he wrote in 1859 as an account of his own journey thinly disguised as a novel. In it the character who represented himself says that 'his keenest wish was to visit the homeland of Walter Scott' to 'soak in with all his senses the poetic essence of that enchanted land'. It seems to have rained almost continuously, but that did not dampen his enthusiasm for visiting the settings of the Waverley novels or for Scotland itself, which he called 'that brave, proud nation that still suffers under English domination.'[15] It is, of course, well known that even before the novels appeared Scott's poetry had brought a flood of visitors to Scotland. You might say that he started the tourist industry in Scotland.

Since Scott, no other Scottish writer, and perhaps no other novelist or poet at all, has had such influence or so affected the image of Scotland. This year the Stevenson centenary is being celebrated in America, Japan, Samoa and France, as well as Scotland. He has certainly given wide currency to the Scottish idea of the divided self. He has also explored the Scottish psyche in his Scottish novels and in essays, letters and poetry in Scots. Outside Scotland, I do not think that these are read as much as *Treasure Island*, *Dr Jekyll and Mr Hyde* and the South Sea stories, and for this reason I do not think that he has greatly affected the external image of Scotland. The Kailyard school had an influence for a short time; but since 1901, when it was shattered by George Douglas's *The House with the Green Shutters*, quite a different tendency has prevailed. Urban deprivation and violence has displaced rural innocence and aspiration. This has certainly had an effect on the controllers of television in London to whom only *Rab C Nesbitt* or *Taggart* and the like seem to be acceptable as images of Scotland. Perhaps they gratify southern assumptions of superiority. I do not know to what extent they are accepted as typical by the English audience.

Since a country without its own government is invisible to the rest of the world, Scotland at present has only a very shadowy international existence. But there are still people in many countries in the world who may never have read a word of Macpherson or even Scott, but have an attitude to Scotland which ultimately derives from their influence.

THE INTERNAL IMAGE

I turn now to the effect of literature on the image of Scotland in the eyes of its own people. To reduce the subject to manageable proportions, I shall concentrate on the last three centuries; but first a few preliminary remarks about an earlier period. Scotland since John Knox's *First Book of Discipline*, Scotland has aspired to a school in every parish. We have had a literate population for far longer than most other countries. For about 300 years the most familiar book was the Authorised Version of the Bible.

It was translated on the instructions of James VI, but after he had moved to England and the book was therefore in English at a time when the language was powerful and poetic. Its use in Scotland as the most influential book of all had a profound effect on language and attitudes. No doubt, much of the effect was positive, but it did tend to suggest that English was a language of superior status and the most suitable one to take the place of Latin for serious discourse. One effect of this was to undermine the self-confidence of the Lowland Scots in their own language and culture.

There were, of course, also influences in the opposite direction. In Burns's autobiographical letter to John Moore he says that one of the first books that he read for himself was the history of William Wallace and that it 'poured a Scottish prejudice in my veins which will boil along there till the flood-gates of life shut in eternal rest.'[16] He was referring to a version of Blin Hary's epic poem, *The Wallas*, which had been for centuries after the Bible, and a long way after, the book most likely to be found in Scottish houses. So we have examples of the two opposing influences which have affected Scottish life and attitudes since James flitted to London in 1603, and affect them still, Anglicisation and assimilation on one hand and resistance and assertion of Scottish distinctiveness on the other. You might call them the unionist and the nationalist points of view.

By about the middle of the 18th century the survival of Scotland as a nation was in doubt. The Union of 1707 had been brought about by means which were too shameful to contemplate. The Treaty had given some guarantees for the survival of the Scottish church, legal system, local government and education; but by subjecting everything to a Parliament in which the Scottish members were an insignificant minority, Scotland was left without defence, without an international identity and without means of coherent expression. When the Union was made, it was opposed by the great majority of the Scottish people. Even the Scottish politicians who had helped to bring it about, soon changed their minds and tried to have it repealed. They were made to realise that, in the words of the speaker of the House of Commons, that England had caught Scotland and would not let her go. The suppression of the Highlands after Culloden emphasised the powerlessness of Scotland even more emphatically. The whole power of the state in money, patronage and military force was controlled from London. A Jacobite rising had offered a chance of escape, but that involved the risk of the restitution of arbitrary royal power associated with Catholicism or Episcopalianism. Scots with democratic aspirations or Presbyterian convictions might conclude that even an English dominated Parliament was preferable. The Scots were faced with two unpalatable alternatives.

In these circumstances it is not surprising that many Scots should have concluded in the second half of the eighteenth century that their best course was to make the best of a bad situation, to face the reality of the weakness of Scotland under the Union, to forget the past and to try to become as English as possible. This did not mean that the English were ready to accept them.

David Hume wrote from Paris to Gilbert Elliot of Minto on 22 September 1764:

> 'I do not believe there is one Englishman in fifty, who, if he heard that I had broke my Neck tonight, woud not be rejoic'd with it. Some hate me because I am not a Tory, some because I am not a Whig, some because I am not a Christian, and all because I am A Scotsman. Can you seriously talk of my continuing an Englishman? Am I, or are, an Englishman? Will they allow us to be so? Do they not treat with Derision our Pretensions to that name, and with Hatred our just Pretensions to surpass and govern them?'[17]

David Hume, as you may see from that example, was frank in his letters, and no doubt in his conversation, about his Scottish feelings and his opinion of the English, whom he called 'the barbarians who inhabit the banks of the Thames.'[18] But in his writing for publication he, and the other literati of the Scottish Enlightenment, not only avoided Scottish expressions, but, nearly always, any reference to Scotland at all. Very often they were discussing social change and must have had Scotland in mind, but they drew their examples from ancient Greece and Rome or even from North American Indians. To judge from their writings, you might think that Scotland had ceased to exist. As indeed it would have done if this habit had been allowed to continue unchecked.

This is why so many people have spoken of the debt of gratitude that Scotland owes to Burns and Scott. It is because they are two of the most powerful voices which have been raised to resist the disappearance of Scotland. Both of them did this deliberately and consciously. Burns, for instance, in his lines *To the Guidwife of Wauchope-House* wrote:

> Ev'n then, a wish (I mind its pow'r),
> A wish, that to my latest hour
> Shall strongly heave my breast
> That I for poor auld Scotland's sake
> Some usefu plan or beuk could make,
> Or sing a sang at least.

His strenuous efforts in collecting every scrap of Scottish song which he could find was a patriotic endeavour carried out in this spirit. So was Scott's work on the ballads of the Scottish Border. He ended his Introduction to that collection with these words:

> By such efforts, feeble as they are, I may contribute something to the history of my native country, the peculiar features of whose manners and character are daily melting and dissolving into those of her sister and ally. And, trivial as may appear such an offering to the Manes of a Kingdom, once proud and independent, I hang it upon her altar with a mixture of feeling which I shall not attempt to describe.

There is no mistaking, Edwin Muir said, the emotion in these words.[19]

Burns reinforced the national character of Scotland, egalitarianism, sense of social justice, irreverence, gusto and spirit, by expressing it in words which embodied it so perfectly they themselves became part of our identity. He gave new vigour to the Scots tongue by using it with force, intelligence and wit.

Walter Scott, whose best writing is also in Scots in dialogue of the novels, vitally contributed to the survival Scotland by restoring an awareness of our own past. His son in law, biographer J.G.Lockhart, discussed this in an account of a visit to Scott at Abbotsford. He said that many events had conspired to take Scots away from their own past, 'the unpleasant nature of some of events that have befallen them, the neighbourhood of triumphant eclipsing England.' He thought that this was a misfortune because 'the folly of slighting and concealing what remains concealed within herself, is one of the worst and most pernicious that can beset a country.' Fortunately Scott had now shown Scotland that 'her own national character' was 'a mine of intellectual wealth.'

But in Lockhart's view, Scott had restored more than a sense of history alone. The writers of the generation of Hume and Smith had shown the force of the national intellect, but had left the national mode of feeling unexplored. Scott, he says, had 'grappled boldly with the feelings of his countrymen' and was 'the sole saviour of all the richer and warmer spirit of literature in Scotland.'[20] Of course, Scott was not alone. There was Burns for one thing and he was following the lead of Ramsay and Fergusson and the traditions of several centuries of Scottish poetry. Both John Galt and James Hogg were writing at the same time as Scott and they too grappled with the Scottish, past, character and feeling. George Davie in his celebrated book, *The Democratic Intellect*, said that since the Union 'the distinctive national inheritance was more than once brought to the very brink of ruin only to be saved at the last minute by a sudden burst of reviving energy.'[21] This is true but these revivals are generally the work of several hands, even when one or two individuals have given the lead.

Another example in more recent times is the Scottish Renaissance of which Hugh MacDiarmid was the core. He too gave a new impetus to poetry in Scots, but he did more than that. Although inconsistent in many things, he was consistent in his tireless campaign for a revival of Scotland. He believed that Scotland had lost its way as a consequence of the Union with England. The English Ascendancy, in his phrase, had attempted to replace everything Scottish with a poor imitation of the English model. Scotland had to fight back by re-establishing control of her own affairs, by re-opening direct contact with the rest of Europe and the world at large, and by the cultivation of her own literature, languages and history. We had to restore self-confidence by the recovery of our own distinctive and valuable culture.

Not all of these objectives have so far been achieved, but since MacDiarmid started his campaign in the 1920s nearly everything in Scotland has changed in the direction that he wanted. It is now axiomatic that Scotland is a nation with a distinctive contribution to make to the world. Even the present Government in their 'taking-stock' White Paper of March 1993 said that there should be a 'more concerted recognition of Scotland's status as a nation' and that the Scottish identity should be 'recognised, understood and respected'.[22] Whether they realised it or not, they were responding to the influence of MacDiarmid. As David Murison has said: 'After MacDiarmid, as after Knox, Scotland will never be the same place again.'[23]

Of course, there are many things apart from literature which affect the image of a nation, music, architecture, social, military and political behaviour, clothes, food, sport and so on. I suggest that literature is the most potent because it is the most comprehensive and explicit. It comes to terms with all the other factors, reacts to them and describes them. It can be said to include all the rest. Certainly in the case of Scotland, I think that it is clear that the writers, especially the poets and the novelists, have largely created the image of Scotland, both in the rest of the world and at home. Andrew Fletcher of Saltoun said that he knew a wise man who 'believed if a man were permitted to make all the ballads, he need not care who should make the laws of a nation.'[24] There is a sense in which the wise man was right.

The Author

Following a distinguished career as a diplomat, Paul Scott returned to Scotland in 1980 to become a leading campaigner for Scottish culture. He is Convenor of the Advisory Council for the Arts in Scotland and Vice-Chairman of the Saltire Society, being Panel Convenor for its Scottish Book of the Year Award. He is a prolific writer and his latest book is *Defoe in Edinburgh and Other Papers (1994)*.

References

1 Quoted in Wain, J. (ed), *Johnson on Johnson*, London, 1976, p 46
2 Quoted by Allan Massie in an address to the Edinburgh Sir Walter Scott Club in 1990. Text in Campbell I., and Garside, P. (eds), *Talking About Scott*, Edinburgh, 1994, p 133
3 Op. Cit. Edition of 1835, p.820
4 Greig, J.Y.T. (ed), *Letters of David Hume*, Oxford, 1932 (2 Vols), Vol 1, p 255
5 Buckle, H.T., *On Scotland and the Scotch Intellect*, Hanham, H.J. (ed), Chicago, 1970, p 264
6 Harvie, C., *Scotland and Nationalism*, London, 1977, p 18
7 Op. Cit. Everyman's Library Edition. London, 1932, p 90
8 Broadie,A, *The Tradition of Scottish Philosophy*, Edinburgh
9 Stafford, F., *The Sublime Savage*, Edinburgh, 1988, passim, especially pp 28–33

[10] Smollett,T., *Humphrey Clinker*, Many editions. Reference is to J. Melford's letter of 3rd Sept

[11] Fiske, R., *Scotland and Music*, Cambridge, 1983, especially pp 33 and 73

[12] MacDiarmid, H., *Burns Today and Tomorrow*, Edinburgh, 1959, p.73

[13] Lord Byron, *Don Juan*. Many editions. Canto X/XVII

[14] Quoted by Eric Anderson in *Talking About Scott* (As 2 above) p 36

[15] Verne, J., *Backwards to Britain*, Edinburgh, 1992, pp 1 and 128

[16] de Lancey Fergusson, J. (ed), *Letters of Robert Burns*, Oxford, 1931, 2 Vols, Vol I pp 1067

[17] *Letters of David Hume* (As 4. above) Vol I p.470

[18] Ibid. vol. 1 p.436

[19] Muir, E., *Scott and Scotland*, London, 1936, p 137

[20] Lockhart, J.G., *Peter's Letters to his Kinsfolk*, Edition of 1977, Edinburgh, pp. 145–148

[21] Davie, G. E., *The Democratic Intellect*, Edinburgh, 1961, p xvi

[22] *Scotland in the Union* Government White Paper, Cm. 2225. HMPO, Edinburgh, 1993, pp 38 and 39

[23] Murison, D., in *Lines Review*, December, 1978

[24] Daiches, D. (ed), *Fletcher of Saltoun, Selected Writings*, Edinburgh, 1979, p 108

Books for further reading.

Scott, P.H., *In Bed with an Elephant*, Saltire Society, 1985

Scott, P.H. (ed), *Scotland: A Concise Cultural History*, Mainstream, Edinburgh, 1993

Watson,R., *The Literature of Scotland*, Macmillan, 1984

Figure 3 Hugh McDiarmid.

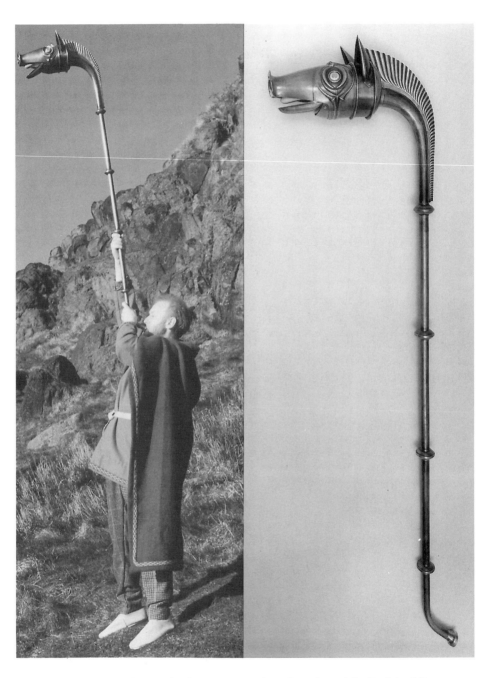

Figure 1 John Kenny playing the Carnyx.
© *National Museums of Scotland.*

Figure 2 Replica of the Deskford Carnyx.
© *National Museums of Scotland.*

31

HOMECOMING OF
THE DESKFORD CARNYX
After 2000 Years of Silence

John Purser

Now and again the good dreams come true. A magnificent building like Chatelherault is restored; a long lost manuscript is rediscovered; a salmon spawns in a river cleansed of its infertility; a remote community survives, knowing its own true nature and being true to the best of it.

Perhaps the reconstruction of the carnyx does not have such a claim on our delight, but it does allow us to hear the sounds of two thousand years ago, and it was one of my best dreams and it has come true, and already it has proved itself to be a vital and fascinating link with our past, for all sorts of different people. The archaeologists became skittish, craftsmen rubbed their pates with hands expressive of wonderment at the beauty of its manufacture, acousticians sucked meditatively on their lower lips, metallurgists got lost in the mines of their enquiries, players of brass instruments wounded their embouchures to make it speak, musicologists gurgled insanely in the corners of their studies, and the ethnologists woke up to the presence of a matter of import on their own doorstep rather than in the depths of Amazonia; and children in schools, as children do, took to its re-emergence with the natural acceptance of, and rather less caution than birds at a feeding table.

The reconstruction was made possible by a Glenfiddich Living Scotland Award (on which account we should regularly toast the directors' healths in their own product), the balance being provided by the National Museums of Scotland for whom the replica was destined. Their co-operation in the scheme was not only essential, but was given unstintingly (especially from Fraser Hunter and Mike Spearman) so that the whole process was a pleasure from start to finish, not least for the superb craftsman, John Creed, who made it; the brilliant musician, John Kenny, who first played it; and myself as consultant musicologist.

THE DESKFORD FIND

The Carnyx was a Celtic trumpet/horn type of instrument made of beaten bronze (as well as brass in the Scottish example) and known probably throughout Europe and wherever else the Celtic tribes went into battle. Fragments of carnyxes survived in what are now Germany, France, Scotland, and England in which latter country the artefact they discovered in Tattershall, Lincolnshire, was examined in the 18th century and then melted down in order to determine its composition, no English jokes please.

The most substantial surviving fragment is the *bell* end, in the form of a boar's head, which was discovered at Deskford in Scotland, and now housed in the Royal Museum, Edinburgh. It provides the only evidence that the instrument once possessed a hinged wooden tongue, though it did not survive its excavation and no trace of it now remains. Here is the report of its finding in The New Statistical Account, Volume 13, 1845:

> There was found, about twenty years ago, on the confines of a farm called Leichestown, the resemblance of a swine's head in brass, of the ordinary size, with a wooden tongue moveable by springs. It had also eyes, and the resemblance in every respect was wonderfully exact.

ITS FORM DEDUCED

It was Professor Piggott who was the first to demonstrate that this object was part of a carnyx, suggesting how the original would have been attached to the missing tubing and placing it in the context of other finds. Deducing the rest of the instrument, at least in broad outline, was therefore not too difficult.

In particular there are three carnyx players depicted in magnificent repoussé work on the famous Gundestrup Bowl (circa 200BC), found in Denmark, but thought to have originated in the Danube basin. Although the scale of the instruments and the humans cannot be taken too literally on such small and fine work, it is clear that the carnyx was nearly as long as a man is tall and was held vertically with the zoomorphic head facing forward. The joints in the main tubing are clear, and these involved reinforcing elements which were also decorative and could serve to assist the player in raising and holding the instrument, much easier than is usually imagined, the instrument being nicely balanced almost directly above an erect person's centre of gravity. In this position it can not only be held and played with one hand, but it is possible to do so while marching forward, which allows for hands to be swapped when the blood drains too much out of the one in use. That there were carnyxes of various length is clear from a number of depictions of it on coins, Roman, French and British, in which the zoomorphic element is frequently prominent, with raised crest, pricked ears and gaping jaws.

Figure 3 The Gundestrup Bowl showing contemporary images of the Carnyx in use.
By kind permission of the Danish National Museum.

Figure 4 The original relic excavated at Deskford 200 years ago.
© *National Museums of Scotland.*

The carnyx was contemporary with the Roman invasions and was also known to the Romans, but it was not a Roman instrument. In fact it terrified them, according to Polybius, when describing the battle of Telamon in the second century BC:

> The Romans were terrified by the fine order of the Celtic army and the dreadful din, for there were innumerable trumpeters and horn blowers, and, as the whole army were shouting their war-cries at the same time, there was such a tumult of sound that it seemed that not only the trumpets and the soldiers but all the country around had got a voice and caught up the cry.

There is no question that the instrument was used in battle. On the coins it is shown in the hands of mounted warriors at full gallop (arguing for great integral strength in the design of the instrument), in association with shields and Gaulish warriors. That the Deskford carnyx was used in similar situations by the proto-Picts is made likely by the interesting discovery by the Museum that, on analysing the metal, brass had been used as well as bronze. Brass was a Roman metal. The proto-Picts, though sophisticated metallurgists, had yet to produce it and must have imported or stolen the material from the Roman invaders, melted it down and incorporated it in their own design, using its colour contrast with the bronze to heighten the effect of the head. Fraser Hunter has observed that this gives a date for the construction of the Deskford Carnyx between the 2nd and 4th centuries AD, and this fits in with the decorative and design style which is typical of North-East Scotland of the period. He has suggested that the development of local design types, especially using a Roman metal, can be seen as 'a way of displaying and enforcing an independent identity in the face of the Roman threat.' (National Museum of Scotland exhibition, 1993).

The carnyx is capable of producing a sound of immense power. It can be as loud as a modern trombone, the most powerful instrument in the symphony orchestra. What is more, the manner in which it is held means that the sound travels unimpeded from the instrument well over the heads of the surrounding armies and could have been used to terrify the opposition, encourage the lads, or to convey signals. Indeed, we could imagine a sneaky proto-Pict making his way at night to the bottom of the Antonine wall, raising the head of the carnyx over the wooden pallisade which surmounted it, and scaring the Roman sentries into rapid involuntary bowel evacuation with a few fearsome blasts, before disappearing into the mists. In my more fanciful moments I like to think of the carnyx as the weapon which turned the tide against the Roman empire, the proto-Picts being the most expert musicians compared with the Celts in the rest of Europe, but this opinion is sadly open to the suggestion of bias and downright chauvinism, so we had better let it pass.

Of course aggression and defiance need not have been the carnyx's only function. It is capable of producing sounds of warmth and beauty, even delicacy. The Gundestrup bowl shows it in a quite different context from that of war, even though it is being played at the rear of a procession of warriors bearing shields and supporting a tree (the tree of the clan?) on their spears. At the left hand end of this procession, a figure so much larger than the others as to suggest very much greater power, heroic or even god-like status, is either lowering into or withdrawing a person from a cauldron type of vessel. This has been interpreted as a sacrifice, but could just as well be a ceremony of healing or rebirth, or even the boiling away of the flesh from a body to leave only the bones for burial. The most likely seems to be healing or rebirth as the top half of the scene shows mounted warriors proceeding in the opposite direction from those with the tree. The horse was regularly used to symbolise transition to the other world, but could also be a simple device to illustrate the increased power of the warriors after being immersed in whatever was in the vessel.

We know from the *Tain Bo Fraoch* (a Celtic tale popular in Ireland and Scotland, appearing in early mediaeval manuscripts and quite possibly contemporary with the heyday of the carnyx) that horns, of a type unspecified, were used to accompany a healing ceremony. In this ceremony Fraoch, suffering from multiple abrasions, contusions and cuts after being mauled by a water monster, was immersed in a bath of pork and calf's flesh. If these animals were recently slaughtered and cut up, the traumatised flesh would have produced high quantities of clotting factor which could have assisted recovery, albeit marginally and at a price which would not have been readily met by the then NHS. However, Fraoch was a hero and was no doubt on an expensive private medical insurance scheme which will also have covered the nine horn players who played so beautifully that thirty of King Aillil's warriors died of rapture. A price of a calf, a pig and thirty warriors to one hero, is indeed expensive medicine, unless it was simply that the thirty warriors swooned away. It is possible that the warriors on the Gundestrup Bowl are singing, their mouths being quite distinct from the narrow slits shown for the carnyx players. This being the case, they may well have been using techniques, still practised in the Middle East, which involve hyper-ventilating in order to induce a trance-like state which can lead to swooning.

It is also very unlikely that an instrument such as the carnyx, of highly developed design and sophisticated beauty and imagery would have been used in one context only. Of course the imagery of the wild boar bears upon the qualities of ferocity, courageousness and cunning. Pigs are intelligent, and the wild ones particularly so, and very fast. But they were an important part of diet (vide Obelix) and, according to many Celtic tales from Ireland and Scotland, were regularly herded if not partially domesticated. Some had magical properties, notably the wild boar whose poisonous bristles caused the death of Diarmuid, again a tale common to Ireland and Scotland.

379

Magnificent images of boars feature prominently in Pictish and Celtic artwork.

John MacQueen has convincingly argued that the wild boar could be understood to act as an intermediary between this world and the next, citing examples from Welsh mythology as well as from Jocelin's *Life of St Kentigern*. This would allow for the use of the carnyx at other ceremonies such as funerals and initiations, possibly even at births. Interestingly, the people of the Orkneys take their name from that of the pig, the *Arcaibh* or pig people, it being their totemic creature and traditionally featuring in their dreams, an association which would give extra force to an artefact from North-Eastern Scotland, assuming association between the two peoples of those parts.

THE SPECIAL QUALITIES OF THE DESKFORD CARNYX

The first and most striking thing about the Deskford Carnyx is the wonderful sense of animal life which it conveys. This is true of the original artefact, though it is missing its tongue, its ears, its bristling mane, and has only holes for its eyes.

But the hinged jaw is a unique feature, the only other surviving carnyx head from Mandeure (Musee du chateau des Ducs de Wurtemberg), having the jaw fixed open, and being zoomorphologically unclear.

When it comes to the reconstruction, the effect is almost of a living thing. We know from the original that not only was the jaw hinged, but there was a free-moving tongue operated by springs. In the reconstruction, it takes scarcely any movement of the instrument to set the tongue and jaw in motion. The instrument seems to breathe and speak, and in less solemn moments it looks as though it desperately wants a drink. The original palate survives, and this is ridged (as are our own palates) to reflect the dramatically deep ridging in the palates of pigs. The eye sockets were clearly designed to hold enamel eyes and, a pig's eye being red in appearance and red enamel being in common use at the time, we are able to recreate the eyes with a fair degree of accuracy.

The exquisite and technically brilliantly executed repoussé work around the eyes and jaw are not only of beautiful flowing shape, but reflect the natural lines of the bristles of the wild boar around the eyes and fold of flesh under the chin. Given this truth to life, albeit refined and abstracted with stunning artistic confidence, the reconstruction of the ears and bristling mane which the wild boar raises when angry, could be undertaken in the same spirit. So John Creed who has met these challenges with great skill and sensitivity, wended forth to an estate in the wilds of the Trossachs to meet up with some wild boar, and produced a final object which has its own character and integrity while being a natural growth from and extension of the original.

People always ask me how we can possibly know what music was played on the carnyx. The answer is that the instrument itself can teach us. Clearly there must be an element of speculation, but only a limited number of notes is available and how they are used is more a factor of the skill of the individual player than a question of picking a tune out of it. It is reasonable to assume that such valuable instruments were not played by amateurs. Whoever had the right to perform on them, especially given their role in military and ceremonial and other functions, must have been good enough to add something to the occasion rather than detract from it. Almost certainly these players will have been basically full-time professionals although, as with pipers and drummers today, they will have carried out other functions compatible with their speciality as musicians. If this is accepted, then it is reasonable to explore a wide variety of techniques on the assumption that the musicians of the past will have done so. It may well be that there were different styles, even schools of carnyx playing throughout Europe, just as there are among, say, horn players today.

That the instruments were played in consort is known to us from the Gundestrup Bowl where there are three playing simultaneously. That there may have been comings and goings between musicians from different tribes, even races, is as reasonable as it is today. That there may even have been a standard pitch to which instruments over a wide area were tuned is made at least worthy of consideration by the fact that the 8th century BC bronze age horns of Ireland were all tuned to a standard pitch, although recovered from widely different areas of the island. That techniques such as circular breathing may have been used is made possible by the knowledge that the end-blown bronze age horns cannot be successfully played without the technique. Whether that technique was remembered through the centuries is another matter, but the possibility should not be discounted, especially since we know the technique must have been used by Pictish triple pipe players in the ninth and tenth centuries.

A critical problem had to be faced with respect to the actual form of the tube and, in particular, the mouthpiece. The decision with the present replica was to make the lengths of tube cylindrical, but each one slightly wider than the last, thus creating a slight degree of expansion which, over the five foot length decided upon, married up nicely with the head at one end and the natural size the tube needed to be to accommodate a mouthpiece at the narrow end. This seemed to fit in with the appearance of the instruments on the Gundestrup bowl as well as with the 18th century illustration of the melted-down Tattershall carnyx. The resultant note spectrum comes sufficiently close to the natural harmonic series produced by most instruments, to suggest that any future reconstruction should actually aim to produce the series.

As presently constructed, the carnyx produces the following notes:

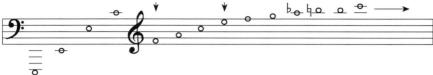

Of course we cannot be certain that the harmonic series was intended. It is fairly readily produced from the Scandinavian lurs, but the earlier bronze age horns do not approximate to it. Nor does the Caprington horn, a cast bronze conical instrument from Ayrshire which, despite possible shortening when repaired at some unknown date, is still eminently playable. It is probably contemporary with the Deskford carnyx, and has an integrally cast mouthpiece of cup form with sharp rim and narrow hole leading into the main tube.

On any lip reed instrument the mouthpiece is crucial because, as the classification indicates, it is human lips which activate the air column to produce the sound, rather than a piece or pieces of reed. The shape of the mouthpiece affects the shape of the lips, the embouchure, as well as the way in which the vibrations are transmitted into the main tube, so that although the acoustic properties of the main tube remain in theory unchanged unless it is altered in design, a change of mouthpiece can change the apparent acoustical properties simply because it can permit or deny certain possibilities to the lips.

No carnyx mouthpiece survives. It may be that, as with the bulk of the bronze age horns, they were ritually destroyed when deposited, so that they could never be played by the profane. However, we know from surviving mouthpieces on Scandinavian lurs (late bronze age) as well as Roman lituus and other mouthpieces, that a wide variety had at one time or another been in use in Europe. In the event, the decision was to make several types of mouthpiece and select the one which seemed to work best with the instrument and the player, a practice which is normal among today's musicians and which allows us to explore the potential of the instrument more thoroughly than would a cut-and-dried decision.

When it comes to an assessment of the quality of the sound, it has to be borne in mind that the carnyx was made of beaten bronze, whereas with the exception of the Irish Loughnashade Trumpet, and a similar instrument found in Nice (neither of which can be played or has been reconstructed), all the surviving bronze and brass instruments of this period are cast. Despite great refinement in the casting techniques, such instruments cannot possibly be made as thin as beaten metal, which naturally vibrates more freely if properly designed and executed, the metal being no thicker than 0.7 of a millimetre, the general average being half a millimetre. The power of the carnyx is certainly partly a consequence of this lightness, which also makes holding it vertically much easier. The relative ease with which it can be set in vibration also allows for the production of a rich warm and gentle sound which can be sustained without much difficulty.

John Kenny, an outstanding trombone player, as well as performer on a wide variety of esoteric wind instruments ranging from didgeridoo to alp horn, was an ideal person to try out the instrument. He was vastly impressed with its musical potential, and we all believe that further reconstructions could be made to produce even better results with more, rather than less truth to the assumed originals. We very much hope that funding will be found to commission more reconstructions, not only in order to refine the instrument, but also to enable us to hear it played in consort.

ITS IMPORTANCE TODAY

The above descriptions of the carnyx should already have made it clear that it has relevance to a wide variety of disciplines. Archaeology, music, metallurgy, jewellery, bronze smithing, acoustics, ethnology, European military history, Roman history, religion, medicine and, of course, local history. John Kenny and I were invited by the Rector of Milne's High School in Fochabers, near Deskford, to demonstrate the instrument, both in the school and at the site where it was found. We also took part in a play based upon its use against the Romans. Dressed respectively and scantily in sacks as Asterix and Obelix (we declined the role of Cacofonix) we had the greatest of fun, and so did the children. Their interest and enthusiasm was the reward we had most sought for our efforts in bringing the carnyx to life. The rector, Mr Matheson, thoughtfully sent us copies of letters he had from primary school children who had been bussed in to share in the carnyx mania of the day. At the risk of breaching copyright, I reproduce part of a letter from Willie:

> The carnyx was very very very very very very very loud. When I was watching the play I saw how it was then. it was fun. felt like I wanted to jump on to the stage and blow the carnyx. The mu[s]ic was lovely . . I say GREAT.

As the only playable carnyx replica in existence, beyond its local community value, it represents an important national icon of Scottish culture. It is an evocative symbol of a culture that was, and still is, shared with the rest of Europe, and it could therefore also be said to be of international significance. It resides in the collection of the National Museum of Scotland to be on show to tourists from overseas and local residents alike on suitable occasions. This paper has enabled me to put it on the agenda of an international conference held to debate cultural tourism, and it is hoped that those who attended the 1994 Heritage Convention in Elgin will long remember the 2000 year old sound of the Deskford Carnyx as artfully produced by John Kenny. The last time it was played in North East Scotland to an international audience, was when the Picts chased the Romans out to sea for their voyage home. This time it was played in honour of old scars and in defiance of the wounds of time.

Acknowledgements

In his endeavours to make the project of a replica carnyx a reality, the author is grateful for the encouragement, help and support from the following organisations and individuals: Glenfiddich Living Scotland Awards; The National Museums of Scotland; The Scottish Music Information Centre; Mike Spearman, archaeologist; Fraser Hunter, archaeologist; Stuart Piggott, archaeologist; John Creed, metal smith and jeweller; John Kenny, trombonist and carnyx player; Lindsay Matheson, rector; and staff at Milne's High School, Fochabers.

The Author

Dr John Purser is a polymath of Renaissance stature. A highly respected composer, musician, poet, dramatist, broadcaster, writer and university lecturer, he is most widely known for his BBC Radio Scotland programmes on the history of Scottish Music, and he wrote *Scotland's Music (1991)*.

References

The most complete bibliography of the carnyx is to be found in the Catalogue of the exhibition *Le Carnyx et la Lyre*, Besancon Musee des Beaux-Arts et d' Archeologie, 4 septembre – 22 novembre 1993; Orleans Musee Historique et Archeologique de l'Orleanais, 18 decembre 1993 – 23 fevrier 1994; Evreux Musee de l'Ancien Eveche, 26 mars – 30 mai 1994.

Fraser Hunter of the Royal Museum, Queen Street, Edinburgh, has a full description of the original Deskford carnyx in preparation.

MacQueen, J., *Myth And The Legends Of Lowland Scottish Saints*, in Scottish Studies 24, 1980
Piggott, S., *The Carnyx In Early Iron Age Britain*, in the Antiquaries Journal 39, OUP, 1959

32

EUROPEAN CULINARY CAPITAL
The Subversive Sausage

Elisabeth Luard

Of all the arts associated with cultural tourism, cookery is perhaps the least understood. As a cookery writer, I have noticed a curious phenomenon about my line of work. When I am asked what I do, in the way that modern manners require, by my neighbour at dinner, and I confess how I earn my daily bread, my questioner usually says nervously: 'How interesting. You must talk to my wife: she has dozens of cookbooks.'

'Ah yes,' I reply politely – and we talk of lighter matters. Politics. History. Philosophy. But sometimes, if I am in combative mood, I reply: 'You imagine my subject to be frivolous – a mere ribbon on life's petticoat. It is no such thing. Food is the only serious subject.'

It seems to me that the area most neglected by historians and students of world affairs has always been the lives of ordinary people, and how they are affected by what might seem to be pure domesticity. Politically, it can be a dangerous area to ignore. At the time the Soviet Union was falling apart, Mikhail Gorbachev discovered this in Lithuania when he sought to defuse the situation with a joke. 'Shall our great Union,' he enquired, smiling, 'be broken up because of sausage?'

'You bet your hobnailed boots it shall.' the angry crowd replied, and meant it.

The Union could be broken up not for porridge, not even for bread or potatoes, but for just one link of that spicy larder-store which transforms mere belly-fodder into a dish worth a thousand bowls of gruel. At the most basic level, a starving nation cannot ferment revolution, any more than Napoleon could storm Moscow with his supply lines overstretched. Real hunger leaves no strength for politics. But once the stomach is comforted with the bare essentials, then what goes into the pot becomes the stuff of insurrection.

An examination of that same subversive sausage which the leader of all the Russias dismissed so lightly reveals that this basic larder-store takes many forms, some 3,000 of them at the last count, including our very own haggis. Traditionally, the sausage is a mixture of animal protein (meat or blood) mixed with grains and stuffed into a casing of animal innards, providing an instant, ready-prepared meal which is portable, economical, and can be cured for winter storage.

To return to Mr Gorbachev's mistake: the sausage, although important in every nation's larder, is the cornerstone of the German culinary tradition, a cultural influence which extends over those ex-Soviet Socialist Republics which lie west of the Urals. The oriental slant, the spice in the sausage, was provided by the Tartars, rulers of much of Russia for two centuries. It was they, too, who introduced soured foods to the western culinary repertoire: curd cheese, soured cream, and the secret of salted soured cabbage. The basic Russian one-pot meal, cabbage soup with sausage made with fresh cabbage in summer and sauerkraut in winter, is a shotgun marriage of two culinary traditions. Sauerkraut greets sausage where East meets West.

A brief glance round the kitchens of the former satellites of Russia will serve to illustrate how national identity can be read in the culinary landscape. The Slavs of the Ukraine (where borscht comes from), Byelorussia and Moldavia betray their Viking allegiances with berry soups, meat accompanied or combined with fruit, and preserved fish, particularly salted herrings served as the central dish of the zakuski, the Russian version of smorgasbord. A taste for kasha, a dry-cooked buckwheat porridge, distinguishes the Poles.

In the Caucasus, buckwheat is replaced with rice, cooked in much the same way as kasha, but including such eastern ingredients as raisins and saffron. In the southern states of the old Russian Empire, the basic culinary habit is Turko-Persian: meat for feast days is cooked with pounded nuts and spices, and baklava-style nut-and-honey pastries are the special treat. You can tell an Armenian by his Bulgar pilaf, his seasonings of lemon and olive oil, and his soured milk soups.

By our dinners shall we be known, and reported, in Ceaucescu's Romania, to the secret police. Of all the twentieth century's despots, Ceaucescu was the most subtle in his understanding of the subversive nature of culinary habit. He early moved the battle to destroy his country's ethnic minorities into the kitchen. In the autumn of 1985 his campaign deprived me of much useful material when, researching Eastern Europe's cuisine, I visited the old market town of Sibiu.

The catering manager of the tourist hotel (the only place where a ration book was not required) explained the lack of regional dishes on the menu as the result of a government edict, which required public catering to conform to the precise recipes in the official cookery manual. This standardisation, he said, was designed to eradicate all ethnic culinary differences among the multi-cultured Romanians. *Cuisine du terroire* was reduced at a stroke to one pork chop and a spoonful of mash. The cabbages, frivolous greens, had all been sent for export. Then he proudly took me to view a floodlit grotto

Figure 1 The Subversive Sausage   *drawing by Elisabeth Luard.*

packed from floor to ceiling with huge jars of pickled vegetables: scarlet peppers, emerald cucumbers, purple aubergines in technicolor profusion. After admiring the display, I enquired if perhaps I might purchase a jar to supplement the thin commons the market yielded for my daily picnics? Good heavens, no. These were icons, symbols of the new order, to be admired but not consumed.

The evening I arrived I had a generous invitation to take supper with the wife and granddaughters of Sibiu's Lutheran Saxon bishop, whose sturdy stone church and school co-existed round the old market square with the edifices which housed five other denominations. These roughly reflected the ethnic mix of the town, including the Hungarian Catholics whose treatment was four years later to light the fuse of revolt. Frau Klein laid out a fine supper of boiled eggs, rye bread, sheep's cheese and pickles, with an apology that I could not taste her famous home-cured wurst, the pride of all Saxon housewives. The spiced sausage, she explained, was a casualty of the Government's Romanianization programme.

The town's 'Turkish' market, a corner of the market-place forever Ottoman where coffee, spices and carpets had been sold for centuries, had been closed down. No one could get the pepper and nutmeg which the traditional recipe required. Importation of all foreign ingredients was forbidden. For the first time in Frau Klein's life, the ancient German-speaking community of Saxons (seven villages subsequently flattened by the dictator's bulldozers) could not make their wurst for the winter, and no spice could be added to the stew. The meat was not the problem: that could be got at a price on the black market. Her flock, said Frau Klein, found the deprivation of sausage an even greater hardship than the hunger everyone was often forced to endure.

The contents of the stew pot sets armies on the march, or holds them in their barracks. The Ottoman Turkish army was given to kicking over their cooking pots as a sign of disapproval of the conduct of their officers. Napoleon valued his chefs above his generals: I confidently expect that some historian will come up with the news that Marshal Blucher was late for Waterloo because he had a prior engagement with a stuffed dumpling. The English complained that the Scots got the edge at the battle of Bannockburn because the Highlanders ate cold porridge on the run instead of taking the time to stew up a potage.

It was not to fill the granaries of Europe that Henry the Navigator's merchant sailors, Elizabeth of England's pirates, Isabella of Castile's protégé, Don Cristobal Colon, risked falling off the edge of the world, but to supply Europe's cooks with so seemingly inessential an ingredient as a pinch of spice. If men will risk their lives over the contents of the pot, politicians who ignore the flavour of the soup invite revolution.

So how do you identify that which is so distinctive, so precious, that it can move nations to defend their right to it? We are used to dividing our dinners into two culinary traditions of bourgeois cookery and haute cuisine. We tend to disregard the third, underlying the other two, highly individual and of localised habit, that of peasant cookery: a tradition limited by what could be

388

grown, herded, gathered or hunted locally, plus those few imported luxuries which trade-routes could provide.

Let me define briefly the differences between the three traditions: *bourgeois cookery* is the cookery of the town-dweller, someone without direct access to his own raw materials in that he does not plant, husband or hunt what he eats. An economically vertical distribution of ingredients characterises the dishes of the town. The rich ate the prime cuts of meat, taking their pick according to their pocket; the poor would make dishes with the tripe and the cheaper cuts. Vegetables and fruits were transported over vast distances to provide city-dwellers with out-of-season goods. This led to a tradition of *made dishes* with a great many ingredients which were not dictated by regional or seasonal considerations.

Where anything and everything is available at a price, ingredients are sometimes new and strange and not much understood, and recipes have to be invented to accommodate them. So tripe *a la mode de Caen* and kiwifruit cheesecake are always bourgeois dishes. I found one rather delightful tradition within this genre: leather-tanning towns, such as Cordoba in southern Spain or Bermondsey on the outskirts of London, share a tradition of ox-tail stews, since the skins for tanning were delivered with tail still attached, providing the main ingredient free. Find a tanning town, and you will get oxtail dishes. In ship-victualling ports you will find dishes made with perishable leftovers from the salt-meat barrel: Marseille's *pieds et paquets*; the black puddings and pig's trotters of Cork. In 18th century Cork, a cooper was entitled to seven pounds of offal a day in addition to his wages. Cork no longer barrels meat for the English navy, but it still consumes three times the national average of offal.

Haute cuisine, on the other hand is the offspring of the mediaeval banquet and grandchild of the extravagant cooks of Rome. It is essentially a palace kitchen and restaurant tradition, with grand display the major consideration: the dishes set out for public view must reflect the status of the host and guests. Requirements are different from those of home-cooking, either peasant or bourgeois. A certain amount of theatre is essential to the production, now to be seen in the self-conscious plating and theatricality of fashionable restaurant chefs. An emphasis on imported and deliberately non-seasonal ingredients, strawberries in Norway in December, smoked salmon in Madrid in July, ensures an international, non-regional base. Even if some regional dishes do feature on the menu, no chef can resist adding his own individual flourish of luxury. So shepherd's pie made with goose conserve and truffles, grouse cooked in cabbage leaves, are now the *dernier cri* in Paris restaurants.

If neither bourgeois nor restaurant cooking truly reflect regionality, we are left with *peasant cookery* as the true litmus-paper of national culinary habit: a tangible, visible, edible record of regional differences. Ask an Azerbajani what he has for supper, and you will probably find out why he hates his Armenian neighbour. Climate, landscape and season order and dictate the peasant tradition, even today, however seemingly uniform in the matter of sliced bread and frozen peas are the contents of the Global Village's supermarkets. Nor is a peasant household necessarily poor.

When I lived in Spain, one of my neighbours, a smallholder known as Manolo-the-dustman since he was retained by the local municipality to collect the community's rubbish, doubled up as the community's banker. He made loans for major purchases such as cars and livestock, and charged interest, with the great advantage that he had the most intimate knowledge of his customers' credit-worthiness through his inspection of their rubbish. He lived almost entirely off the produce of his land, a fertile valley five miles from any road, held on the Spanish system of ownership by default, when after ten years of harvesting unclaimed land, title was granted to the incumbent.

His wife and four daughters were the pride and envy of the community. Stupendous women, with brawn to match their bulk, they were sent for when a recalcitrant bull needed corralling or a herd of the fierce little red half-wild pigs was on the loose. When the time came for the daughters to be courted, all the young men were in a high state of excitement. There was no doubt the young women were value for money, would be generously dowered, and that their acquisition would reflect glory on the suitor ambitious enough to go for it. But, as one young man put it to me while rhapsodising over their charms, think of the maintenance.

When I embarked on my three books on European peasant cookery in 1985, I already knew, after a dozen years of living in deep rural isolation in Spain and France with my growing family, the basics of the peasant tradition. But sometimes new ingredients replace old, in modern times, the social and political importance of the arrival, post-Columbus, of the New World vegetables cannot be overestimated. Maize replaced chestnuts in the polenta recipes of Italy and Provence. The nutritious haricot bean replaced the broad bean in baked-bean dishes such as the *ollas* of Spain and the *cassoulets* of France. Tomatoes became the mainstay of the Italian kitchen. Paprika peppers, a prime source of vitamin C in a northern climate, went to Hungary in the luggage of the occupying Ottoman Turks, as did filo pastry to wrap the German dumpling to give Austrians their strudel.

The Turks were everywhere. When I was travelling through Sweden and asked for simple country dishes, I was offered *kaldomar*, cabbage leaves stuffed with rice, a staple grain of the south, not grown anywhere nearer than the Danube basin, which were the direct adaption, even down to the name, of the Turkish *dolmas* rice-stuffed vine-leaves, a habit apparently brought back, along with his Turkish creditors, by the adventuring Charles XII.

Then there is that arch-revolutionary, the potato, responsible for the rise and success of the Inca civilisation. The potato flourishes in poor soil and at inhospitably high altitudes. One acre of marginal land planted with potatoes yields enough to feed a family, with enough over for the household pig. It also needs no more than two weeks labour a year. After a slow start as an ornamental pot plant, the tuber took off and became the mainstay of the European peasant kitchen, particularly since, unlike grain, its perishability guaranteed all supplies did not get shipped out to feed the towns. There were, of course, a few famous bad patches such as the failure of the crop in Ireland where the population had nevertheless already tripled in the previous good years. Overall in Europe, the rural infant mortality dropped as dramatically as the workload. Food and leisure: the stuff of revolution, and quite explosive enough to fuel the social upheavals of the nineteenth and twentieth centuries.

Of such is the daily diet. But, for greeting visitors, we like to set out the best. This is a natural human response, and accounts for a reluctance to offer strangers the simple food we ourselves appreciate. Festivals and the feasts which mark them are the apotheosis of our domestic habit. We instinctively celebrate with scarce or imported foods and complicated recipes to demonstrate not only that we have taken time and trouble in the preparation, but that we are thoroughly up-to-date and aware of gastronomic fashion. Traditional cooking is especially vulnerable to a loss of skill: a simple dish which relies on the excellence of the raw materials suffers most at the hand of the indifferent caterer. We are all familiar with menus which promise real home cooking and deliver something whose only contact with the home-cook's hand is a finger on the switch of the microwave.

Regional culinary habit is all too easy to reduce to a cartoon version of itself, particularly when, as in modern times in Ceaucescu's Romania, or in Scotland after the '45, there is a political reason to suppress ethnic identity, leading to the breaking-down of oral traditions and the loss of practical knowledge and skills. Once lost, these habits are not easy to resurrect, the memory of what would now be called political incorrectness remains, a ghost at the feast. When I make field trips across Europe to research regional food and cookery, I often use painting and sketching as a means of communication, particularly in countries where I do not speak the language. Policemen know a subversive document when they see it: my sketchbook has been confiscated on the Turko-Bulgarian border, I have been taken for a secret policeman in Bucharest, come close to being arrested as a Russian spy in a Norwegian fjord. Quite right. I deal in matters of life and death.

As I will occasionally point out to my neighbour at dinner, politicians stir the cooking pot at their peril. The tumbrels rolled for the Austrian-born Queen who suggested to the bread-hungry French that they should eat the foreigner's kugelhupf. Mr Gorbachev made a common mistake in Lithuania: he forgot that sausage has never been a laughing matter.

The Author

Elisabeth Luard is a wildlife artist and an internationally renowned writer and broadcaster on the ethnology of cooking. Her books include *European Peasant Cookery (1986)*, and she won the coveted Glenfiddich Award for the best cookery book of the year in 1992. Elisabeth Luard's 13-part series, *The Rich Tradition of European Peasant Cookery*, was shown on BBC 1 in July and August 1994.

References

Baerlein, H., *Baltic Paradise*, Muller, 1943
Ballou, M. M., *Due North: Glimpses of Scandinavia and Russia*, Boston, 1887
van Bath, and Slicher, B.S., *The Agrarian History of Western Europe*, London, 1963
Blum, J., *The End of the Old Order in Rural Europe*, Princeton, 1978
Blum, J.(ed), *Our Forgotten Past*, Thames & Hudson, London, 1982
Camporesi, P., *Bread of Dreams*, Polity Press, 1989
Dabitesse, M.L., *Revolution silencieuse*, Paris, 1931
Franklin, S.H., *The European Peasantry*, London, 1969
Gyula, I., *The People of the Pushta*, Budapest, 1967
Hobhouse, H., *Seeds of Change*, Sidgewick & Jackson, 1985
Le Roy Ladurie, E., *Les Paysans du Languedoc*, Paris, 1966
Luard, E., *European Peasant Cookery*, Bantam, 1986
Luard, E., *The Barricaded Larder*, Bantam, 1988
Luard, E., *European Festival Food*, Bantam, 1990
Stratilesco, T., *From Carpathia to Pindus*, London, 1906
Viski, Ka'roly., *Hungarian Peasant Customs*, Budapest, 1932

33

A TASTE OF SCOTLAND'S FOOD

Catherine Brown

On a country estate of rolling farmlands on the North East shoulder of Corstorphine Hill, the laird of Ravelston, John Foulis, sits down at his desk each day to write up the details of his expenditure in a leather-bound book[1]. Unlike many others who also keep detailed household books, he adds notes, diary-like: 'some bricks have fallen out of the bread oven... a new kitchen chimney is built... he is off to an Edinburgh tavern for an oyster supper... to Leith for a game of golf...'

The pleasant task of journeying back to this period (1671–1707), when Edinburgh was still surrounded by a medieval wall with a twenty-four hour guard, began with the question: what was life like for this kindly, socially aware bon viveur who fishes the Cramond river; regularly visits his wine merchant in Leith; frequently buys his wife sweetmeats and his children chestnuts and gingerbread for a treat; and takes many jaunts into Edinburgh for a night of gambling with friends in the taverns of the Old Town? Before long, with the help of other material, a tangible picture began to emerge of a way of life and a cooking and eating pattern which might be described as the roots of Scotland's food.

Though the first Scottish cookery book by Mrs McLintock[2] was not published until 1736, a manuscript collection of recipes by Martha Brown of Ayrshire dated 1710[3] provided help with the kind of dishes which might have been popular. There was also help from the better-known recipe manuscript by Lady Castlehill of Cambusnethan, dated 1712: some four hundred hand-written recipes bound in leather and held in the Mitchell Library (Glasgow), a quarter of which were published in 1976.[4]

The aim, however, was principally to savour a taste of what Scotland's food might have been like for a lowland laird's family in the period immediately prior to the loss of parliamentary independence in 1707.

What emerges is an eating pattern which clearly exploited every available resource from land and sea in the local vicinity. Yet the people were not entirely self-sufficient. Spices and citrus fruits, for instance, were certainly not produced in Scotland. There are also cheeses from Ireland. But the most substantial imported addition to the Ravelston diet was the mature claret and fine brandy imported from France which cost John Foulis more in a year than the combined cost of maintaining his house and farm. His cook, he tells us, is called Marie.

So what was in her larder and what did she cook? From the vegetable garden came parsnips, leeks, turnips, potatoes, asparagus, carrots, salad vegetables, parsley and syboes. Apples, pears, plums and apricots came from the orchard. By way of food-storing for winter, besides the pickles and preserves made at the end of the summer, there are preserved hams, 15lb Irish cheeses, barrels of salt herring, pickled oysters, dried fish, *solan geese* (gannets) and anchovies.

There is a permanent supply of loaf sugar, butter, salad oil, vinegar and salt, while occasionally dried figs, prunes, raisins, nuts, aniseed, chestnuts, lemons, oranges, pomegranates, cinnamon, mustard seed, cumin, cardamoms and fenugreek, are used. She sees little tea, coffee or chocolate which are only bought rarely and in very small quantities. Wheat bread is very expensive, and is bought only rarely from an Edinburgh baker. The home farm provides grain, mostly barley and oats, also beef and lamb while tenants pay their rent in *kain* (kind) with chickens and grain.

Her cooking equipment consists of a three gallon iron pot over an open fire, a flat metal plate, which also hangs over the open fire where she *girdle-bakes*. A brick-lined oven is heated with wood faggots for bread-baking and an open spit is for roasting in front of the fire.

17TH CENTURY LOWLAND CAULDRON BROTH

The dawn is just breaking in the late summer of 1690 when Marie hitches the handle of the muckle black pot onto a hook over the open coal fire in the basket grate. The smoke catches her throat and waters her eyes whilst coiling upwards and, hopefully, out of the hole in the roof (she eventually gets a new, more efficient chimney which does not cover the kitchen, and the food, in soot whenever the wind blows in the wrong direction). She fills the pot almost full with three gallons of cold water carried from the well in a wooden *luggie* and it heats up slowly.

A wide baronial archway separates fire and pot from the main kitchen where she goes now to cut the meat from a leg of fresh beef. Large chunks of beef, the bones, three onions stuck with a dozen cloves and a bundle of sweet herbs go into the pot. There is a lid for protection from soot drips coming down the chimney. She has been up since five o'clock getting the fire lit, the water in, the vegetables washed, the breakfast organised. By the time the family sit down to their morning brose at eight, this first part of her broth-making procedure will be almost completed.

Throughout this part of the cooking, and also during the second finishing of the broth, she makes sure that it cooks softly with a gentle heat. Broth-making is an instinctive part of her cooking life, the basis for the family's everyday food. Success is a long, slow, careful simmer over a slow fire. By the middle of the morning the onions are in a mush, the beef is tender and the resulting liquid is rich and concentrated with many flavours.

She strains it and lifts out the beef, putting it onto a cold marble shelf in the larder. Onions and herbs have done their task of flavouring and go out. Bones are either given to animals or kept for beggars at the back door. The highly flavoured strained liquid, which we recognise as *stock*, she describes as a *strong broth*.

While it might seem an unusual sophistication to make a basic stock first, this method, which is also firmly rooted in French cuisine, became an instinctive part of the Scottish broth-making tradition appearing in subsequent cookery books and was undoubtedly the foundation of the Scottish broth-making tradition. The fact that the two countries had close ties for many centuries, along with the absorption into Scots of French words like *gigot* and *ashet*, makes it likely that the Scots refined their broth-making techniques by picking up the French system of starting with a *pot au feu* stock pot; the highly flavourful liquid and then using this to adventure further. At any rate it is clear from recipe evidence[5] that Scottish broths employed this method and that it was the source of a repertoire of many original and notable Scottish broths still popular today.

But now Marie proceeds with the second stage, adding barley, which has been soaked and which will *lithe* (thicken) the broth; a number of celery heads which have been finely chopped; some handfuls of marigold petals to give it a golden colour; and several scraggy *old kain hens*, handed into the kitchen from the laird's tenants, as rent.

By twelve-thirty the broth is smelling good. She adds a few handfuls of fresh young sorrel leaves as a final touch, and makes sure it is well seasoned, before pouring it into an immense *charger*. The steaming liquid scents the kitchen with delicious aromas.

It is carried by one of the man servants through to the laird's dining table and placed before him, to be served out to family and servants. Already the ashet of cold beef, removed earlier from the strong broth has been taken through, also a *kebbuck* (whole cheese) from their own farm, a stone jar of freshly churned butter, baskets of soft bannocks, a bowl of ripe plums from the house orchard and a heap of oysters from the Forth piled up on a wooden board.

Pewter broth-trenchers are set round the table at everyone's place. Sir John presides in his high backed chair at one end with his family around him, while the indoor servants are at the other end. Everyone is served a share of the ambrosial liquid along with a morsel of hen and a slice of beef. The servants drink home-brewed ale, the family and children drink claret from a pewter stoup (flagon) taken from hogshead (barrel) in the cellar.

This is the main hot meal of the day.

A HIGHLAND TABLE

Move forward to 1715 and to another Scottish family, who not only live in a house and surrounding area which is in complete contrast to the leisurely lifestyle of our claret-drinking Lowland laird, but who also speak a different language. The head of the household does not sit down each day to write up his household books so there are no recordings of day-to-day expenditures preserved for posterity. But the MacDougall clan chief lives in the six-foot thick walled tower fortress of Dunollie on the edge of a sea cliff overlooking the northern entrance to Oban Bay, which unlike the house at Ravelston, still stands. And there are letters.[6] Also inventories of the castle's contents, which are made each time an old clan chief dies and a new one inherits.

Equipped with the information in the family letters, plus details in inventories and some understanding of the political situation in the late summer of 1715 for a family whose sympathies lie with a Jacobite cause, it is not too difficult to stand in the old hall in Dunollie and imagine.

The roof beams may be gone but the fire hearths on opposite walls remain. One was for people to congregate round, the other for cooking. Besides her cauldron, the clanswoman-cook has two big and two small *potts*; two small copper *skillets*; two brass pans; a frying pan; an old *girdle*; a *brander* (grill); three pairs of tongs; a ladle; a strainer; and a grater.

In the fireplace there is a roasting rack and three long spits which rest on hooks above the stone arch when not in use. There are shelved stone recesses in the walls to store everyday essentials like salt and meal. The rest of the hall is not lavishly furnished but there are the essentials of comfort. The carved wooden trestle table is set with linen, fine delftware and silver, pewter plates, wooden bowls, horn spoons, a dealing spoon, a salt dish and a mustard dish.

BREAKFAST

The day's work begins with first light: peat-cutting on the hill; water-carrying from the burn; going out to milk the cattle in the fields; the children going out to search for newly laid eggs in the nooks and crannies of outbuildings and courtyard. The pot of mealy porridge has been heaving and bubbling for several hours before everyone congregates in the hall for their first hot meal of the day which will last them through until evening.

They stand round, supping with their horn spoons from the communal pot, dipping the hot spoonfuls into a bowl of thick fresh cream. The good contrast of hot porridge and cold cream is so satisfying, and yet there are still some freshly boiled eggs to crack and eat with a soft bannock, a slice of soft goat's milk cheese, ale and buttermilk to drink. For those whose meal is not complete without a swig of potent whisky, a stone bottle of the *usquebae* sits permanently on the table.

This is an everyday breakfast which will be augmented with other delicacies when there are special guests: cold roasts, fried fish, pickled meats and fruit preserves. If there are some special guests, they will also make a special drink known as *Auld Man's Milk* with eggs and milk beaten together in the Delph bowl, sweetened with honey and zested with whisky, brandy or rum. These spirits are among the luxuries bartered from foreign luggers sailing into remote Highland sea lochs and exchanged, tax free (no crime is so common or respectable as 'fair trading'), for salt herring and local cheese. The MacDougall larder is also augmented, in a similar way, with Dutch tea and coffee, Oriental spices, dried figs, raisins, liquorice and sweet candies.

18TH CENTURY HIGHLAND CAULDRON BROTH

Like Marie at Ravelston, the cook here is dependent on her cauldron broth for feeding the large, and often fluctuating, number of eaters who assemble daily in the great hall. It is an ideal food resource in the circumstances. It is the most common day-to-day item in the Scottish diet, varying according to the location and wealth of the family. At Dunollie, the summer broth simmering over the slow-burning peat, is rich with herbs, garlic, sorrel and watercress which are all growing wild for the picking. There are also tender young shoots of seaweed which can be gathered when the tide ebbs. The seeds, which have been sent from Glasgow in March, have grown, in the enclosed castle garden, into cabbages, carrots, parsnips, turnips, beetroot, parsley and radishes. There is no shortage of meat with well-hung venison and other game in the cellar as well as salted, smoked and dried meat and fish.

She has just put the scrag ends, the bones and skinned head from a deer carcass into the pot and will leave them to simmer for several hours. Then she will strain off the rich liquid into one of the large potts and add some barley for thickening. Thin *collops* (slices) of venison from the haunch will be fried in butter in the copper skillet until well browned before being tipped into the thickened broth. Just before it is served, some chopped sorrel and *syboes* (spring onions) will be added to the broth; the sharpness of the sorrel balancing the richness of the dark brown gamy soup-stew. The meat, which comes from the cheeks, and is a great delicacy, will be picked from the cooked head, to be put into the large pot, served up in the centre of the table as the focal point of the meal.

Beside it are the cold remains of a boiled salmon, some barley bannocks cooked on the girdle, butter, sheep's milk cheese, a large bowl of fresh cream to mix with newly picked blaeberries. Depending on the success of the hunters, there may be partridge, grouse, hare, mallard, woodcock or snipe turning and roasting on the spit.

The family are not wealthy in money terms. The total value of the house contents when the Iain Ciar (dark John) twenty-second chief of the clan MacDougall dies, is only £50, while the laird of Ravelston can afford to buy 'occasional items of furniture' at £200. The Highland Jacobite sympathisers lose their castle and lands, the head of the clan is exiled and finally imprisoned. The night before he is to be transported to Barbados along with Stewart of Appin and Rob Roy MacGregor, he receives the King's pardon. When he returns to the ownership of Dunollie Castle his lands are still confiscated and for the last ten years of his life, until he dies in 1737, he lives with his wife and children at the castle, dependent on their own, rather than the extended clan's efforts, to survive.

While the plenty of the past had been created by a sophisticated system which made the best use of the natural assets of land and sea by a judicious pulling of manpower and resources, the future brings a less successful system to the Highlands. When clan chiefs are dispossessed of their lands, everything is split up into uneconomic units (crofts). Agricultural improvements are taking place in other parts of the country but the capital investment is not forthcoming to develop the agricultural resources of the Highlands. The old ruling class have neither the resources, nor the political power, to save the land, and so the food resources fall into a decline, from which they never recover.

In the years before the clan chiefs depart to take up the Stewart cause, others like MacDougall manage the day-to-day provisioning of their clanspeople by casting a net, ingeniously, in search of food which gave them a table of rich Highland plenty appreciated, and extensively recorded, by many famous and not so famous travellers from foreign lands.

19TH CENTURY OLD AND NEW

Back now to Edinburgh, where the old and the new are in conflict. Not just in habits and manners, but in a transfer from the old camaraderie of tenement houses, *houffs* and taverns of the town's medieval centre, to a New Town of spacious classical houses, symmetrical squares and circuses. Are old Scottish cooking pots still hanging over open fires, simmering and stewing the heady aromas?

They are certainly still the focal point of eating in the cramped taverns of the Old Town where housing is also so cramped that the population are obliged to use the tavern for not only eating and socialising but also for doing business, even doctors have their surgeries in taverns.

It is not uncommon to come across a pair of cronies sharing a large bowlful of thick broth. The rib chops of an old sheep have been left whole in the broth and the bone end is grasped by the eater as a convenient handle. But do those who have moved into more sophisticated housing across the North Bridge still continue with these old ways?

In a magazine column, *Noctes Ambrosianae*, which appeared in the popular Blackwood's Edinburgh Magazine (The Maga) from 1817 to 1835,[7] John Wilson provides a vivid, racy, imaginative dialogue between Christopher North (Wilson), James Hogg (Walter Scott's friend, *The Ettrick Shepherd*) and Timothy Tickler (Robert Sym, Wilson's uncle). The old-style artless supper, as opposed to the new formal dinner, is the preference of the *Noctes epicures*. Like others, they despise the *corner dishes* which have started appearing as *table fillers*.

'I like,' said the Shepherd, 'to bring the haill power o' my stamach to bear on vittles that's worthy o't, and no fritter't awa on side dishes, sic as pates and trash o' that sort.'

The well-filled ashets of *roast and boiled* were enough of an attraction in themselves, they thought. Placed, all at once on the table, to avoid the interruption of *instalments,* they enjoyed a wide repertoire of dishes cooked by douce, civil, judicious Ambrose, the cook. They liked mustard with their steaks, apple sauce and mashed potatoes with their roast goose, their turkey devilled, their potatoes mealy, their cheese well-ripened and toasted, their mince pies soaked with brandy and set alight, their oysters by the hundred.

One night the Shepherd gets onto the subject of broths: 'That's hotch-potch[8], and that's cocky-leeky[9] the twa best soups in natur. Broon soup's moss-water – and white soup's like scaudded milk wi' worms in't. But see, sirs, hoo the ladle stauns o' itsel in the potch – and I wish Mr Tickler could see himsel the noo in a glass, curlin up his nose, wi' his een glistenin, and his mouth watering, at the sight and smell o' the leeky.'

If the roots of Scotland's food begin with a pot hanging over the fire, the good bowls of broth which have followed are in part due to the cook, but also to the enthusiasm of the eaters. The Shepherd articulates the effect on the appetite of wisps of aromatic steam rising from a restorative broth. It is possible to 'nose' a broth and tell something of its character and how it has been made. The elemental extraction of flavour from food into a liquid when you make 'strong broth' first produces original results. As a starting point, it gives the cook the versatility to sally forth into individual styles, while at the same time remaining within the idiom.

It is not a complicated or difficult procedure, not even an expensive one, but still a classic ground rule in the professional kitchen. Without it, as Escoffier once said, nothing can be achieved. For the modern kitchen the advantages are that it not only provides, in the first instance, a clear, light, aromatic soup (fat and salt-free if preferred), but also a spin-off in terms of the ready-cooked meats which can form an endless permutation of future meals. The sustaining broth-pot of the future may take on different aromas, as times, people, habits and foods change, but it will never lose its place in the scheme of Scotland's food as a valuable restorative for the inhabitants of a cold Northern country.

The Author

Catherine Brown is an author and freelance journalist who writes regular columns in both The Herald and Scottish Field. She has worked as a professional cook in the hotel industry and as a catering lecturer at Elgin Technical College. She was the senior researcher for the University of Strathclyde's research project: *The British Culinary Code*, a four year study of Britain's natural food resources and regional cooking traditions (published in 1976 as *British Cookery*). Her other publications include *A Taste of Scotland, Chef's Manual* (Scottish Tourist Board, 1973), *Scottish Regional Recipes* (1981), *Scottish Cookery* (1986), *A Flavour of Edinburgh* (1986) and *Broths to Bannocks* (1990).

References

[1] Foulis, Sir J., *Foulis of Ravelston's Account Book: 1671 1707*, Scottish History Society, 1894

[2] McLintock, Mrs, *Receipts for Cookery and Pastry-Work*, 1736. The first published cookery book in Scotland, nothing is known of either the Glasgow publisher or the author. Facsimile published by Aberdeen University Press, Introduction by Iseabail Macleod, 1986

> To make a Soup: Make a strong Broth of a Thigh of Beef, and a Nuckle of Veal cut in pieces, put it in the Pot full of Water, and some hail Spice with a Blade of Mace, three great whole Onions, stuck with cloves, and a Bunch of Sweet Herbs, boil all together on a slow fire, till the Meat be all in Pieces, then strain the broth thro' a callendar, and take some collops of Beef, dust them with flower, and fry them very brown, take the Fat off the strong Broth, then put in the collops among the broth, and let them soke over a slow fire; and have ready some Pieces of tosted Bread for your Soup Dish, put in a Marrow Bone in the middle, or in the Broth on the Bread, but keep out the collops and serve it up.

[3] Unpublished manuscript recipes dated 1710, by Martha Brown, private collection in Ayr and Cunningham Public Library

> To make Strong Broth: Take 12 quarts of water and 3 knuckles of veal and a hough of beef and two pair of calves feet and chickens and rabbits and a faggot of sweet herbs and 2 onions and some leimond peil and boile these together until it comes to 6 quarts and when this is strained it is fit for all Sauces and pottages.

[4] Manuscript recipes by Martha Lockhart, The Lady Castlehill, 1712, collection in Mitchell Library, Glasgow. About a quarter of the recipes edited by Hamish Whyte as Lady Castlehill's Receipt Book, Molindinar, 1976

[5] Carter, C., *The Complete Practical Cook*, 1730. (Cook to the Duke of Argyll)

To make a STOCK of STRONG BROTH of FLESH: Take a Leg of Beef, and a Knuckle of Veal, and a Neck of Mutton; wash all well: Put a large Pot on the Fire with fair Water, and then change the Pot with your Meat: When it boils take care to scum it well; put in a Carrot or two and a Turnip, and a good Faggot of Sweet Herbs, some whole Onions peeled, and season it with whole pepper, Salt, some Blades of Mace, and some Cloves stuck in a Piece of Bacon; boil in it the Crust of a French Manchet, and when it is well boil'd, strain it out for Use.

Glasse, H., *The Art of Cookery Made Plain and Easy*, 1738, 17th Edinburgh edition

To Make Scots Barley Broth: Take a leg of beef, chop it all to pieces, boil it in three gallons of water with a piece of carrot and a crust of bread, till it is half boiled away; then strain it off, and put it into the pot again with half a pound of barley, four or five heads of celery washed clean and cut small, a large onion, a bundle of sweet herbs, a little parsley chopped small, and a few marigolds. Let this boil an hour. Take a cock or large fowl, clean picked and washed, and put into the pot; boil it till the broth be quite good, then season with salt, and send it to the table with the fowl in the middle, this broth is very good without the fowl. Take out the onion and sweet herbs, before you send it to table.

Some make this broth with a sheep's head instead of a leg of beef, and it is very good; but your must chop the head all to pieces. The thick flank (about six pounds to six quarts of water) makes good broth; then put in the above ingredients, with turnips and carrots clean and scrape and pared, and cut in little pieces. Boil all together softly, till the broth is very good; then season it with salt, and send it to table, with the beef in the middle, turnips and carrots round, and pour the broth over all.

Dods, Mistress Margaret (Meg), *The Cook and Housewife's Manual*, 1826

Stock broth: to every pound of fresh, juicy, rump beef, or a shin broken, allow a quart of soft water, and to this add any fresh trimmings of lean mutton, veal poultry, or game, which the larder affords. An old fowl, a rabbit, or a knuckle of veal, are excellent additions, and with these less meat will serve. When the broth is rendered pellucid by boiling, skimming, and clearing, as directed in the observations on boiling, put to it three or four carrots, two turnips, four large onions, four cloves, some good leeks, a faggot of herbs, if you like their flavour, and a head or two of celery. Let the soup stew slowly by the fire for from four to six hours, according to the quantity. If left too long on the fire, the flavour of the vegetables will become too powerful, the colour will spoil, and the broth become ropy. When done, let it settle, skim off the fat, (which will be useful for moistening braises, enriching vegetables etc.) pour it from the sediment: strain it through a fine search or wetting cloth, and set it aside for use.

[6] MacDougall, J., *Highland Postbag*, the Correspondence of Four MacDougall Chiefs 1715 – 1865, Shepheard-Walwyn, London 1984

[7] Wilson, J., *Noctes Ambrosianae*, 4 vols, Blackwood 1855

[8] and [9] Dods, Meg, *The Cook and Housewife's Manual*, 1826

Scotch hotch-potch: Make the stock of sweet fresh mutton. Cut down four pounds of ribs of lamb into small steaks, trimming off superfluous fat, and put them to the strained stock. Grate the zest of two or three large carrots; slice down as many more. Slice down also young turnips, young onions, lettuce, and parsley. Have a full quart of these things when shred, and another of young green pease. Put in the vegetables, withholding half the pease till near the end of the process. Boil well and skim carefully; add the remaining pease, white pepper, and salt; and when thick enough, serve the steaks in the tureen with the hotch-potch; trim the fat from the steaks. – Obs. The excellence of this favourite dish depends mainly on the meat, whether beef or mutton, be perfectly fresh, and the vegetables being all young, and full of sweet juices. The sweet white turnips is best for hotch-potch, or the small, round, smooth-grained yellow kind peculiar to Scotland, and almost equal to the genuine Navet of France. Mutton makes excellent hotch-potch without any lamb-steaks. Parsley shred, white cabbage, asparagus points, or lettuce, may be added to the other vegetables or not at pleasure.

Cock-a-leekie: Boil from four to six pounds of good shin-beef, well broken, till the liquor is very good. Strain it, and put to it a capon, or large fowl, trussed for boiling, and, when it boils, half the quantity of blanched leeks intended to be used, well cleaned, and cut in inch-lengths, or longer. Skim this carefully. In a half-hour add the remaining part of the leeks, and a seasoning of pepper and salt. The soup must be very thick of leeks, and the first part of them must be boiled down into the soup till it become a green lubricious compound, Sometimes the capon is served in the tureen with the cock-a-leekie. This is good leek-soup without the fowl. Obs. Some people thicken cock-a-leekie with the fine part of oatmeal. This who dislike so much of the leeks may substitute shred greens, or spinage and parsley, for one half of them. Reject the coarse green part of the leeks. Prunes wont be put to this soup. The practice is obsolete.

Note: *According to other 19th and 20th century sources, prunes, or raisins, were added to sweeten the flavour if old coarse leeks had been used. Though MD seems to think the practice 'obsolete', prunes continue to be included in recipes. Today they are regarded as a matter of taste rather than correctness.* *CB*

For a complete bibliography see those compiled by Catherine Brown in:
Broths to Bannocks: cooking in Scotland 1690 to the present day, John Murray, 1990
Scottish Regional Recipes, Chambers, 3rd reprint 1992
Scottish Cookery, Chambers, 3rd reprint 1993

34

THE FOOD OF
NORTH EAST OF SCOTLAND

Donald Carney

Traditional ways of life change over time and so do eating habits. The world has now become every region's market and every region a distribution point. However, many aspects of our past, including our eating habits, still remain as present examples of a region's reputation. Local produce, local skills, settings and environment still work together to form regional character. This is equally true for places and people, and their food.

My own approach to food ethnology is in part sentimental because I have strong local connections. Yet, it is also a hard headed business approach. Sentiment and practicality are characteristic of the North East and both are essential when we understand ethnology, not just as it relates to food, but also as it relates to the whole life of the region.

THE CONCEPT OF FOOD ETHNOLOGY

Food ethnology deals with the foods which are characteristic of a given locality. We can list the influences of climate, agriculture, soil type, landform, local economy, ownership, law, technology, social class, trade, tradition, tastes and customs, plus the range of locally produced products. Ethnology is the complex relationship of many features in a region and by its nature it is never fixed. For a region to understand its food ethnology and present it coherently, it is necessary to appreciate the complex ways in which food links different groups in the local community. To think that food ethnology is only about food misses the point. Moreover, it misses an important opportunity to exploit it fully.

Scottish cooking of the past was seen as simple and wholesome. Although the humble rural poor did not eat as well as the Laird and each social class had its own eating habits they shared a common social context of local foods and traditions.

The early foods of the first settlers were based on what could either be hunted or gathered. The cattle drovers of 200 years ago still applied that principle but also used the common commodities of the time. One such commodity was oats ground into oatmeal. This was doused with whisky before leaving home, and eaten by the drovers and their dogs as they walked the drove roads with the cattle. This was their main diet. Whisky was seen as another staple food. Both oatmeal and whisky were local resources. Mixed together, these two foods stayed palatable during the drover's travels and did not deteriorate. A drover simply took some out of his sack, slaked it with stream water and ate it cold and uncooked, often at the *stances* where groups of drovers stopped for the night.

In a sense, the self catering provision for these early drovers led to the development of the *Hospitality Industry*. Local people gave hospitality freely. To supplement the drovers' diet they brought oatcakes, cheeses, broths and scones, all cooked in the pot or bake steen on an open peat fire. This improved diet was valued by the drovers and has developed over time into the food service industries we know today.

The drovers were among the first commercial travellers and would sample different local foods as they travelled through Scotland to the market towns of the Borders. Each community provided food typical of its own ethnology. These dishes for the early traveller included an abundance of fresh river or sea fish. Meat from beef and mutton was actually seldom eaten and when it was, usually stewed or boiled in the three legged pot. Sadly, today's travelling tourist finds very little taste of Scotland's regions on the standardised nation-wide menu.

As tenant farming developed from the old *ridge and furrow* or the *runrig* system fewer people had direct access to growing their own foods. By the time of the late industrial revolution we can identify shifts in society's use of food. Town dwellers were at the mercy of market forces and faced spartan meals, mainly based on oatmeal. As the Industrial Revolution continued, more and better foods became available. Manufactured items and greater hospitality provision developed: after the drovers, the coaching inns, followed by the posthouse inns developed for the mail carriers. The impact of the railway and the influence of Queen Victoria's links with *Huntin' Shootin' and Fishin'* at Balmoral helped to expand and develop the region's food. Before imported foreign foods became common, the main changes were in local food availability, and extremes of poverty and plenty were still present even as new social classes emerged.

THE DIET OF THE LAIRD

During the time of the Industrial Revolution, before it and after it, too, the rich of any region did not go hungry. Their lifestyle was based on travel from region to region, and being hosted by the closed circle of rich friends within any district. Accommodation was in the grand houses of the region where massive spreads of the best produce in the area were laid on. The style of eating was different and it was extravagant: thirteen- to twenty-course banquets were not uncommon. Before the introduction of crockery, foods were served on dishes made of bread. Once these dishes began to get soggy they were taken outside the house or castle and distributed to the poor who had gathered for such a hand out. The rich of the time did a great deal to develop early cooking methods and styles in Scotland. Keeping up with the Jones's is nothing new. Indeed, today's food industry is still exploiting their research and developments. It is interesting to note that the ice creams and water ices of today date back to the first sugar imports of this time.

The French approach to cooking was very strong among the rich. Master chefs like Escoffier. and Careme spread the influence of French Classical cuisine to England and, later, Scotland. With the *Taste of Scotland* on our menus today, a modern chef can show off regional foods in the grand manner, with a local flavour and an international appeal. Indeed, in April of this year the Culinary Olympics were held in Singapore and the Scottish team won eight gold medals, eight silver medals and two bronze medals. The foods which they exploited were truly Scottish. Our regional food traditions are clearly alive and kicking here in modern Scotland and, on the modern world stage too.

THE TECHNOLOGY OF FOOD

Part of the changing nature of food ethnology is linked to technology. The horn spoon was state of the art technology in its day. The technological developments which effect meal provision can also be charted before, during and after the Industrial Revolution. Early spit roasting, baking and grilling used simple methods like wooden spits or the use of flat *bake steens*. Metal utensils came with the introduction of cast iron pots. Later came the *girdle*, the *kail pot* or three legged pot, *jelly pans* for jam making, and the *pot oven* which could all be covered with hot peat so the ingredients inside could be heated evenly. Eventually the *swie* and the open method of cooking was replaced with the beehive-style oven and, latterly, the closed range. The introduction of coal gave a further impetus to cooking techniques. Today the modern kitchen (or hospitality unit) is perhaps the most technically equipped room in the house. Every innovation, from wooden spits to fan-assisted ovens, has shaped our approach to food: how we prepare it, present it and eat it. Likewise the tools, simple or sophisticated, which we have to hand shape the food we eat, and will continue to do so.

FROM TRADITION INTO TOURISM

The food we eat reflects features of both our past and our present: farming, rural traditions, the avalability of meat or vegetables. Our past survives through local dishes whose ingredients were produced locally for generations and whose names grew out of that earlier way of life. Today many of these surviving dishes are firm favourites with local and tourists alike. They now support a wider employment and economic base than when they were first created. That new economic base needs to be effectively managed. The culture of our traditional foods, its dishes and its local food sources all depend on the structure of the local economy which includes aspects of heritage as much as those of agriculture, income and diet. Loss of any one aspect can mean irrecoverable loss of the others.

If we are going to move regional food traditions into the present and find a niche for them in today's society, we must first focus on just what society demands of food, tradition and regional character. Scotland competes in the world markets for tourism, produce and manfactured goods. It can only do this successfully if it takes an holistic approach. The interdependent features of such an approach include: food ethnology as a component of tourism, strategic marketing, the role of education the dynamics of international commerce and economics with regional food processing, the future for traditional foods in integrated planning.

THE IMPERATIVE OF QUALITY

Any region must have the ability to attract tourists and make them *Stop, Stay and Spend*. This is what generates real income for the regional economy. No tourist provider can do everything and be all things to all tourists: the secret of success lies in partnership. Everyone who interacts with the tourist during their visit has the potential to create an impression. One bad experience can turn that person away from what a whole region can offer. Tourist providers rely on each other: local foods may be delicious and distinctive but, if they are poorly represented in the local museum, an opportunity to market them is missed. If food provision is poor, or simply neglected, then other excellent facilities may suffer by association. Quality is essential. It is not enough to provide food, *good* food is what is important. Likewise good food may appear mediocre when delivered with only adequate service. Value added products give competitive edge and increase sales and profit. In food preparation added value, like regional character, gives it distinction.

In tourism and hospitality provision, of course, good training and skills are vital to quality. Whatever else they are interested in, tourists need food. Staff skilled in preparation, presentation and service ensure that each tourist experiences the best in the area. A well-fed and satisfied customer is more likely to remain satisfied on the next stage of their visit. Food and good hospitality matters. Measuring the quality of this experience depends on rigorous evaluation. Providers must work together to regulate their practices through professional forums and quality circles. Standards can be maintained, and the best practices identified and made public. It is even more important to understand the customer: knowing that a tourist in Buckie will expect quayside fish and one in Tomintoul will expect game is only the start.

Our understanding must be detailed and up to date. Customer feedback is vital. Providers need to hear when the experience does not match the marketing, customers need to be encouraged to share their views and to know they will be listened to. Tourism is a subjective experience and deals with feelings and impressions as much as with souvenirs and craft products. Positive experiences can sell the tangible products of tourism just as these products can help promote the experience of food and food traditions. What matters most of all is that providers and suppliers work together and understand their part in this complex mix and how to introduce regional character of high quality to it.

The quality North East meal encompasses the whole range of regional culture. Aberdeen Angus steak, for example, is nominally a regional dish, but has lost its true regional character through being exported all over the world and cooked in the style of the importing country. A North East chef would choose a more distinctly local dish and add other regional embellishments, perhaps, by making the sauce whisky based and serving with it quinelles of haggis. The table staff would use the local dialect with the robust social style of the North East. The restaurant layout might feature tartan and heather, and guests could dance to a Scottish dance band. Each guest would leave the meal with a souvenir menu and the recipes, having met the chef and made new friends, not only with other guests but with the staff too. As a result, the tourist gains knowledge and understanding of the region and forges closer links with its culture.

STRATEGIC MARKETING

If the traditions of food are to feature as part of how we package the heritage of an area, then we must understand fully the needs of the tourist market and which segments of that market we are trying to attract. Marketing requires that we consider how, where, when and what we market, and how we measure effectiveness. We need to be clear, too, about who makes the decisions and who will pay for marketing when it takes place. Strategic thinking also requires us to balance apparently conflicting demands. To some extent we must be guided by our own vision of what we want to achieve, but, at the same time, we must recognise those things that a tourist may want Regional food may be just one component of this. In purely economic terms, we can promote precisely whatever a piece of market research says we should sell. In strategic terms, however, we must balance complex sets of demands from different market segments, the views and standards of other tourist providers, the quality components of satisfaction, enthusiasm and loyalty.

Sometimes we undersell what seems commonplace and familiar to us on home ground. We cannot see the wood for the trees. Not every country can boast of the North East's natural and built heritage, yet our common practices can be of great interest to visitors and of unique value as a tourist product. Authenticity and a fresh outlook is one of the key ingredients of success. Scottish chefs can be as creative as French chefs. It is important to realise that cookery is both art and science. The end product must be unique to the provider and might include, for example, a dish with roots in local cultural, a souvenir menu and recipes for the tourist to keep, a memorable meal which fits into the complete tourist experience.

THE ROLE OF EDUCATION

The hospitality industry is generally poorly perceived of by the public. 'If you cannot get a job anywhere else you will find one in the catering industry.' This general feeling is one which needs to change. If the hospitality industry is to pull its weight as a provider of goods and services, it must ensure that such goods and services are of a quality to match the quality of our other tourist attractions.

We must educate the industry. Recruitment, selection, training and operation must all strive to achieve high professional standards. Much has changed recently, and the new breed of catering managers now realise that mediocrity in their service must be a thing of the past. With the passing of the CNAA, colleges and universities who provide and validate their own courses must build their academic reputations on course content. This may allow each university to develop its own regional expertise and interpretation of what hospitality industry students need to know. It could, for example, place less emphasis on the standard menus which make up the average sweet trolley, which is normally limited in skilled preparation and short on local produce. There will always be a place for some convenience foods, but consumers are no longer willing to pay high prices for what can be bought in a supermarket. However,they are willing to pay for good quality value added produce.

We must also educate the consumer. When we look at our past food ethnology, we see the use of beef, pork, lamb, game, poultry, sea foods, river fish, dairy produce, oats, cereals and vegetables. We must brand these quality local ingredients with a regional identity for the wider market. The North East of Scotland must continue to sell itself as a major world food provider. The best place to taste regional products is where they come from. To make this possible, the local hospitality industry must ensure that authentic North East styles of cooking, presenting and customer care are provided locally by imaginative chefs, cooks and managers. The North East of Scotland is an area with a huge potential, where food and drink features high on a scale of uniqueness both for resident and tourist.

The Robert Gordon University has been one of the first to ensure that its Hospitality Degree course links with local environments, local produce, past culture and history of the area as a niche market. The modern caterer must become more aware of their own area's culture and use their skills to develop new and existing market opportunities. The University also supports the need for local and regional groups of providers to work together toward excellence and develop a holistic approach to serving the needs of our customers. We are aware that no part of the area can be truly successful in isolation.

TODAY'S COSMOPOLITAN INFLUENCES

Menus today are cosmopolitan and show a wide ethnic mix. While we must strive to ensure that Scottish dishes gain the prominent positions enjoyed by culinary menues in some other countries of the world, we need to be aware of how local methods stamp a style and identity of even imported dishes. Lasagne, for example, appears on most UK menus, without doubt evolving as a result of tourism. Its ingredients are mince, garlic, tomatoes, bechamel sauce and cheese. If I were to ask four Scottish chefs to prepare and present it, I would get four different dishes. These styles would look and taste different from the Italian lasagne. Our region will stamp its style and identity on foods from other regions, based on our local products, economy, tastes, skill, resources and tradition. In this way the ethnology of a region is the foundation for individual creativity in each hospitality establishment.

There are always threats to traditions which are handed down from one generation to another. My childhood on a North East farm, allowed me to watch my mother cook on a coal fire, then on an electric cooker. She baked bread, bannocks and scones, she cooked soups using vegetables from the garden and old hens or rabbits, we also consumed various *brose* types. My mother also worked on the farm, and was always with us. We watched what she used from the kale yard and how she cooked it, so we learned directly through her actions and influence. In our house today, my wife's work takes her away from the home and we pass on far fewer cooking skills to our children than even one generation previously. It is much harder for today's children to inherit past culinary traditions directly. For them packet biscuits and convenience foods are the norm. As society becomes cosmopolitan, local tastes change. Traditional dishes can be dismissed as inconsistent with a cosmopolitan menu and if a business fails to respond to customers' food preferences it will go out of business. This is how the foods which represent the North East tradition become the foods which the customers are happy with. Yet, the caterer can choose to package foods attractively, inventively and preserve their traditional roots at the same time.

The market place is a powerful shaper of culinary habits. In Aberdeen, greengrocers quickly progressed from supplying only local vegetables such as potatoes, onions, carrots, peas and cabbage, to being able to source any vegetable from any country. The ethnology of food changes as society and the foodstuff available to it changes. There is greater scope now for any city to have a mix of food traditions. That is healthy, but it is driven by a certain kind of market force. Paradoxically, there is no authentic Scottish restaurant in Aberdeen. This does not mean there is no demand for one, nor that we have passed over our own traditions and regional identity for more cosmopolitan ones. The complexities of the market place have had this effect. These same forces can be used to reverse it. The traditions of Scottish or North East food can be applied positively with the wide range of produce available, treated thematically for the benefit of tourists. Thematic events have been shown to improve levels of trade. There is no reason why Scottish, or North East food cannot offer creativity and innovation in the context of world products and respect its own strong roots.

COMMERCIAL APPLICATIONS

Manufacturers can help to re-establish these food traditions, and at the same time expand their market by integrating the tourist into it. Baxter's of Speyside is an excellent example. They show the customer how the ingredients are worked into a value added product, provide a visitor centre with a viewing gallery in the production area and opportunities for tasting. You never know who the tourist might be: even major product buyers take holidays. If we can impress them on holiday, then they may come back as customers. We could share our traditions with a world-wide market, and develop our region's economic base at the same time, and food theme visitor centres would achieve a greater reputation as tourist attractions in the area. Scottish restaurants such as the Peat Inn in Fife, and the Bouquet Garni are Scottish restaurants par excellence, featuring local foods cooked in a uniquely Scottish style. They are successful examples of Scottish identity being openly marketed.

A STRATEGY FOR FOOD ETHNOLOGY.

Change will continue in the future and we need to keep under constant review our traditional foods and our approaches to them. Food will remain a fundamental part of a growing tourism industry which will encompass an ever expanding cultural diversity across the world. To secure our position at the top table of culinary nations, strategies for future development need to be devised now. Some of the key points are listed here as a framework for action.

1. Standards of provision, for food and accommodation, should be improved across all sections of the catering and hospitality industries.

2.. Hospitality must become more locally articulate in order to offer, in a holistic way, what is authentic and special to the North East.

3. Product development should become a central part of the training of all chefs. The basic training for chefs and cooks should include a platform to develop local themes. Students should be shown the potential of mixing and matching flavours to create new regional dishes to help sustain the modern food ethnology in their area.

5. Food is perhaps the most critical factors in any tourism package. Our natural and built tourist attractions are all of a high standard and food provision should match that standard. Food must not be the weak link.

6. When you market a region in cultural, heritage or ethnological terms, then it is vital that marketing campaigns target the correct groups of tourist.

7. A strategic framework for heritage interpretation should be set up to develop the region's overall strengths (see Fladmark, 1993). From here priority funding should be used to prime the building of an infrastructure to move into the future, still featuring our strong links with the past.

It is not just food which needs to be marketed: we must market the whole experience in a regional partnership to create a lasting and sustainable identity for the North East. We will only succeed if we follow such an integrated approach within an alliance of interested parties dedicated to the care of our tourists and our culture.

Food is a business and for a business to be successful it must make the best use of available resources. The North East can produce top quality raw materials, from the simple whelk to the prized lobster. It is important that food production is fully supported. However, we must not lose sight of the fact that Scottish and North East food provision is always under threat from modern day pollution. Recent reports about North Sea fish being deformed as a result of pollution highlights the need to protect the environment not only as a direct tourism asset but also as a primary source of economic stability. The North East, just like any other region, needs to continually develop its production base. At the same time its local produce, local traditions, local setting and environment are rooted in history. There is no contradiction in developing new products for food. This region, like all regions, exists within society and when society changes, the traditions change. What was new may wither away or become another part of our tradition. The surviving features of food ethnology, indeed any tradition, become what sustains and perpetuates the traditions of a region, its foods and its essential character.

The Author

A Lecturer in the School of Food and Consumer Studies at the Robert Gordon University, Don Carney is an authority on the ethnology of cooking in the North East of Scotland. He is also working on a programme for BBC Television based on his extensive video recordings of traditional rural life.

References

Aberdeen Education Authority, *Cookery Book*, 1929
Brown, C., *Scottish Cookery*, Richard Dew
Brown, C., *Broths to Bannocks: Cooking in Scotland 1690 to the Present Day*, John Murray, 1990
Fenton, *Food in Change*, John Donald
Ferguson, S., *Food*, Batsford
King, A., *Scottish Cookery*, Faber
McNeil, *The Scots Kitchen*, Blackie
Robert Gordon's Technical College, *Plain Cookery Recipes*, Aberdeen School of Domestic Science, 1916
Warren, *A Feast of Scotland*, Bantam
Warren, *Caledonian Feast*, BBC

TRADITIONAL DISHES OF THE NORTH EAST

Soups

COCK-A-LEEKIE SOUP: water, leeks and seasoning, later an old hen/cockerel and prunes were added.

CULLEN SKINK: Findon haddock, onion, butter, milk, and mashed potatoes.

GAME SOUP: any game type, onions, carrots, and water.

BROSE: kail, oatmeal and seasoning.

POWSOWDIE OR SHEEP HEAD BROTH: split sheep's head, mixed vegetables, barley and seasoning, picking meat from head to serve with the flavoursome stock.

SORREL SOUP: sorrel leaves in summer, butter stock, cream potato and seasoning.

Fish

HERRINGS IN OATMEAL: salmon and trout baked, fried or grilled.

LOBSTER: in pie or served with cold salad.

GUDDLED TROUT AND NETTLE SAUCE: hand caught stream trout poached in fresh nettles and served with *chappit* nettles.

Meat

MUTTON POT OVEN STEW: diced mutton, garden roots, fresh water and potatoes for thickening.

PORK STEAK AND BRAMBLES: pork loin baked on a *bake steen* with fresh bramble berries.

Game stews

HAGGIS: sheep's pluck, ie liver, lungs, heart, suet, oatmeal, onion, and seasoning, served in the sheep's stomach.

POTTED HEID OR HOUGH: ox cheeks (heid) or shin of beef (hough) and seasoning, to simmer gently, then strain and reduce liquid to concentrate the natural gelatine setting agent, chop the meat and mix, and allow to set.

Meatless Dishes

SKIRLIE: oatmeal, dripping, onion and seasoning.

STOVIES: potatoes, onions, dripping and seasoning (today meat is added).

CLOUTIE DUMPLING: flour, suet, sugar, currants, sultanas, raisins, spices, water and charms for the bairns.